W9-CFI-934

The
Four-Season
Landscape

The
Four-Season
Landscape

Easy-Care
Plants and Plans
for Year-Round Color

Susan A. Roth

Photography by the Author

Rodale Press, Emmaus, Pennsylvania

To Conni and Jim Cross,
with immeasurable thanks.

Our Mission

We publish books that empower people's lives.

RODALE BOOKS

The information in this book has been carefully researched, and all efforts have been made to ensure accuracy. Rodale Press, Inc., assumes no responsibility for any injuries suffered or damages or losses incurred during use of or as a result of following this information. It is important to study all directions carefully before taking any action based on the information and advice presented in this book. When using any commercial product, *always* read and follow label directions. Where trade names are used, no discrimination is intended and no endorsement by Rodale Press, Inc., is implied.

Copyright © 1994 by Susan A. Roth

All rights reserved. No part of this publication may be reproduced or transmitted in any form or by any means, electronic or mechanical, including photocopy, recording, or any other information storage and retrieval system, without the written permission of the publisher.

Printed in the United States of America

on acid-free ∞ , recycled ♺ paper

Executive Editor: Margaret Lydic Balitas
Managing Editor: Barbara W. Ellis
Editors: Ellen Phillips and Deborah L. Martin
Contributing Editors: Joan Benjamin and Sarah F. Price
Copy Editor: Robyn Bem
Indexer: Ed Yeager
Senior Research Associate: Heidi A. Stonehill
Administrative Assistant: Susan Nickol
Office Manager: Karen Earl-Braymer
Editorial assistance: Debbie Weisel

Book design by Darlene Schneck
Illustrations by Elayne Sears and Jean Emmons
Photographs by Susan A. Roth

If you have any questions or comments concerning this book, please write to:
Rodale Press
Book Readers' Service
33 East Minor Street
Emmaus, PA 18098

Library of Congress Cataloging-in-Publication Data

Roth, Susan A.
    The four-season landscape / easy-care plants and plans for year-round color / Susan A. Roth.
        p.   cm.
    Includes bibliographical references and index.
        ISBN 0–87596–556–3   hardcover
        ISBN 0–87596–740–X   paperback

        1. Landscape gardening. 2. Color in gardening.
3. Low maintenance gardening. 4. Gardens–Design.
5. Landscape plants. 6. Seasons. I. Title
SB473.R65   1994   93–6141
712'.6—dc20   CIP

Distributed in the book trade by St. Martin's Press
    6 8 10 9 7 5   hardcover
2 4 6 8 10 9 7 5 3 1   paperback

Contents

Acknowledgments vi

Welcome to the Four-Season Landscape 1
Chapter 1: Landscaping for Four Seasons 3
Chapter 2: Winter in the Four-Season Landscape 18
Chapter 3: Spring in the Four-Season Landscape 75
Chapter 4: Summer in the Four-Season Landscape 134
Chapter 5: Autumn in the Four-Season Landscape 181
Chapter 6: Designing a Year-Round Landscape 229
Chapter 7: An Encyclopedia of Four-Season Plants 254

Resources for Four-Season Landscapes 328
Recommended Reading 332
USDA Plant Hardiness Zone Map 334
Index 335

Acknowledgments

I wish to especially thank Eleanor Lahr for her friendship and encouragement during the sometimes arduous task of preparing this book. Her delight in my writing and my subject reignited my enthusiasm, propelling me forward when I needed it most.

Thanks go to the following people for opening their gardens to my camera and for their friendship, encouragement, personal stories, and expert advice: Suzanne Bales, Donna Bickley, Virginia Blacklock, Bob Carlson, Conni Cross, Jim Cross, Barbara Damrosch, Ruth Dix, Joe Eck, Sally Ferguson, Edith Friedman, Angela Garguila, Tom Greene, Gail Harrigan, Mary Jean Harris, Mark Horvatich, Randy Johnson, Steve Kyner, David Leach, Patty McGuigan, Elwin Orton, Maggie Oster, Jane Owens, Liz Shepherd, Bob Simpson, Randy Summerlin, and Wayne Winterrowd.

Many thanks to editors Ellen Phillips, who first read the book proposal and encouraged me from beginning to end, and Deb Martin, whose eagle eye kept me on the straight and narrow.

And last, but certainly not least, wheelbarrows of gratitude to my wonderful husband, Mark Schneider, who digs the holes.

Welcome to the Four-Season Landscape

My passion for gardening evolved as an inevitable offshoot of my love of nature, an appreciation that began during my childhood. When I was 12, my family moved from southern California to Connecticut; we traded a residential urban neighborhood for a suburban development carved out of the woods. Tall, lanky palm trees with tufts of fronds decorating their tops had lined the streets where we lived in L.A.; in Connecticut, spreading oaks, white-barked birches, and huge-canopied maples shaded the expansive yards. And rather than high-rises in the distance, forest served as a backdrop for the homes across the street. These woods became my playground.

Though there was certainly plenty of wilderness in southern California when I lived there, I saw little of it. Family outings consisted of going to the beach and romping in the surf with thousands of others seeking refuge from the heat and smog, rather than quiet excursions to the deserts or the mountains. All of the plants I saw were cultivated and owed their lives to automatic underground sprinklers. The wooded New England landscape represented a profound visual change and sowed the seeds of a love of nature that matured and blossomed later in my life, in part as a passion for gardening.

The rolling acres surrounding my new neighborhood belonged to the watershed for a large reservoir that provided water for the city of Hartford. Included were wild habitats unlike anything I had ever experienced—mature deciduous forest, a brook feeding several ponds, a swamp, a moist meadow, and the huge reservoir, complete with a hemlock forest along its edge. This land seemed virtually unexplored, and it beckoned to a 12-year-old bent on escape but imprisoned in suburbia. I achieved a new freedom and peace denied to me by urban life as I explored those wooded acres and learned to recognize and cherish the wildflowers that graced each habitat.

Those woods represented a very special and private place to me. I sought refuge there no matter what the season, soaking up the intricacies and details of the natural land-scape around me as if it were nourishment for my young soul. I knew the woodland every month of the year, trekking there even during the most bitter winter weather when the stream seemed flash-frozen into a bas-relief of ripples and the naked trees towered as dark silhou-ettes against the winter sky. Well before spring brought out a haze of chartreuse from the treetops, I was walking with eyes focused on the ground, frequenting the locations I knew would soon offer up furry-stemmed hepatica blossoms as a harbinger of spring.

Each season offered something different to look at, to experience, to feel. Each season possessed its own fragrance, colors, and textures. Each season basked in a different angle of light. And each season delighted me as much as the last.

Now, my garden captivates me throughout the year as much as my childhood retreat did. I designed the landscape for seasonal beauty, selecting garden plants for the same features that had entranced me through the seasons in the woodland: the colors and textures of flowers, foliage, and bark, as well as the architectural effect of a plant's form and silhouette.

I'd like this book to be a gift to gardeners everywhere who want their gardens to be an oasis of beauty every month of the year. This book will help you transform your yard and garden into a beautiful four-season landscape. I'll point you in the right direction, providing the knowledge that will keep your landscape colorful when most are plain green or brown. You'll learn which plants perform for four sea-sons and which bloom at odd times of the year. You'll discover which shrubs and trees offer the best fall color and which ones hold onto their eye-catching berries well into winter. And finally, you'll learn to put it all together into a pretty picture—a dynamic picture that changes throughout the year, from season to season, but nevertheless a picture that's as lovely in January as it is in July.

Susan A. Roth

CHAPTER 1

Landscaping for Four Seasons

Paint a Beautiful Garden Picture Every Month of the Year

Gardening is an art form, and a beautiful garden exists as a work of living art. As with artwork, its execution may seem inspired, but in actuality very little is left to chance. Most unplanned gardens offer the bounty of their beauty during a short, intense flowering period in spring and early summer. To enjoy the seasons to their fullest, you need to carefully plan your four-season landscape so it will excite interest every day of the year, whether seen from indoors or out. Creating a decorative garden full of color and interest throughout the year takes both planning and knowledge.

Flowers—annuals and perennials—come first to most people's minds when they think of garden color. But a year-round landscape must be much more than a flower bed, as the American gardener is learning. A four-season landscape relies on a continual parade of exciting plants—plants that offer color or intriguing textures and patterns, not for just a single short blooming period, but for several seasons of the year. Each plant chosen for a four-season landscape ought to contribute to the garden's beauty for at least two seasons, or during a time of the year when little else offers color or interest.

Woody plants—trees, shrubs, and some vines and groundcovers—give a garden permanent appeal and structure. I can't emphasize enough how important these are to the year-round beauty of your garden. The most successful year-round gardens I've seen rely less on the usual garden annuals and perennials and more on a diversity of flowering trees, shrubs, and vines for a colorful show. These plants, as well as evergreen shrubs and trees, also give the garden a permanent structure—they don't die to the ground in winter, and they're not dull when out of bloom. Their foliage and form command attention all year.

Drawing on an extensive palette of plants—a palette that will take you beyond the commonplace flowers—you can paint a series of ever-changing garden scenes that, taken together, constitute a *four-season landscape*. Designed and planted to be beautiful every day, your four-season landscape will celebrate the best nature has to offer.

3

Making My Four-Season Landscape

Creating a colorful garden in spring and high summer has rarely been a problem for most gardeners, but late summer, autumn, and winter are often dull, lifeless times in the average home landscape. With planning, though, boredom doesn't need to define the landscape during the off-season. I discovered this for myself when designing a four-season landscape for my home on Long Island, which is located in USDA Plant Hardiness Zone 7. The landscape features an assortment of plants that provide a progression of bloom beginning in late winter and continuing right through to Thanksgiving.

Almost every plant chosen for my garden fulfills a seasonal purpose, and many offer year-round beauty. Very few contribute to the garden's beauty during only one season. I concentrated on getting the most from my half-acre property, seeking out shrubs and trees with attention-getting aspects in at least two seasons. Some display noteworthy features every month of the year; others are at their best at times when traditional gardens seem hard-pressed for interest.

Foliage for Long-Lasting Color and Form

Where flowers don't provide interest, I use foliage to draw the eye, creating lovely color and texture combinations that last from spring through fall. I like to create colorful foliage combinations by intermingling burgundy-foliaged plants, such as 'Crimson Pygmy' barberry (*Berberis thunbergii* var. *atropurpurea* 'Crimson Pygmy'), with yellow-green- or golden-leaved plants, such as 'Limemound' spirea (*Spiraea* × *bumalda* 'Limemound'). I paint a garden with the many different leaf colors of hostas and use the dark purple foliage of 'Palace Purple' coralbells (*Heuchera micrantha* 'Palace Purple') to contrast with the grass green leaves of other perennials.

Most of the flowering perennials I've chosen for my flower beds or tucked in the shrub borders offer more than just pretty flowers, which are fleeting at best. I expect their foliage and form to add substance, texture, or color to the garden during the months they are out of bloom.

Bearded iris, for instance, produces its sumptuous flowers for perhaps two weeks of the year. But after the flowers wither, the plant's stiff swordlike foliage endures until frost, creating a jaunty vertical contrast to the softer, bushier plants nearby.

Special Plants for Seasonal Highlights

Plants that lack two- to four-season appeal may slip into my garden if they bloom or offer a colorful feature at a difficult time of year. For instance, many of the early-spring bulbs contribute little more than their flowers to the garden, because their foliage yellows and withers in early summer. But masses of early-spring bulbs rollicking through the landscape brighten the otherwise barren ground, forming an important aspect of a four-season garden.

I gratefully welcome these cheerful blooms in March and early April, when so much of the garden lies dormant and a long winter has wrought its depressing effects on my psyche. Whatever trouble it takes to camouflage the homely foliage later in the season is made up for by the earlier show.

Creating Seasonal Groupings

In my four-season landscape, I try to group plants that bloom sequentially so that each area of the garden remains in bloom for as long as possible. For instance, the graceful native flowering dogwood (*Cornus florida*) blooms for three weeks in May; soon after its white or pink flowers give way to foliage, the lesser-known Kousa dogwood (*Cornus kousa*) bursts into bloom for four weeks in June. By planting these trees together, the canopy of spring flowers lasts for over two months.

To make an even more colorful garden picture, combine these trees with other plants that bloom at the same time. You might underplant a group of flowering dogwoods with azaleas and small-leaved rhododendrons. Then cover the ground with cold-hardy annuals such as pansies and violas, and early perennials such as violets, bleeding hearts (*Dicentra spectabilis*), and Virginia bluebells (*Mertensia virginica*). Finish your picture with rivers of bulbs such as daffodils (*Narcissus* spp.), grape hyacinths (*Muscari* spp.), and summer snowflakes (*Leucojum aestivum*).

To accompany the Kousa dogwood, use shrubs such as European cranberrybush viburnum (*Viburnum opulus*), old-fashioned weigela (*Weigela florida*), and mountain laurel (*Kalmia latifolia*). Complement the dogwood and shrubs with perennials such as coralbells (*Heuchera sanguinea*), snow-in-summer (*Cerastium tomentosum*), and Siberian iris (*Iris sibirica*), and bulbs such as Spanish bluebells (*Hyacinthoides hispanicus,* also sold as *Endymion hispanicus* and *Scilla campanulata*). Try planting the bulbs and perennials in a thick groundcover of leadwort (*Ceratostigma plumbaginoides*), which makes up for its late-spring emergence with an autumn profusion of pure blue flowers set against deep red-tinged foliage.

Winter—A Time of Subtle Beauty

The winter garden may be stark and spare compared to the rest of the year, but it can still have color and interest. Even in December and January, when flowers remain few and far between, bunches of red, purple, and gold berries line the bare branches of many of the deciduous shrubs and trees. Evergreen foliage sparkles with a dusting of hoarfrost. Trees and shrubs selected for textured or brightly colored bark or unusual branching patterns command attention. Seedpods and grasses left standing adorn the garden through the winter, resembling giant bouquets of everlastings.

Color for the Dormant Season

The growing season brims with beautiful flowering plants in any garden. But the dormant season—often several long, bleak months of gray skies and bare limbs—comes alive with subtle colors in the four-season landscape. You can learn to skillfully combine the needled and broadleaved evergreens to create a beautiful winter scene. By planting several colorful evergreens beside a doorway, you can adorn the entrance with a focal point that's exciting throughout the year.

In the distant view from the kitchen window, try arranging a grouping of red- and yellow-stemmed dogwoods (*Cornus sericea* cultivars) for a joyful panorama of brilliant bark colors in winter. Hollies (*Ilex* spp.) and heavenly bamboo (*Nandina domestica*) offer evergreen foliage and long-lasting, shimmering red berries. Just when winter's edge has worn thin, you will welcome the first flowers—winterhazels (*Corylopsis* spp.), witch hazels (*Hamamelis* spp.), Cornelian cherry (*Cornus mas*), and Christmas rose (*Helleborus niger*)—that bloom even while snow covers the ground.

Each year since it was planted, my 'Arnold Promise' witch hazel (*Hamamelis* × *intermedia* 'Arnold Promise') has unfurled its fragrant yellow ribbons as if on cue on February 1, beginning an eight-week season of bloom. Carpets of crocuses and snowdrops (*Galanthus nivalis*) soon join the witch hazel. By the time spring arrives, my garden has been blooming for weeks.

FOUR-SEASON ISLAND BED

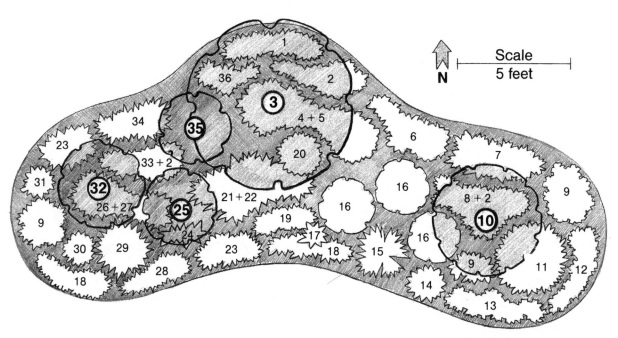

Plot plan for an island bed. 1. *Ajuga reptans* 'Bronze Beauty' ('Bronze Beauty' bugleweed) **2.** *Ceratostigma plumbaginoides* (leadwort) **3.** *Crataegus viridis* 'Winter King' ('Winter King' hawthorn) **4.** *Crocus* spp. (crocuses) **5.** *Hosta plantaginea* 'Elegans' ('Elegans' August lily) **6.** *Campanula portenschlagiana* (Dalmatian bellflower) **7.** *Astilbe × arendsii* (astilbe) **8.** *Scilla siberica* (Siberian squill) **9.** *Coreopsis* 'Moonbeam' ('Moonbeam' coreopsis) **10.** *Acer palmatum* 'Aoyagi' (green-bark Japanese maple) **11.** *Rhododendron carolinianum* (Carolina rhododendron) **12.** *Nepeta × faassenii* (catmint) **13.** *Juniperus horizontalis* (creeping juniper) **14.** *Sedum* 'Vera Jameson' ('Vera Jameson' sedum) **15.** *Pennisetum alopecuroides* 'Hameln' ('Hameln' fountain grass) **16.** *Mahonia bealei* (leatherleaf mahonia) **17.** *Iris sibirica* 'Papillion' ('Papillion' Siberian iris) **18.** *Prunella × webbiana* 'Loveliness' ('Loveliness' self-heal) **19.** *Chrysanthe-* *mum zawadskii* var. *latilobum* 'Mary Stoker' ('Mary Stoker' hardy garden chrysanthemum) **20.** *Helleborus orientalis* (Lenten rose) **21.** *Hemerocallis* spp. (daylilies) **22.** *Narcissus* 'February Gold' ('February Gold' narcissus) **23.** *Stachys byzantina* (lamb's-ears) **24.** *Tulipa kaufmaniana* (waterlily tulip) **25.** *Enkianthus campanulatus* (red-vein enkianthus) **26.** *Galanthus nivalis* (common snowdrop) **27.** *Liriope muscari* 'Gold Banded' ('Gold Banded' blue lilyturf) **28.** *Imperata cylindrica* 'Red Baron' ('Red Baron' bloodgrass) **29.** *Pinus mugo* (mugo pine) **30.** *Sedum* 'Autumn Joy' ('Autumn Joy' sedum) **31.** *Sedum cauticola* **32.** *Viburnum* 'Mohawk' ('Mohawk' viburnum) **33.** *Hyacinthoides hispanica* (Spanish squill) **34.** *Astilbe chinensis* 'Pumila' (dwarf Chinese astilbe) **35.** *Pieris japonica* 'Dorothy Wycoff' ('Dorothy Wycoff' Japanese pieris) **36.** *Dicentra eximia* (fringed bleeding heart)

Island bed in late summer. After shrubs, trees, and bulbs have finished their late-winter and spring flower show, perennials and groundcovers carry the garden through summer. Highlights include such long-blooming favorites as 'Moonbeam' coreopsis, daylilies, leadwort, astilbes, chrysanthemums, and catmint. Lamb's-ears, bloodgrass, and variegated lilyturf add season-spanning foliage color.

(continued)

FOUR-SEASON ISLAND BED—Continued

Island bed in late winter. Even in winter, this island bed creates a memorable picture. Evergreens provide greenery and mass to give the garden presence. The 'Aoyagi' Japanese maple offers bright green bark, and the hawthorn and viburnum display eye-catching clusters of gleaming red berries. Late winter brings on the mahonia's yellow flowers, pink flowers from the Japanese pieris, and a carpet of blooming bulbs to light up the garden floor.

Spring—Fresh Tints and Profuse Flowers

Spring, the season of birth, lets you rejoice in a haze of new foliage and a profusion of flowers—sunny daffodils, elegant tulips, and beguiling bleeding hearts (*Dicentra spectabilis*), to name only a few. April and May bring an orchestrated crescendo of blooms and spring green foliage to my garden.

The planned sequence of early perennials, bulbs, and flowering shrubs and trees in my landscape practically leaves me breathless. Masses of pink azaleas fill the shade beneath cloudlike dogwood branches, and fragrant Koreanspice viburnums (*Viburnum carlesii*) are covered with snowballs. Ferns unfurl their fiddleheads, stretching out new foliage over the sweet violets nearby.

Most of the spring bloomers in my garden remain attractive come summer—their foliage, berries, or form will continue to contribute to the landscape long after their flowers fade. And I've avoided mass-planting spring bloomers in favor of leaving plenty of room in my garden for shrubs that bloom during other seasons, especially late summer and fall.

When planning your garden, keep the lilacs (*Syringa* spp.), with their sorry fall color, to a minimum and seek out shrubs that offer color in spring and other seasons. (If lilacs or similar one-season shrubs are your favorites, locate them away from center stage, where you don't have to look at them during the rest of the year.)

One of my favorite shrubs for spring and fall color is dwarf fothergilla (*Fothergilla gardenii*). In spring, before its leaves have fully unfolded, fothergilla displays creamy white bottlebrush flowers that sparkle in the sunshine. Autumn brings a conflagration of fiery hues to the foliage: rusty red, burnished gold, and clear pumpkin orange.

Save Space for Late Bloomers

Spring is known to be a season of garden riches. It's difficult to prevent spring fever from sending you into a gardening frenzy, and harder still to resist a shopping spree when the nurseries lure customers to the cash register with their seductive displays.

Nursery managers know all too well that most people equate the planting season with spring and early summer, and that blooming plants will practically walk out of the store, while those out of bloom are a harder sell. Nurseries stock up heavily on the spring and early-summer bloomers, sometimes making it difficult to even find later-blooming shrubs and perennials.

Resist the temptation to fill your garden to overflowing with spring beauties, leaving no room for plants that bloom in other seasons. Instead, seek out the out-of-bloom shrubs and

perennials like viburnums and asters that are sulking for lack of attention in the far corners of the garden center. These Cinderellas will reward you with glorious bloom later in the year.

If your nursery hasn't yet stocked any of the later bloomers, be sure to leave room for them in your garden plan. Plant the garden with readily available spring bloomers but then visit the garden center monthly to scout out new arrivals, especially blooming ones, to pop into the empty spaces.

Summer—A Deluge of Flowers and Deep Green Foliage

Summer, generally considered to be the growing season, brings a wealth of flowers to most gardens. As the fragile young foliage of spring gives way to the deep green of summer, the garden develops more substance and fullness. Roses abound, while perennials and shrubs add hotter flower colors to complement the earlier pastels.

But without careful planning, a perennial garden often reaches its peak in midsummer and then suddenly ceases to perform. One day it's garbed in full glory, the next it's in rags. My perennial garden keeps right on blooming through August and into September and October, because I chose plants especially for their long season of bloom. I also included a generous assortment of late summer- and fall-blooming perennials and bulbs.

Seek Flowers, Foliage, and Form

In summer, the shrubs and trees in most landscapes usually retreat into greenery, but they hold their own in a garden designed for year-round beauty. My four-season landscape displays groups of shrubs and trees that surround the garden with fragrance and color even in summer.

The summer-blooming trees and shrubs bear delightful flowers in the canopy overhead and at eye level, enveloping the garden with color and fragrance. Two of my favorite shrubs create a commotion of blue flowers in late summer and fall: bluebeard (*Caryopteris × clandonensis* 'Blue Mist') and butterfly bush (*Buddleia davidii*).

I chose other woody plants for the summer border not so much for their flowers but for their form and variegated, gold, or burgundy foliage. The wine-hued foliage of my 'Bloodgood' Japanese maple (*Acer palmatum* 'Bloodgood') commands attention all summer against the leafy green canopy of taller trees.

Autumn—A Celebration of Color

Autumn doesn't signal death in the four-season garden but sets off a celebration of flamboyant color. As summer progresses into autumn, purple, gold, lavender, and red flowers and berries predominate, painting the garden with warm hues that presage the imminent fire of fall foliage.

Bridge the Seasons with Color

Late-summer perennials, such as Frikart's aster (*Aster × frikartii*), purple coneflowers (*Echinacea purpurea*), and 'Goldsturm' black-eyed Susans (*Rudbeckia fulgida* var. *sullivantii* 'Goldsturm'), keep flowering until frost. The numerous types of ornamental grasses also may bridge the seasons. Fall-blooming perennials, such as Japanese anemones (*Anemone × hybrida*), New York asters (*Aster novi-belgii*), bugbanes (*Cimicifuga* spp.), and chrysanthemums, are stars of the autumn border.

Don't overlook autumn crocuses (*Colchicum autumnale*) and other fall-blooming bulbs, which create a spectacular effect flowering through the crisp fallen leaves. And many frost-tolerant annuals, such as sweet alyssum (*Lobularia maritima*), rebloom in late summer and fall as the nights cool off. Surprisingly, they can provide a mass of dependable color into December, even where I live.

Specially selected for their dependable fall display, deciduous shrubs and trees begin assuming their fiery hues at the end of the growing season, but the last colorful leaves don't drop until close to Thanksgiving. All this glowing color is perfectly set off by a backdrop of evergreens.

Defining the Seasons

I live in a climate well suited to gardening. Long Island boasts four seasons, none of them severe or overlong. The latitude is reasonable, providing an adequate amount of daylight in every season, though winter's days do seem a bit too short and dim. However, I'm not complaining after learning that my friends in Alaska don't see the sun in winter for months on end, and they endure the roar of their neighbor's lawn mower at midnight because the July sun shines about 22 hours a day!

No matter where you live, the solstices and equinoxes occur on the same dates: approximately March 21, June 21, September 21, and December 21. If you live in Maine, you may feel it's a cruel joke when the weather forecaster announces on March 21 that it's the first day of spring—snow is swirling around the house and visibility is about zero. Those first crocuses are about a month away, and your last frost can be expected around Memorial Day. On the other hand, if you live along the Gulf Coast or in southern California, spring flowers may have been blooming for as long as six weeks before the official announcement of spring.

Elevation also influences the arrival of spring and the advent of the other seasons. In mountainous or hilly regions, local differences in elevation, and thus temperature and frosts, may significantly change the length of the seasons. The crabapples may be blooming where you work in the valley but be two weeks behind where you live up in the mountains.

Friends of mine who live in the mountains of Colorado may suffer a killing frost in August without seeing another frost until late October!

Seasons in the Garden

Where I live, the seasons pretty much match up with their "official" starting dates. But for me, the real start of the seasons occurs in relation to what's happening in the garden. I think of spring beginning about the second week of April, when forsythia suddenly gilds the neighborhood overnight. By then, the soil has warmed enough for the dandelions to bloom and the grass to green up. The fresh look of spring lasts for about two and a half months in my garden.

Summer arrives in mid- to late June with the rose blossoms and the maturing of the tree foliage from bright to dark green. My garden flowers abundantly throughout July and August and into September, again closely matching the solar calendar.

Autumn begins in mid- to late September, when the angle of light is noticeably lower in the sky, the air feels deliciously crisp, and the sky seems bluer as summer's humidity disappears. With this change in weather, the dogwoods take on their first hint of red. The fall foliage colors take their time developing. Our foliage peak is usually in late October.

While the weather often remains mild well into December (never mind the 8-inch snowfall on Thanksgiving Day in 1989 and the record-breaking low temperatures in December of that year), I usually think of winter as starting when the last foliage falls in mid- to late November. No matter what the temperature, the leafless landscape spells winter. The dormant season has arrived.

In this book, when I speak in specific terms of the different seasons, I'll be referring to the times of year these seasons visit my garden in the borderline of USDA Plant Hardiness Zones 6 and 7. The dates of bloom and the lengths of the seasons in my garden are likely to differ from those in yours, but for general discussion purposes this need not worry you. When it comes down to particulars, you may need to recalculate and make adjustments according to your location and climate. I've observed that with every 100 miles south I travel, spring arrives an entire week earlier and fall, a week later.

Designing the Bare Bones

Garden designers talk a lot about bones. The bones of the garden—its trees, shrubs, fences, walls, hard surfaces, and outlines, rather than the finery of flowers and foliage—endow the landscape with structure and form and, ultimately, with year-round beauty.

Successful year-round gardens owe their appearance to an attractive backbone of plants and garden structures. These "bones" provide a sculptural, three-dimensional quality that acts as a framework and backdrop for displaying foliage and flowers. Garden bones also frame our views of the garden as a whole.

Without a good structure to support it, a garden can't hold its own throughout the year. It will look especially desolate from late fall through midspring, when its bare bones—or lack of them—are most apparent. Garden designers always plan a garden's bones before anything else. After they put the bones in place, then, and only then, do they dress up the garden.

Creating the bones of a garden so that it looks as inviting in January as in June takes planning and thinking on a larger scale than most gardeners are used to. Don't think just in terms of the small plants in your flower beds and borders. Instead, think in terms of the shrubbery, fences, and walls behind them,

SEASONAL FEATURES
OF A YEAR-ROUND LANDSCAPE

In the four-season landscape, year-round color and appeal come from a specially orchestrated parade of plants, many of which enhance the landscape during more than one season. The following checklist describes the most prominent garden and landscape features in each season so you can choose your favorites.

Winter

▶ Evergreen foliage takes center stage in shades of bright and dark green, blue-green, gold, and rust

▶ Variegated evergreen foliage adds variety

▶ Berries of deciduous trees, shrubs, and vines add red, blue, and orange sparkle

▶ Colorful and textured bark adds interest

▶ Striking silhouettes and branching patterns of deciduous trees, shrubs, and vines add drama

▶ Bleached and dried seed stalks and foliage of ornamental grasses create contrast to darker tones and add movement

▶ Very early-flowering shrubs add color

▶ Very early-flowering bulbs create a bright carpet

▶ Very early-flowering perennials often bloom in unusually brilliant colors

▶ Forms, textures, and colors of garden structures and hardscape materials such as brick and rock contrast with the plants

Spring

▶ Greens of evergreen trees, shrubs, and groundcovers are still a keynote

▶ Flowering trees, shrubs, groundcovers, and vines add layers of color

▶ Spring-flowering bulbs create a brilliantly colored tapestry

▶ Early-blooming perennials add striking form and cool pastel colors

▶ Cool-season annuals like pansies add deeper colors to the spring palette

▶ Woodland wildflowers light up the shade

▶ Fresh colors of emerging tree and shrub foliage brighten their silhouettes

▶ Fresh green lawns are a hallmark of spring

Summer

▶ Midseason-flowering trees, shrubs, and vines add continuing color

▶ Flowering perennials brighten the border

▶ The deep green of shade tree foliage provides a cooling canopy of color

▶ The deep green of lawns creates a soothing backdrop to brilliant flower colors

▶ Burgundy, gold, and silver of colored and variegated foliage provide a welcome change

▶ Annuals come into their own with a season-long kaleidoscope of color

Autumn

▶ Red, yellow, purple, orange, and rust of fall foliage make the garden blaze

▶ Berries and fruits of trees, shrubs, and vines add bright clusters of color

▶ Evergreen foliage makes a striking backdrop to the bright deciduous foliage

▶ Fall-flowering perennials echo the deciduous foliage palette, adding lilac and blue as accents

▶ Cool-season annuals add more jewel tones to the fall color scheme

▶ Earthy colors of seedpods and ornamental grasses provide a beautiful contrast to the brighter colors of flowers and foliage

---

and of the trees spreading out overhead and standing in the background.

Think in terms of planting and designing your entire yard from ground level right up to the sky, because that's the area encompassed by your landscape. And that's the landscape you'll be viewing for 12 months of the year. Stand back from the garden and study it as a picture—the most effective gardens offer a series of views or frames that can stand on their own and be combined into a larger framework.

Borders: All Mixed Up

The traditional American yard sadly lacks an attractive structure. All too often, a stiff hedge, pruned into unnatural flat-walled neatness, or a stark board fence bounds the yard. A couple of tall trees and a smattering of flowering shrubs and small flowering trees dot the lawn, each standing in pathetic isolation. A row of stiffly regimented evergreens, tortured into balls, cones, and coffins, lines the house foundation. Annuals fill the flower beds with gaudy colors for two or three months, then wither with the frost, leaving a noticeable vacancy the rest of the year.

The answer to endowing your landscape with a strong structure is the mixed border, a coalition of small trees, shrubs, perennials, groundcovers, bulbs, and vines. Mixed borders combine an assortment of different plants into a pleasing arrangement. The arrangement has a backbone of trees and shrubs, with layers of branches giving the garden a year-round continuity.

The first step in creating a mixed border is simply to avoid planting shrubs and trees in isolation: Begin planting them in compatible groups instead. Don't arrange plants in segregated beds, borders, and hedges. Instead, mix your plantings up, combining herbaceous plants with trees and shrubs, and evergreens with deciduous plants. Don't relegate annuals or perennials to traditional flower borders that will lie barren and boring during the dormant months. Weave masses of them among groups of shrubs.

The basic mixed border can be used to landscape every part of your property, from the yard's boundaries to the home's foundation, from the garden's shady nooks to its sunny expanses. Mixed borders can be of either formal or informal design. Or you might create a naturalistic arrangement that mimics a real woodland. Keep in mind that the more perennials you plant, the more maintenance you'll need to keep the border tidy. This is especially true for neatniks, but if you thrive on carefree chaos, then you'll be happy with less order and thus less maintenance. (I'll go into more detail about how to design mixed borders in Chapter 6.)

Advice from an Expert Garden Designer

I learned a great deal about mixed borders and garden structure from my friend Conni Cross, a sought-after garden designer. Conni's own garden consistently evokes exclamations of awe from anyone who visits it at any time of year. Her garden constantly changes but never lacks excitement.

Something is always happening in every part of Conni's property, and the scenes change and evolve when viewed from different angles throughout the year. One week, bright pink honeysuckle flowers stud the gray fence surrounding the pool. The next week, mounds of frothy white sweet autumn clematis (*Clematis maximowicziana*) spill over the fence, changing the mood and grabbing the viewer's attention. Tiny bulbs peek out from behind rocks in spring, while a few months later, the same spot features a tapestry of groundcovers mingled with a sea of ever-changing perennials.

Conni is adamant about bones: "For bringing out the full potential of a garden, you must have structure. First put in the evergreens," she advises, "then plant the deciduous trees and shrubs, and place the walls and fences. After that, the rest will fall into place." Conni also admonishes that you "must know your plants" if the garden is to be lively and stimulating throughout the year and from year to year. She advises taking a close look at the plants you're considering using in a mixed border, especially the woody ones, and asking yourself a few questions:

▶ What is the plant's overall form, and how does it combine with other plants and its surroundings?

▶ What are a plant's branching structure and growth rate, and how will these affect nearby plants?

▶ Will the foliage contribute to the garden even when the plant is not in bloom?

▶ When does a plant flower, and what color are the flowers? How will the flowers look with the colors of nearby plants and the colors in the hardscape?

▶ Will the bark add color and interest during winter? How does the bark texture combine with the rest of the garden?

After you've evaluated a potential candidate, decide if the plant excites enough year-round interest or possesses other special attributes to deserve a place in your garden. If you have limited garden space, you won't want to waste much on plants that can't earn their keep.

The encyclopedia of plants in Chapter 7 describes the best plants to use for a four-season landscape and lists their seasonal attractions. By drawing on this encyclopedia of very special plants, you can give your landscape sparkle every month of the year.

Once you've selected the landscape plants that will perform longest in your garden, your next challenge will be to arrange them in pleasing combinations—combinations that work throughout the year, both visually and culturally. Even if two plants make a good-looking couple, the marriage won't last long unless your site's sun, soil, and climate suit them both.

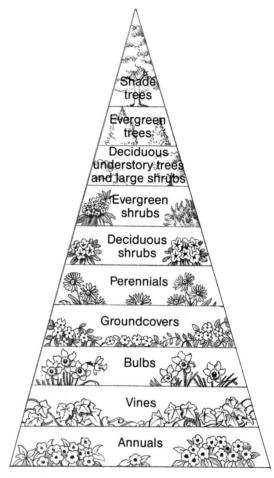

Planting pyramid. Designer Conni Cross's method of garden design involves selecting plants according to a hierarchy she calls a planting pyramid. She starts with the top of the pyramid and moves down, choosing plants that need the same care and conditions and can be used in the same way. Because the lowest-level plants are smallest, you can have more of them and use a greater selection.

Planting Pyramids

My friend Conni follows an almost foolproof method for designing a landscape's bones and selecting the plant combinations that make the garden a special place throughout the year. She calls her method "planting in pyramids." Depending on the size of the garden or landscape she's designing, Conni may create one to several different, but compatible, pyramids to fill the garden space. In large landscapes, she may repeat some pyramids several times next to each other to create an effective mass planting.

Assuming the site already has mature shade trees, she starts at the top of the pyramid, selecting a single small- to medium-height deciduous tree or large conifer. The tree forms the beginning of the garden's skeleton. Then she chooses the evergreen shrubs to be planted in the tree's sphere of influence—beneath or near its canopy. (See "Spheres of Influence" on page 244 for more information on this subject.) These evergreens form an important part of the garden's structure, especially in winter. Next comes a selection of deciduous flowering shrubs, often compact or dwarf forms, to be arranged between the groups of evergreens.

After Conni chooses the structural plants, she considers which groundcovers will work well with the woody plants. Then she adds groups or specimens of perennials, planted directly into the groundcover. These may add the most color and brilliance to the garden over the longest season but provide little year-round structure. The spring-flowering bulbs—those ephemeral flowers that are here today and gone tomorrow but loudly celebrated during their brief stay in spring—aren't chosen until the larger plants go in.

Last, but not least, Conni accessorizes the garden with woody vines. She adds vines to drape over walls and fences, twist their way into trees, or clamber into shrubs where they bring summer or fall flowers to eye level or higher.

Conni leaves plenty of room in the garden design for flowering annuals and tropical vines, though these aren't part of its permanent structure. Tropical vines, such as mandevilla (*Mandevilla* × *amabilis*), passionflowers (*Passiflora* spp.), and moonflower (*Ipomoea alba*), grow rampantly during summer, blooming constantly until frost cuts them down. A lavish allotment of annuals and tropical vines provides an opportunity to be creative each year—changing a color scheme or visual effect. These annual plants usually bloom constantly from early summer until frost, providing a dependable sweep of color to complement the changing perennials.

As we move down the pyramid from the narrow top to the widening bottom—from trees to bulbs—the number of each type of plant, and the number of different species of each type, increases. The planting pyramid progresses from tallest to shortest plants. Because the lowest-level plants are the smallest, you can have more of them and use a greater selection.

Mastering Bloom Sequence

When planning planting pyramids and plant combinations, keep in mind that the garden and individual plants will change through the year. You may wish to design your landscape so that different sections shine in different seasons. For instance, you could create a winter garden outside the kitchen window and a summer garden surrounding the patio or pool.

You really don't want *everything* in a garden—or section of it—blooming at the same time. This would be visually overpowering. Arrange plants so that evergreens or out-of-bloom perennials and shrubs provide islands

THE BASICS OF FOUR-SEASON LANDSCAPING

A garden that excites interest and commands attention throughout the year doesn't just happen—it's planned. Use these basic principles for creating a year-round landscape; you'll find more about them in this and the following chapters.

Develop garden bones. Create a landscape foundation with evergreen trees and shrubs and an attractive hardscape of walls, fences, paths, and patios.

Use mixed borders. Rely on borders of trees, shrubs, groundcovers, perennials, and bulbs to provide year-round structure.

Plant evergreens. Needled and broad-leaved evergreens give year-round greenery and privacy. They also form a background for brighter plants.

Emphasize outlines. Plant deciduous trees where their winter outlines are silhouetted against the sky.

Look for lengthy bloomers. Choose perennials with long blooming seasons to keep the perennial border in flower.

Seek added features. Choose flowering plants with foliage or fruits that add interest to the garden after flowers fade.

Use your views. Plant early bloomers within sight of a window or near an entrance, where you can see them from indoors and as you come and go.

Plant multiseason shrubs. Choose deciduous shrubs with attractive flowers and colorful fall foliage or berries for several seasons of garden color.

Mix things up. Place plants with colored or variegated foliage amid green-leaved plants to liven up the garden's color scheme.

of green between masses of blooming plants. The foliage provides a bit of tranquility without obliterating the garden's excitement.

Ideally, those out-of-bloom plants should come into bloom in sequence with the ones that are presently in bloom, so the garden changes but remains colorful. To make sure this happens, you need to know the blooming seasons of your plant palette very well. You should know not only in which season a plant blooms, but also when it blooms within that season and how long its display lasts. You also need to know if a plant dies back after flowering or needs to be cut back, leaving an empty hole in the garden, or if its foliage remains handsome after its flowers fade.

In the following chapters I'll describe successful combinations you might wish to duplicate in your landscape. If you wish to create your own combinations, consult the encyclopedia of plants in Chapter 7.

Learning from Mistakes

I've learned that it's not always a simple matter to combine plants attractively. One of my worst mistakes was to plant masses of bearded iris next to Siberian iris (*Iris sibirica*). I thought they would bloom sequentially, but their two-week flowering periods overlapped by a week.

Though separately these flowers embellish almost any perennial border, planted side by side they destroyed each other. The opulent bearded irises became a vulgar spectacle blooming beside the more delicate Siberians, which in turn lost their charm and grace, appearing weak and feeble.

Fortunately, most mistakes with perennials are easily remedied. Transplanting the Siberian irises to a different site with more suitable companions proved the solution to the war of the irises. Transplanting large established shrubs, however, is another matter, although young shrubs can be moved easily enough during their first year or two in a garden. I usually keep on trying until I get them arranged in a pleasing composition, but it's better to plan ahead and site permanent large plants very carefully.

Choosing Good Companions

When selecting garden companions, consider each plant's physical attributes, performance schedule, and cultural requirements. Choose plants that bloom at the same time for drama and those that bloom sequentially for a long season of color.

Consider whether the flower colors and shapes complement or detract from each other's looks. Some plants—like some people—just can't get along with each other no matter how hard they try. When this happens, keep them apart by placing other plants in between, or better yet, don't invite them to the same garden party.

Finally, ask yourself whether your plant choices look good together when out of bloom—contrasting plant shapes and foliage textures and colors go a long way toward creating garden interest and are just as important as flower combinations. Gray, silver, or burgundy foliage often works wonders by subduing other colors.

One of my favorite combinations consists of late-blooming evergreen azaleas, such as 'Gumpo White', with the dwarf yellow-flowered daylily 'Stella d'Oro' and blue-flowered Serbian bellflower (*Campanula poscharskyana*) nestled together in front. All three bloom in late spring and early summer, but they also form an attractive combination out of bloom. The swordlike daylily foliage arches over the mounds of scalloped bellflower leaves, while the handsome oval azalea leaves provide a dark green background.

Painting a Lovely Picture

In the next four chapters, I'll describe many of the best plants and planting combinations for each season of the year. You will learn how to choose and combine plants so that your garden will look lovely all year. I'll tell you how to plant your property for winter brightness as well as for summer jubilee. And when sections of your garden are temporarily out of bloom, the garden's luxuriant foliage and good bones will carry the day so you won't even miss the flowers. Whether your property is small or large, by following this simple method you can enjoy your garden 12 months of the year.

If you intend for your garden to be a work of art, observe it closely. Consider whether you've actually created a beautiful picture or merely planted a collection of beautiful flowers. With careful observation through the seasons, you can develop the skill to combine lovely plants into an even lovelier garden scene.

CHAPTER 2

Winter in the Four-Season Landscape

Wake Up the Dormant Season with Berries, Bark, Evergreens, and Flowers

From my vantage point at the top of our hilly property, I sometimes feel as if I'm living in a tree house. From most of the upstairs rooms I can look directly into the canopies of the surrounding trees. The views change dramatically with the onset of winter. When the leaves have dropped from the trees and shrubs, the landscape takes on a transparent, see-through quality.

Vistas and expanses of sky that are blocked by a solid mass of leaves in other seasons open up, viewed through winter's veil of bare branches. The beauty of the winter scenery relies on a combination of solid and transparent elements. The solidity of evergreens, walls, and fences contrasts with the transparency of deciduous trees and shrubs, creating drama and excitement.

When you look at your landscape in winter, you'll see that when deciduous trees and hedges become see-through, they no longer hold your eye: You look through and beyond them. This transparent quality gives the landscape an open feeling that's quite unlike the enclosed lushness of summer.

While this openness often reveals beautiful views, such as a distant landscape or a hidden garden scene, sometimes you're not so lucky. In some cases, the views opened up turn out to be objectionable eyesores. A screen of summer greenery may hide a neighbor's woodpile, garbage cans, or compost pile, but come winter, suddenly the eyesores come into full view.

The woods behind my property effectively screen off my neighbors' backyards much of the year. But, come winter, the expanded view includes a huge trailered boat wrapped up like a Christmas present in a protective blue plastic tarpaulin. Strategically placed hemlocks (*Tsuga canadensis*), white pines (*Pinus strobus*), Catawba rhododendrons (*Rhododendron catawbiense*), and mountain laurels (*Kalmia latifolia*) will eventually grow tall enough to solve this problem, but I hope my neighbor tires of the boat sooner than it takes my evergreens to mature!

The Beautiful Bones of Winter

As you might guess, for winter beauty, a garden relies less on color and more on form and structure. The things that make up a garden's structure—its trees, walls, paths, evergreen shrubs, benches, and so on—are often called its bones. If you look at your own garden in winter, you can see how these "bones" work together to create an attractive landscape. If, on the other hand, the structural elements are badly placed or there aren't enough of them, your garden will look barren or unattractive.

Evergreens, because they look the same all year, can give continuity to your garden's design while forming the most prominent part of its winter bone structure. Deciduous trees and shrubs will contribute to the skeleton, but they carry much less visual weight and importance during the leafless months than during the growing season. Garden structures, such as fences, walls, arbors, and statuary, also play a more important role in the winter garden.

One of the keys to designing a good-looking landscape is siting the deciduous and evergreen trees and shrubs where they'll look best. Your goal is to plant deciduous trees and shrubs so you can enjoy distant scenery through the veil of their naked branches, or to locate them where they form a dramatic silhouette to be enjoyed for its own sake. You'll need to decide where to place masses of evergreens to effectively screen off undesirable views, frame desirable ones, or act as a solid background for deciduous plantings. For more on planting evergreens, see "Guidelines for Placing Evergreens" on page 244.

Remember to mix deciduous trees and shrubs with your evergreens. A deciduous plant, situated as a solitary element among evergreens, looks forlorn—perhaps even dead—surrounded by a lot of greenery. When creating your garden, try to keep a balance between the evergreens and the deciduous trees and shrubs. Arrange them in groups, balancing the visual weight of the evergreen shrubs with a greater mass of lightweight deciduous shrubs. You'll find more about creating balance and using visual weight in garden design in Chapter 6.

One of the easiest ways to add interest to the winter landscape is to choose trees and shrubs that have structural interest. You can choose a plant for its dramatic silhouette, for its unusual way of branching, or for its ability to hold snow in interesting sculptural patterns. Let's look at each option in detail.

Shapely Silhouettes

You can create great effects in a winter garden by repeating, combining, and contrasting vertical and wide-reaching shapes. Mix plants with fine and bold textures, regular and irregular outlines, and heavy and light visual weights when designing your garden's bones.

To choose trees and shrubs with appealing winter outlines, pay a winter visit to a large arboretum or botanical garden, where plants are identified. Stroll around and familiarize yourself with the shapes, textures, and branching patterns of the various plants. Once you've identified the plants, step back far enough to see how they look in silhouette. Each tree and shrub has a characteristic branching structure, so choose the ones that will work best in your landscape. (You'll find four-season trees with effective silhouettes in "Plants with Dramatic Winter Silhouettes" on page 20.)

PLANTS WITH DRAMATIC WINTER SILHOUETTES

In the more open winter landscape, many woody plants reveal the dramatic beauty of their branching patterns. Deciduous trees and shrubs create striking silhouettes when displayed against a clear blue sky, an orange sunset, or an evergreen backdrop.

Deciduous Trees with Horizontal Branches

Albizia julibrissin (mimosa), Zones 6–9
Cercis canadensis (redbud), Zones 5–9
Cornus alternifolia (pagoda dogwood), Zones 4–7
C. florida (flowering dogwood), Zones 5–9
C. kousa (Kousa dogwood), Zones 5–7
Crataegus spp. (hawthorns), Zones 4–9
Nyssa sylvatica (black gum), Zones 5–9
Quercus alba (white oak), Zones 4–9
Q. palustris (pin oak), Zones 5–8

Deciduous Trees with Weeping Branches

Betula pendula 'Tristis' and 'Youngii' (weeping European birches), Zones 3–5
Carpinus betulus 'Pendula' (weeping European hornbeam), Zones 5–7
Cornus florida 'Pendula' (weeping flowering dogwood), Zones 5–8
Fagus sylvatica 'Pendula' (weeping green beech) and 'Purpurea-Pendula' (weeping purple beech), Zones 5–9
Prunus subhirtella var. *pendula* (weeping Higan cherry), Zones 6–8
Pyrus salicifolia 'Silver Frost' ('Silver Frost' weeping pear), Zones 5–8
Salix alba 'Tristis' (golden weeping willow), Zones 4–9

Pyramidal Deciduous Trees

Betula spp. (birches), Zones 2–9
Liquidambar styraciflua (sweet gum), Zones 5–9
Oxydendrum arboreum (sourwood), Zones 5–9
Pyrus calleryana (callery pear), Zones 5–9
Quercus palustris (pin oak), Zones 5–8
Taxodium distichum (bald cypress), Zones 5–9
Tilia cordata (littleleaf linden), Zones 3–8

Evergreen Trees with Horizontal Branches

Cedrus atlantica (atlas cedar), Zones 7–9
Metasequoia glyptostroboides (dawn redwood), Zones 5–9
Pinus densiflora (Japanese red pine), Zones 5–7
P. sylvestris (Scotch pine), Zones 3–8
Pseudolarix kaempferi (golden larch), Zones 6–7

Evergreen Trees with Weeping Branches

Cedrus libani 'Pendula' (weeping cedar-of-Lebanon), Zones 5–9
Picea pungens 'Pendula' (weeping Colorado spruce), Zones 3–7
Pinus strobus 'Pendula' (weeping white pine), Zones 3–9
Pseudotsuga menziesii 'Pendula' (weeping Douglas fir), Zones 3–6
Tsuga canadensis 'Pendula' (weeping Canada hemlock), Zones 3–8

Pyramidal Evergreen Trees

Ilex aquifolium (English holly), Zones 7–9
I. opaca (American holly), Zones 6–9
Juniperus virginiana (eastern red cedar), Zones 3–9
Magnolia grandiflora (southern magnolia), Zones 6–9
Picea spp. (spruces), Zones 3–8

Deciduous Trees and Shrubs with Striking Branching Patterns

Corylus avellana 'Contorta' (Harry Lauder's walking stick), Zones 4–8
Cotoneaster horizontalis (rockspray cotoneaster), Zones 5–8
Salix matsudana 'Tortulosa' (corkscrew willow), Zones 5–9
Stephanandra incisa 'Crispa' (cutleaf stephanandra), Zones 5–8
Viburnum plicatum var. *tomentosum* (doublefile viburnum), Zones 5–8

When you start looking at trees in winter, you'll see how heavily branched trees with massive scaffolds appear much more commanding than trees with slender, fine-textured branches borne in a regular pattern. Some trees have especially dramatic winter silhouettes. I always admire the cascading branches of the weeping Higan cherry (*Prunus subhirtella* var. *pendula*) and the perfect oval crown of the littleleaf linden (*Tilia cordata*).

A stout-trunked, heavy-limbed English oak (*Quercus robur*) will send its rugged branches out at wide angles, forming a dark, massive, craggy outline against the winter sky. Such a tree works well in an informal or naturalistic setting. On the other hand, the elegant oval outline of a 'Bradford' pear (*Pyrus calleryana* 'Bradford') has much less visual weight and a more refined appearance than the oak's. Its pattern and texture suit a more formal or intimate setting.

The undulating horizontal branching structure of the flowering dogwood (*Cornus florida*) is so special that the pattern has its own name: sympodial branching. The dogwood's branches form graceful tiers of outreaching waves studded with fat, round flower buds. For a pretty winter grouping, try a cluster of dogwoods, with their strong horizontal pattern, underplanted with rounded shrubs, such as pinxterbloom azaleas (*Rhododendron periclymenoides*), for a contrast of line and pattern.

Other effective ways to use silhouettes play up the exclamation-point excitement of columnar trees and shrubs. You can plant them in a short line in a formal landscape, or use one as a single contrasting element in a group of rounded or spreading plants. But don't plant long rows of severely shaped plants as a border or edging unless a formal design anchors them to the rest of the landscape. Some of the worst examples of landscaping I've seen use a line of columnar evergreens against a wall or along the edge of a driveway or lawn. In such situations, the repetition of the strong vertical shape looks too rigid, like prisoners in a lineup.

Evergreen trees and shrubs, though solid-looking in winter, also add their shapely silhouettes to the winter scenery. Standing solid and dark against a lighter background, such as the sky or a snow-covered lawn, evergreens anchor the scenery, contrasting with the openness of nearby deciduous plants. Their very solidity gives their silhouettes a geometrical look—conical, columnar, horizontal, or rounded.

To get the most from your winter landscape, place a deciduous or evergreen specimen with a dramatic shape in an open, uncluttered setting where its outline can be fully appreciated. Don't hide it in a grove, but let it stand on its own, with no competing elements nearby or in the background. If you situate a dramatic tree such as a white oak (*Quercus alba*), atlas cedar (*Cedrus atlantica*), or European beech (*Fagus sylvatica*) against the western sky, you'll be rewarded with the spectacular sight of its handsome, dark silhouette displayed against a backdrop of fire as the sun sets.

Since slow-growing trees, such as atlas cedar and beech, can take 50 years to mature into noble specimens—and need considerable room in which to grow to perfection—you may never see the results of your thoughtful planting. If you're lucky enough to inherit a mature specimen of cedar, beech, pine, or oak, then by all means clean up the background, if need be, to fully appreciate the beauty of the pattern and texture of the tree's silhouette.

Twisted Personalities

Weird but lovable plants with oddly twisted and spiraled branches really come into their own in winter. The best-known of these twisted

Wrong

Right

Using tree silhouettes. *Wrong:* The silhouette of this weeping tree disappears among the interfering branches of the neighboring trees, which detract from the weeper's splendid shape. *Right:* This weeping tree is the tallest element of the design, with mounded and spreading plants beneath, so that its silhouette stands out.

trees and shrubs are Harry Lauder's walking stick (*Corylus avellena* 'Contorta') and corkscrew willow (*Salix matsudana* 'Tortuosa'). When leafless, their crazy-quilt branching patterns may not be beautiful, but they certainly score high in the "odd and curious" category. Use one of these plant oddities as a playful element to liven up a somber winter scene.

In summer, the rough-textured foliage of Harry Lauder's walking stick totally obscures the plant's weird branching pattern. I've seen specimens that look like large, green heaps of leaves in summer. But as the foliage turns golden and shrivels in autumn, the twisted nature of the branches becomes more apparent. This zigzaggy plant looks delightful in winter, especially when coated with ice or snow, or when its rain-darkened bark is set off against a lighter background. In late winter, long yellow catkins dangle like Christmas ornaments from the curly boughs.

To get the full effect of a contorted plant, isolate one and locate it as a focal point in a winter garden. When mashed into a border with plants of the same size or set against a busy background, the odd outlines are lost. Plant the weird thing as the tallest plant in a group of low-spreading shrubs and groundcovers with simple, perhaps horizontal, lines. And be sure your twisted plant has a plain background, such as a wall or an evergreen hedge, to act as a backdrop for its silhouette.

My friend Claudia Scholtz planted a Harry Lauder's walking stick in a whiskey barrel located beside her garden shed. From her kitchen window, Claudia can admire the curious branch pattern set off against the light-colored boards of the shed's siding.

Contorted plants such as Harry Lauder's walking stick result from mutations. Specimens with branches twisted corkscrew-style occur from time to time in almost any plant species. Many of these oddities are offered by nurseries or mail-order catalogs; you can often recognize them by the cultivar name 'Contorta'. ("Plants with Dramatic Winter Silhouettes" on page 20 lists some readily available types.)

Snow-Catchers

A snowfall can transform a desolate winter landscape into an architectural marvel in a matter of minutes. Snow frosts surfaces with light-reflecting whiteness, giving a tired landscape a quick face-lift. Snow can improve an unattractive site, concealing winter's mud and other eyesores.

Snow also emphasizes the garden's structure, or lack thereof, by painting white edges along all the dark outlines. A flat property without much structural interest simply disappears under the snow cover, resulting in a boring white scene. On the other hand, a well-designed landscape featuring handsome clusters of skeletal trees and shrubs becomes a lovely high-contrast study in black and white.

When fluffy white snow catches in all the nooks and crannies of branches and fences, the garden's bones become all the more apparent and important. Rising from the drifts, the dark silhouettes of trees and shrubs give the garden dimension.

Trees and shrubs also act as snow-catchers, holding out their branches to collect and display the crystals. I especially love the tiered branches of flowering dogwoods when lightly crusted with snow or ice—they look as pretty as a wedding cake. Evergreens are good snow-catchers, too. When snow clings to their needles or broad dark leaves, they seem dressed for a holiday party.

You'll appreciate snow more if you study the patterns it makes in your garden. I think a light snow—just an inch or two—looks perfect. This amount is enough to blanket the ground and stack up along tree limbs and fence posts, but it's not enough to hide low stone walls, boulders, and planters. Stalks and seedpods of leftover perennials burst through the snow cover, creating intricate patterns.

In my own garden, I like to look at how and where the snow piles up along the notches of my trellises and clings to the rough bark of the oak trees. I especially cherish the forlorn look of my Adirondack chairs when several inches of snow stand on their wide armrests and seat slats. These snow-clad chairs, as desolate as they seem, offer a promise of the season to come. They remind me of the pleasant hours I will soon be spending, sitting surrounded by a blooming garden. And for now, they reinforce the coziness I feel inside my warm home on a cold winter's day.

Your Garden's Winter Color Scheme

Color plays as important a role in the winter garden as it does during the other seasons. It may even be more important, since we crave it so much more during winter.

Even in the coldest regions where snow comes early and stays late, colorful evergreens can add blue, green, rust, and gold to the garden. It's true that, except for the azure sky, winter's pigments may seem decidedly subdued. But you can design your garden with winter color in mind, aiming to intensify nature's palette with a careful selection of four-season plants.

Color Clues from Nature

The natural winter landscape offers many clues to creating a colorful garden during the dormant season. Although subtle, the colors in a winter garden can be quite alluring. You can draw inspiration from nature, scaling down the scope of the scene to fit into your own backyard.

Winter transforms the grasses and wildflowers clustered along the roadside and inhabiting old fields to a patchwork of wonderful earth-colored stems and foliage. The little bluestem (*Schizachyrium scoparium*), a native prairie grass, forms fine-textured patches of vivid peachy orange blades that stand out against the greens, browns, and straw colors of other grasses and dried flower stalks.

Clusters of river birch (*Betula nigra*), another midwestern wetland tree, go mostly unnoticed from a distance in summer when cloaked with foliage. Come winter, when wearing only their shaggy coats of colorful bark, these same trees command attention. The bark peels away in gleaming curls of metallic bronze and copper with hints of salmon and pink. A blanket of snow sets off the bark to perfection.

Choosing Your Winter Palette

Any winter garden gets most of its color from the foliage of evergreen plants. Never forget that green is a color, too—the most important color of all in the garden! Complement the color of your evergreens with carefully selected deciduous plants. You can add deciduous color by choosing trees and shrubs with red and orange berries clinging to their branches or with colorful, highly textured bark.

Complete your winter palette with dried grasses and perennials in shades of almond, russet, ash blond, and wheat. If you live in a mild climate, your winter garden might even boast an unusual sight—winter-blooming flowers. We'll discuss all these features, and which plants to choose to get them, on the following pages.

Essential Evergreens

Psychologists who study human responses to color say that green is one of the most restful, calming colors. But we tend to over-look green as a garden color because green surrounds us—it's everywhere. Green becomes the canvas we paint the "color" on in our summer gardens. But not in winter. In winter, green beckons. Green signifies life. Green becomes the most welcome color, providing relief from mud brown.

Evergreen trees, shrubs, and groundcovers form both the flesh and bones of the winter garden. They're as essential to the garden for their mass and form as for their color. Green-ery from conifers and broadleaved evergreens contributes the primary color to the winter landscape, with broadleaved evergreens pre-dominating in southern areas and conifers in colder regions.

Most conifer species grow naturally into large trees, limiting the number the average home landscape can accommodate. All too often a homeowner plants a cute blue spruce or Douglas fir as a specimen in the front lawn, only to find it, 20 years later, gobbling up the yard and lurking over the house like some monster unleashed on the unsuspecting landscape. Enter dwarf conifers—slow-growing or miniature versions of normal evergreen species.

Delightful Dwarfs

Dwarf conifers grow at a much slower rate than would be expected of the species, but that doesn't necessarily mean they mature into small plants. Take a Colorado spruce (*Picea pungens*), which matures at 135 feet tall, and its slow-growing cultivar 'Fat Albert' (*P. pungens* 'Fat Albert'), which grows at half the speed. The so-called "dwarf" may reach its ultimate height of 75 feet in 50 years.

Exact information on the mature size of most dwarf conifers is hard to come by, but if you expect them to grow at half the rate and to half the size of their species, you should be

---

BACKBONE EVERGREEN SHRUBS FOR FOUR-SEASON LANDSCAPES

Evergreen shrubs give a winter garden structure and mass, while creating an impor-tant backbone throughout the year. Choose the following coniferous and broadleaved ever-green shrubs as the essential backbone plants in your mixed border.

Coniferous Shrubs

Chamaecyparis obtusa (Hinoki false cypress), Zones 5–8
Juniperus chinensis (Chinese juniper), Zones 4–9
Pinus mugo (mugo pine), Zones 3–7
Taxus baccata (English yew), Zones 6–8
T. cuspidata (Japanese yew), Zones 4–7
T. × media (Anglojapanese yew), Zones 5–7

Broadleaved Shrubs

Buxus microphylla var. *koreana* 'Wintergreen' ('Wintergreen' littleleaf box), Zones 5–8
B. sempervirens (common boxwood), Zones 6–8
Daphne odora (winter daphne), Zones 8–10
Ilex cornuta (Chinese holly), Zones 7–9
I. crenata (Japanese holly), Zones 6–9
I. glabra (inkberry), Zones 5–9
I. × meserveae (blue holly), Zones 4–8
Kalmia latifolia (mountain laurel), Zones 5–9
Rhododendron carolinianum (Carolina rhodo-dendron), Zones 5–7
R. × indicum (evergreen azalea hybrids), Zones 6–9
R. 'P.J.M.' ('P.J.M.' rhododendron), Zones 5–7
R. yakusimanum, (yako rhododendron), Zones 6–8

---

safe. Some, however, are much slower and smaller: These can often be spotted by the cultivar name 'Nana', derived from the Latin word for dwarf. Broadleaved shrubs are available in dwarf or compact-growing cultivars, too. The Dwarf Conifer Society is developing

(continued on page 28)

WINTER ENTRANCE GARDEN

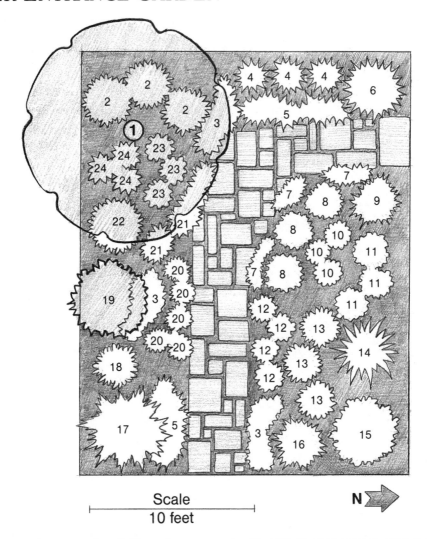

Scale
10 feet

N ➤

Plot plan for an entrance garden. 1. *Stewartia pseudocamellia* (Japanese stewartia) **2.** *Pieris japonica* 'Red Mill' ('Red Mill' Japanese pieris) **3.** *Galanthus nivalis* (common snowdrop) **4.** *Cupressus arizonica* 'Blue Pyramid' ('Blue Pyramid' Arizona cypress) **5.** *Juniperus horizontalis* 'Livida' **6.** *Chamaecyparis pisifera* 'Filifera Aurea' (golden-threadleaf Sawara false cypress) **7.** *Crocus chrysanthus* (snow crocus) **8.** *Leucothoe fontanesiana* 'Scarletta' (scarlet leucothoe) **9.** *Picea pungens* 'Montgomery' ('Montgomery' dwarf blue spruce) **10.** *Sedum* 'Autumn Joy' ('Autumn Joy' sedum) **11.** *Rudbeckia fulgida* var. *sullivantii* 'Goldsturm' ('Goldsturm' black-eyed Susan) **12.** *Calluna vulgaris* 'Silver Knight' ('Silver Knight' heather) **13.** *Daphne odora* (winter daphne) **14.** *Miscanthus sinensis* 'Gracillimus' (maiden grass) **15.** *Callicarpa bodinieri* 'Profusion' ('Profusion' Bodinier beautyberry) **16.** *Pinus strobus* 'Blue Shag' ('Blue Shag' white pine) **17.** *Pinus densiflora* 'Oculus-draconis' (dragon-eye pine) **18.** *Rhododendron yakusimanum* (Yako rhododendron) **19.** *Hamamelis* × *intermedia* 'Arnold Promise' ('Arnold Promise' witch hazel) **20.** *Erica carnea* 'Winter Beauty' ('Winter Beauty' heath) **21.** *Chionodoxa luciliae* (glory-of-the-snow) **22.** *Rhododendron* 'Aglo' ('Aglo' rhododendron) **23.** *Helleborus orientalis* (Lenten rose) **24.** *Arum italicum* 'Pictum' (Italian arum)

Entrance garden. On close view all year, this entrance garden is designed for impact during the long winter months. Winter features include beauty-berry, a shrub with bright lavender berries; Japanese stewartia, a tree with colorful patchwork bark; ever-greens that take on rich gold, blue, or ruby red colors in cold weather; winter-blooming shrubs, perennials, and bulbs; and dried grasses and seedpods. The garden makes a splash the rest of the year, too, with an assortment of seasonal flowers.

standardized categories, based on growth rates, for dwarf conifers. Let's hope this information will soon be included on nursery plant labels.

You won't go wrong by using dwarf conifers and compact cultivars of broadleaved evergreens as backbone plants for the mixed borders of your four-season landscape. Their diversity of form, color, and texture excites year-round interest, and because of their slower growth and smaller size, you'll be able to fit a wider selection into your garden. These compact choices can also reduce maintenance; they are less likely to require pruning to keep them from outgrowing their garden sites.

Don't plant the really slow-growing dwarfs, which grow only into tiny mounds a few inches tall in a mixed border; they are quickly overpowered by the perennials and groundcovers. Concentrate instead on the slow-growing, compact types, or the weeping or ground-hugging forms. Save the pygmies for specialty sites such as rock gardens, where their diminutive stature seems appropriate. (The best evergreen trees and shrubs for winter color in four-season landscapes and mixed borders are listed in "Evergreen Shrubs with Colorful Foliage" on the opposite page, "Evergreens with Purplish, Red, or Bronze Winter Color" on page 30, and "Evergreen Trees and Shrubs with Variegated Foliage" on page 36.)

The Many Shades of Evergreen

Evergreen foliage comes in many hues. Tints and shades of basic green abound, ranging from blue-green through gray-green to yellow-green, and from dark, somber shades to light, cheerful hues. And then, of course, we must consider the foliage that could hardly be called green at all—foliage that I call "evergold" and "everblue," to create more apt descriptions than evergreen.

Three genera stand out among the conifers for their amazing range of blue and golden cultivars: junipers (*Juniperus* spp.), false cypress (*Chamaecyparis* spp.), and spruces (*Picea* spp.). The golden and yellow-green cultivars of common green conifers warm up the winter garden with their reminders of summer sunshine. Such beauties as 'Golden Mop' and golden threadleaf Sawara false cypress (*Chamaecyparis pisifera* 'Golden Mop' and *C. pisifera* 'Filifera Aurea') make radiant contrasts throughout the year but are especially welcome in winter because of their sunny color.

Some garden designers consider the conifer cultivars with blue-green, steel blue, and gray-green foliage too cold-looking for the winter landscape. But I find that their steely blue color looks especially lovely under a somber winter sky.

Winter light enhances the color of conifers such as Colorado blue spruce (*Picea pungens* 'Glauca'), blue atlas cedar (*Cedrus atlantica* 'Glauca'), and 'Blue Star' juniper (*Juniperus squamata* 'Blue Star'). Freshly fallen snow settling along the branches seems even whiter and purer when juxtaposed with the waxy blue needles. Many junipers, especially those descended from the highly variable Chinese juniper (*Juniperus chinensis*), bear blue-green or blue-gray needles on upright, spreading, or ground-hugging shrubs.

The best color companions for blue-green conifers are dark green yews (*Taxus* spp.), boxwoods (*Buxus* spp.), or hollies (*Ilex* spp.), and broadleaved evergreens with foliage that turns burgundy in cold weather, such as pieris (*Pieris* spp.). The blues also look crisp and clean combined with white-variegated evergreens, such as 'Emerald Gaiety' wintercreeper (*Euonymus fortunei* 'Emerald Gaiety'), variegated Japanese pieris (*Pieris japonica* 'Variegata'), or 'Silver Queen' English holly (*Ilex aquifolium* 'Silver Queen'). But I don't find them good mates for the golden or yellowish green types.

EVERGREEN SHRUBS WITH COLORFUL FOLIAGE

Better termed "evergold" or "everblue," many needled or broadleaved evergreens add vivid foliage color to a winter landscape.

Gold-Needled

Chamaecyparis obtusa 'Fernspray Gold', 'Golden Drop', and 'Golden Sprite' (golden Hinoki false cypresses), Zones 5–8

C. pisifera 'Filifera Aurea' (golden threadleaved Sawara false cypress), Zones 5–8

C. pisifera 'Golden Mop' ('Golden Mop' Sawara false cypress), Zones 5–8

Juniperus chinensis 'Pfitzeriana Aurea' (golden Pfitzer juniper), Zones 4–9

J. horizontalis 'Mother Lode' ('Mother Lode' creep ing juniper), Zones 4–9

Picea orientalis 'Aurea Compacta' (compact golden oriental spruce), Zones 5–8

Taxus baccata 'Aurea' (golden English yew), Zones 6–8

T. baccata 'Standishii' (Standish golden English yew), Zones 6–8

T. cuspidata 'Aurescens' (golden Japanese yew), Zones 4–7

Golden Broadleaved

Abelia × *grandiflora* 'Francis Mason' ('Francis Mason' glossy abelia), Zones 6–9

Ilex crenata 'Golden Gem' ('Golden Gem' Japanese holly), Zones 6–9

Blue- or Blue-Gray-Needled

Chamaecyparis pisifera 'Boulevard' (blue moss Sawara false cypress), Zones 5–8

C. pisifera 'Mikko' ('Mikko' Sawara false cypress), Zones 5–8

Juniperus horizontalis 'Bar Harbor' ('Bar Harbor' juniper), Zones 3–8

J. horizontalis 'Wiltonii' (blue rug juniper), Zones 3–8

Picea pungens 'Fat Albert' and 'Montgomery' ('Fat Albert' and 'Montgomery' dwarf blue spruces), Zones 3–7

Getting into the Chameleon Act

The foliage of evergreens, whatever its predominant hue, does not always remain colorfast. Many evergreens, both coniferous and broadleaved, perform a chameleon routine in winter, changing color subtly or even dramatically with the onset of the cold months. This color change enhances some evergreens and detracts from others. (Evergreens noted for attractive winter color are listed in "Evergreens with Purplish, Red, or Bronze Winter Color" on page 30.)

Certain junipers, such as eastern red cedar (*Juniperus virginiana*), change from handsome green to a dirty brownish green in winter. Although this trait seems to occur in individual plants and not consistently throughout the species, such specimens only reinforce winter's bleakness, hibernating as they do under a cloak of off-color needles that seem more dead than alive.

Seek out junipers like 'Livida' creeping juniper (*Juniperus horizontalis* 'Livida') that enhance the winter landscape by turning a plum color rather than a dying green. These plants can make useful contrasts to junipers and other conifers that stay green, such as dwarf prostrate Chinese juniper (*Juniperus chinensis* var. *procumbens* 'Nana').

Many of the broadleaved evergreens take on deep red and purplish hues during the cold months. These colors become richest in a sunny location, but keep in mind that most broadleaved evergreens appreciate some shade in summer, especially in the South. A spot under deciduous trees may suit their seasonal needs best. Broadleaved evergreens may also suffer leaf burn from harsh winds and bright sun reflected off snow in northerly sites when the soil is frozen. Try to choose a protected spot out of the wind and with only half a day of full winter sun in the coldest regions.

EVERGREENS WITH PURPLISH, RED, OR BRONZE WINTER COLOR

Some evergreens change color with the seasons. They often deepen from green to a rich purplish burgundy or bronze during the cold months, especially when sited in full sun. One familiar example is the eastern red cedar (*Juniperus virginiana*). Here are some others to try:

Broadleaved Shrubs and Groundcovers

Arctostaphylos uva-ursi 'Massachusetts' ('Massachusetts' bearberry), Zones 3–5

Bergenia cordifolia (heartleaf bergenia), Zones 3–8

Euonymus fortunei 'Colorata' (purple-leaf wintercreeper), Zones 4–8

E. fortunei 'Harlequin' ('Harlequin' wintercreeper), Zones 4–8

Leucothoe fontanesiana 'Scarletta' ('Scarletta' leucothoe), Zones 5–9

L. keiskei (Keisk's leucothoe), Zones 6–9

Mahonia aquifolium (Oregon grape holly), Zones 5–9

Pieris japonica 'Red Mill' ('Red Mill' Japanese pieris), Zones 5–9

P. japonica 'Variegata' (variegated Japanese pieris), Zones 6–8

Rhododendron × 'Marilee' ('Marilee' Polly Hill azalea), Zones 6–8

R. 'P.J.M.' ('P.J.M.' rhododendron), Zones 5–7

Thuja orientalis 'Juniperoides' (juniper oriental arborvitae), Zones 6–8

Vaccinium crassifolium 'Wells Delight' ('Wells Delight' creeping blueberry), Zones 4–9

Coniferous Shrubs and Groundcovers

Juniperus horizontalis 'Douglasii' (Waukegan juniper), Zones 3–8

J. horizontalis 'Livida' ('Livida' creeping juniper), Zones 3–8

Microbiota decussata (Siberian carpet cypress), Zones 2–8

The foliage at the branch tips of some cultivars of Japanese pieris (*Pieris japonica*) and mountain pieris (*P. floribunda*) becomes gleaming red, ruby, or burgundy after the first frost. The reddest winter foliage—and also the reddest new spring growth—occurs in Japanese pieris cultivars with red or pink flowers rather than the species, which bears pure white flowers. Favorites for winter foliage color include *P. japonica* 'Dorothy Wycoff' and 'Coleman'.

Long ornamental chains of small, round flower buds form at the branch tips of pieris plants in fall and remain all winter. These bud chains are usually light green in white-flowered cultivars but may be highly colored, especially in red- and pink-flowered cultivars. Pieris flowers open in late winter and last six to eight weeks. They are often followed or accompanied by colorful new growth, earning pieris a place among my top ten four-season plants!

Japanese pieris cultivars noted for the reddest winter flower buds include 'Coleman', 'Dorothy Wycoff', 'Valentine's Day', 'Valley Rose', and 'Valley Valentine'. 'Wada's Pink' has deep pink buds and clear pink flowers, and 'White Cascade' has pure white flowers and rose-colored buds.

According to rhododendron specialist Bob Carlson of Carlson's Gardens, in South Salem, New York, many of the compact and dwarf rhododendron cultivars that have the Dahurian rhododendron (*Rhododendron dauricum*) in their family tree change from green to wine red. As with pieris, this occurs most often in magenta-, pink-, or red-flowered cultivars that receive winter sun.

Some of the best of these rhododendrons are plants from the group known as the 'P.J.M.' hybrids, whose 4-inch oblong leaves deepen to a purple so dark it's almost black. This trait makes these popular rhododendron cultivars effective winter foliage plants. The masses of purplish pink flowers in early spring aren't bad either, though some people find them garish. (White- and light pink-flowering cultivars are now available, too.)

Tidy summer and fall greenery, added to their winter and spring traits, make the 'P.J.M.' rhododendrons and similar compact cultivars desirable plants for the four-season landscape. Mr. Carlson also recommends 'P.J.M. Aglo', 'P.J.M. Black Satin', 'P.J.M. Olga Mezitt', and 'April Reign' for their winter foliage, noting that they look most attractive in winter when planted near contrasting green-leaved rhododendrons and azaleas.

Heaths (*Erica* spp.) and heathers (*Calluna* spp.) also make the top-ten hit parade. These shrubby groundcovers are evergreens with needlelike leaves. Even if they didn't bloom, heaths and heathers would be worth having for their foliage alone: Species and cultivars boast colors from lime green to grass green to gray to blue-green in summer, turning reddish orange, rust, gold, or plum in winter. The dainty flowers—little white, pink, lavender, or red bells—bloom anytime from winter to fall, depending on the cultivar. These four-season plants shine throughout the year, but especially in winter.

Conni and Jim Cross grow an assortment of heath and heather cultivars in their wholesale nursery on Long Island. Conni incorporates these plants in many of the gardens she designs. For her own home, she created a patchwork quilt of heaths and heathers nestled up against the picture window of the dining room and rounding the bend alongside the patio. I first saw this planting in late winter, and the sight was as rich and appealing as any flower garden.

When mass-planted, heaths and heathers make a grand statement, but they also work well when used in small-scale settings or as specimens in a mixed border. (See "Heaths and Heathers for Year-Round Color" on page 32 for Conni's favorite four-season heaths and heathers.)

Unfortunately, heaths and heathers have a well-deserved reputation for being difficult to grow. They demand perfectly drained sandy or even poor soil, high in organic matter but low in nutrients. And they don't tolerate either wet feet or desiccating winters with southern or western exposures. But if you have the right conditions or are willing to coddle them, these beauties are well worth growing.

Multicolored Evergreens

Variegated foliage—spotted, flecked, striped, banded, or edged with a contrasting color or two—adds landscape excitement through the bright surprise of its color combinations. Many broadleaved evergreens—and a few conifers—have variegated cultivars that result from mutations.

Variegated plants lack chlorophyll or other pigments in the nongreen parts of the leaves. A total lack of pigment causes the tissue to appear white or creamy—often along the leaf margins or in the center of the leaf—while a reduction in normal amounts of chlorophyll allows the leaf's yellow and red pigments to predominate or tint the leaf color. Because they suffer a chlorophyll deficit, many variegated plants grow more slowly and succumb more easily to sunburn than their all-green counterparts, and they may not be as cold-hardy.

Although evergreen foliage in its variegated forms can jazz up a winter landscape, too many multicolored plants can create a busy carnival atmosphere in your garden. As a general rule of thumb, the more wildly colored the foliage, the less of it you should use.

Plant highly variegated shrubs as single specimens, rather than mass-planting them. One such showstopper is 'Gold Spot' winter-

(continued on page 34)

HEATHS AND HEATHERS FOR YEAR-ROUND COLOR

When designing a heath and heather garden for your year-round landscape, design for winter foliage beauty—the rest of the seasons will fall naturally into place, according to garden designer Conni Cross, because the pink, lavender, and white flowers of heaths and heathers look charming together no matter how they are grouped. Conni advises creating a colorful patchwork of winter foliage by grouping several red and gold heaths together with silver ones behind. Separate these with patches of dark and light green heaths or heathers. Repeat the red, gold, and silver combinations so you get a lovely patchwork of colorful foliage. Place dwarf conifers in the garden to give it height and structure, and surround them with winter-blooming heaths to catch your attention for a special winter effect.

Heather (Scotch Heather)

Heather (*Calluna vulgaris*) flowers in mid- to late summer and often has colorfully changing evergreen foliage, especially vivid in winter. It grows best in full sun in acid, well-drained but moist soil in a cool, moist climate. You can grow heathers in Zones 5 to 7. Here are some of the best cultivars, organized by winter foliage color so it will be easy for you to choose some for your winter garden.

SILVER OR GRAY WINTER FOLIAGE
Cultivar: 'Anthony Davis'
Flowers: white, midseason
Foliage: gray-green in summer, gray in winter
Height and Form: 15"–18", upright

Cultivar: 'Dainty Bess Minor'
Flowers: mauve, midseason
Foliage: silver in summer, silver-gray in winter
Height and Form: dwarf, tight mound

Cultivar: 'Peter Sparks'
Flowers: rose-pink, midseason

Foliage: gray in summer, grayer in winter
Height and Form: 12"–15", upright

Cultivar: 'Silver Knight'
Flowers: lavender, midseason
Foliage: steel gray in winter, silver in summer
Height and Form: 15"–18", upright

Cultivar: 'Silver Queen'
Flowers: lavender, midseason
Foliage: silver in summer, gray in winter
Height and Form: 12", spreading

Cultivar: 'Sister Anne'
Flowers: pale mauve
Foliage: silver in summer, silver-gray in winter
Height and Form: 4"–6", large bun

GOLD FOLIAGE IN WINTER
Cultivar: 'Gold Haze'
Flowers: white
Foliage: gold in summer and winter
Height and Form: 9"–12", spreading mound

RED FOLIAGE IN WINTER
Cultivar: 'Aurea'
Flowers: mauve
Foliage: gold in summer, orange-red in winter
Height and Form: 15", spreading

Cultivar: 'Blazeaway'
Flowers: lavender, midseason
Foliage: gold in summer, orange-red in winter
Height and Form: 12", spreading

Cultivar: 'Cuprea'
Flowers: lavender, midseason
Foliage: copper in summer, rust in winter
Height and Form: 15"–18", upright

Cultivar: 'Multicolor'
Flowers: mauve
Foliage: yellow in summer, yellow and orange-red in winter
Height and Form: 12", spreading

Cultivar: 'Red Haze'
Flowers: lavender, midseason
Foliage: gold in summer, red-speckled in winter
Height and Form: 15", spreading

GREEN FOLIAGE IN WINTER

Cultivar: 'Alice Sutcliff'
Flowers: pale lavender, midseason
Foliage: green all year
Height and Form: low and flat

Cultivar: 'Caerotton White'
Flowers: white, early
Foliage: bright green all year
Height and Form: 12″, spreading mound

Cultivar: 'County Wicklow'
Flowers: double light pink, midseason
Foliage: medium green in summer, very dark green in winter
Height and Form: 12″, spreading mound

Cultivar: 'Crammond'
Flowers: double light pink, midseason
Foliage: medium green in summer, silvery green in winter
Height and Form: 15″–18″, upright

Cultivar: 'E. F. Brown'
Flowers: lavender-pink, late; beige seedheads, winter
Foliage: bright green all year
Height and Form: 12″–15″, spreading

Cultivar: 'Hibernica'
Flowers: pale mauve, late; beige seedheads in winter
Foliage: medium green all year
Height and Form: 12″

Cultivar: 'J. H. Hamilton'
Flowers: double medium pink, midseason
Foliage: medium green in summer, almost black in winter
Height and Form: 9″, low-spreading

Cultivar: 'Kinlochruel'
Flowers: double white, midseason
Foliage: medium green in summer, very dark green in winter
Height and Form: 12″, spreading mound

Cultivar: 'Kuphaldi'
Flowers: lavender-pink, midseason
Foliage: green all year
Height and Form: very flat

Cultivar: 'Mairs Variety'
Flowers: white
Foliage: bright green all year
Height and Form: 18″, upright

Cultivar: 'Molecule'
Flowers: lilac, midseason
Foliage: green all year
Height and Form: tiny globe

Cultivar: 'Mrs. Ronald Gray'
Flowers: mauve, midseason
Foliage: medium green in summer, dark green in winter
Height and Form: prostrate

Cultivar: 'Rigida'
Flowers: white, midseason
Foliage: bright green all year
Height and Form: 12″, spreading

Cultivar: 'Schurigi's Sensation'
Flowers: double light pink
Foliage: medium green all year
Height and Form: 15″–18″, upright

Cultivar: 'Tenius'
Flowers: magenta, early–late
Foliage: medium green all year
Height and Form: 9″

Cultivar: 'Tib'
Flowers: double magenta, early–late; tan seedheads in winter
Foliage: medium green all year
Height and Form: 12″, spreading

Cultivar: 'Toralosa'
Flowers: white, late
Foliage: bright green all year
Height and Form: 12″, upright

Cultivar: 'White Lawn'
Flowers: white, midseason
Foliage: bright green in summer, green in winter
Height and Form: prostrate

Heath

Heaths (*Erica carnea*) are low evergreens, valued for their winter or early-spring flowers and their fine-textured needlelike leaves. They

(continued)

HEATHS AND HEATHERS FOR YEAR-ROUND COLOR—CONTINUED

grow best in full sun in acid, well-drained but moist soil in a cool, moist climate. You can grow heaths in Zones 5 to 7. Here are some of the best cultivars, listed by bloom season.

EARLY-WINTER TO EARLY-SPRING BLOOM
Cultivar: 'Silberschmeltz' (Zones 6–7)
Flowers: white, aging to pink
Foliage: green
Height: 18"–24"

Cultivar: 'Winter Beauty'
Flowers: lavender-pink
Foliage: green
Height: 24"

EARLY-WINTER BLOOM
Cultivar: 'King George'
Flowers: deep pink
Foliage: green
Height: 9"

MID- TO LATE-WINTER BLOOM
Cultivar: 'Praecox Rubra'
Flowers: ruby
Foliage: green
Height: 9"

LATE-WINTER TO EARLY-SPRING BLOOM
Cultivar: 'Ann Sparkes'
Flowers: pink
Foliage: gold
Height: 9"

Cultivar: 'Myertoun Ruby'
Flowers: red-purple
Foliage: green
Height: 5"

Cultivar: 'Pink Spangles'
Flowers: pink
Foliage: green
Height: 4"–8"

Cultivar: 'Porter's Red'
Flowers: red-purple
Foliage: green
Height: 6"–9"

Cultivar: 'Ruby Glo'
Flowers: ruby
Foliage: light green
Height: 3"–5"

Cultivar: 'Springwood Pink'
Flowers: pink
Foliage: green
Height: 4"–8"

Cultivar: 'Springwood White'
Flowers: white
Foliage: green
Height: 4"–8"

Cultivar: 'Vivelli'
Flowers: magenta
Foliage: dark green; black in winter
Height: 9"

creeper (*Euonymus fortunei* 'Gold Spot'), which has large green leaves with bright yellow centers. Some groundcovers are gaudy, too, including the yellow-, green-, and white-variegated 'Maculata' English ivy (*Hedera helix* 'Maculata'). Try tucking these among all-green groundcovers, where they will create bursts of color.

More refined variegated plants include variegated winter daphne (*Daphne odora* 'Aureo-Marginata'), with dark green leaves that are edged in white or cream. Don't be afraid to plant such well-bred, restrained shrubs in greater quantity than their aggressively garbed cousins. Their luxuriant light-reflecting foliage will add sparkle to the garden during the somber months and never seem overdone.

From a distance, some variegated foliage doesn't appear multicolored at all but seems to be a uniform color. This is true of variegated Japanese pachysandra (*Pachysandra terminalis* 'Variegata'), with blue-green leaves and creamy margins. From across the yard, its foliage appears to be a pleasing glaucous gray. Variegated Japanese pachysandra makes a better groundcover for a dim spot than the dark green species, because its lighter color brightens up the shadows instead of deepening them.

One of my favorite variegated coniferous trees is the dragon's eye pine (*Pinus densiflora* 'Oculus-Draconis'). Two or more pale yellow bands encircle each needle of this Japanese red pine cultivar, giving the tree a creamy glow from a distance. This slow-growing evergreen has a loosely branched, craggy outline and eventually reaches 30 feet tall, but it remains shrubby for many years.

Variegated evergreens can enhance your garden's color scheme and draw the eye with their flashy contrasts. Try using their colorful variegation to enhance the subtle shades of green of the evergreens in your four-season landscape. The golden-hued conifers become even sunnier when combined with a yellow-and-green variegated broadleaved shrub such as the golden-edged English holly (*Ilex aquifolium* 'Aureo-Marginata').

Blue-greens and gray-greens seem bluer when paired or underplanted with white-and-green variegated plants. Tricolor combinations featuring red, reddish purple, or pink in their foliage patterns enrich the burgundy winter colors of select cultivars of pieris, rhododendron, and leucothoe (*Leucothoe* spp.), as well as *Euonymus fortunei* 'Colorata'. (See "Evergreens with Purplish, Red, or Bronze Winter Color" on page 30.)

Winter Lawns and Groundcovers

When visiting Charleston, South Carolina, one January, I was surprised by the brown lawns, especially when so many broadleaved evergreen shrubs and trees were providing such rich greenery. In the colder regions where I've lived (Zones 5, 6, and 7), lawns often remain green throughout the winter—admittedly a dull or yellowish green when compared to the spring color, but green nevertheless. A green lawn in winter looks decidedly more cheerful than a brown one, and its shape adds structure—the lawn may be the largest expanse of color in your garden.

You can take measures to ensure a green winter lawn by growing cool-season grasses if you live outside the South. Avoid warm-season types, such as zoysia grass (*Zoysia* spp.), that survive in the North but are brown three seasons of the year. Zoysia grass remains an ugly camel's-hair-coat tan from fall through spring, greening up about a month later than neighboring cool-season lawns.

Cool-season grasses grow vigorously in the spring and fall months in northern climates but tend to slow down or even turn brown during the summer unless well watered. But they usually remain green (or greenish) during winter, often revealing beautiful emerald colors from beneath the melting snow. Keep your cool-season lawn healthy and vigorous—and green—through winter by feeding it in the fall with a balanced organic fertilizer.

In the warmer zones (8, 9, and 10), where warm-season grasses predominate, lawns go dormant in the winter, turning straw-colored. To have a beautiful green lawn in winter as well as summer in these regions, each fall overseed the warm-season lawn grass with annual ryegrass (winter rye). The ryegrass will germinate quickly and stay green all winter long without harming the permanent lawn.

In beds and borders, a green carpet of groundcovers goes a long way toward brightening the scene and covering the mud. Traditional evergreen groundcovers that are ideal for planting under shrubbery and in large beds

EVERGREEN TREES AND SHRUBS WITH VARIEGATED FOLIAGE

Foliage that's banded, streaked, edged, or splashed with contrasting colors cheers up many a stark winter scene. Used sparingly, the following plants will create a lovely focal point of color in the garden.

Coniferous

Cedrus deodara 'Snow Sprite' ('Snow Sprite' deodar cedar), Zones 7–9

Juniperus chinensis 'Kaizuka Variegata' ('Kaizuka Variegata' Chinese juniper), Zones 4–9

Pinus densiflora 'Oculus-Draconis' (dragon's-eye pine), Zones 6–7

Broadleaved

Aucuba japonica (Japanese aucuba), Zones 7–9

Buxus sempervirens 'Elegantissima' (variegated boxwood), Zones 6–8

Daphne × *burkwoodii* 'Carol Mackie' ('Carol Mackie' burkwood daphne), Zones 4–7

D. odora 'Aureo-Marginata' (variegated winter daphne), Zones 8–10

Euonymus fortunei 'Silver Queen' ('Silver Queen' wintercreeper), Zones 6–9

E. japonica 'Gold Spot' ('Gold Spot' Japanese euonymus), Zones 8–9

E. japonica 'Silver King' ('Silver King' Japanese euonymus), Zones 8–9

Ilex aquifolium 'Argenteo-Marginata' (silver-edge English holly), Zones 7–9

Leucothoe fontanesiana 'Rainbow' ('Rainbow' leucothoe), Zones 5–9

include common periwinkle (*Vinca minor*), Japanese pachysandra (*Pachysandra terminalis*), and English ivy (*Hedera helix*). These vigorous plants will cover lots of ground with a floor of year-round greenery that sets off bright stems and evergreen boughs. Keep in mind, however, that Japanese pachysandra and English ivy can be very invasive. (The smaller cultivars of ivy grow less aggressively than the species, so choose them for small gardens.)

For smaller sites, many other evergreen groundcovers offer landscape solutions. For small sites—and even large-scales ones—you might choose from such shrubby groundcovers as the many feathery cultivars of creeping juniper (*Juniperus horizontalis*). Or try Siberian carpet cypress (*Microbiota decussata*), a cypress relative that resembles a groundcover juniper. Most junipers require a sunny location, while Siberian carpet cypress will grow in shady sites hostile to junipers.

In more shaded spots, choose the North Tisbury azalea cultivars, which make a beautiful winter groundcover with evergreen foliage and creeping stems, or any of the wintercreepers (*Euonymus fortunei* cultivars). Epimediums (*Epimedium* spp.) are semievergreen; they're good choices for sites in dry shade, where they spread readily.

Bark Is Beautiful

Once their leaves drop, many trees and shrubs reveal highly ornamental bark. Olive green, snow white, blood red, golden yellow, eggplant purple, and cinnamon brown are just some of the bark colors that may be evident in the winter garden.

Besides being beautifully colored, bark may be beautifully textured, too. Many of the highly colored specimens feature flaking or peeling patches (called exfoliation) where the outer bark peels away to reveal a colorful inner bark, often in a patchwork pattern of various colors. The peeling bark may cling to the tree, curling back in intriguing ribbons that children can't resist tugging. Or it may fall away completely to reveal a surface as smooth as leather. Shaggy textures, smooth sinewy curves, highly polished surfaces, and deeply furrowed grooves are all bark options.

Although you may notice attractive bark, especially on tree trunks, throughout the year, the color and texture seem most apparent in winter, when there's less competition from foliage and flowers. You can enhance your four-season landscape by planting several specimens with ornamental bark where you'll see them often, relieving the winter doldrums. The trees and shrubs described in "Plants with Ornamental Bark" on page 38 have outstanding bark.

The Wonder of White Bark

As I've traveled throughout the country, I've noticed that each region has its own native white-barked trees. These trees stand out like beacons in winter against a background of somber evergreens, gray stones, or brown trunks. The paper birches (*Betula papyrifera*) of the New England woods are legendary; their bark is the color of snow. Aspens (*Populus* spp.) form extensive stands of gray-white or greenish white trunks in the mountains of the West, ranging from the Rockies to the Sierras and north to the Alaska Range.

American sycamores (*Platanus occidentalis*) stud the bottomlands of the Midwest, while Arizona sycamores (*P. wrightii*) inhabit the washes of the desert Southwest. Though not all these trees make ideal garden subjects— sycamores litter the yard with messy fruits and grow too large, aspens send up annoying suckers, and some birches suffer disfiguring insect damage—you can follow nature's lead by using white bark to enhance your winter landscape.

European white birch (*Betula pendula*) and paper birch (*B. papyrifera*) are the most commonly planted white-barked trees. Because these suffer so badly from leaf miners and bronze birch borers, many gardeners have shied away from planting them in recent years. Instead, horticulturists have focused on recently available white-barked Asian birches that resist drought, heat, and insects better than American and European species. (See "Plants with Ornamental Bark" on page 38.) Some of these may be difficult to come by, but they're worth searching out.

Of special note is the 'Whitespire' birch (*Betula platyphylla* var. *japonica* 'Whitespire'). This readily available cultivar resists the common birch pests and features chalk white bark and golden fall color. Unfortunately, it takes several years until young trees begin to form their famous white bark.

Another birch cultivar, the 'Heritage' river birch (*Betula nigra* 'Heritage'), has gained cult status in recent years. A highly ornamental selection of a tree native to our midwestern bottomlands, this tree defies wet and dry soil, heat and cold, and the worst birch insects. I've planted a multitrunked specimen where we can see it from the breakfast-nook window. We enjoy the creamy white bark, which curls back to reveal patches of salmon pink and beige inner bark.

'Heritage' grows faster and has glossier leaves, more vivid yellow fall color, and a much whiter bark than the species, which sports coppery curls with a metallic sheen. The trunk of the species also loses its ornamental quality as it matures. In the Midwest and South, where heat spells the demise of other white birches, 'Heritage' thrives. It makes a beautiful four-season specimen in almost any part of the country.

Variations on Basic Brown

Another favorite four-season tree of bark admirers is the paperbark maple (*Acer griseum*). The bark of this choice small garden tree reminds me of cinnamon sticks, except that the bark shines like polished furniture. The color is the same—rich reddish brown—and the outer bark peels back in tight curls just like cinnamon sticks. The trunk's bark begins

(continued on page 42)

PLANTS WITH ORNAMENTAL BARK

Trees and shrubs with colorful or dramatically textured bark break up the monotony of the winter landscape. The following plants feature bold and beautiful bark that is especially noticeable in winter, when gardeners yearn for some color.

TREE	BARK
Acer davidii (David maple) and *A. pensylvanicum* (striped-bark maple, moosewood)	Dark green bark striped vertically with white on trunk and branches
Acer griseum (paperbark maple)	Mahogany-brown bark peels back to reveal shiny cinnamon brown underbark on trunk and branches
Acer palmatum (Japanese maple)	Red to reddish purple twigs and young branches
Acer palmatum 'Sango Kaku' (coral-bark maple)	Brilliant coral-red, smooth bark on trunks and branches
Acer pensylvanicum 'Erythrocladum' ('Erythrocladum' striped maple)	Twigs vivid scarlet with white stripes; trunk green and older branches green with white stripes
Acer tegmentosum 'White Tigress' (Manchurian snakebark maple)	Smooth rich green to purple-green bark with vertical white stripes
Acer triflorum (three-flower maple)	Shaggy outer bark peels back to reveal creamy white inner bark.
Arbutus unedo (strawberry tree)	Smooth bark flakes off to reveal bright red inner bark on trunk and branches.
Betula alba-sinensis (Chinese paper birch)	Outstanding orange-red to terra-cotta bark peels off in tissue-paper-thin sheets.
Betula jacquemontii (white-bark Himalayan birch)	Perhaps the best white-barked birch
Betula maximowicziana (monarch birch)	Yellowish white bark

TREE	BARK
Betula nigra 'Heritage' ('Heritage' river birch)	Magnificent shiny salmon or coppery bark peels in large curls from trunks to reveal creamy white inner bark.
Betula papyrifera (canoe birch, paper birch, white birch)	Creamy white bark peels off in paper-thin sheets on trunk and branches; whitest of the birches
Betula pendula, syn. *B. alba* (European birch), and *B. pendula* 'Tristis' and 'Youngii' (weeping European birches)	Bright chalk white, peeling bark on trunk and branches; white trunk at young age, but lower trunk turns black with age
Betula platyphylla var. *japonica* 'Whitespire' ('Whitespire' birch)	Bright chalk white bark on trunk and branches
Carya ovata (shagbark hickory)	Brown bark peels back from the trunk in large shaggy pieces.
Chionanthus retusus (Chinese fringetree)	Attractively textured gray-brown bark is ridged and furrowed, sometimes exfoliating.
Cladrastis lutea (American yellowwood)	Smooth silver-gray bark on sinuous trunks
Clethra barbinervis (Japanese tree clethra) and *C. acuminata* (American clethra)	Softly mottled blend of pink, green, cream, and terra-cotta in the Japanese species; peeling cinnamon brown in the native tree
Cornus kousa (Kousa dogwood)	Smooth bark mottled with gray, tan, and maroon becomes more striking with age.
Cornus officinalis (Japanese cornel dogwood)	Exfoliating bark reveals patches of gray, tan, and creamy white.
Fagus grandifolia (American beech) and *F. sylvatica* (European beech)	Smooth silver-gray bark on massive muscular-looking trunks and branches
Franklinia alatamaha (Franklin tree)	Dark gray sinuous trunk striped with light gray

(continued)

PLANTS WITH ORNAMENTAL BARK—CONTINUED

TREE	BARK
Lagerstroemia indica (crape myrtle)	Smooth silver-gray bark with pinkish tan streaks on sinewy trunks and branches; 'Lipan' and 'Osage' with colorful patchwork bark
Liquidambar styraciflua (sweet gum)	Small branches silver-gray and edged with unusual corky wings
Parkinsonia aculeata (Mexican palo verde)	Bright yellowish green bark on twigs, main branches, and young trunks
Parrotia persica (parrotia)	Dark reddish brown bark flakes off to reveal creamy patches.
Pinus bungeana (lacebark pine)	Colorful patchwork bark of green, yellow, gray and reddish tan becomes more beautiful with age, developing white patches.
Pinus densiflora (Japanese red pine)	Peeling brilliant orange-red bark on trunk and branches
Pinus nigra (Austrian pine)	White bark marked with cream, beige, pink, and gray and ridged with deep black furrows
Platanus occidentalis (sycamore, American plane tree) and *P.* × *acerifolia* (London plane tree)	Smooth light brown bark exfoliates in large plates, revealing creamy white inner bark.
Populus alba (white poplar) and *P. tremuloides* (quaking aspen)	Dull white to greenish white bark on trunk and branches
Prunus mackii (golden chokecherry, Amur cherry) and *P. serrula* (paperbark cherry)	Outstanding metallic mahogany-red bark with horizontal tan bands peels off in thin strips.
Prunus serrulata (Japanese flowering cherry)	Lustrous deep reddish brown bark with prominent light brown horizontal bands
Salix alba 'Tristis' and 'Vitellina' (golden weeping willows)	Bright yellow twigs and young branches; brighter on 'Vitellina'

TREE	BARK
Sophora japonica (pagodatree, scholartree)	Olive green twigs and young branches
Stewartia koreana (Korean stewartia), *S. pseudo-camellia* (Japanese stewartia), and *S. ovata* (mountain stewartia)	Smooth tan bark flakes off to reveal a patchwork of green and salmon inner bark.
Stewartia monadelpha (Hime-Sayara stewartia)	Metallic orange bark
Ulmus parvifolia (lacebark elm)	Bark flakes off trunks, revealing patches of silver, green, buff, gold, or orange.
Zelkova sinica (Chinese zelkova)	Bumpy green bark mottled with gray, tan, and coppery orange on trunk

SHRUB	BARK
Cephalanthus occidentalis (buttonbush)	Red twigs
Cornus alba (Tartarian dogwood) and *C. sericea*, syn. *C. stolonifera* (red osier dogwood)	Young stems and branches brilliant to dark red or deep coral
Cornus sericea 'Flaviramea', syn. *C. stolonifera* 'Flaviramea' (golden-twig dogwood)	Golden yellow young stems and branches
Cytisus spp. (brooms)	Green to olive green stems and branches
Euonymus alata (winged euonymus, burning bush)	Prominent corky projections along the twigs and branches create an unusual texture and hold snow in intriguing patterns.
Hydrangea quercifolia (oakleaf hydrangea)	Cinnamon brown bark peels off in long, shaggy strips.
Jasminum nudiflorum (winter jessamine)	Green branches

(continued)

PLANTS WITH ORNAMENTAL BARK—CONTINUED

SHRUB	BARK
Kerria japonica (Japanese kerria) and *K. japonica* var. *aureo-vittata*	Bright yellowish green bark on stems and branches, yellow on var. *aureo-vittata*
Poncirus trifoliata (hardy orange, trifoliate orange)	Bright green twigs, branches, and large thorns
Rosa virginiana (Virginia rose)	Red twigs
Rubus lasiostylus var. *hubeinesis* (ghost bramble)	Chalk white canes with rusty red prickles form a fountainlike arrangement.
Salix alba 'Britzensis'	Brilliant orange-red stems
Salix daphnoides (violet willow)	Bright violet twigs and buds
Salix × *erdingeri*	Coppery bark with a bluish white waxy bloom
Salix lucida (shining willow)	Lustrous orange bark and buds
Salix purpurea var. *nana* (dwarf purple osier)	Slender lustrous purple branches
Vaccinium corymbosum (blueberry)	Twigs bright to dark red
Viburnum opulus (cranberrybush viburnum)	Red twigs

peeling while the tree is very young, and even small limbs and twigs feature this ornamental trait.

Because of its tidy size and year-round appeal—the three-lobed leaves are dark green in summer, turning a wonderful red in fall—paperbark maple makes an ideal tree for a mixed border. I planted my specimen in the widest part of the border surrounding the front yard. In this prominent location, where afternoon sunlight bounces off the polished bark, the tree becomes a winter focal point.

Several four-season trees, such as the Kousa dogwood (*Cornus kousa*), stewartias (*Stewartia* spp.), and fringetrees (*Chionanthus* spp.), may be admired first for their lovely flowers, but their bark is remarkable, too. These trees relieve the winter tedium with mottled wrappers of colorful bark. Their bark colors include varying shades of brown and gray with creamy spots and splashes of pink and beige mixed in. Give them a prominent location.

The lacebark pine (*Pinus bungeana*) has perhaps the most spectacular bark of all. The stout trunk sloughs off its rough outer bark to reveal a jigsaw puzzle of white, gray, and tan with generous splashes of maroon, silver, and green. This Chinese pine may grow as a single- or multi-trunked tree with a picturesque open outline, making it a tree for all seasons. Lacebark pine grows very slowly to its ultimate 30- to 50-foot height, adding as little as 3 feet in ten years. If the branches of your lacebark pine obscure the beautiful bark on the trunk, selectively prune some of the lower branches to show it off.

The Most Colorful Barks of All

The smooth, blood red bark of the red osier dogwood (*Cornus sericea*) and tartarian dogwood (*C. alba*) makes a stunning show in winter when mass-planted in a sunny location. These shrubby plants form a network of slender upright stems with small side branches that are visible in the winter landscape even when seen from quite a distance.

The golden-twig dogwood (*Cornus sericea* 'Flaviramea') features slick, bright golden yellow twigs. It looks spectacular planted along with its red-barked cousin. These colorful shrubby dogwoods have been adopted by highway departments in the Northeast and are widely planted for their winter effect in highway median strips.

Red- and yellow-twigged dogwoods develop the richest hues on young growth when grown in full sun. To keep them their showiest, prune off about a third of the oldest stems at ground level every year in spring. This will encourage vigorous—and brightly colored—new growth. Without this regular pruning, the bark becomes dingy and the shrubs may grow too tall.

Though spectacular in winter, these shrubs aren't much to look at during the other seasons, unless you plant one of the variegated cultivars. *Cornus sericea* 'Silver and Gold' offers foliage decorated with an irregular edge of creamy white along the leaf margins and gleaming yellow bark. *C. alba* 'Argenteo-Marginata' has similar leaves and red stems.

Plant red osier dogwoods in a thicket, rather than single file, so the red stems are clustered, intensifying their vividness. You might also echo the yellow and red bark by planting some of the gold-needled dwarf conifers and red-berried shrubs such as winterberry (*Ilex verticillata*) nearby.

Other trees and shrubs, such as red-stemmed 'Britzensis' white willow (*Salix alba* 'Britzensis'), coral-bark maple (*Acer palmatum* 'Sango Kaku'), purple osier (*Salix purpurea*), and striped maples (the native *Acer pensylvanicum* and similar Asian species), brighten dreary winter landscapes with unexpected color. I particularly cherish the yellow twigs of the golden weeping willows (*Salix alba* 'Tristis' and 'Vitellina'). They gleam on wet winter days when other trees are rain-darkened.

The Bright Berries of Winter

Many berries that redden and ripen in summer and fall would persist into winter if they didn't appeal to hungry birds, who devour the fruits so quickly that you may never realize the plant produces berries at all. The summer and fall fruits that birds ignore often shrivel or drop to the ground come winter and add little to the garden scene. But the berries that hang onto twig and limb through winter add splashes of bright color to the winter garden, echoing colored bark and adding sparkle to evergreen foliage.

Birds delve into sweet, juicy fruits first, often turning up their beaks at dry, mealy berries if they have a choice. These they leave for leaner times in January and February, when alternate freezing and thawing have softened or even fermented the fruits into more tasty fare. But some berries are so unpalatable that they cling to plants from fall through winter, until new growth forces them to drop.

For winter gardens, it pays to seek out those trees and shrubs that hold their bright fruits the longest. (Shrubs and small trees noted for their winter berry display are listed in "Plants with Showy Winter Berries" on page 46.)

One of my favorite shrubs for winter fruit color is winterberry (*Ilex verticillata*), a deciduous holly whose branches display great clusters of decorative coral-red berries. These color up about the time the foliage turns butter yellow in fall and usually last well into midwinter.

Many improved cultivars of this woodland shrub, which enjoys partial shade, feature larger, more persistent berries in various shades of red. I was particularly taken with a mass planting of the large-fruited 'Afterglow' alongside a pond on the Indiana University campus in southern Indiana. On a cold, dreary Thanksgiving weekend, these plants were the brightest things around.

Many of the viburnums produce summer fruits that hide behind a cloak of foliage and then fall victim to hungry critters; other species make fall displays that don't persist into winter, but several highly ornamental species reliably hold onto their showy fruits. These include European cranberrybush viburnum (*Viburnum opulus*), which does indeed possess translucent fruits the size and color of ripe cranberries, and the similar American cranberrybush viburnum (*V. trilobum*). Yellow-fruited cultivars of *V. opulus* are also available.

Resembling tiny ruby earrings, the teardrop-shaped red berries of barberries (*Berberis* spp.) dangle from long stems along the undersides of the spreading branches. Korean barberry (*B. koreana*) and Japanese barberry (*B. thunbergii*) produce the most striking displays. Their berries last from fall into January and February, when the fruits turn raisinlike and finally become bird food.

White-fruited snowberry (*Symphoricarpos albus*) bears clusters of opaque, marble-sized fruits, adding a new color to the berry repertoire. And the gleaming lavender-blue berries of the beautyberries (*Callicarpa* spp.) are so unusual they stop people in their tracks. The fruits on my beautyberry, planted near the street where I can admire it as I go to and from my mailbox, remained colorful well into February this year. Last year, they shriveled at Thanksgiving when the temperature suddenly dropped to below zero.

One of the longest-lasting fruit displays occurs on the native bayberry (*Myrica pensylvanica*), even though many species of birds feed on them. I suspect the berries last so long because the waxy blue-gray spheres provide the food of last resort for these birds. The rough-textured, leathery berries, which form only on female plants, may last until new growth displaces them in spring. The Colonists melted these berries down to make fragrant bayberry candles; sometimes you can still find real bayberry candles.

The red-berried evergreen hollies (*Ilex* spp.) are practically synonymous with the Christmas season. They make wonderful displays as long as the berry-producing female plants have a nearby male specimen to ensure pollination. Locate prickly leaved types away from walkways, where they may snag clothing, and be sure to give the tree hollies enough growing space.

The best four-season flowering trees for winter berry color include the hawthorns (*Crataegus* spp.), with dangling clusters of orange-red berries on thorny branches; crab-apples (*Malus* spp.), with yellow or red fruits of varying sizes; and mountain ashes (*Sorbus* spp.), which produce huge clusters of red or orange berries in fall that can last well into winter. Locate one of these four-season plants where you can admire it every day of the year.

One of the best trees for holding its berries all winter, according to Indiana nurseryman Bob Simpson, is white-flowered 'Winter King' green hawthorn (*C. viridis* 'Winter King'). I've seen trees that retain their exceptionally large orange-red berries right up until new spring growth pushes them off. The silvery gray trunk catches the eye in winter, providing a perfect foil for the berries. Bark of older trees may exfoliate to reveal patches of orange inner bark.

Berry-Saving Tactics

One late fall day when I was admiring my clever placement of a winterberry—a wild one that I had dug up on my property and strategically transplanted into the breakfast-nook view—a boisterous flock of migrating robins descended on it. The shrub blazed with yellow leaves and a crop of orange-red fruits, but within the space of five minutes the voracious robins had stripped the branches clean of every berry!

Don't count on the berries of any plant for a dependable show, or you may be disappointed. The display on even the most reliable fruit-bearers, such as firethorns (*Pyracantha* spp.), can be variable: One year birds and squirrels may ravish them, and another year pass them over; during wet seasons fungus may rot the berries; and in other years the fruit set may be poor from lack of pollination.

To safeguard the berries you do get, a few tricks may pay off. Red fruits attract birds, so if you plant yellow- or golden-fruited forms of typically red-fruited plants, the berries may survive longer into winter. A beautiful golden-fruited shrub is 'Golden Girl' blue holly (*Ilex* × *meserveae* 'Golden Girl'). The highly polished evergreen leaves set off the dark yellow berries like jewels on velvet, to be admired by the gardener but passed over by birds.

Planting berried shrubs close to the house near a busy entrance or window may also discourage the more timid feeders. You might also try providing birds with alternate sources of food, such as a well-supplied feeder, where you can enjoy their comings and goings. As a last resort, try changing your attitude. Think of your berry display as a wonderful gift and enjoy it—and the visiting wildlife—while it lasts.

Backdrops for Your Berries

Effectively displaying winter-berried plants—especially deciduous ones that lack a built-in green backdrop—creates a greater impact from fewer berries. Situate the trees or shrubs against a uniform background, such as an evergreen hedge or screen, a fence or wall, or even the open sky, so the clusters of fruits won't be lost amid a busy background.

As with the bright-stemmed red osier dogwoods (*Cornus sericea*), berried plants look showier when planted in groups so the berries are seen massed together for an intense color impact. This rule holds especially true for plantings to be viewed from a distant window or walk, rather than ones to be enjoyed close at hand. When planted in the distance, orange-red berries look showier than dark red types, because the brighter color carries better.

PLANTS WITH SHOWY WINTER BERRIES

Many shrubs and trees produce colorful clusters of berries, which ripen anytime from midsummer through fall. Some last only a short period on the branches before dropping or being devoured by birds. The following shrubs and trees usually retain their showy fruits throughout winter, brightening the landscape.

Trees and Shrubs with Red Berries in Winter

Aronia arbutifolia (red chokeberry), Zones 4–9
Berberis koreana (Korean barberry), Zones 3–8
B. thunbergii (Japanese barberry), Zones 4–9
Cotoneaster microphylla (small-leaf cotoneaster), Zones 6–9
C. salicifolius (willowleaf cotoneaster), Zones 6–9
Elaeagnus umbellata (autumn olive), Zones 5–9
Ilex aquifolium (English holly), Zones 7–9
I. cornuta (Chinese holly), Zones 7–9
I. opaca (American holly), Zones 6–9
I. verticillata 'Winter Red' ('Winter Red' winterberry), Zones 4–9
Nandina domestica (heavenly bamboo), Zones 7–9
Pyracantha coccinea (scarlet firethorn), Zones 5/6–9
P. angustifolia (narrow-leaf firethorn), Zones 7–9
P. atalantioides (Gibbs firethorn), Zones 7–9
Rhus copallina (shiny sumac), Zones 4–9
R. typhina (staghorn sumac), Zones 3–8
Rosa blanda (meadow rose), Zones 2/3–6
R. × incarnata (cottage rose), Zones 5–9
R. setigera (prairie rose), Zones 4–9
R. virginiana (Virginia rose), Zones 5–7
Viburnum dilatatum (Linden viburnum), Zones 5–8
V. opulus (cranberrybush viburnum), Zones 3–8
V. trilobum (American cranberrybush), Zones 3–8

Shrubs with Blue or Purple Fruits in Winter

Callicarpa americana (American beautyberry), Zones 7–9

C. bodinieri (Bodinier beautyberry), Zones 5–7
C. dichotoma (Chinese beautyberry), Zones 5–8
C. japonica (Japanese beautyberry), Zones 5–8
Fatsia japonica (Japanese fatsia), Zones 7–9

Shrubs with White or Gray Berries in Winter

Callicarpa americana var. *alba* (white-berried American beautyberry), Zones 7–9
C. japonica var. *lactea* (white-berried Japanese beautyberry), Zones 5–8
Ilex serrata var. *leucocarpa* (white-berried Japanese winterberry), Zones 6–9
Myrica pensylvanica (bayberry), Zones 4–9
Nandina domestica 'Alba' (white-berried heavenly bamboo), Zones 7–9
Symphorocarpus albus var. *laevigatus,* syn. *S. rivularis* (snowberry), Zones 4–7
S. orbiculatus var. *leucocarpus* (white-berried coralberry), Zones 3–9

Shrubs with Yellow, Gold, or Orange Fruits in Winter

Ilex aquifolium var. *xanthocarpum* (yellow-fruited English holly), Zones 7–9
I. laevigata 'Hervey Robinson' ('Hervey Robinson' smooth winterberry), Zones 4–7
I. × meserveae 'Golden Girl' ('Golden Girl' blue holly), Zones 4–8
I. verticillata 'Aurantiaca' (orange-berried winterberry), Zones 4–9
I. verticillata 'Chrysocarpa' (yellow-berried winterberry), Zones 4–9
Pyracantha coccinea 'Shawnee' (yellow-fruited firethorn), Zones 5–9
Viburnum dilatatum 'Xanthocarpum' (yellow-fruited linden viburnum), Zones 5–8
V. opulus 'Xanthocarpum' (yellow-fruited cranberrybush viburnum), Zones 3–8
V. setigerum 'Aurantiacum' (orange-fruited tea viburnum), Zones 6–8

Small Trees with Red Fruits in Winter

Crataegus crus-galli (cockspur thorn), Zones 4–6
C. laevigata, syn. *C. oxyacantha* (English hawthorn), Zones 5–7

C. nitida (glossy hawthorn), Zones 5–9
C. phaenopyrum (Washington hawthorn), Zones 5–9
Ilex aquifolium (English holly), Zones 7–9
I. opaca (American holly), Zones 6–9
Malus 'Adams' ('Adams' crabapple), Zones 4–7
M. 'Donald Wyman' ('Donald Wyman' crabapple), Zones 4–7
M. 'Makamik' ('Makamik' crabapple), Zones 3–7
M. 'Red Jade' ('Red Jade' crabapple), Zones 3–7
M. 'Sisspuk' ('Sisspuk' crabapple), Zones 3–7
M. 'Sugar Tyme' ('Sugar Tyme' crabapple), Zones 4–7
M. zumi var. *calocarpa* (zumi crabapple), Zones 3–7
Sorbus alnifolia (Korean mountain ash), Zones 4–7
S. aucuparia (European mountain ash), Zones 3–7

Small Trees with Yellow or Orange Fruits in Winter

Ilex opaca var. *xanthocarpa* (yellow-fruited American holly), Zones 6–9
Malus 'Bob White' ('Bob White' crabapple), Zones 4–8
M. 'Dorothea' ('Dorothea' crabapple), Zones 4–7

Small Trees with Black Fruits in Winter

Liquidambar styraciflua (sweet gum), Zones 5–9
Viburnum prunifolium (black haw), Zones 3–9

Evergreen Trees with Showy Cones in Winter

Cedrus atlantica (atlas cedar), Zones 7–9
C. libani (cedar-of-Lebanon), Zones 5–9
Larix decidua (larch), Zones 4–6
Picea spp. (spruces), Zones 3–8
Pinus spp. (pines), Zones 2–9
Pseudotsuga menziesii (Douglas fir), Zones 3–6

Winter's Surprising Flowers

Would you believe flowers in winter? It's hard to believe, but even during the so-called dormant season, your garden can come to life with flowers! Having flowers in your garden each month of the year may be commonplace in California, Florida, and other semitropical climates. But in regions where winter proves to be a real, not a make-believe, season, winter flowers are an unusual sight.

In cold climates, you can use little-known winter-flowering plants that bloom from December to February. A winter display can't possibly equal the lavish bloom of a summer border, but given the bleak alternative, no one's complaining.

In milder regions characterized by four climatic seasons, such as the South or Pacific Northwest, gardeners who select and plan carefully can have a considerable flower display every month of winter. In colder areas—Zones 6 and 5—you might need to locate the winter bloomers in warm planting pockets. Give them a sheltered site in front of a south-facing wall, hedge, or fence to coax the early bloomers into January and February flower. In Zones 4 and colder, winter flowers won't be possible during the season's harshest months but will bloom during the tail end of a long winter as welcome harbingers of a still far-off spring.

These early bloomers defy winter by their own unique devices. Most are dependable, flowering on warm or sunny days in January, February, or March. The open flowers of plants such as the fall- and winter-blooming autumn-flowering Higan cherry (*Prunus subhirtella* var. *autumnalis*) may get zapped by frost or a freeze, but new flower buds wait in the wings to open with the next mild spell. Other flowers, such as those of the witch hazels (*Hamamelis* spp.), are cold-hardy and remain unblemished by plunging mercury.

Unfortunately, the flowers of some late-winter bloomers, such as the star magnolia (*Magnolia stellata*), do not tolerate cold temperatures. The first warm weather in late winter encourages them to bloom beautifully, so the entire tree is fully cloaked with gorgeous satiny petals. But then an inevitable drop below the freezing point turns the flowers dead brown. In some areas, such as southern Indiana (Zone 6), the magnolia trees themselves are perfectly hardy, but it is a rare year that the blooms outlast a frost.

With these winter bloomers, you'll have the chance to enjoy a full two weeks of bloom if you locate the trees in a cold spot, one that *delays* bloom, and if you choose later-blooming cultivars designed to outsmart Jack Frost. But these delaying tactics also transform winter bloomers into early-spring bloomers, reducing the potential winter show.

Weather-Defying Trees and Shrubs

Some of my favorite winter-flowering plants are trees and shrubs that bloom when most plants are dormant. Because they bloom at eye level and above, these plants form an important part of the winter planting pyramid.

The earliest-blooming shrubs include several species of witch hazel (*Hamamelis* spp.). Often multistemmed, witch hazels can reach 12 to 20 feet tall with time and may function as small trees in the landscape. Flourishing in partly shaded sites, witch hazels top my list of favorite four-season plants. I admire them for their winter flowers, handsome summer foliage, and excellent fall color.

Witch hazel blooms are small fringe-petaled things that cluster along the branches. The petals react to temperature by unfurling on an unexpectedly warm day in winter—during a January thaw, for instance. When cold weather returns, they temporarily curl up like shrinking violets. The delightful fragrance of some cultivars is doubly pleasant during the winter months.

Adapted to Zones 5 to 9, Chinese witch hazel (*Hamamelis mollis*) is a tall wide-spreading shrub with large heart-shaped gray-green leaves in summer. It blooms in February in Zone 5, earlier in warmer regions. Choose the cultivar 'Pallida', because the glowing clear yellow flowers are extra large and extra showy. The native vernal witch hazel (*H. vernalis*) blooms even earlier but is far less showy.

'Arnold Promise' witch hazel (*Hamamelis × intermedia* 'Arnold Promise') resembles a forsythia blooming on Valentine's Day. The golden yellow mopheads herald spring for almost two months in my garden—February through March. Unlike the Chinese witch hazel, which with maturity can exceed 30 feet tall and wide, this hybrid of *H. mollis* and *H. japonica* forms a 15- to 20-foot-tall, vase-shaped shrub. Another attractive *H. × intermedia* cultivar is 'Jelena', which produces large orange-pink flowers that look pretty when seen close up but don't show up well from a distance. Plant this cultivar near a path or walk.

More treelike than shrubby, cornelian cherry (*Cornus mas*) blooms a bit later than witch hazels, producing a mist of yellow flowers on bare limbs in late February or March in my garden. This four-season tree offers tan-and-gray-mottled bark, neat glossy green foliage in summer, red foliage in fall, and from late summer until they're eaten by birds or humans, large, high-gloss red berries as appealing as real cherries.

I've added a winter honeysuckle bush (*Lonicera fragrantissima*) to my shopping list, even though its tiny white blooms aren't much to look at. My friend Donna Bickley, who's converting her entire Maryland property into a four-season garden, says, "The fragrance is *wonderful*. We planted ours near the vegetable garden so we can enjoy the perfume when we plant our peas and early cole crops." I'll situate the shrub where we can enjoy its intense fragrance as we come and go from the house.

Another fragrant winter-blooming shrub that I've included on my must-have list is wintersweet (*Chimonanthus praecox*). Blooming in late December or early January, the yellowish green 1-inch blooms produce a powerful orange-blossom perfume and look fairly showy displayed along the bare branches. If you can find it, plant the much prettier cultivar, *C. praecox* 'Luteus', which offers gorgeous deep yellow flowers with a color and scent you won't fail to notice. Another choice winter bloomer is buttercup winterhazel (*Corylopsis pauciflora*), a yellow-flowered shrub that puts forsythia to shame.

Evergreens for Winter Bloom

Several broadleaved evergreens adorn winter gardens with both flowers *and* foliage. My favorites for acid-soil areas are cultivars of Japanese pieris (*Pieris japonica*). The neat, glossy foliage often takes on beautiful winter colors, as do the decorative clusters of beadlike flower buds. Bell-shaped white or pink blooms open in early March in my garden and continue for six to eight weeks, often lasting through the early and midseason bulbs. Winter daphne (*Daphne odora*) forms neat mounds of foliage and clusters of highly scented, pinkish white flowers in February and March.

Two species of camellia, the common camellia (*Camellia japonica*) and sasanqua camellia (*C. sasanqua*), are synonymous with the South, having adorned stately southern gardens with their red, pink, or white blooms since Colonial times. These glossy-leaved ever-green shrubs bloom during the cool season, the huge waxy-flowered common camellia from October through March and the more delicate-flowered sasanqua from September until heavy frost in December. They are normally hardy in Zones 7 to 9, but more cold-hardy cultivars have been developed, which may extend camellias' possibilities into protected sites in Zone 6. "Winter-Flowering Plants" on page 54 lists more winter-blooming choices that finish flowering before spring foliage makes an appearance.

Persistent Leaves

Some deciduous trees and shrubs make a different kind of contribution to the winter garden. Their persistent foliage creates an ornamental effect. The American beech (*Fagus grandifolia*) and European beech (*F. sylvatica*) retain much of their dead foliage through the winter, dropping it only when new spring growth pushes the leaves off. Turning golden yellow or orange-brown in autumn, the foliage slowly bleaches to pale apricot by the end of winter. Like bright feathers caught in the branches, the oval, toothed leaves glow in the soft winter light, making a bright contrast to the rain-darkened gray trunks.

Some species of oak—notably the pin oak (*Quercus palustris*)—tend to hang on to their dead foliage the way the beech does. Oak leaves don't bleach but remain a rich coppery brown until displaced by spring greenery. Pin oaks have an elegant pyramidal silhouette with a skirt of downswept lower branches, which further adds to their winter beauty. These elegant trees do best in acidic soils and may languish in midwestern sites, where pH levels are less to their liking.

The ground-covering shrub 'Hidcote' St.-John's-wort (*Hypericum patulum* 'Hidcote'), noted for its lovely blue-green leaves and bright yellow summer flowers, holds its dried leaves throughout winter. These turn a sumptuous shade of copper that adds rich color to the winter scene. Spicebush (*Lindera benzoin*), an early bloomer that's at home in a woodland site, brightens the woods with pale peachy beige leaves that persist until new growth pushes them off in late winter.

Winsome Winter Bulbs

Spread a carpet of early-blooming bulbs beneath the boughs of your winter-blooming shrubs and trees, and you'll create a colorful sight to lift the winter doldrums. Because most late-winter and spring bulbs have a short growing season—blooming, growing, and dying back before deciduous trees and shrubs have leafed out—they're the perfect plants to grow under deciduous woodies. By the time the trees and shrubs are shading the ground in summer, the bulbs will have gone dormant.

For four-season interest, interplant winter and spring bulbs with groundcovers and flowering perennials. They can push up through most groundcovers and will have finished with their growth cycle when the perennials are just beginning theirs. Evergreen groundcovers, such as bugleweed (*Ajuga reptans*), common periwinkle (*Vinca minor*), and English ivy (*Hedera helix*), show off the flowers against a pretty background while keeping rain from splashing the blooms with mud.

Common snowdrops (*Galanthus nivalis*) and winter aconites (*Eranthis* spp.) fearlessly defy winter, blooming proudly through melting snow and shrugging off ice. You can count on these rugged characters to begin blooming about the same time as witch hazel. Because they bloom so early, snowdrops and winter aconites make perfect garden companions for shrubs and trees like witch hazels and Japanese quince (*Chaenomeles japonica*), which bloom in early January in garden writer Sandra Ladendorf's North Carolina garden.

Snowdrops naturalize readily by both reseeding and increasing their clumps. When happily situated in rich, humusy soil—a woodland is a perfect spot—snowdrops form lovely, 6-inch-tall clumps of blue-green foliage with nodding white-petaled flowers. Spreading rapidly from expanding tubers and by reseeding, winter aconites remain low to the ground, forming a cheerful winter groundcover. A collar of ruffly green leaves surrounds each buttercup-like flower, forming a green-and-yellow swirly carpet when mass-planted.

Following on the heels of the earliest bloomers, several species of crocuses, often collectively called snow crocuses, offer their delicate chalicelike flowers for a month or more in January, February, or March, depending on your region. As sun fades or snow crushes the first blooms, more buds and flowers emerge from each corm. Species crocuses bear numerous small flowers but lack the wallop of the later-blooming Dutch crocus hybrids. The smaller species crocuses don't show up as well from a distance but make a delightful display massed in a rock garden or along a frequently visited path where they can be enjoyed at close range.

Favorite species crocuses for garden situations include the many cultivars of golden crocus (*C. chrysanthus*), which come in shades of light blue, butter yellow, bicolored purple and white, and creamy yellow. The flowers of Tommasini's crocus (*C. tommasinianus*) begin as silvery lavender spires cutting through the snow and open to white-throated lilac to purple flowers on sunny days. Sieber crocus (*C. sieberi*) has rich lilac flowers with yellow throats. Unlike many bulbs, all these crocus species do well in summer-moist soil and thus adapt well to garden situations.

Several bulbous species of tiny irises bloom along with the crocuses in February or March in the North and in January in the South. These beautifully splotched flowers arise

Winter-blooming bulbs. Bulbs that bloom through melting snow in mid- to late winter provide the greatest impact if you plant them in large patches beneath winter-blooming shrubs. Here two of the earliest bloomers, common snowdrops (*Galanthus nivalis*) and winter aconites (*Eranthis hyemalis*), carpet the ground beneath a Chinese witch hazel (*Hamamelis mollis*).

directly from the ground, often surrounded by the low spikes of their emerging foliage. The slender leaves later elongate to 12 inches tall.

Unfortunately, none of these species spreads very well in most gardens, probably because they demand gritty, well-drained soil and baking sun in summer. They may even be short-lived to the point of needing to be replaced every year. In my garden, squirrels devoured the blooms as eagerly as they ate the crocuses, and slugs may be a problem in the South or Northwest. But their bright colors and lovely form make them earn their place in the garden — even as annuals.

The earliest-blooming iris is probably the lovely blue-flowered harput iris (*Iris histrioides*), which races the snowdrops, winter aconites, and species crocuses to the starting line. The winner often depends on how much snow blankets the garden. If snow lies late, these bulbs may all bloom in unison, but in snowless years, the winter aconites and snowdrops beat the crocuses and irises.

The bright yellow Danford iris (*Iris danfordiae*) and the blue or purple Baker iris (*I. bakeriana*) soon follow the harput iris. The most elegant of these elfin irises is the reticulated iris (*I. reticulata*), offering velvety purple or soft blue flowers with yellow crests. These bloom while their leaves are only just poking through the ground, so try interplanting them with evergreen groundcovers such as woolly thyme (*Thymus pseudolanuginosus*) or lemon thyme (*T.* × *citriodorus*).

Sandra Ladendorf reports from North Carolina that her winter iris (*I. unguicularis*) produces its yellow-crested violet flowers throughout winter, beginning in early January. A white form is also available. It's best to cut back the tips of the foliage of this early-leafing iris, if necessary, to prevent them from hiding the flowers.

I love blue flowers, and winter-blooming bulbs provide several delightful choices for my garden. Siberian squill (*Scilla siberica*) produces short stalks of bluebells in mid- to late winter. The less common tubergen squill (*Scilla mischtschenkoana,* syn. *S. tubergeniana*) flowers even earlier, with fringed pastel blue bell-shaped blooms. Two-leaved squill (*S. bifolia*) also flowers earlier than Siberian squill, with rich blue blooms. Glory-of-the-snow (*Chionodoxa luciliae*) has starlike flowers with petals that are china blue with white bases, creating a subtle two-tone effect. All these bulbs will naturalize, creating great drifts of blue in late winter.

Most daffodils bloom in early spring, but several species and early-blooming hybrids display their sunny yellow flowers in late winter. The best early bloomers are the miniatures — the tiny and very early species *Narcissus asturiensis* and *N. cyclamineus,* and hybrids such as 'February Gold', 'Little Gem', and 'Tête-à-Tête', all of which are dwarf versions of full-sized April-blooming daffodils.

Conversation pieces, such as the hoop-petticoat narcissus (*N. bulbocodium*) with its oddly shaped corolla-less flowers, look delightful in a rock garden. These early narcissi make colorful companions for the winter heaths (*Erica* spp.) and Dutch crocus hybrids. I especially enjoy the blue-and-yellow color scheme they

create when combined with Virginia bluebells (*Mertensia virginica*) and glory-of-the-snow.

For more winter-blooming bulb choices, see "Winter-Flowering Plants" on page 54.

Early Perennial Pleasures

A number of perennials bloom with the melting snow in late winter in the North or as early as Christmas in milder climates. These intrepid perennials are good company for sweeps of early bulbs and groupings of winter-blooming trees and shrubs. Combine them in a corner of your yard, and you'll create a garden sensation when most yards display only mud and dead-looking stems.

Most noteworthy among these winter-blooming perennials are the hellebores (*Helleborus* spp.). Several species of these evergreen to semi-evergreen perennials ornament gardens from Maine to Georgia with their cold-hardy, roselike flowers and leathery, glossy green, deeply cut leaves. Christmas rose (*H. niger*) is most widely known, blooming in mid- to late winter (not really at Christmas, except in the most southerly parts of its range, but often before the snowdrops).

Christmas rose produces clusters of 2- to 3-inch-wide, nodding, creamy white flowers with centers filled by showy golden stamens. The waxy blooms last perfectly for months, defying the snow, and eventually age to an old rose color. A mature specimen of Christmas rose glows with as much elegance and substance as any summer flower: This is not one of those paltry winter bloomers that couldn't compete out of season. The equally admirable Lenten rose (*H. orientalis*) usually opens in midwinter, several weeks after the Christmas rose. Its foliage is a very dark—almost black—shiny green; the cup-shaped flowers range from creamy white to dusky maroon and may be stippled or spotted with other hues.

The green-flowered stinking hellebore (*H. foetidus*)—which gets its name from its bad-smelling root, not its flowers—makes a charming sight with its apple green flowers edged with maroon. These are borne on 2-foot-tall upright stalks decked out with fernlike foliage, making a beautiful foliage plant. Corsican hellebore (*H. argutifolius,* also listed as *H. corsicus*) bears apple green flowers and foliage marbled with darker shades. It's the least hardy hellebore, surviving only to Zone 6.

The trick to growing hellebores, if there is one, is to provide the plants with rich, woodsy soil in semishade and mulch them well with leaf litter or compost. Don't let the soil dry out, especially when getting them established (plants can often be slow to establish).

You can allow the flowers to set seed, and these will germinate and set up a happy colony if the conditions are to their liking. (But note that all hellebore species seem to hybridize freely, so if you grow several species, the offspring may be hybrids.) You might also wish to cut off the overwintered foliage as new foliage emerges in spring. All parts of hellebore plants are poisonous if eaten, and the sap may give some people a rash.

Emerging from the soil quite early and blooming well before their silver-spotted leaves have fully expanded, the flowers of common lungwort (*Pulmonaria officinalis*) and Bethlehem sage (*P. saccharata*) resemble Virginia bluebells (*Mertensia virginica*). Their clusters of bell-shaped flowers develop from curled-up hairy stems that unwind to reveal pink-tinged buds, eventually producing blue flowers. These late-winter bloomers, appearing in March in my garden, naturalize well and thrive in moist, shady, or woodsy sites.

Amur adonis (*Adonis amurensis*), blooming in late February, and spring adonis (*A. vernalis*), blooming a few weeks later, thrive in the same locations favored by the lungworts, so they make good companions. I admire the fernlike, feathery foliage of the adonises and their yellow or white flowers, which shine like sunstruck satin.

Though they go dormant and disappear from view by midsummer, these plants have fibrous roots and are not bulbs. Plant them in a low groundcover such as common periwinkle (*Vinca minor*) or sweet woodruff (*Galium odoratum*), or with ferns or other late-emerging foliage or flowering plants that will leaf out to cover the ground when the adonises go dormant in summer.

More winter-blooming herbaceous perennials are featured in "Winter-Flowering Plants" on page 54 and described beginning on page 300 in Chapter 7.

Designer Perennials

Several perennials—ones I've nicknamed "designer perennials" due to their overwhelming popularity among garden designers in the know—deserve special notice for their winter form and color. All are four-season plants deserving a place in any garden. And all their seed heads look great in winter, so don't cut them down until spring.

Autumn Joy sedum (*Sedum* 'Autumn Joy') is a four-season perennial if there ever was one! Jade green succulent foliage emerges from the ground in spring and deepens in color by midsummer, when flat clusters of pale green flower buds top the plant. By late summer these flowers bloom rosy pink, eventually turning rusty red with the onset of autumn's cold. Though freezing weather finishes off the foliage, clusters of 1½-foot-tall stems remain standing all winter, holding up the richly colored dried flower heads, which make magnificent snow-catchers.

Thread-leaved coreopsis (*Coreopsis verticillata*), especially the pale yellow cultivar 'Moonbeam' and the bright yellow 'Golden

WINTER-FLOWERING PLANTS

Unusual as it may seem, flowers can embellish the winter garden. Some bloom in the dead of winter, others on the cusp of spring, but all the plants listed below finish flowering during the transparent season, well before new spring foliage emerges on the shade trees.

Trees

Acer rubrum (red maple), Zones 3–9
Cornus mas (cornelian cherry), Zones 5–8
C. officinalis (Japanese cornel dogwood), Zones 5–8
Parrotia persica (Persian parrotia), Zones 6–9
Prunus mume (Japanese apricot), Zones 7–9
P. subhirtella var. *autumnalis* (autumn-flowering Higan cherry), Zones 5–8

Shrubs

Abeliophyllum distichum (white forsythia), Zones 4–9
Camellia japonica (common camellia), Zones 7–9
C. sasanqua (sasanqua camellia), Zones 7–9
Chaenomeles japonica (flowering quince), Zones 4–9
Chimonanthus praecox (wintersweet), Zones 7–9
Corylopsis pauciflora (buttercup winterhazel), Zones 6–8
Corylus avellana 'Contorta' (Harry Lauder's walking stick), Zones 3–8
Daphne mezureum (February daphne), Zones 3–7
D. odora (winter daphne), Zones 8–10
Elaeagnus × *ebbengei* (hybrid elaeagnus), Zones 7–9
Garrya elliptica (tasselbush), Zones 8–10
Hamamelis × *intermedia* (hybrid witch hazel), Zones 5–9
H. mollis (Chinese witch hazel), Zones 5–9
H. vernalis (vernal witch hazel), Zones 4–8
Lonicera fragrantissima (winter honeysuckle), Zones 5–8
Mahonia bealei (leatherleaf mahonia), Zones 6–9
M. lomarifolia (Chinese mahonia), Zones 6–9
Pieris japonica (Japanese pieris), Zones 5–9
Sarcocca hookerana var. *humilis* (sweet box), Zones 7–9
Viburnum × *bodnantense* 'Dawn' (fragrant dawn viburnum), Zones 7–9
V. tinus (laurustinus), Zones 8–9

Groundcovers and Vines

Bergenia crassifolia (leather bergenia), Zones 4–9
B. × *schmidtii* (hybrid bergenia), Zones 3–8
Clematis cirrhosa var. *ballearica*, Zones 7–9
Erica cultivars (winter heaths), Zones 7–8 (See "Heaths and Heathers for Year-Round Color" on page 32.)
Jasminum nudiflorum (winter jessamine), Zones 6–9

Perennials

Adonis amurensis (Amur adonis), Zones 4–7
A. vernalis (spring adonis), Zones 4–7
Anemone sylvestris (snowdrop anemone), Zones 4–8
Arum italicum var. *pictum* (Italian arum), Zones 6–9
Helleborus atrorubens (purple hellebore), Zones 5–9
H. corsicus (Corsican hellebore), Zones 6–8
H. foetidus (stinking hellebore), Zones 5–9
H. niger (Christmas rose), Zones 3–8
H. orientalis (Lenten rose), Zones 4–9
Hepatica americana (liverleaf hepatica), Zones 3–9
Primula vulgaris (English primrose), Zones 5–8
Pulmonaria saccharata (Bethlehem sage), Zones 4–8

Bulbs

Anemone blanda (Grecian windflower), Zones 4–8

A. coronaria (poppy anemone), Zones 6–9
Chionodoxa luciliae (glory-of-the-snow), Zones 4–8
Colchicum luteum (golden colchicum), Zones 7–9
Crocus ancyrensis (golden bunch crocus), Zones 3–9
C. chrysanthus (golden crocus), Zones 4–9
C. flavus, Zones 5–8
C. imperatii (Italian crocus), Zones 6–9
C. sieberi (Sieber crocus), Zones 4–8
C. tommasinianus (Tommasini's crocus), Zones 3–8
Cyclamen coum (cyclamen), Zones 6–8
Eranthis hymenalis (winter aconite), Zones 3–7
Fritillaria imperialis (crown imperial), Zones 5–8
Galanthus elwesii (giant snowdrop), Zones 4–7
G. nivalis (common snowdrop), Zones 3–7
Ipheion uniflorum (starflower), Zones 5–9
Iris danfordiae (Danford iris), Zones 5–9
I. histrioides (harput iris), Zones 5–9
I. reticulata (reticulated iris), Zones 5–9
I. unguicularis (winter iris), Zones 8–10
Leucojum vernum (spring snowflake), Zones 5–9
Narcissus asturiensis, Zones 3–9
N. bulbocodium (hoop-petticoat narcissus), Zones 6–9
N. cyclameneus 'February Gold' ('February Gold' narcissus), Zones 6–9
N. cyclameneus 'February Silver' ('February Silver' narcissus), Zones 6–9
N. cyclameneus 'March Sunshine' ('March Sunshine' narcissus), Zones 6–9
N. cyclameneus 'Tête-à-Tête' ('Tête-à-Tête' narcissus), Zones 6–9
Puschkinia scilloides (striped squill), Zones 4–9
Scilla bifolia (two-leaved squill), Zones 4–8
S. mischtschenkoana, syn. *S. tubergeniana* (tubergen squill), Zones 4–8
S. siberica (Siberian squill), Zones 2–8

Showers', deserves a place in most gardens. These plants spread enthusiastically, making pretty patches of fine-textured, knee-high foliage. The small starry flowers begin blooming in midsummer and keep at it until the middle of fall—without your ever having to deadhead them.

Frost turns coreopsis plants yellow and eventually the needlelike leaves drop, leaving behind wiry black stems decked out with buttonlike, dark brown seedpods. These are too fine-textured to catch much snow, but they spear through a soft snowfall, making a charming silhouette.

Standing 3 to 3½ feet tall, the dark stems of 'Goldsturm' black-eyed Susan (*Rudbeckia fulgida* var. *sullivantii* 'Goldsturm') form impressive clumps of chocolate brown seedheads that last all winter. Strong and sturdy, this cultivar of a native American plant begins producing abundant golden flowers resembling large black-eyed Susans in late summer and continuing through fall. The purple coneflower (*Echinacea purpurea*) puts on a similar performance but bears purplish pink, dark-centered flowers on 5-foot stems. This native prairie plant also has a stark architectural appeal when the dried stems and seedpods are left during winter.

If you're like me and choose to let grasses and flowers remain in your garden throughout the winter, make sure you tidy up in March before new growth begins.

Great Ornamental Grasses

Ornamental grasses fall into the "designer plant" category these days, whether planted in expansive stylized meadows or used in drifts or as specimens in a mixed border. Part of their allure is their winter beauty. Some grasses stand tall over the winter, their narrow leaves bleaching and curling into wonderful rustly arrangements topped with feathery dried plumes; others lack the substance to withstand winter wind and storms, and are flattened or demolished by unruly weather.

Carole Ottesen, author of *Ornamental Grasses: The Amber Wave,* recommends the following grasses for their winter effect: Feather reed grass (*Calamagrostis acutiflora* 'Stricta') bleaches almost white in winter, forming 4-foot-tall clumps of straight stems. Japanese silver grass (*Miscanthus sinensis*) gradually blanches over the winter to the color of dried cornstalks and is topped with white plumes, forming an elegant vase-shaped clump about 5 feet tall. Flame grass (*Miscanthus sinensis* 'Purpurascens') forms 5-foot-tall, upright clumps that turn orange-red in fall and soften to glowing orange in winter, creating a compelling winter color, especially when set out against evergreens.

Fountain grass (*Pennisetum alopecuroides*) is a grass with a lot of volume—it fills up a space about 3½ feet square with graceful cascading blades and purple-tinted late-fall plumes. Fountain grass holds its shape in winter, even after it has changed to bright ash blond, effectively keeping the garden from looking empty. Suitable either as a specimen in a border or mass-planted in a meadow, fountain grass is one of the best grasses for four-season interest.

Gardener's-garters or ribbon grass (*Phalaris arundinacea* var. *picta*) pleases me to no end with its charming green-and-white-striped summer foliage, which makes a pretty groundcover about 2 to 2½ feet tall. Semi-evergreen, the blades eventually bleach to a warm wheat color, adding a ray of sunshine to the winter garden. This aggressively spreading grass needs to be restrained in neat gardens, but where it can be left to form an expansive groundcover, you won't be disappointed with

its winter effect. (These and other grasses are discussed in more detail beginning on page 316 in Chapter 7.)

Then, of course, there are the bamboos— those tall grasses that can form towering groves of elegant reedlike stems and feathery evergreen foliage. In most landscapes, it's best to plant clump-forming bamboos, such as clump bamboo (*Fargesia nitida,* syn. *Sinarundinaria nitida*). Bamboos that spread by runners, such as golden bamboo (*Phyllostachys aurea*), are among the most invasive plants around. They have been known to push up through asphalt, and almost nothing will stop most of them.

One exception is a very pretty cold-hardy dwarf bamboo for winter effect, Kuma-zasa or Kuma bamboo (*Sasa veitchii*). Though it spreads by runners, it is not overly aggressive. The knee-high swirls of foliage, which are green all summer, become variegated in winter. The leaves' edges dry into broad almond bands, giving the plant a light-reflecting brightness in the shady sites it prefers. In spring, cut the old foliage to the ground to make room for new growth.

Creating a Special Winter Garden

Your year-round garden will be most effective if, when planning it, you first study your garden and landscape in winter. Note where evergreens are particularly needed to block or frame views or provide a weighty mass, and note, too, which areas of the garden come most into view from the house, drive, or walks during the winter months.

Developing the bones of a mixed border is a continuing process. The process will evolve over the course of several years. You'll add plants and perhaps subtract some as the landscape grows and fills in, as you correct errors

Susan's winter view. Viewed from a picture window in the eat-in kitchen, the author's side yard provides visual excitement all year. The 'Heritage' river birch (*Betula nigra* 'Heritage'), with its colorful salmon and cream bark, creates the focal point. It's set off against broadleaf evergreens and surrounded by Lenten roses (*Helleborus orientalis*) and reticulated iris (*Iris reticulata*).

or oversights, and as your gardener's eye becomes more critical and discerning.

With a good bone structure in place, all of your property should hold garden interest during winter. But you might wish to concentrate those plants with great winter interest in locations where you'll appreciate them most, such as near the most-often-used door or in view from a frequently used window.

I have planted two areas of our property, the foundation planting along the front walk and the side yard that opens off the kitchen door, with a high concentration of winter-interest plants. We view the small side yard, where we garden intensively, from a picture window in the breakfast nook. The perennial and wild-flower garden we planted in the side yard looked beautiful through fall. But during our first winter, we found ourselves with only a naked board fence to study during breakfast. We quickly fixed that by turning the flower border into a mixed border.

In winter, the border gets its bones from a low stone wall separating the curving border and planting area from the small lawn and from deciduous trees and evergreen and deciduous shrubs. A shallow terra-cotta dish set on a low rough-hewn stump provides water for birds, while acting as a focal point in the part of the garden most devoted to perennials. Bird feeders attract a colorful band of visitors to entertain us when we find ourselves housebound.

A main attraction in the side garden is the lovely white-and-salmon bark of the 'Heritage' river birch (*Betula nigra* 'Heritage') set to one side of the view. Color and mass derive from the red osier dogwood (*Cornus sericea*); the broadleaved evergreens, which include

'P.J.M.' hybrid rhododendrons (*Rhododendron* 'P.J.M.') with their burgundy winter foliage; the glossy dark green foliage of Burford holly (*Ilex cornuta* 'Burfordii'); and the golden green, scalelike needles of the golden threadleaf Sawara false cypress (*Chamaecyparis pisifera* 'Filifera Aurea').

The bright red berries of winterberry (*Ilex verticillata*) sparkle into early winter if they survive the birds. Winter flowers provide more color when 'Arnold Promise' witch hazel (*Hamamelis* × *intermedia* 'Arnold Promise'), winter daphne (*Daphne odora*), and Christmas rose (*Helleborus niger*) begin to bloom, accompanied by carpets of common snowdrops (*Galanthus nivalis*) and winter aconite (*Eranthis hyemalis*). The garden floor stays green from the patch of lawn and sweeps of bugleweed (*Ajuga reptans*), Allegheny foamflower (*Tiarella cordifolia*), common periwinkle (*Vinca minor*), English ivy (*Hedera helix*), and Japanese pachysandra (*Pachysandra terminalis*).

In its most dreary months, winter possesses its own stark grandeur, which I have come to appreciate and admire, even if the weather keeps me housebound. You may count yourself among the gardeners who, as I once did, find winter a dead and dreary time of year. But once you've encountered the surprise of colorful barks and berries, the varied hues of evergreens, and the bright but unpredictable cold-hardy blooms available to brighten your winter garden, you'll never think of this season in quite the same way. Winter will no longer be the bereft season in your garden but will become the season of quiet revelation, the season of scrutiny, the season of delicate harmonies, the season of surprise.

Winter

Winter has its own subtle beauty, featuring the vibrant colors of evergreens, glossy berries, beautiful bark, and the few but prized winter flowers. If you design a garden with a good winter bone structure, it will look lovely in all seasons.

A light snowfall transforms this hillside into a study in black and white, emphasizing the design's strong bone structure. Slender white-barked trunks form a mass of vertical lines balanced by the roundness of the path's stones. Garden design: Conni Cross.

▲ Snow adds a surprise to this flower-lined path in March. *Narcissus* 'February Gold', an early-blooming daffodil, is flanked by 'Springwood Pink' heath (*Erica carnea* 'Springwood Pink'), with 'Lemon Drop' false cypress (*Chamaecyparis pisifera* 'Lemon Drop') in the back. Garden design: Conni Cross.

▶ The brilliant orange berries of 'Mohave' firethorn (*Pyracantha coccinea* 'Mohave') last from fall through winter, forming an almost solid wall of color when trained against a building or fence.

◀ Winter reveals the smooth gray bark of the European beech (*Betula sylvatica*), which hides behind a thick mantle of glossy green leaves in summer. Give this slow-growing tree plenty of space in an open lawn, for it will ultimately reach majestic proportions.

▲ Unfurling their temperature-sensitive petals during warm spells in mid- to late winter, the mophead flowers of 'Arnold Promise' witch hazel (*Hamamelis* × *intermedia* 'Arnold Promise') bloom here on a sunny day after a February snowfall, perfuming the air with a sweet fragrance.

◀ Every garden deserves at least one witch hazel (*Hamamelis* spp.). Plant it in a prominent location, where you can view and enjoy it from indoors during winter's gloomy days. The cheerful flowers bloom for as long as two months, beginning in January in the South and February or March in the North. Garden design: Conni Cross.

Junipers and pines provide a green background that shows off the fruiting display of 'Profusion' beautyberry (*Callicarpa bodinieri* 'Profusion') along the street in the author's garden. The startling lilac-purple berries are showy from September through February.

Reticulated iris (*Iris reticulata*) and snowdrops (*Galanthus nivalis*) compete with each other for the title of winter's earliest-blooming bulb—snowdrops usually win during cold years and iris during warm ones.

▲ This February landscape, featuring garden color from bark, berries, foliage, flowers, and structures, demonstrates all that a garden can be, even in the dead of winter. Plants include heaths and heathers in the foreground; weeping larch and golden false cypress in the midground; cotoneasters and weeping birch along the fence; and European birch and variegated Japanese cryptomeria in the far background. Garden design: Conni Cross.

► Startlingly colorful throughout the winter, the blood red bark of red osier dogwood (*Cornus sericea*) actually deepens in color with the cold. These plants look most effective when mass-planted, intensifying their impact. 'Flaviramea', in the background, is a gold-barked cultivar.

▲ Naturalized in a lawn, glory-of-the-snow (*Chionodoxa luciliae*) self-sows with abandon to provide an expanse of bright flowers at winter's end. Bulbs will flourish if you wait to mow the lawn until six weeks after they bloom.

◀ Christmas rose (*Helleborus niger*) blooms in mid- to late winter and remains showy for months. This handsome perennial thrives if sited in moist, humusy soil in partial shade.

▶ An open sky makes an effective backdrop for the frosted branches of the corkscrew willow (*Salix matsudana* 'Tortuosa'), allowing the twisting branch structure to stand out uncluttered by competing elements.

One of our most graceful native conifers, white pine (*Pinus strobus*), is truly white only when frosted by a light snow. Best when they're allowed to grow into tall specimens or planted as a screen with branches to the ground, mature trees can also be limbed up to provide garden space beneath.

▲ The gold bands on the needles of dragon's-eye pine (*Pinus densiflora* 'Oculus-Draconis') become more golden in winter, making a stunning contrast to dark green neighboring plants.

▼ The delicate effect created by variegated Japanese pieris (*Pieris japonica* 'Variegata') is welcome every month of the year in a garden designed for four-season appeal.

▶ Before they bloom, the dark rose-red flower buds of 'Valley Valentine', a pink-flowered cultivar of Japanese pieris (*Pieris japonica*), adorn the evergreen foliage like strings of garnet beads. The buds expand in February or March, opening into pink flowers that bloom for six to eight weeks in late winter and early spring.

◄ A useful backbone plant throughout much of the year, 'Blue Maid' holly (*Ilex* × *meserveae* 'Blue Maid') comes into its own in winter, when bright red fruits sparkle among the glossy evergreen foliage. Evergreens bring much-needed color and substance to a winter landscape, which would be brown and lifeless without them.

▼ Winter is hardly a dull season with a view like this from your window! White-barked weeping European birch (*Betula pendula*) and variegated Japanese crypto-meria (*Cryptomeria japonica* 'Aurea') form a backdrop for a clump of 'Brookside' Japanese silver grass (*Miscanthus sinensis* 'Brookside'), which forms a commanding focal point. Rugged rocks give further structure to the scene. Garden design: Conni Cross.

Winter color comes primarily from the not-necessarily-green foliage of evergreen plants. Here golden false cypress (*Chamaecyparis obtusa* 'Nana Aurea') glows behind a foreground of the heather *Calluna vulgaris* 'Cuprea', with copper needles that turn rusty red in winter. Garden design: Conni Cross.

▲ Bleached to a light-reflecting, wheat-colored fountain of dried foliage and flowers, Japanese silver grass (*Miscanthus sinensis*) stands tall and showy all winter. It turns this otherwise bleak landscape into an eye-catching scene.

▶ A tough, insect-resistant tree, the 'Heritage' river birch (*Betula nigra* 'Heritage') brings much-appreciated color to a four-season landscape. The English ivy (*Hedera helix*) must be carefully pruned so the vines don't obscure the ornamental birch bark.

◀ A choice tree for a mixed border, Japanese stewartia (*Stewartia pseudocamellia*) displays colorful patchwork bark all year, showy white flowers in midsummer, and rich red to purple foliage in autumn.

▲ Especially long-lasting if they escape the ravages of migrating birds, the red fruits of winterberry (*Ilex verticillata*) provide an exciting splash of winter color. Improved cultivars of this native deciduous holly are laden with large berries, but like the species, only female plants produce fruit, and they must be pollinated by a male plant to do so.

◄ Carpeting the ground with golden yellow, buttercup-like blossoms, winter aconite (*Eranthis hyemalis*) seems to melt away the last snows of winter. Winter aconite self-sows readily to form large drifts that look especially pretty beneath deciduous shrubs. This tuberous-rooted perennial goes dormant during summer.

CHAPTER 3

Spring in the Four-Season Landscape

Make the Most of the Translucent Season's Beauty

The crabapple tree in my front yard acts as my barometer for the seasons, its cycles of flower, foliage, and fruit marking the movement of the year. From my second-story office, I observe the tree's canopy, noting its progress from fruit-studded winter branches to a mist of ruby-blushed spring greenery. At these initial signs of green I begin my countdown to spring. First, I anticipate the rosy flower buds in early spring, and then their opening in midspring to become bouquets of pink blooms. Over the next two weeks, the crab's flowers will gradually fade to white, completing the spring show.

Spring's arrival seems as much a sentimental event as a visual one. The sun feels warmer and the breeze less chilly, the sky seems bluer and the days noticeably longer. Clamorous bird song greets the dawn. When this happens, regardless of what's in bloom, I *know* spring has arrived. Often all these signs

of spring coincide with the golden yellow banners of border forsythia (*Forsythia × intermedia*), which signal spring's arrival.

Stretching their blooming period from the end of winter, when the landscape still stands transparent and leafless, into the first week or so of spring, when greenery begins to shade the horizon, forsythias and other early-blooming plants blur the edges of winter and spring. These are the transition plants that wake the garden out of its dormant season.

The Elusive Season

If gardeners have a universal complaint about spring, it is that the season is here today, gone tomorrow. I hear all too many gardening friends, from all over the country, claim, "We hardly have any spring here. It seems it's winter one day and summer the next. Spring just doesn't last long enough!"

No matter how long the season actually lasts, no matter how much we get, it doesn't satisfy. The freshness and drama of the season pass too soon—the baby leaves grow into matronly foliage, the wild floral colors drop to the ground. I cannot capture enough of this elusive season—it comes and goes almost in the blink of an eye—but by carefully choosing plants that bloom for long periods and at each end of the season, I can stretch spring's beauty to its fullest potential.

The Three Seasons of Spring

Spring's bloom parade falls into three miniseasons—early, mid-, and late spring—because each plant has its own timetable and sequence of development, some leafing out earlier, some later than the rest. Some bloom before their foliage emerges, while others flower and leaf out simultaneously.

Early-spring bloomers, such as eastern redbud (*Cercis canadensis*) and the transition plants, usually flower well before their leaves emerge. They make a strong color impact because no green foliage dilutes or softens their flowers' bright pigments. Blooming on bare branches does not necessarily relegate such plants to winter, however; in early spring, many other plants are leafing out around them to act as foliage foils.

Midspring bloomers, such as Koreanspice viburnum (*Viburnum carlesii*), usually produce flowers as their leaf buds begin to unfurl, creating a pretty picture of flowers and soft foliage. Late-spring blooms, like those of doublefile viburnum (*Viburnum plicatum* var. *tomentosum*), are surrounded by well-developed but still fresh and tender foliage.

Some summer-blooming woody plants, such as mimosa (*Albizia julibrissin*) and crape myrtle (*Lagerstroemia indica*), leaf out so late that you may fear that they're dead. Some perennials, notably balloon flower (*Platycodon grandiflorus*) and butterfly weed (*Asclepias tuberosa*), poke through the ground so late that they're in danger of being forgotten and dug up when you start to plant something in the "bare spot."

Peonies, though they bloom in late spring or early summer, push up their ruby red new stems and curled-up foliage very early, developing into a mound of glossy leaves. They've turned into sturdy, bush-sized plants by the time their knobby flower buds begin to expand in late spring and early summer.

When selecting spring plants for your four-season landscape, keeping these three phases of spring in mind provides assurance that you'll get the most from this season. As the early bloomers fade, the midseason beauties take over the show, in turn giving way to the late bloomers.

Don't Forget Foliage

Spring's young foliage transmits light like stained glass—solid enough to veil the see-through quality of winter views, but sheer enough to let sunlight pass, bathing the garden in green light. If winter is the transparent season, then spring is the translucent season.

Foliage marks the transition from winter to spring as the new leaves unfold a delicate yellow-green. By midspring the trees' foliage has fully expanded, blocking the open winter views, fleshing out the bare bones and silhouettes, but allowing light to pass through the still-tender growth in sparkling rays. Foliage begins to enclose the garden by midspring, creating a cozy, private feeling and a deepening green foil for the season's colorful flowers.

Layers of Bloom

A well-planned spring garden surrounds you with flowers from head to foot. Unlike the blooms of summer and autumn, which consist mostly of perennials and annuals flowering below eye level, spring's blooms layer themselves profusely from top to bottom of the planting pyramid. Drawn overhead by the flower-laden branches of blooming trees, your vision travels down to eye-level flowering shrubs, then drops below those to meet the bouquets of bulbs, perennials, and groundcovers that carpet the pyramid's base.

The vast majority of flowering trees and shrubs bloom in spring, bringing color up off the ground to eye level and above. I'd venture to say that when we think of spring flowers, it's the dogwoods, magnolias, crabapples, viburnums, lilacs, azaleas, and spireas that first come to mind—the flowers of the permanent, *woody* plants that form the bones and structure of the landscape—rather than the ground-level perennials, bulbs, and groundcovers.

A Skyline Progression

The top of the planting pyramid begins its springtime show with the unfolding foliage of the tall shade trees—whose catkins and flowers are usually green and insignificant, and may actually be mistaken for young leaves—and the opening blooms of the small flowering trees.

The flowering trees in their spring glory command our attention. Usually growing as understory trees in their native habitats, small flowering trees—such as the dogwoods and redbuds of southern Indiana—are adapted to the filtered shade of the forest and the half-day shade of the woodland edges. In the landscape, the trees flourish in partially shaded

conditions, but many also do well when planted in full sun, perhaps blooming even more profusely in sunny conditions.

The Early-Spring Canopy

Nothing uplifts me from the winter doldrums in earliest spring like the sight of magnolia blooms displayed against a bright blue sky. The delicate-looking star magnolia (*Magnolia stellata*), a shrubby, multitrunked tree, blooms very early, often in late winter, cloaking its bare gray branches with many-petaled, 6-inch-wide, creamy white flowers. The flowers, whose 20 petals make them appear to be double, emit an enchanting sweet fragrance. Though the tree itself is one of the most cold-hardy magnolias (hardy to Zone 5), its tender blooms often fall prey to frost.

The Kobus magnolia (*M. kobus*) resembles the star magnolia and is equally cold-hardy but grows larger. The hybrid between the two, Loebner magnolia (*M.* × *loebneri*), blooms at a much younger age than the Kobus magnolia, and so it is preferred.

Following on the heels of the star and Loebner magnolias comes the saucer magnolia (*Magnolia* × *soulangiana*), with huge, waxy, saucer-shaped blooms appearing on smooth bare gray branches. Often the flowers are bicolored, with the outer surfaces of the petals, and hence the flower buds, colored deep beet purple or purplish pink and the insides of the petals creamy white. The flowers open chalice-like to reveal a cluster of showy yellow stamens in their centers.

Saucer magnolia is probably the most widely planted of all magnolias. It's the magnolia that most northerners picture when thinking of magnolias, despite the fact that it, too, can be deadheaded by a cruel frost.

Though magnolias possess three seasons of beauty (they unfortunately lack fall color), I

(continued on page 80)

A SPRING WILDFLOWER GARDEN

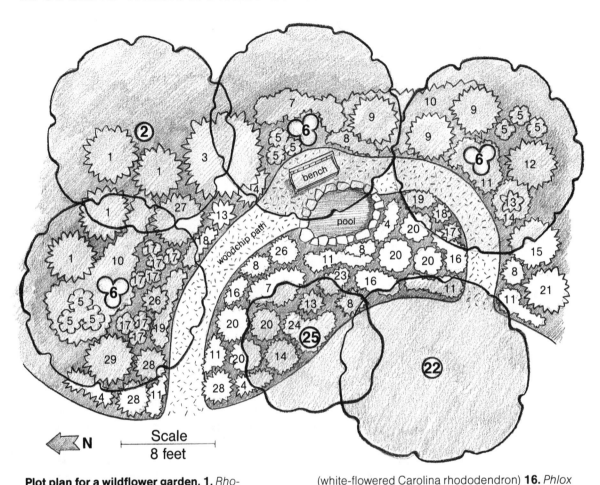

N   Scale
8 feet

Plot plan for a wildflower garden. 1. *Rhododendron carolinianum* (Carolina rhododendron) **2.** *Cercis canadensis* (eastern redbud) **3.** *Rhododendron catawbiense* (catawba rhododendron) **4.** *Iris cristata* (crested iris) **5.** *Osmunda cinnamomea* (cinnamon fern) **6.** *Amelanchier arborea* (downy serviceberry) **7.** *Cimicifuga simplex* (Kamchatka bugbane) **8.** *Dicentra eximia* (fringed bleeding heart) **9.** *Kalmia latifolia* (mountain laurel) **10.** *Galium odoratum* (sweet woodruff) **11.** *Tiarella cordifolia* (Allegheny foamflower) **12.** *Rhododendron periclymenoides* (pinxterbloom azalea) **13.** *Trillium grandiflorum* (large-flowered white trillium) **14.** *Phlox stolonifera* 'Blue Ridge' ('Blue Ridge' creeping phlox) **15.** *Rhododendron carolinianum* var. *album* (white-flowered Carolina rhododendron) **16.** *Phlox divaricata* (wild blue phlox) **17.** *Polystichum acrostichoides* (Christmas fern) **18.** *Viola labradorica* var. *purpurea* (purple-leaf Labrador violet) **19.** *Phlox stolonifera* 'Bruce's White' ('Bruce's White' creeping phlox) **20.** *Fothergilla gardenii* (dwarf fothergilla) **21.** *Clethra alnifolia* 'Rosea' (pink summersweet) **22.** *Cornus florida* (flowering dogwood) **23.** *Sanguisorba canadensis* (bloodroot) **24.** *Phlox stolonifera* 'Home Fires' ('Home Fires' creeping phlox) **25.** *Halesia carolina* (Carolina silverbell) **26.** *Adiantum pedatum* (maidenhair fern) **27.** *Rhododendron atlanticum* (coast azalea) **28.** *Pieris floribunda* (mountain pieris) **29.** *Rhododendron roseum* (roseshell azalea)

A wildflower garden. The flowers, shrubs, and trees used in this design are native to the woodlands of the eastern United States. Planted along a path that leads to a bench and restful pool, these wildflowers create a shade-filled garden that comes alive with color in spring. Other seasons are quieter but have a charm of their own: Summer brings a jewel-like sprinkling of flowers amid cool greenery; autumn features brilliant fall foliage; and winter offers evergreen and deciduous shrubs for strong textural impact.

usually advise people to forgo planting early-blooming species in areas where late frosts pose a problem. Or I tell them to plant one in a cold microclimate, such as a northern exposure, which slows down the flower buds so the tree blooms later, hopefully after the last freeze.

If you really love magnolias and would be bereft without one in your garden, you might choose a cultivar bred to bloom late and escape frost. In a way, this defeats the purpose of planting the tree, because you won't have early blooms, but you will at least have your magnolia!

Of course, my husband Mark and I don't always practice what we preach. We planted a specimen of 'Alexandrina' saucer magnolia (*Magnolia* × *soulangiana* 'Alexandrina'), a popular purple-and-white bicolor, the first fall we lived in our present home. We chose the barren southeastern corner of our house, where I had ripped out an ungainly fir tree whose branches had been obscuring the windows and lounging on the roof, as the spot most in need of the magnolia.

We bought the plant on impulse one fall weekend when passing a nursery with huge sale banners flying—Mark loves magnolias *and* loves a bargain. The tree has bloomed magnificently (knock on wood) each spring since without any frost damage. And it has put out enormous growth. I've underplanted it with white daffodils, which bloom at the same time, and later-blooming perennials.

Four cherries (*Prunus* spp.) with outstanding flowers, foliage, and bark bloom with the star magnolias and serviceberries (*Amelanchier* spp.) but are cold-tolerant enough to escape frost blast. Weeping Higan cherry (*Prunus subhirtella* var. *pendula*), delicate pink in bloom, commands attention throughout the year because of its graceful, pendulous branches. Be sure to locate it as a focal point in your garden and don't obscure the silhouette in a crowded setting. One of the prettiest weeping

cherries I've seen was planted beside a large garden pond where its reflection doubled its beauty.

Blooming for three full weeks in late March or early April in the Mid-Atlantic states, 'Okame' cherry (*Prunus* 'Okame', a cross between *P. incisa* and *P. campanulata*) cloaks itself with deep maroon buds that open into small pink blooms, making it a favorite season-stretcher, according to garden designer Conni Cross. Not commonly grown, this tree was honored with an award of merit from the Pennsylvania Horticultural Society.

Sargent cherry (*Prunus sargentii*) is another early-blooming cherry for year-round beauty. In early spring, clusters of single, deep pink blooms festoon the branches, coinciding with the flowers of the star magnolias. Cherries, of course, spell springtime in Washington, D.C. Performing in the famous cherry blossom display at the Tidal Basin, the Yoshino cherry (*Prunus* × *yedoensis*) bears fragrant white flowers, which, though single, are among the showiest of all cherry blossoms.

Purple-leaf plums or flowering plums (*Prunus cerasifera* 'Atropurpurea' and related hybrids) are members of the same genus as cherries. Not only do they offer a delicate display of white or pink early-spring flowers, their foliage is tinted maroon or burgundy, adding to the spring display and carrying on throughout summer. Double pink purple-leaf plum (*P.* × *blireana*) is a double-pink flowering plum that blooms before it leafs out—about the time forsythias bloom. Its purple-bronze foliage retains good color in summer. It bears purplish red fruits.

Ornamental pears, notably the popular 'Bradford' callery pear (*Pyrus calleryana* 'Bradford'), accompany the saucer magnolias in early spring. Urban landscapers throughout the country once embraced this cultivar for its four-season beauty and its well-behaved

EARLY-SPRING BLOOMERS
FOR FOUR-SEASON LANDSCAPES

These plants adorn gardens and landscapes with their blooms in early spring, beginning about when the forsythia is losing its petals, and trees and shrubs are beginning to leaf out.

Early-Spring Trees

Acer platanoides (Norway maple), Zones 4–7
Amelanchier spp. (serviceberries, shadblows), Zones 3–8
Cercis canadensis (eastern redbud), Zones 4–9
C. chinensis (Chinese redbud), Zones 6–9
Prunus cerasifera var. *atropurpurea* (purple-leaf plum), Zones 4–9
P. sargentii (Sargent cherry), Zones 5–9
P. yedoensis (Potomac cherry), Zones 6–8

Early-Spring Deciduous Shrubs

Cytisus × *praecox* (Warminster broom), Zones 6–9
Fothergilla spp. (fothergillas), Zones 5–9
Rhododendron schlippenbachii (royal azalea), Zones 5–8

Early-Spring Evergreen Shrubs

Daphne cneorum (garland daphne), Zones 4–7
Rhododendron carolinianum (Carolina rhododendron), Zones 5–7
Rhododendron hybrids (dwarf small-leaved rhododendrons), Zones 5–7

Early-Spring Perennials

Arabis albida (rock cress), Zones 4–7
Aubrieta deltoidea (rock cress), Zones 4–8
Aurinia saxatile, syn. *Alyssum saxatile* (basket-of-gold), Zones 3–7
Dicentra eximia (fringed bleeding heart), Zones 3–9
D. spectabilis (old-fashioned bleeding heart), Zones 2–9
Iberis sempervirens (evergreen candytuft), Zones 3–9
Mertensia virginica (Virginia bluebells), Zones 3–9
Phlox stolonifera (creeping phlox), Zones 2–8

P. subulata (moss pink), Zones 2–9
Primula denticulata (drumstick primrose), Zones 4–8
Viola papilionacea (Confederate violet), Zones 3–9

Early-Spring Bulbs

Allium neopolitanum (Naples onion), Zones 7–9
Hyacinthus orientalis (Dutch hyacinth), Zones 3–7
Leucojum vernum (spring snowflake), Zones 3–9
Muscari armeniacum (Armenian grape hyacinth), Zones 4–9
M. botryoides (common grape hyacinth), Zones 2–8
Narcissus hybrids (midseason daffodils and narcissi), Zones 4–9
Pushkinia scilliodes, syn. *P. libanotica* (striped squill), Zones 2–8
Tulipa batalini (Batalin tulip), Zones 3–8
T. greigii hybrids, Zones 3–7
Tulipa hybrids (single and double early tulips), Zones 3–7
T. linifolia (slimleaf tulip), Zones 4–8
T. maximowicziana, Zones 4–8
T. pulchella var. *violacea,* Zones 5–8
T. tarda, Zones 4–8

Early-Spring Groundcovers

Bergenia spp. (bergenias), Zones 3–8
Galium odoratum (sweet woodruff), Zones 4–8
Lamium maculatum (spotted deadnettle), Zones 3–8
Pachysandra terminalis (Japanese pachysandra), Zones 5–7
Vinca minor (periwinkle myrtle), Zones 4–8
Waldsteinia fragarioides (barren strawberry), Zones 4–7

Early-Spring Vines

Gelsemium sempervirens (Carolina jessamine), Zones 8–9

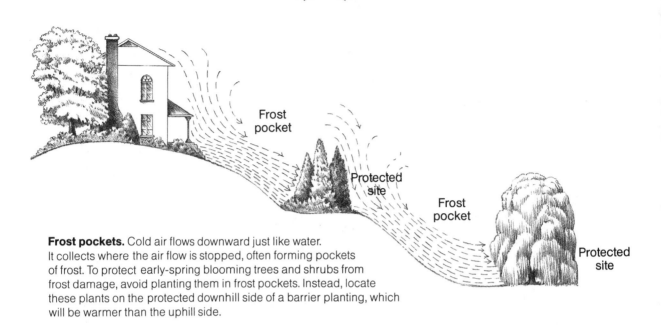

Frost pockets. Cold air flows downward just like water. It collects where the air flow is stopped, often forming pockets of frost. To protect early-spring blooming trees and shrubs from frost damage, avoid planting them in frost pockets. Instead, locate these plants on the protected downhill side of a barrier planting, which will be warmer than the uphill side.

shape, which seemed to make it an ideal street tree. A profusion of dainty but malodorous white flowers transforms the bare branches into a shimmery mist for about two weeks in early spring, until reddish-tinged new green foliage begins to fill in the silhouette.

'Bradford' pear is a handsome tree in a four-season landscape where a formal shape is called for. Note that I said "where a formal shape is called for." Many garden designers hate this tree. They find it overused and too often planted in the wrong places, where its stiff shape seems unfriendly. And now that all those 'Bradford' street trees, planted in large numbers two or three decades ago, are maturing, urban landscapers aren't so pleased. 'Bradford' pear's tailored mature shape makes it vulnerable to the weight of ice and snow, with broken branches and snapped crowns a heavy price for perfect symmetry.

Similar cultivars with broader or narrower shapes and wider branch angles may make a better specimen for your garden than 'Bradford'. 'Bradford' pear's sturdier cousin, 'Chanticleer' pear (*P. calleryana* 'Chanticleer'), may be the best; it has a very formal, tightly pyramidal shape, but branches emerge from the main trunk at wider and stronger angles.

'Aristocrat' grows less dense and may be the best pear for informal garden settings, but it produces few flowers when young, a disadvantage if you're an impatient gardener. 'Capital' forms a narrow column, and 'Whitehouse' forms a narrow pyramidal crown; both are suited to tight locations.

The eastern redbud (*Cercis canadensis*) — the tree I loved in the Indiana woodlands — inhabits woodlands throughout most of the eastern United States and as far west as Texas and Nebraska. Tolerant of widely varying conditions, eastern redbuds need hot summers to prepare them for winter.

Two other redbuds, the Texas redbud (*C. reniformis*) and Mexican redbud (*C. mexicana*), found in the Southwest, are similar to the eastern species. Instead of large, matte green heart-shaped leaves, Texas redbud features 2- to 4-inch-wide, very leathery, glossy dark green leaves. The cultivar 'Oklahoma', a hard-to-find plant, is worth looking for. Its flowers bloom dark reddish purple—the reddest of all the redbuds—and the high-gloss foliage makes a summer statement. This plant can be propagated only by grafting, so be sure you're getting the real thing. The Mexican redbud is a dense, shrubby plant with glossy foliage that develops beautiful wavy margins on mature plants.

In the Pacific Northwest, the mild climate leaves eastern redbuds unprepared for winter, and they often freeze when exposed to winter temperatures that would not hurt them on the East Coast. In this region, choose western redbud (*C. occidentalis*), which forms a dense multistemmed shrub or small tree in Mediterranean-type climates. Magenta-pink blooms are followed by bluish green heart-shaped leaves.

Chinese redbud (*C. chinensis*) blooms more profusely and a week or two earlier than the American species and usually forms a shrubby plant, though in the wild it may reach 50 feet. The magenta buds of the cultivar 'Avondale' appear so profusely that they entirely hide the branches and trunks, creating a more solid color display than that of the eastern redbud. I've only seen a small specimen of this tree, and I have to admit that, though others find it attractive, I find it overdone, preferring instead the grace and gentleness of our native species.

Along with the redbuds, the serviceberries, juneberries, or shadbushes (*Amelanchier* spp.) are among the first bloomers of early spring, producing a haze of white flowers, often accompanied by unfolding leaves, against their pinkish gray bark. A reddish bronze blush tints the new foliage of serviceberry (*A. laevis*),

providing a pretty contrast to its white flowers and the haze of green foliage of other trees. *A. laevis* 'Allegheny Shadblow' has the largest flowers and best fall color of the genus.

The many species of *Amelanchier* are native to different regions of North America. The largest-growing and showiest is shadblow or downy serviceberry (*A. arborea*), whose large flowers are mopheads of gleaming white strap-shaped petals. All species feature edible, purplish blue to black berries in early summer, which attract birds, and nice fall color along with handsome gray or pinkish bark. Unfortunately, the flowers are ephemeral, blooming only about one week. They create a romantic sight when blooming with the redbuds, as I saw them once in the Tennessee woodlands.

The Midspring Canopy

Midspring brings a flood of showy trees into bloom just about the time that tree and shrub foliage has developed enough to provide a beautiful bright green background to offset the eye-catching blooms. Unlike early-spring bloomers, whose flowers seem to hang in the air, midspring bloomers look fuller and more robust.

Crabapples (*Malus* species and cultivars) are among the showiest midspring flowering trees for full-sun situations. The best cultivars command attention throughout the year. The worst cultivars turn unsightly with foliar disease and drop messy, slippery fruits. If you've ever grown one of these older cultivars, it may have left such an indelible impression that you refuse to even consider planting a crabapple again. You're in good company; many homeowners, not knowing that newer cultivars aren't so ill-behaved as those of yesteryear, mistakenly ignore crabapples when planning landscape additions.

Though several of the species and older cultivars are exceptionally beautiful and

MIDSPRING BLOOMERS
FOR FOUR-SEASON LANDSCAPES

These plants open their flowers at the height of spring, when the landscape is fresh with new foliage, but they perform beautifully throughout the year.

Midspring Trees

Cornus florida (flowering dogwood), Zones 5–9
Halesia carolina (Carolina silverbell), Zones 5–9
Malus cultivars (crabapples), Zones 4–9
Prunus maackii (Amur chokecherry), Zones 3–7
P. sargentii (Sargent cherry), Zones 5–9
P. serrula (paperbark cherry), Zones 6–8
P. serrulata 'Shirotae', 'Shogetsu', and 'Shirofugen' (Japanese flowering cherry), Zones 6–8

Midspring Deciduous Shrubs

Berberis koreana (Korean barberry), Zones 3–8
B. thunbergii (Japanese barberry), Zones 4–9
Enkianthus campanulatus (red-vein enkianthus), Zones 5–8
Kerria japonica (Japanese kerria), Zones 5–9
Rhododendron luteum, syn. *R. flavum* (Pontic azalea), Zones 4–8
R. schlippenbachii (royal azalea), Zones 5–8
R. vaseyi (pinkshell azalea), Zones 5–8
R. yedonense var. *poukahanense* (Korean azalea), Zones 5–8
Viburnum × *burkwoodii* (Burkwood viburnum), Zones 5–8
V. × *carlcephalum* (fragrant snowball), Zones 5–8
V. carlesii (Koreanspice viburnum), Zones 4–8
V. × *juddii* (Judd viburnum), Zones 4–8

Midspring Evergreen Shrubs

Berberis julianae (wintergreen barberry), Zones 6–9
Mahonia aquifolium (Oregon grape holly), Zones 5–9
Raphiolepis indica (Indian hawthorn), Zones 8–9

Rhododendron carolinianum (Carolina rhododendron), Zones 5–7
R. Glenn Dale hybrid azaleas, Zones 7–9
R. × *indicum* (evergreen azalea hybrids), Zones 5–9
R. × *kaempferi* hybrids (kaempferi azaleas), Zones 6–9
R. × *obtusum* hybrids (Kurume and Gable azaleas), Zones 5–9

Midspring Perennials

Aquilegia × *hybrida* (columbine), Zones 3–9
Corydalis lutea (yellow corydalis), Zones 5–7
Dianthus deltoides (maiden pinks), Zones 3–9
Geranium sanguineum (blood-red cranesbill), Zones 3–9
Iris cristata (crested iris), Zones 3–9
Phlox divaricata (woodland phlox), Zones 3–9
Phlox subulata (creeping phlox), Zones 3–8

Midspring Groundcovers

Arctostaphylos uva-ursi (bearberry), Zones 3–7
Epimedium spp. (barrenworts), Zones 3–8
Galium odoratum (sweet woodruff), Zones 5–9
Tiarella cordifolia (foamflower), Zones 3–8

Midspring Bulbs

Fritillaria imperialis (crown imperial), Zones 4–7
F. meleagris (checkered lily), Zones 3–9
Ipheion uniflorum (spring starflower), Zones 5–9
Leucojum aestivum (summer snowflake), Zones 4–9
Tulipa clusiana (candystripe tulip), Zones 3–10
T. clusiana var. *chrysantha* (chrysantha tulip), Zones 3–9
Tulipa hybrids (Triumph and Darwin hybrid tulips), Zones 3–7 (8–10 with special care)
T. saxatilis (cliff tulip), Zones 4–10

Midspring Vines

Wisteria chinensis (Chinese wisteria), Zones 5–9

disease-free, recent breeding work has brought us disease-resistant modern hybrids noted for their four-season appeal: beautiful blooms that last for two to three weeks, handsome disease-free summer foliage, and small to medium-sized fruits that ornament the tree after leaf-fall and cling to the branches well into winter, finally shriveling or being eaten by birds without making a mess.

Be sure when purchasing a crabapple that you select one of these commendable plants; many nurseries, unfortunately, still stock the undesirable types that gave these trees such a hard-to-shake bad rap. (See "Plants with Showy Winter Berries" on page 46 for crabapples with both good floral and good fruit displays.)

There are so many improved cultivars that it makes selection a difficult task. They range from wide-spreading shrubby plants to tall trees. Blooms may be white or all shades of pink, rose, and red, and even two-toned. Crabapple flower colors are eye-catching but may clash terribly with the magenta-pink of nearby redbuds or with azaleas coming into bloom. Choose cultivars with both color compatibility and disease resistance in mind.

Dr. Tom Green, executive director of the International Crabapple Society, cautions that in selecting a crabapple it pays to know if diseases pose a real problem in your area. Then you can select cultivars particularly resistant to local problems. In the Northeast and the Pacific Northwest, leaf scab may defoliate trees; in the Rocky Mountains and around Washington, D.C., fire blight can be severe; powdery mildew disfigures crabapples in the South. In the upper Midwest, choose trees grafted to particularly cold-hardy rootstocks.

Spring simply wouldn't be spring in the South without the flowering dogwood (*Cornus florida*). The state tree in both North Carolina and Virginia, this American native reaches lovely large proportions in these states. I had the memorable opportunity to visit the Dixie states one spring when these trees were at their peak. And though Long Island boasts numerous dogwoods, they can't compare to the magnificent cloudlike specimens with their low-spreading branches and elegant notched blooms that grace North Carolina and Virginia.

Flowering dogwoods reach full bloom in midspring, about the same time as crabapples, but their showy notched bracts keep on looking great through almost any type of weather until they finally become full-blown and then fall three to four weeks later at spring's end. I especially cherish the white cultivars, which resemble great cumulus clouds when their flowers are fully expanded. 'Cloud 9', 'Cherokee Princess', and 'Springtime' are extremely floriferous; the mature 'Cloud 9' specimen I've seen in a Long Island garden certainly lives up to its reputation.

Pink-flowered cultivars range from the pastel pink of 'Apple Blossom', a luminous shade that glows at dusk almost as eerily as the white kinds, to the bright shocking pink of 'Rubra', a color that competes with the crabapples for drama. So-called red-flowered forms, such as 'Cherokee Chief', appear in catalogs. Don't be fooled into thinking these are really red. They are actually a very deep rosy pink.

Cultivars with variegated leaves are not uncommon and offer the advantage of beautiful spring flowers and colorful summer foliage. 'Cherokee Sunset' has the same ruby red flowers as 'Cherokee Chief' and foliage splashed rose in spring, maturing to yellow and green, and then putting on a spectacular fall show splashed with yellow, maroon, pink, and red.

(continued on page 88)

CHOOSING A CRABAPPLE
FOR FOUR-SEASON DISPLAY

With over 700 crabapple cultivars available, choosing the right one for your landscape may seem a hit-or-miss proposition. The following cultivars are favorites of Dr. Tom Green, a researcher at the Morton Arboretum in Lisle, Illinois, and executive director of the International Crabapple Society. These trees resist disease and display lovely flowers, graceful shapes, and persistent fruit to guarantee their year-round appeal. All perform well in Zones 3 to 7.

Name: *Malus* 'Adams'
Flowers: Carmine red buds open to red flowers, fade to pink
Fall Foliage: Excellent orange, dark red, and purple
Fruit: Glossy, dark red, ⅝ inch, keep color all winter
Silhouette: Dense and rounded, to 20 feet tall and wide

Name: *M.* 'Amberina'
Flowers: rosy pink buds, open to fragrant pure white, slightly ruffled flowers
Fall Foliage: Flaming red and gold
Fruit: Cardinal red, ⅜ inch, turn oxblood red and persist
Silhouette: Upright to oval, reaching 15 feet tall

Name: *M.* 'Bob White'
Flowers: Pink buds open to white flowers
Fall Foliage: Golden yellow to warm orange-brown
Fruit: Yellow, ½–⅝ inch, persist but often eaten by birds
Silhouette: Rounded and dense, to 20 feet tall and wide

Name: *M.* 'David'
Flowers: Red buds open to white flowers
Fall Foliage: Bright yellow
Fruit: Glossy cardinal red, ½ inch, persistent through winter
Silhouette: Open and rounded, 15 feet tall and wide

Name: *M.* 'Donald Wyman' (1989 Styer Award of Garden Merit)
Flowers: Delicate rosy pink buds open to white flowers
Fall Foliage: Bronze-yellow to golden
Fruit: Glossy cardinal red, ½ inch, persist all winter with good color
Silhouette: 20–25 feet tall and 30 feet wide

Name: *M.* 'Harvest Gold' ('Hargozam')
Flowers: Red buds open to pale pink flowers and fade to white
Fall Foliage: Golden yellow
Fruit: Light yellow on red stems through fall, ages to cider gold and persists in winter
Silhouette: Upright to spreading, 20 feet tall and 15 feet wide

Name: *M.* 'Indian Magic'
Flowers: Red buds open to pink flowers
Fall Foliage: Reddish orange
Fruit: Red, teardrop-shaped, ½ inch, change to brilliant reddish orange and persist
Silhouette: Rounded, to 15 feet tall and wide

Name: *M.* 'Indian Summer'
Flowers: Carmine red buds open to pink flowers
Fall Foliage: Rusty red with purple
Fruit: Glossy cardinal red, ⅝ inch, persistent through winter
Silhouette: Upright to spreading, 20 feet tall and 25 feet wide

Name: *M.* 'Jewelberry' (1989 Styer Award of Garden Merit)
Flowers: Red buds open to pink and white flowers, fade to white
Fall Foliage: Golden yellow
Fruit: Bright red, ½ inch, persist but may be eaten by birds
Silhouette: Dense rounded shrub, 8 feet tall and 12 feet wide

Name: *M.* 'Molten Lava' ('Molazam')
Flowers: Pink buds open to white flowers
Fall Foliage: Bright yellow
Fruit: Glossy, bright red, ⅜ inch, persist all winter
Silhouette: Wide-arching to weeping, 10–12 feet tall and 10–15 feet wide

Name: *M.* 'Ormiston Roy'
Flowers: Red buds open to white flowers
Fall Foliage: Golden yellow
Fruit: Orange-yellow, ½ inch, become blushed with red and persist with excellent color
Silhouette: Upright and spreading, 20 feet tall and 25 feet wide

Name: *M.* 'Prairifire'
Flowers: Crimson buds open to purplish red, nonfading flowers displayed against reddish young leaves
Fall Foliage: Orange-red and purple fall color
Fruit: Glossy, dark red, ½ inch, persistent
Silhouette: Upright and spreading, to 20 feet tall with red bark

Name: *M.* 'Professor Sprenger'
Flowers: Red buds open to white flowers
Fall Foliage: Golden yellow
Fruit: Brilliant reddish orange, ⅝ inch, persist all winter
Silhouette: Upright and spreading, to 25 feet tall and wide

Name: *M.* 'Red Jade'
Flowers: Deep pink buds open to white flowers
Fall Foliage: Golden yellow
Fruit: Glossy, bright red, ½ inch, persist all winter unless eaten by birds
Silhouette: Weeping, 10–12 feet tall and twice as wide

Name: *M.* 'Red Jewel'
Flowers: Pale pink buds open to white flowers
Fall Foliage: Bright yellow
Fruit: Glossy cardinal red, ⅜ inch, turn oxblood red and persist all winter
Silhouette: Upright to pyramidal, 15 feet tall and 12 feet wide

Name: *M.* 'Snowdrift'
Flowers: Pink buds open to white flowers
Fall Foliage: Golden yellow with some orange
Fruit: Orange deepening to rust red, persist but often eaten by birds
Silhouette: Rounded and dense, to 20 feet tall and wide

Name: *M.* 'Sugar Tyme' ('Sutyzam')
Flowers: Pale pink buds open to white flowers
Fall Foliage: Golden yellow
Fruit: Red, ½ inch, persist through winter
Silhouette: Upright and spreading, to 18 feet tall and 15 feet wide

Name: *M.* 'White Cascade'
Flowers: Pink buds open to white flowers
Fall Foliage: Golden yellow
Fruit: Yellow, ⅜ inch, persistent
Silhouette: Weeping, to 15 feet tall and wide

Name: *M.* × *zumi* 'Calocarpa' (redbud crabapple)
Flowers: Bright red buds fade to pink, open to pure white flowers
Fall Foliage: Golden yellow
Fruit: Bright red, ⅜ inch, colorful all winter
Silhouette: Horizontal, 25–35 feet tall and 35–40 feet wide

'Rainbow' and 'Welchii' also boast tricolored foliage but have white flowers, and 'Daybreak' has green foliage with a wide creamy white edge that turns rosy pink in fall.

Flowering dogwoods perform best when given an eastern exposure so they are protected from hot afternoon sun, a condition that mimics the woodland edges where they naturally flourish. Although dogwoods tolerate full sun, their leaves may curl unattractively except in the coolest parts of their range. Red- and pink-flowered cultivars are not as cold-hardy as the white ones, and the flower buds may be killed at −15°F to −10°F in Zone 5.

Different cherries bloom from early to mid-spring, the latest of the lot being the 'Kwanzan' Japanese flowering cherry (*P. serrulata* 'Kwanzan'), which begins blooming in midspring with the late crabapples and carries on through late spring. It is the most cold-hardy of the double-flowered cherries (Zones 5 or 6 to 8), and the flowers have up to 30 petals each, more than any white-flowered cultivar.

This tree is commonly trained so that it has a stout straight trunk with branches beginning at about 5 or 6 feet and forming a flaring vase shape that makes an ideal small street tree. Shiny reddish bark wraps the conspicuous trunk, and the branches are coated with shocking pink, double flowers arranged in pendant clusters, accompanied by bright reddish copper young leaves. The tree puts on a fine fall foliage display, making it a four-season favorite.

The garden snobs among us consider 'Kwanzan' cherry a bit too much, bordering on the vulgar—subtle it is not. But when sited properly and carefully combined with complementary plants, this cherry may steal the show from more sedate plants. I thought I was above liking this cherry until I saw it used as a street tree in Vancouver, where specimens lined the streets in two parallel lines pointing their way toward a cornflower blue sky and snow-capped horizon. Two hundred of these cherries bloom at the Tidal Basin in Washington, D.C., surely a sight to behold.

Other cultivars of *Prunus serrulata* bloom a bit earlier and in white or less vivid shades of pink than 'Kwanzan'. The white-flowered 'Shirotae' may be the finest of all the double-flowered cherries. The fragrant flowers bear ruffled petals that shimmer when caught by the angled rays of spring sunshine. The blooms of pale pink cultivars, such as the wide, flat-topped 'Shogetsu' and the bronze-foliaged 'Shirofugen', quickly fade to white, creating the same shimmery effect.

Prunus maackii, the Amur chokecherry, isn't as showy as the Japanese flowering cherries but does put on a nice display of 3-inch-long racemes of tiny white flowers in mid- to late spring. A four-season tree most admired for its spectacular coppery bark in winter, this plant has fans in very cold regions, such as Zones 3 and 4, where other cherries aren't hardy.

I first saw Carolina silverbell (*Halesia carolina*) growing beside a woodland path in a Delaware garden. Its branches arched over the path, framing it with a shower of dainty white bells dangling from the undersides of the branches. Transmitting light like fine silk, the flowers painted a pretty picture against the blue sky. This and the similar mountain silverbell (*H. montana*) bloom in midspring, just about tulip time, as the trees' young foliage expands.

Growing into fairly large trees with rounded heads and horizontal branches, Carolina and mountain silverbells are best in a woodland setting where they can get the rich, organic soil they prefer and where their quiet beauty doesn't have to compete with flashier garden hybrids. I've also seen several Carolina silverbell trees planted as a hillside grove in a Pennsylvania garden—where their flowers are displayed to perfection—and underplanted with blue and white wildflowers.

The Late-Spring Canopy

Late spring—the end of May in my garden—brings a collection of lesser-known trees into bloom. By this time of the season, foliage is well developed, so the blooms of late-flowering trees aren't quite as showy as those blooming before or simultaneously with emerging greenery. But they do add color and fragrance to help ease the transition into summer. Be sure to include at least one late bloomer in your garden to prolong spring's overhead display.

Blooming in late spring and into early summer (late May into June in New England), hawthorns (*Crataegus* spp.) are cold-hardy trees bearing little bridal bouquets of tiny flowers along the tops of their thorny branches. The scallop-edged leaves gleam glossy green in summer and often develop pleasing colors in fall; a profusion of small red or orange berries makes a great show in fall and winter, and most species display a strong horizontal branching pattern that adds to their beauty.

Unfortunately, nothing is ever quite perfect, and indeed these perfect-sounding trees have their drawbacks. Vicious thorns the size of darning needles arm the branches and trunks of many species, and some hawthorns have malodorous flowers. And as members of the rose family, hawthorns fall prey to numerous pests and diseases, including leaf-spot diseases that can defoliate trees in midsummer.

One hawthorn stands out above all the others for year-round beauty and disease resistance. Noted for its profuse, long-lasting clusters of extra-large, orange-red winter berries, 'Winter King' hawthorn (*C. viridis* 'Winter King') holds its own in late spring with a fine display of white flowers, according to Indiana nurseryman Bob Simpson, who discovered and named the tree in 1951.

Mr. Simpson claims 'Winter King' is the most disease-resistant of the hawthorns and the best for winter color. With showy silvery bark and only small thorns, this selection of a native tree won the prestigious Styer Award from the Pennsylvania Horticultural Society in 1992.

After 25 years of breeding and research, Dr. Elwin Orton of Rutgers University has recently released a series of six exciting new hybrids created from crossing the summer-flowering Kousa dogwood with the flowering dogwood, which blooms in midspring. Called the stellar dogwood (*Cornus* × *rutgersenensis*), the new hybrid begins flowering in late spring in between the bloom times of its parents.

The stellar dogwood hybrids include 'Aurora' and 'Galaxy', with large, rounded white flower bracts that overlap to form magnificently showy blooms. The bracts of 'Constellation' and 'Stardust' remain more separate, creating a delicate show. 'Constellation' forms a narrow tree, perfect for tight spaces.

'Stellar Pink', the only pink cultivar, displays brightly blushed pink blooms on a rounded tree. 'Ruth Ellen' and 'Stardust' most resemble the flowering dogwood in form, with horizontal branches extending low to the ground. All have excellent fall foliage color and grow much more vigorously than either parent. I'm particularly excited about these new dogwoods because they resist disease and insects, taking both anthracnose and dogwood borers in stride, and because they bloom in spring with the later azaleas.

LATE-SPRING BLOOMERS
FOR FOUR-SEASON LANDSCAPES

Blooming when the landscape is fully leafed out, these plants wrap up the spring season with their flowers. They continue to ornament the landscape in other seasons with their fine foliage, berries, or handsome shapes.

Late-Spring Trees

Aesculus × *carnea* (red horse chestnut), Zones 5–8

Chionanthus virginicus (American fringetree), Zones 5–9

Cladrastis lutea (American yellowwood), Zones 4–8

Cornus alternifolia (pagoda dogwood), Zones 4–7

C. × *rutgersenensis* (stellar dogwood), Zones 5–8

Crataegus laevigata 'Crimson Cloud' ('Crimson Cloud' English hawthorn), Zones 5–8

C. phaenopyrum (Washington hawthorn), Zones 4–8

C. viridis 'Winter King' ('Winter King' hawthorn), Zones 4–9

Laburnum × *watereri* (golden-chain tree), Zones 6–8

Liriodendron tulipifera (tulip tree), Zones 5–9

Poncirus trifoliatus (hardy orange), Zones 6–9

Prunus maackii (Amur chokecherry), Zones 3–7

P. serrulata 'Kwanzan' ('Kwanzan' Japanese flowering cherry), Zones 6–8

Sorbus alnifolia (Korean mountain ash), Zones 4–7

S. aucuparia (European mountain ash), Zones 3–7

Late-Spring Deciduous Shrubs

Cotoneaster spp. (cotoneasters), Zones 5–8

Rhododendron atlanticum (coast azalea), Zones 5–9

R. calendulaceum (flame azalea), Zones 5–8

R. Exbury hybrid azaleas, Zones 5–8

R. Ghent hybrid azaleas, Zones 4–7

R. Northern Lights hybrid azaleas, Zones 3–6

R. nudiflorum, syn. *R. periclymenoides* (pinxterbloom azalea), Zones 5–8

R. occidentale (western azalea), Zones 5–8

Syringa meyeri, syn. *S. palabiniana* (Meyer lilac), Zones 4–7

S. patula 'Miss Kim' ('Miss Kim' dwarf lilac), Zones 3–7

S. × *persica* (Persian lilac), Zones 4–8

Viburnum dilatatum (linden viburnum), Zones 5–8

V. opulus (cranberrybush viburnum), Zones 3–8

V. plicatum var. *tomentosum* (doublefile viburnum), Zones 5–8

V. setigerum (tea viburnum), Zones 6–8

V. trilobum (American cranberrybush viburnum), Zones 2–8

Late-Spring Evergreen Shrubs

Daphne × *burkwoodii* (Burkwood daphne), Zones 4–7

Leucothoe fontanesiana (fountain leucothoe), Zones 5–9

Nandina domestica (heavenly bamboo), Zones 7–9

Photinia × *fraseri* (Fraser photinia), Zones 8–9

Rhododendron catawbiense (catawba rhododendron), Zones 4–8

Rhododendron hybrids (large-leaf rhododendron hybrids), Zones 4–8

R. yakusimanum (Yako rhododendron), Zones 6–8

Late-Spring Perennials

Baptisia australis (wild blue indigo), Zones 3–9

Campanula garganica (Gargano bellflower), Zones 6–8

C. glomerata (clustered bellflower), Zones 3–8

C. portenschlagiana (Dalmatian bellflower), Zones 4–8

C. poscharskyana (Serbian bellflower), Zones 3–7

Centaurea montana (mountain bluet), Zones 3–8

Cerastium tomentosum (snow-in-summer), Zones 2–7

Iris Bearded hybrids (bearded iris), Zones 3–10

I. sibirica (Siberian iris), Zones 3–9

Linum perenne (blue flax), Zones 4–9

Papaver orientale (Oriental poppy), Zones 2–7

Late-Spring Groundcovers

Ajuga reptans (bugleweed), Zones 3–9

Cotoneaster horizontalis (rockspray cotoneaster), Zones 5–8

Mazus reptans, Zones 5–9

Sedum acre (goldmoss stonecrop), Zones 4–9

Late-Spring Bulbs

Allium aflatunense (Persian onion), Zones 4–8

A. giganteum (giant onion), Zones 4–8

A. karataviense (Turkistan onion), Zones 4–9

A. moly (lily leek), into early summer, Zones 3–9

Camassia esculenta, syn C. cusickii (quamash, camass), Zones 3–9

Convallaria majalis (lily-of-the-valley), Zones 2–8

Hyacinthoides hispanica, syn. Scilla hispanica, S. campanulata (Spanish squill, Spanish bluebells), Zones 4–8

Muscari comosum (tassel grape hyacinth), Zones 4–8

Ornithogalum umbellatum (star-of-Bethlehem), Zones 4–9

Tulipa bakeri, Zones 5–9

Tulipa hybrids (Cottage, Lily-Flowered, Double Late, Parrot Tulips), Zones 4–7 (8–10 with special treatment)

Late-Spring Vines

Clematis armandii (Armand clematis), Zones 7–9

C. montana (anemone clematis), Zones 6–8

Hydrangea anomala subsp. petiolaris (climbing hydrangea), Zones 5–7

Wisteria floribunda (Japanese wisteria), Zones 5–9

The red horse chestnut (*Aesculus × carnea*) is a drought-tolerant tree with spectacular candelabras of reddish pink flowers set atop a base of large palmate leaves. It blooms in late spring a week or two after the common horse chestnut. This hybrid doesn't suffer the same disfiguring diseases that blight the larger common horse chestnut. I love the polished mahogany nuts that fall from horse chestnut trees in autumn, though many people find them a cleanup nuisance.

The red horse chestnut cultivar 'Briotii' produces double-flowered inflorescences with a deeper tint than the original hybrid, and it is virtually sterile, so it produces no nuts. It forms a compact 40-foot-tall tree—one of the largest of the ornamental flowering trees—so plant it to double as a shade tree.

Probably one of the most unusual spring-flowering trees is the golden-chain tree (*Laburnum × watereri*), which blooms in late May in my area. It's especially eye-catching because, while most spring-flowering trees blossom in white or shades of pink, the golden-chain tree drips with bright golden yellow, wisteria-like clusters.

This yellow-flowered beauty stops traffic because it is so rarely seen. Unfortunately, the flowers are at their peak for only about a week, two at the most. Though it lacks appreciable fall foliage color, golden-chain tree does stand out in winter: The bark on the stems and branches is smooth and olive green, adding interest to the winter landscape.

Choose the cultivar 'Vossii', rather than the hybrid, because it produces the largest and fullest flower clusters, up to 20 inches long, and it has the most attractive shape. A golden-chain tree looks best planted in a mixed border that camouflages its coltlike legs. Its yellow flowers offer wonderful possibilities for color schemes not commonly found in the spring border.

Dogwood and azaleas. Make midspring's crescendo of blooms all the more alluring by grouping the showiest bloomers into a high-impact design. Here, flowering dogwood (*Cornus florida*), azaleas (*Rhododendron × indicum*), tulips (*Tulipa* hybrids), and Spanish bluebells (*Hyacinthoides hispanicus*) show off in a groundcover of periwinkle (*Vinca minor*).

Shrubs for Eye-Level Color

While the flowering trees envelop us with boughs of overhead bloom, flowering shrubs bring their blooms right into our faces. We meet them eye to eye, nose to nose. Shrubs are the filler plants of the landscape, creating mass and weight and giving the garden an appealing year-round structure—if you design it right.

More shrub species bloom in spring than in any other season—the selection can be enormous and even intimidating. When choosing spring-blooming shrubs for your four-season garden, don't be seduced by the flowers alone. Consider the 50 or so weeks of the year when the plant's not in bloom, and base your choice on year-round appeal.

When you avoid shrubs that offer only one-season impact, you'll find that a number of common spring bloomers, such as flowering quince, common lilac, bridalwreath spirea, and even forsythia, won't make the cut. Aim to balance your spring-blooming shrub choices so you'll have eye-level action from early through late spring. But then be sure to make a conscious effort to save some space for the scarcer summer and fall bloomers, because it's easy to overdo the spring display at the expense of later seasons.

Season-Spanning Shrubs

The transition shrubs of late winter and early spring blur the edges of the seasons, blinding us with their bright colors and sudden light. Blooming about the time the lawn wakes up to its fresh emerald greenery, these earliest of shrubs make a fine accompaniment to the earliest trees. Combine several of them into a garden picture with spring-blooming bulbs and perennials, and you've dispatched winter in no uncertain terms.

For yellow color in earliest spring without the brassiness of forsythia's strident blooms—and for year-round interest—many garden designers prefer the little-known winterhazels (*Corylopsis* spp.) over forsythia. Relatives of witch hazels, the winterhazels also bloom precociously, their two- to three-week-long show beginning just before forsythia's. The pale yellow color of the flowers has a hint of green in it—a pleasing color in spring. When in full bloom, a winterhazel can be quite showy, with pastel flower clusters dangling like earrings from the outstretched branches.

I am thrilled with my specimen of buttercup winterhazel (*Corylopsis pauciflora*), which I transplanted several times until I found the perfect location in a south-facing alcove created by a cluster of white pines. The year-round pine greenery forms a perfect backdrop for the winterhazel's dainty spring flowers;

sets off the small, blue-green, heart-shaped leaves in summer; and silhouettes the zigzagging, light brown, smooth-barked branches in winter.

One of my favorite spring pictures includes the Korean azalea (*Rhododendron mucronulatum*). Korean azalea, a harbinger of spring that blooms on bare limbs before any sign of foliage appears, bears pale rosy purple or lavender blooms in outward-facing clusters at the stem tips. Examined up close, the bowl-shaped flowers reveal an arrangement of steel gray anthers. The upright shrub possesses a pleasing twiggy character in winter and leathery green summer foliage that turns wine red or gold in late fall before dropping.

Blooming just about the time forsythia unleashes itself upon spring, Korean azalea is the very first of the cold-hardy deciduous azaleas to flower. Planted in a mass or as a single specimen, the shrub commands considerable attention.

Once not commonly grown, this azalea now populates yards and foundation plantings everywhere I go on Long Island. I think this is because several local growers started producing the plant in quantity, and the nurseries created a demand by featuring containerized blooming *R. mucronulatum* plants up front, right beside the checkout counter, eliciting that "I gotta have one of those!" response from winter-weary customers.

Unfortunately, the lucid color of the blooms—lavender bordering on magenta—clashes with many other plants. When blooming side by side with the brassy golden yellow forsythia, the rosy purple of the Korean azalea looks anything but subtle. I prefer to combine Korean azalea with winterhazel—the softer yellow complements the purplish cast of the azalea flowers, making each more beautiful.

For those who abhor the color of the Korean azalea—and I do not count myself among them—the cultivar 'Cornell Pink' may hold more appeal. Lacking any hint of blue or purple, the flowers are a pure, bright pink, a shade just as bold as that of the species, but more pleasing to many people. Though I find pure pink a wonderful color, I feel it combines less well than the original lavender tones of the species with the yellow shrubs and bulbs that bloom at the same time.

Other less common cultivars of *R. mucronulatum* are easier to use. You'll find the softer shades of pure pink in 'Pink Peignoir' and 'Cama', and 'Alba' has white flowers. The dwarf lavender-flowered form, 'Nana', grows only a few feet tall—perfect for a mixed border.

An Asian relative of the more commonly grown winter-blooming Japanese pieris (*P. japonica*), Himalaya pieris (*P. formosa*) has the largest flower clusters of all the pieris. Bunches of showy, pendulous white flowers open in early spring and continue to be showy into midspring when the bright red new foliage joins them. The cultivar 'Wakehurst' boasts exceptionally bright red new growth, as arresting as any blooms. (See "Wine Red New Growth" on page 131 for more about pieris foliage colors.) Himalaya pieris, unfortunately, is hardy only to Zone 8.

Pieris floribunda (mountain pieris) is the American relative of these beautiful Asian species and is cold-hardy at least to Zone 5. A low-spreading broadleaved evergreen, mountain pieris may reach 5 feet in width while remaining only about a foot and a half tall. The panicles of white, lily-of-the-valley-like blooms stand upright, rather than drooping as they do in the Japanese and Chinese species, and make a stunning sight against the dark foliage. Like other species of pieris, this one offers showy flower buds all winter and year-round green foliage, but it lacks the colorful new growth of its relatives.

Pieris species evolved in open forests, so they need shade, even soil moisture, and acid soil rich in organic matter. If grown poorly, they'll suffer from leaf scald and lace bugs. I've planted several specimens in the border along my steep driveway, where their attractive foliage and flowers provide year-round color beneath the dogwoods, pines, and maples that shade the area.

Most viburnum species bloom in mid- to late spring, although a few surprise us with earlier blooms. Among the early performers is *Viburnum tinus* (laurustinus), a broadleaved evergreen that flourishes in Zones 8 to 9 and tolerates salt spray and shade. The clusters of pink buds open to fragrant white blooms in earliest spring. A plant for four seasons with dark glossy green foliage and conspicuous bright blue berries, laurustinus belongs in every four-season garden in the regions where it thrives. 'Spring Bouquet', a dwarf cultivar, will grow in Zone 7.

Early-Spring Shrubs

The shrubs of early spring display their wares about the time that green suffuses the network of tree branches, marking the landscape's transition from transparent to translucent. This transformation begins about the second week of April where I live on Long Island. Many early-spring flowering shrubs bloom on bare branches or unfold flowers and leaves simultaneously. Usually by the time their floral show has finished, their leaves have begun to develop, and later-blooming shrubs have leafed out.

My favorite early-spring shrub is *Rhododendron schlippenbachii* (royal azalea), the earliest of the large-flowered deciduous azaleas. Diaphanous pale pink petals, of a pink so pure it hasn't a trace of purple, make up the open-faced, 3-inch-wide blooms. With contrasting dots sprinkled down their throats like a dusting of brown sugar, the flowers resemble a congregation of moths gathered together all over the bare limbs.

This rhododendron—gardeners call the plant an azalea because the leaves are deciduous, but botanists term it a rhododendron because the flowers have ten stamens rather than five—grows into a large, upright plant of considerable elegance. Like other ericaceous plants, royal azalea, a native of Korea, thrives in light shade and humusy, acid soil, though it does better in neutral or near-neutral soil than most of its relatives.

To fully enjoy the impact of royal azalea's delicate spring flowers and smashing fall foliage, you might wish to use it as an isolated focal point in a shade garden or as a mass planting. Whatever you do, don't crowd it in with a lot of dissimilar plants. This shrub deserves a place of prominence. In Conni Cross's garden, a single royal azalea grows along a path beneath the high shade of a stand of native trees. The entire woodland features a sea of sweet woodruff (*Galium odoratum*), with constellations of white flowers and whorls of bright green leaves that wash across the ground, reflecting light up toward the shimmery azalea blooms.

Keep rhododendron and azalea bloom seasons in mind when planning for year-round garden structure and a long season of bloom. Most small-leaved rhododendrons—valued for their compact growth and lovely flowers—bloom in early spring. Their show ends before most of the evergreen azaleas bloom in mid- to late spring, and before most of the large-leaved, tall-growing rhododendron hybrids bloom in late spring. You'll find that the small size of the small-leaved rhododendrons makes them right at home in mixed borders and foundation plantings, as well as in naturalistic shade gardens.

Like the very early-blooming Korean azalea, *Rhododendron* 'P.J.M.' (named after the Massachusetts nurseryman Peter J. Mezitt)

emerged from obscurity several years ago and now populates yards and gardens throughout Long Island, New England, and the Mid-Atlantic states. And, as with the Korean azalea, many gardeners decry this rhododendron for its flowers' garish color—a lavender-pink bordering on magenta. Your personal likes and dislikes, and the colors you use in the surrounding garden, will determine whether or not 'P.J.M.' would be a garden jewel or garden rubbish in your landscape.

A broadleaved evergreen with tidy leaves only 2 to 3 inches long, 'P.J.M.' counts itself among the dwarf or compact rhododendrons, slowly reaching about 4 feet tall and wide at maturity. The leathery foliage turns burgundy to almost black in winter, adding considerable winter interest when contrasted with green foliage. And the bouquets of flowers sit tidily at the branch tips in early spring before the leaves have changed to their summer green.

Selections of 'P.J.M.' are sometimes available. I bought one labeled 'P.J.M.-pink' and another 'P.J.M.-white', and they differ (as expected) from the lavender-purple. 'P.J.M. Black Satin' features coal black winter foliage and purple flowers; 'P.J.M. Elite' blooms a bit later with bright lavender-pink blooms; 'P.J.M. Victor' blooms very early with lavender-pink blooms and somewhat smaller leaves. 'Laurie', a 'P.J.M.' hybrid, blooms just after its parents with very light pink trusses. 'Praecox' is another early bloomer with rosy lilac flowers.

For rare blue-flowering spring shrubs, don't overlook the dwarf rhododendrons. On the West Coast, a plethora of blue-flowered types seem to flourish, such as 'Bluette' with light blue trusses and olive green foliage, a plant I noticed in yards all over Seattle. On the East Coast we settle for 'Purple Gem', a tiny-leaved 2- to 3-foot-tall plant. Its equally tiny flowers engulf the plant with abundant pale purple clusters. But you might try the hard-to-find

A spring combination. Glowing with white and pink flowers in midspring, this combination features a Carolina silverbell (*Halesia carolina*), royal azalea (*Rhododendron schlippenbachii*), and fringed bleeding hearts (*Dicentra eximia*) in a carpet of sweet woodruff (*Galium odoratum*).

'Blue Diamond' or 'Blaney's Blue' on the East Coast for light blue flowers without a purple cast.

Other favorite early-blooming small-leaved rhododendrons include 'Pioneer', noted for its charming light pink blooms, and its offspring 'Pioneer Silvery Pink', with flowers that open a bit later and in a clearer pink than those of 'Pioneer'. This improved version also boasts thicker winter foliage, which turns bright red in fall.

'Windbeam' has a special place in my shade garden. I've included three specimens of this willowy evergreen in the back of the border in front of a fence, where they provide year-round structure and foliage. But it's the pastel apricot-pink flowers in early spring that I love. They glitter in light-catching bouquets all over the stem tips, changing to white as they age. Blooming along with many of the wildflowers, such as trillium, foamflower, and creeping phlox, which I've planted in that area, this rhododendron provides complementary color up off the ground.

'Mary Fleming', a small-leaved dwarf rhododendron, blooms in perhaps the most unusual color for a rhododendron. The compact plant bears yellow flowers blushed with salmon in the early to mid-spring, and its ever-green foliage turns dark bronze in winter.

'Mary Fleming' flowers are a difficult color to use. Though beautiful, the salmon-pink flush looks awful with purplish pinks and clear pinks. Try using it next to white or pure pale yellow. I had to transplant my three specimens from the front of the house to the rear hillside because their early-spring bloom overlapped with the midseason bright magenta-purple azaleas left behind by the previous owners (I won't claim them). The combination was hideous.

These are only a fraction of the small-leaved rhododendron cultivars available. I mentioned the most readily available types, but if you're a fan of these useful and attractive four-season shrubs, consult a specialty mail-order grower, such as Weston Nurseries, Carlson's Gardens, or Roslyn Nurseries. (See "Resources for Four-Season Landscapes" on page 328 for addresses.)

My next-favorite early-spring shrub is fothergilla (*Fothergilla* spp.), another member of the witch hazel family. What I particularly like about all the fothergillas is the way the creamy white, bottlebrush-shaped flowers catch and scatter sunlight. These honey-scented flowers rise up all over the branch tips just before the foliage starts to grow. When the spring sunshine backlights this display, the flowers trap the light like prisms, scattering rays all over the garden. Fothergillas also have spectacular fall foliage in a mix of red and golden orange.

Dwarf fothergilla (*F. gardenii*) is a charming plant native to the Deep South. Of compact habit—it grows only about 3 feet tall—dwarf fothergilla has many landscape uses because it is well-behaved. You might locate several plants along a woodland path, in a shady foundation planting, or even in a mixed border, where you'll be captivated by the spring flowers and spectacular fall foliage display. The cultivar 'Blue Mist', introduced by the Morris Arboretum in Pennsylvania and offered by a few specialty growers, features intense blue-green foliage, which is at its best in a shady spot.

Two other fothergilla species—*F. major* (large fothergilla) and *F. monticola* (Alabama fothergilla)—grace the early-spring garden. They grow much larger and should be located where they have plenty of room—that is, not in a foundation or small border. All the species flower at the same time as another southern native, the redbud (*Cercis canadensis*). Arranged together, these make a pretty plant combination. Use one or more redbuds at the top of your planting pyramid, and fill in below with a handful of dwarf fothergillas.

Rose daphne (*Daphne cneorum*) grows low and spreads wide, forming a neat, broad-leaved evergreen that reaches only a foot tall by twice as wide. The rosy pink flowers, which appear much later than those of February-blooming winter daphne (*Daphne odora*) and are as fragrant, literally smother the leaves. Though sometimes finicky, once established in light sandy soil rose daphne creates a beautiful, no-fuss, groundcover-type shrub to use at the base of taller shrubs.

Midspring Shrubs

Spring simply wouldn't be spring in many parts of the country without the profuse bloom of the hybrid evergreen azaleas (*Rhododendron* hybrids), which bloom simultaneously with flowering dogwoods. Where they're adapted, azaleas adorn the landscape in midspring with masses of white, pink, lavender, purple, magenta, or orange-red blooms—almost every permutation of the rainbow, except yellow and blue. The flowers blanket the branches, obscuring the foliage for a full two weeks in midspring.

Several dozen hybrid groups, with varying cold-hardiness, make up the landscape azaleas, which are part of the complex genus *Rhododendron.* (See "Sorting Out the Evergreen Azaleas" on the opposite page.) When choosing among the many cultivars, consider flower color and shape, the plant's mature height and spread, and how long it will remain evergreen. For a foundation planting, a low-spreading, fully evergreen type that won't top 3 feet—such as one of the Kurume azaleas—looks best. But in a woodland garden, a loose, billowy plant reaching 5 or 6 feet—such as a Kaempferi hybrid—fits the bill.

Those azaleas hardy only in the South have slightly hairy leaves that are larger and more fully evergreen than the foliage of their cold-hardy cousins. In the North, hardy azaleas drop or retain their leaves in response to the winter temperatures where they are growing. In late autumn, the oldest (innermost) leaves of all evergreen azaleas change color and drop off, leaving the younger, outer foliage to clothe the shrubs during winter.

White-flowered azaleas usually develop yellow fall color on the older leaves, while pink-, red-, and purple-flowered cultivars tend to produce red fall foliage—a bonus rarely mentioned in the gardening literature. Overwintering foliage may remain green or may deepen in color to a rich plum or red, especially in cultivars with brightly colored flowers.

Depending on the cultivar, the winter foliage may be thick and lustrous, or so sparse it provides little interest. This can be an important consideration in selecting a cultivar, if a plant's evergreen nature is key to your landscape design. I made a big mistake when I planted a sweep of five Korean azaleas (*R. yedoense* var. *poukhanense,* syn. *R. poukhanense*) on the back hillside of my property.

Their diaphanous lavender flowers create the intended enchanting sight in spring, but in winter only a few sparse leaves remain at the stem tips, leaving the hillside bleak and barren for many months. I am now moving these azaleas to a less prominent spot, where their flowers can be appreciated but their lack of winter greenery won't matter. In their place, I'm planting fully evergreen dwarf mountain laurels.

Extensive hybridization has brought us evergreen azaleas, such as the Gable and Kurume hybrids, which tolerate more cold than the southern Indicas, the first azalea hybrids to come to this country and the ones that grace old plantations in the South. For this we Northeners are grateful. However, it also brought us an azalea color previously unknown to the South: red. For this we should not be grateful. Azalea red is more properly considered magenta-red, not the pure color-wheel red of the painter's palette.

These garish violet-rose-red flowers that breeders try to pass off as red make unfortunate combinations with many spring bloomers. Planted all on their own or combined skillfully with compatible colors, these reds can be stunning, but more often than not they create horrific color clashes. Magenta-reds look especially hideous in front of a red brick house, for instance, or with coral-pink flowers.

Literally thousands of azalea cultivars beckon gardeners, but a recent survey published in *American Nurseryman* indicates that commercial growers prefer to offer 18 sure-fire sellers adapted up and down the East Coast. These favorites unfortunately include the more garish shades of red and magenta such as the Kurume hybrid 'Hinode-Giri', one of the cold-hardiest evergreen azaleas. These garish azaleas have even taken over in the South, where traditional cultivars used to be white, pastel pink, and lavender.

You can mail-order from specialty growers if you aren't satisfied with the limited choices

SORTING OUT THE EVERGREEN AZALEAS

When choosing an azalea from among the thousands of cultivars available, try to find out its hybrid group. This will tell you the plant's expected hardiness, its form, and how evergreen its foliage is.

Spring-Blooming Evergreen Azaleas

Glenn Dale Hybrids: The same large flowers and colors as the Southern Indica azaleas on plants that are more cold-hardy in the Mid-Atlantic states. Bred at the USDA by Dr. B. Y. Morrison, this group of 400 hybrids is variable, with some cultivars loose and airy and others low and compact; some with small leaves, others with large; and some more sun-tolerant than others. Zone 7, many hardy to Zone 6.

Kaempferi Hybrids: The Kaempferi hybrids, of Dutch origin, are 6- to 8-foot-tall plants of open growth. Cold-hardy plants to −10°F, but in coldest areas they retain only sparse foliage in winter. Profuse medium-sized flowers. Hardy to Zones 6 and possibly 5.

Kurume, Gable, and Great Lakes Hybrids: Dense, compact plants with small leaves and masses of small flowers on tiered branches, Kurume hybrids are of Japanese origin and are hardy to −5°F (Zone 7). Gable hybrids are a subgroup of the Kurume azaleas, bred by Joseph B. Gable of Stewartstown, Pennsylvania, to be cold-hardier than the previous Kurume cultivars; they tolerate cold to 0°F (Zone 7) but may lose some foliage. The Great Lakes hybrids were bred in Ohio and Indiana by Peter Girard, Joseph Martin, and Tony Shammarello to be even more cold-hardy than the Gables. These hybrids are the most cold-hardy of the fully evergreen azaleas. Zones 6–9.

Brook's, Gold Cup, and Nuccio Hybrids: Tolerant of the hot, dry climate of California's Central Valley, these hybrids feature large flowers on compact plants. Hardy to 20°F (Zone 8).

Southern and Belgian Indica Hybrids: The famous azaleas of the Deep South, cold-hardy to Zone 7, and tolerant of full sun. These are vigorous, tall-growing shrubs with large pastel or white flowers.

Summer-Blooming Evergreen Azaleas

North Tisbury Hybrids: Bred by Polly Hill of Martha's Vineyard, Massachusetts, these groundcover azaleas may be prostrate or they may form low mounds, spreading to cover a very large area with time. Medium-sized to large flowers and tidy leaves; bloom in June or July. Hardy to Zone 6.

Robin Hill and Gartrell Hybrids: Bred by Robert Gartrell of Wycoff, New Jersey, these compact, mounded shrubs feature huge flowers that bloom in early summer. Offspring of the Satsuki azaleas, these are more cold-hardy, tolerating −10°F without bud damage. Also heat-tolerant. Zones 5–8.

Satsuki and Macrantha Hybrids: Low-growing, large-flowered, dwarf plants that bloom in early summer and are of Japanese origin. Flowers are often streaked or flecked with contrasting colors. Hardy to Zone 7.

---

pervading the mass market. Choose azaleas for your garden carefully, studying the catalog descriptions or consulting a book about azaleas, and select colors, habit, and foliage that combine well with your garden and home.

If the more vivid colors tempt you, don't be shy, but remember to reconcile bright colors by combining them with pure pastel shades. 'Pink Pearl', for instance, is a spectacular soft pink Kurume azalea. Delaware landscape designer Bill Frederick says its flowers are the color of the inside of a rabbit's ear. He uses this azalea to blend brighter azaleas in a mixed planting. He prefers these pale pink flowers to white ones when trying to harmonize a mixed planting. That's because he feels that masses of bright white flowers draw the eye, poking holes in the whole picture, while the pink harmonizes the colors into a rich blend.

Preferring humusy, acid soil, a somewhat shady site, and a moderate climate, azaleas languish in the central part of the country unless they get extra-special coddling. To assure success with azaleas in the Midwest, plant them in shaded raised beds filled with peat-based acid soil.

The latest trend in gardening seems to be getting back to nature and using native plants in naturalistic designs. North America boasts a rich assortment of deciduous azalea species native to the Appalachian and Blue Ridge Mountains.

Deciduous azaleas are more delicate and charming in bloom than the evergreen hybrids and often bloom later in spring and even in summer. They offer many possibilities to a four-season gardener. The earliest to bloom of the American species is the rare and graceful pinkshell azalea (*Rhododendron vaseyi*), native only to four counties in North Carolina.

Blooming in midspring on slender bare branches just as the new foliage begins to enlarge, the fragile-looking flowers of the pinkshell azalea are a winsome sight in a woodland garden. You can also grow this plant in a sunny setting as long as the soil remains moist. The British Royal Horticultural Society honored the pinkshell azalea with an award of merit in 1927.

The lovely Carolina rhododendron (*R. carolinianum*), native to the Appalachian Mountains, blooms in midspring with the pinkshell azalea, before the majority of large-leaved rhododendron hybrids. This tidy plant grows little more than 3 feet tall and spreads to 4 or 5 feet, a perfect size for mixed borders and foundation plantings as well as naturalis-

tic settings. The leathery 3-inch-long green leaves have a pleasing texture and are topped with pale pink or white flowers in rounded clusters for several weeks in midspring.

One of my favorite midspring deciduous azalea species hails from the Caucasus Mountains of eastern Europe. It is the intensely fragrant pontic azalea (*R. luteum,* syn. *R. flavum*). Rich yellow tubular flowers resembling giant honeysuckle blooms form clusters set off against bright green young foliage at the stem tips of this open-branched plant. The pontic azalea gave its sunny color and spicy perfume to the Ghent hybrid azaleas, a showy group of extremely cold-hardy deciduous azaleas bred in Belgium in the 1820s.

The pontic azalea ranks as one of my prized plants, so loved by Mark and me that we have dug up our single specimen and transplanted it each time we moved to a new house. So far, it has survived three moves.

Several other midspring shrubs offer yellow flowers to the garden color scheme. In informal situations, you might wish to plant Japanese kerria (*Kerria japonica*), a rambling shrub with green stems.

The double-flowered cultivar, 'Pleniflora', bears little pompoms of golden yellow flowers lining the slender branches. It used to be more common than the single-flowered species, which I prefer. To my taste, the species looks much finer. Its 2-inch-wide, bright yellow blooms resemble delicate wild roses. And finer still is the variegated cultivar 'Picta', with sharply toothed, silver-edged leaves and single yellow flowers. Whether in or out of bloom, this fine-textured plant lights up a shady spot.

For full-sun situations, choose the barberries for yellow flowers. Wintergreen barberry (*Berberis julianae*) produces the most notable blooms, which hang in chains from the thorny branches, while other species, such as Japanese barberry (*B. thunbergii*), produce less showy—though certainly noticeable—yellow flowers along with their emerging new foliage. These flowers, of course, are precursors of the even showier berries that delight four-season gardeners in fall and winter.

Oregon grape holly (*Mahonia aquifolium*) tops its leathery, bold-textured leaves with long wands of radiant yellow flowers. A four-season plant for full sun to shade, grape holly bears frosty blue berries in grapelike clusters in late summer and fall, and has claret red winter foliage.

One of the midspring shrubs I most look forward to is Koreanspice viburnum (*Viburnum carlesii*). I've planted two, one on each side of the kitchen door, where the flowers' spicy-sweet fragrance permeates the entire side yard and wafts in through the Dutch door. The flower buds become deep pink as they expand in spring and finally open into tight clusters of white flowers as velvety gray-green leaves join them. I chose the cultivar 'Compactum', which nevertheless will need some pruning to keep it in bounds, since it grows to 5 feet—5 feet full of the best-smelling flowers you ever hope to bury your nose in!

The Koreanspice viburnum contributed its fantastic fragrance to a number of hybrids. One of the best-known is the similar-looking fragrant snowball viburnum (*V.* × *carlcephalum*), which surpasses its parent in height and spread and produces grander flower clusters that can reach 5 inches across. Its cultivar 'Cayuga' stays lower, getting about as large as the Koreanspice viburnum.

Other fragrant snowball-type viburnums to look for include the Judd viburnum (*V.* × *juddii*), which won the Royal Horticultural Society's Award of Garden Merit. It's one of the most cold-hardy viburnums, faring well in Zone 4. Burkwood viburnum (*V.* × *burkwoodii*) blooms in early spring with heady, waxy white little snowballs and makes a splash again in

fall with crimson to purple foliage in the North, while remaining evergreen in the South. Its cultivar 'Mohawk' stimulates the senses with currant red flower buds that gradually open to white-centered flowers. Brilliant orange-red fall color makes this a choice plant for the year-round landscape.

Late-Spring Shrubs

Late spring brings out the viburnum blooms in full force. Most viburnums make excellent ornamentals for a four-season garden, but many are known more for their fall and winter berries than for their spring flowers, even though those flowers can make quite a show. I'll describe those special berried beauties in Chapter 5, and stick to those with the most decorative flowers here.

The doublefile viburnum (*V. plicatum* var. *tomentosum*) puts on a stupendous show of spring flowers, bird-attracting summer berries, and colorful fall foliage. In addition, it has a commanding silhouette, all of which make it one of my favorite shrubs for a four-season landscape.

The conspicuous size and character of its flowers surpass all other late-spring bloomers. Delicately textured fertile flowers and a surrounding ring of larger sterile flowers team up to create flat, 2- to 4-inch-wide clusters. These clusters align themselves along the horizontal branches, forming a row on either side of each outstretched branch and icing the crisply veined green leaves and tiered branches with buttercream frosting. The Japanese snowball (*V. plicatum*), a sterile garden variant, produces large snowball-shaped inflorescences but no fruits.

'Mariesii' used to be the preferred cultivar of the doublefile viburnum, admired for its larger flower clusters, but it's been edged out of favor by 'Shasta', a recent introduction from the U.S. National Arboretum. 'Shasta' features abundant snowy white inflorescences and a lower habit than the species. This 1991 Pennsylvania Horticultural Society award-winner ultimately reaches 6 feet tall and twice as wide. A recently selected dwarf seedling of 'Shasta', named 'Shoshoni', grows only 3 feet tall and 5 feet wide.

Even though the common lilac (*Syringa vulgaris*) falls off my list of plants for four-season gardens because it offers only one season of interest, three lilacs do make excellent plants for mixed borders in year-round gardens. These compact beauties ought to satisfy most lilac lovers.

The Meyer lilac (*Syringa meyeri,* syn. *S. palibiniana*) is a fine-textured lilac featuring small panicles of violet-purple fragrant flowers. These transform the plant into a fine-textured purple sensation for a couple of weeks in late spring. The small, bluish green leaves don't mildew like those of its larger cousin, so this lilac thrives in the humid Midwest and along the East Coast. Foliage turns yellow in fall. The Persian lilac (*Syringa* × *persica*) looks similar, with fragrant pale lilac flowers and bluish green foliage.

The Manchurian lilac (*S. patula,* syn. *S. velutina*) looks like a miniature version of the common lilac, growing only to 5 or 6 feet tall and holding its 6-inch-long panicles in pairs at the stem tips, just like its larger cousin. 'Miss Kim' is the preferred cultivar, featuring sweetly scented, pastel purple blooms that gradually fade to a delicate china-doll pink. The leaves of Manchurian lilacs turn rusty red in fall and don't suffer from mildew.

Where soils are acidic and the climate is moderate, the large-leaved rhododendrons (*Rhododendron* hybrids) offer gardeners a wealth of handsome, fully evergreen shrubs with large, leathery leaves and huge clusters of vivid flowers. Like azaleas, these perform best in moist, humusy acid soil with light shade to half shade. Some sun encourages the

best flowering. Protection from full sun on south- and west-facing sites and from winter wind on north-facing sites prevents rhododendron leaves from scorching and flowers from fading.

In general, rhododendrons perform poorly in Georgia and South Carolina and do better in New England, compared to evergreen azaleas, which perform best in the Pacific Northwest. If your soil is neutral or only slightly alkaline, you might be able to grow rhododendrons by amending the soil generously with peat moss or sulfur and mulching heavily with bark chips or leaf compost.

As with the evergreen azaleas, hybridizing mania has brought gardeners a mind-boggling assortment of large-leaved rhododendron cultivars numbering in the thousands. A favorite native species used extensively in hybridization but grown as a species for its own charms is the catawba rhododendron (*Rhododendron catawbiense*). Found as an understory plant in the southern Appalachian Mountains, this is the species whose beguiling lavender-pink flower trusses peek through the mist in Eliott Porter's nature photographs. As many as 20 flowers make up a truss, which rests against a circle of dark green leaves.

The variety *R. catawbiense* var. *album* (not the cultivar 'Catawbiense Album') produces ethereal white flowers with a barely perceptible pink tinge. It makes one of the finest landscape rhododendrons around.

A very cold-hardy shrub, the Catawba rhododendron flourishes in Zones 4 to 7, in protected sites in Zone 3, and in cool-summer areas of Zone 8. Northern gardeners can find no more beautiful or cold-hardy large-leaved rhododendrons than the pink and white forms of this species. However, the many hybrids of the species do not prove as cold-hardy, their flower buds surviving only to Zones 6 or 5. They are known, however, for being tough plants that can withstand hotter and drier summers than many other rhododendrons, performing well in southern and midwestern gardens.

These tough hybrids, sometimes referred to as the "ironclad" rhododendrons, were bred in England during the 1800s and are still widely sold today, despite the fact that far prettier, more recent hybrid rhododendrons are now available. The newer cultivars offer a greater range of flower colors, including purer pink shades, and denser plant shapes.

In prime rhododendron country, you have a much greater choice of adaptable rhododendrons and should avoid the widely grown ironclads such as 'Roseum Elegans', 'Nova Zembla', 'Sappho', 'Catawbiense Album', 'Boule de Neige', and 'Purpureum Grandiflorum'. Instead of frequenting a local nursery that stocks only these mass-produced inferior rhododendrons, find a local specialty grower or go the mail-order route.

Seek out plants hybridized in this century by some of America's famous hybridizers, such as David Leach, Tony Shammarello, Joseph Gable, and Charles Dexter. These hybrids are the aristocrats of the plant world, with enormous trusses of gorgeous bell-shaped flowers, according to Bob Carlson, an azalea and rhododendron nurseryman. He's been growing rhododendrons and azaleas for 20 years, and in his catalog he groups the cultivars according to breeder, making it a handy reference for East Coast and midwestern gardeners seeking the very best plants.

For Mr. Carlson, the only word for the flowers of the Dexter hybrids is "gorgeous." The Dexter hybrids—hybrids of *R. catawbiense* and the Chinese or Fortune rhododendron (*R. fortunei*)—were created by Charles O. Dexter of Sandwich, Massachusetts. He brought us hundreds of very special cold-hardy rhododendrons—all are exceptionally large, reaching 8 to 10 feet tall, and fragrant, but vary in hardiness. Most perform well in Zones 5 to 8.

'Scintillation' is one of the best known of the Dexter hybrids and everyone's favorite, according to Mr. Carlson. This dense plant bears luminous light pink flowers with amber throats and lustrous dark green leaves.

The Gable hybrids, bred by Joe Gable of Stewartstown, Pennsylvania, in general are more cold-hardy and compact than the Dexter hybrids. 'Cadis' is one of Mr. Carlson's favorites, featuring deep pink flower buds that make a beautiful contrast to the light pink, fragrant flowers. 'Mary Belle' grows to only 4 feet and has amazing flowers—they start out coral in bud, open to salmon-peach touched with red, and turn golden as they age.

All of these large-leaved rhododendrons make excellent background plants for a mixed border or shrub garden in formal or informal situations—but be sure to give them plenty of growing room. They are also fine for a woodland garden beneath high-pruned trees. But don't use them to the exclusion of other plants. Remember that their foliage is bold-textured and commanding—too much of it overpowers. For best effect, mix and contrast these handsome shrubs with conifers or finer-textured broadleaved evergreens that bloom in other seasons.

One late-spring-blooming rhododendron to use in the mixed border—rather than behind it—is Yako rhododendron (*R. yakusimanum*). The species and its many cultivars grow as tight mounds of knee-high, boldly textured foliage that form pretty patterns when you look down on them.

Glossy dark green on top, Yako leaves feature a thick, tan, feltlike coating, called an indumentum, on their undersides. New growth emerges covered with woolly white hairs, making an intriguing contrast with the older green leaves. Most gardeners find the felty-coated leaf undersides and new growth attractive, but the felt confuses some, who think the plant has been attacked by an aggressive fungus. One gardener admitted to me that she had tried to scrub the felt off the leaves.

Foliage and form aside, Yako rhododendrons produce astoundingly beautiful trusses made up of apple-bloom pink buds opening to white flowers in the species. Selected cultivars display flowers in varying shades and combinations of pink and red. Most remain elegantly low, never growing more than 3 or so feet high.

Most deciduous azalea species and hybrid groups bloom in late spring as their new growth has leafed out. These plants have much more distinct individual clusters of flowers — similar to a rhododendron's — than the masses of blooms of the evergreen azaleas. But the individual flowers are decidedly azalea-like, charmingly splashed and spotted, and with extremely long, protruding stamens. Cold-hardier than the evergreen azaleas and the large-leaved rhododendrons, deciduous azaleas bring vivacious color to northern gardens as well as to more moderate climates.

Perhaps the best-known hybrid group is the Knap Hill/Exbury azaleas, bred in England during the 1870s by Anthony Waterer, an eminent English horticulturist, at his Knap Hill nursery, and later refined during the 1920s by Lionel de Rothschild at his Exbury estate in Surrey. These hybrids produce the largest flowers of any azalea and come in shades of orange, red, gold, yellow, white, and pink, with up to 20 blooms in a single truss. Hardy throughout Zone 5, the plants can reach 6 feet tall and wide, and some have good fall color.

In Zone 4, try the Ghent azaleas, an older hybrid group from Belgium that is hardy to −25°F. And on the West Coast, try the Occidentale hybrids. The Northern Lights hybrids, developed at the University of Minnesota to withstand the harsh winters of the Northern Plains and Midwest, offer white, pink, yellow, or lavender azaleas to gardeners

in those areas. None of these azaleas performs well in the hot-summer areas of the Midwest or in the South.

Many native American species contributed their genes to the Exbury hybrids, and most of these species make excellent garden plants that are well-suited to woodland or wildflower gardens. The flame azalea (*R. calendulaceum*) turns hillsides ablaze with blooms varying from golden yellow to orange in late spring in the Allegheny Mountains.

The pinxterbloom azalea (*R. periclymenoides*) bears white to pale pink, sweetly scented tubular blooms that resemble those of honeysuckle. The only species native to the West Coast, western azalea (*R. occidentale*) has large distinctive flowers with a squarish flat shape. This white to pink azalea contributed its flower shape to the Exbury hybrids and delights gardeners in northern California, Oregon, Washington, and British Columbia.

Perhaps the best-scented late-spring-blooming native American azalea is the coast azalea (*R. atlanticum*); its natural hybrid with pinxterbloom azalea, 'Choptank River', has pinker flowers with an intense sweet fragrance and, according to Bob Carlson, will grow into a graceful umbrella shape and perfume the entire garden from late spring into summer. All these native species turn glorious colors in fall before dropping their leaves.

You can find other late-spring bloomers in "Late-Spring Bloomers for Four-Season Landscapes" on page 90 and in Chapter 7.

Bulbs and What to Grow with Them

I find no sight quite so cheerful as wide sweeps of sunny yellow daffodils (*Narcissus* hybrids) marching across a garden, turning their faces toward the sun like so many happy children. Beginning about the time forsythias bloom, the early-season trumpet daffodils open in profusion to bridge the gap between winter and spring, edging out the late-winter bloom of Dutch crocuses and creating skirts of color around trees and shrubs.

Many people panic when they notice bulb foliage pushing above the soil in winter. They worry that snow or freezing temperatures will spell the flowers' demise. Not to worry. It's a rare year when hardy bulbs get blasted by cold. Most bulb foliage, and even the flower buds, can withstand temperatures into the 20s or even high teens. According to Chicago bulb hobbyist Michael Nunamaker, a daffodil's flower bud will be unharmed by cold as long as it's still standing straight up at the tip of its stem. But once the bud begins to nod downward, as it does on its way to opening, temperatures lower than the high 20s may cause injury.

Bulbs like daffodils and tulips are not exactly four-season plants, because their very nature motivates them to go dormant and lie invisible beneath the ground for most of the year. Bulbs offer only one season of interest and, after their spectacular spring show, their yellowing foliage can be decidedly unornamental as it ripens in early summer. Despite these drawbacks, spring bulbs play a significant role in a landscape designed for four seasons of beauty, because they bring so much excitement and variety to the garden floor when little else is blooming there.

The hardy bulbs that delight us in spring play their magic best when planted in groups and great swaths—not polka-dotted around the yard like so many lost souls. And because they leave behind a hole in the garden, it pays to plan ahead when planting bulbs and decide what will take their place come summer.

Better yet, suggests Suzanne Bales, author and bulb specialist for W. Atlee Burpee, ask yourself two questions when planting bulbs: What will be the bulbs' companions, and what will be the bulbs' successors? I probe Suzanne's expertise on designing with bulbs on page 251 in Chapter 6, where you can find out her clever answers to these two questions. Her design strategies work perfectly to incorporate these important one-season plants into a four-season landscape.

Keep Suzanne's questions in mind while reading this section, even if you don't know all her secrets yet. Here's a hint about the answers: In a landscape designed for year-round beauty, bulbs work best used in one of two ways—naturalized in a lawn or woodland, or combined with other types of plants in a mixed border. As long as their green leaves are left to ripen until yellow, and they are grown in fertile, well-drained soil, many types of bulbs only get better year after year. They rapidly increase in number, forming larger, more floriferous clumps.

Major League Bulbs

Taking the limelight in spring, daffodils (*Narcissus* cultivars), Dutch hyacinths (*Hyacinthus orientalis* cultivars), and tulips (*Tulipa* cultivars) are the star bulb attractions. These three are called major bulbs, perhaps because of their potential to produce large, vibrantly colored flowers. They have been hybridized extensively over the years. Now so many wonderful cultivars abound (there are about 3,500 named cultivars of tulips on the market!) that choosing bulbs for your garden can make you feel like a small child in a candy store—you simply can't decide!

But don't be tempted to buy only these major bulbs. Give them a supporting cast of minor players—the dozens of lesser-known minor bulbs, such as grape hyacinth (*Muscari* spp.), summer snowflake (*Leucojum aestivum*), and Grecian windflower (*Anemone blanda*).

If you plan it right, major and minor bulbs can perform in your garden from earliest spring until the beginning of summer, and some even bloom in winter. (See "Winsome Winter Bulbs" on page 50 for more on winter bulb bloom.) Time and length of bloom often depend on the weather. Cold nights and cool sunny days in spring will stretch out daffodils' bloom period to four weeks or so, while heavy rain may beat them down, and a fit of summerlike heat in April will fry them to a crisp. A heavy snow cover will keep the earliest bulbs from blooming as early as they would in a warm year, so bloom sequence and plant combinations are often surprising in earliest spring.

Daffy Over Daffodils

The charming, small daffodil species bloom in late winter, carrying on into early spring if the weather remains favorable, but the showy hybrids wait until earliest spring to begin their display, opening with the forsythias. "Nothing is as wonderful as a daffodil," says my husband Mark. "Maybe it's because they start blooming just when you really *need* them."

He and I simply can't have enough daffodils in spring. Masses of them decorate the mixed borders along both sides of our steep driveway, where they form crowds of happy faces to greet us and our guests when we drive up the hill. (Daffodil flowers turn to face the sun, so be sure to plant them where they'll be viewed from a southern, eastern, or western exposure, not a northern one, or you'll be looking at their backsides!)

We naturalized masses of daffodils among the pachysandra beneath the outreaching branches of a mighty oak near our front walk. And we planted a large swath across the back hillside, where they create flashing trails of golden color through the trunks of the 'Whitespire' birches.

Fortunately, daffodils aren't rare or difficult to grow, and they'll increase to form glorious clumps with practically no care at all. As long as their foliage gets plenty of sunshine in spring and the bulbs don't sit in waterlogged soil, the show gets better year after year because the mother bulb remains hefty while going on to make offsets that flower on their own in a year or two.

Choose daffodils for the color, form, and bloom time that please you—combining ones that bloom early, midway, and late in the daffodil season so you can enjoy a display lasting from earliest spring into midspring. Specialty growers, such as the Daffodil Mart in Gloucester, Virginia, are the best sources for the more unusual types of daffodils.

Heady Dutch Hyacinths

Even highly scented paperwhite daffodils can't compete with the Dutch hyacinth for an aroma powerful enough to scent the entire garden. Today's hybrid hyacinths bear massive, tightly packed stalks of flowers in a rainbow of colors.

Though they begin to bloom about the time the major daffodils open up, hyacinths don't have the same sunny aspect. They look decidedly formal and stiff, especially the first year after planting. Many people won't plant Dutch hyacinths because of their overblown nature. I used to feel this way about the bulbs, probably because all too often I saw them set out in rigid, widely spaced rows, like soldiers given their marching orders, which only accentuated their stand-to-attention look.

But seeing a group of pastel blue Dutch hyacinths planted close together in an informal gathering, and underplanted with the loose sprays of intense blue-flowered glory-of-the-snow (*Chionodoxa luciliae*), convinced me that these flowers do have a place in the spring garden. They just need to keep company with

(continued on page 123)

Spring

A season brimming with hope and expectation, spring bursts upon the garden with irrepressible enthusiasm. Sunny flowers, fragile foliage, and sweet fragrance characterize the season.

Here, two native phlox spread readily in the humusy soil of the author's shade garden. Wild blue phlox (*Phlox divaricata*), in back, has notched petals and slender stems. Creeping phlox (*P. stolonifera*), in front, is lower, with yellow-eyed flowers above evergreen leaves; this one is the cultivar 'Home Fires'.

▲ Large-leaved rhododendrons do best in light shade and moist, humusy soil. They provide year-round greenery, great texture, and a bonus of flashy late-spring flowers.

▲ The flowers of 'Vossii' golden-chain tree (*Laburnum* × *watereri* 'Vossii') are yellow—a rare color for a spring-blooming tree. They adorn the pea green branches for a short time in late spring. The leggy, vase-shaped tree looks best with plants such as the blooming fountain leucothoe (*Leucothoe fontanesiana*), shown here, which hides its base and anchors it to the landscape.

◄ Roseshell azalea (*Rhododendron roseum*), a deciduous native azalea, blooms in late spring, producing clove-scented flowers that fill the garden with an enchanting fragrance. Use this shrub in a naturalistic garden, where the delicate pink flowers and blue-green leaves aren't overshadowed by gaudier hybrids.

Midspring is just one of many pictures painted in this four-season landscape. The bone structure created by trees, shrubs, conifers, rock wall, and stone steps is fleshed out with an extravagant and ever-changing show of flowering bulbs and perennials. Garden design: Conni Cross.

▲ Early spring brings a wealth of flowers and foliage to a lightly shaded woodland path. Here, fringed bleeding heart (*Dicentra eximia*) blooms in the foreground, joined by violets, sweet woodruff (*Galium odoratum*), and emerging hosta leaves.

▶ Pasqueflower (*Anemone pulsatilla*) blooms in earliest spring, sometimes bridging the gap between winter and spring. After the petals drop, the flowers form silky, pinwheel-shaped seedpods atop tall stems.

◀ A tree for four seasons, 'Kwanzan' Japanese flowering cherry (*Prunus serrulata* 'Kwanzan') offers stunning hot pink flowers in midspring, handsome summer foliage, orange and gold fall color, and gleaming mahogany bark.

▲ Blooming in spring and continuing through autumn, native green-and-gold (*Chrysogonum virginicum*) makes a brilliant groundcover for a four-season garden. Here it's combined with the changing foliage colors and summer flowers of 'Goldmound' bumald spirea (*Spiraea* × *bumalda* 'Goldmound'). Garden design: Conni Cross.

◀ Red-vein enkianthus (*Enkianthus campanulatus*) makes a terrific four-season shrub, with creamy yellow, red-veined flowers in spring, blue-green foliage in summer, brilliant orange and scarlet leaves in fall, and whorls of slender brown stems in winter.

▶ Blooming in late spring, large-leaved rhododendrons have spectacular displays of huge flower clusters, but their dark green, leathery leaves are effective year-round. Here the foliage contrasts with bright green cinnamon ferns (*Osmunda cinnamomea*).

The garden wall and gate of this Virginia garden are softened with overhanging flowering dogwood branches (*Cornus florida*) and Carolina jessamine vines (*Gelsemium sempervirens*), giving the garden an interesting year-round bone structure. Garden: Mr. and Mrs. Charles Woltz.

▲ In another example of successful interplanting, the slender branches of a blooming scotch broom (*Genista* sp.) make a splendid display, with bold tulips mingling with their dainty flowers. The wiry, green-barked broom stems look attractive against the brick wall during the rest of the year when the shrub is out of bloom.

▶ Saucer magnolia (*Magnolia × soulangiana*) is one of the earliest spring-blooming trees, opening magnificent blooms well before any leaves appear. Because it blooms so early, late frosts may wipe out the tender flowers, even though the cold-hardy tree remains unscathed. Plant yours in a protected location to help safeguard the flowers.

Because eastern redbud (*Cercis canadensis*) blooms in early spring before the foliage leafs out, its numerous, small magenta-pink flowers look best when displayed against a solid background. Purchase locally grown trees to ensure the best cold-hardiness for your area.

This midspring scene features effective layering from sky to ground, a
structure that works well all year. Flowering dogwood (*Cornus florida*)
forms the canopy, rhododendrons and azaleas make up the midlevel, and
yellow flag iris (*Iris virginica*) and waterlilies grow on the lowest level.
Garden design: Mitsuko Collver.

◄ One of the secrets of a successful four-season garden is to interplant perennials with bulbs so that after spring bulbs fade and go dormant, perennials will fill their space. Here, hostas will take over after the daffodils go dormant.

► The native American yellowwood (*Cladrastis kentukea*) offers wisteria-like white flowers in late spring through early summer, bright green summer foliage, and soft yellow fall color. The bark is a smooth silvery gray, resembling a beech.

▼ The bare ground beneath tulips can be dressed up with forget-me-nots (*Myosotis sylvatica*). Scatter their seeds thickly over the tulip bed in autumn.

▲ Pink-flowered stellar dogwood (*Cornus × rutgersenensis* 'Stellar Pink') is a new disease-resistant hybrid tree. Its bloom time falls between the midspring bloom of flowering dogwood (*C. florida*) and early summer bloom of Kousa dogwood (*C. kousa*), its parents.

▶ Foliage can be as exciting as flowers, as you can see by this golden fullmoon maple (*Acer japonicum* 'Aureum'). Its bright chartreuse new foliage matures to lime green in summer and changes to deep gold in autumn.

◀ This colorful midspring scene features native wildflowers, including foamflower (*Tiarella cordifolia*), wild blue phlox (*Phlox divaricata*), creeping phlox (*P. stolonifera*), and Virginia bluebells (*Mertensia virginica*), with a backdrop of dwarf rhododendrons.

◄ An outstanding native shrub for a four-season garden, dwarf fothergilla (*Fothergilla gardenii*) displays bottlebrushes of creamy white flowers in early spring, heavily textured heart-shaped leaves in summer, and flaming orange-red fall color—all on compact plants that fit well into almost any landscape.

▼ Crested iris (*Iris cristata*), a native woodland wildflower, spreads rapidly to form thick carpets in humusy soil and partial shade. Delicate lavender, blue, or white flowers bloom in midspring, and the low sword-shaped leaves provide a bold vertical effect throughout summer and autumn.

▲ Plant cool-season annuals like these pansies (*Viola × wittrockiana*) and primroses (*Primula × hybrida*) in early spring, then replace them with hot-weather annuals when summer arrives so you can enjoy several seasons of flowers in the same spot.

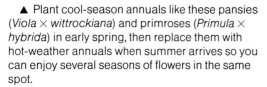

flowers that will encourage them to loosen up a bit.

Actually, Dutch hyacinths will loosen up on their own, if given the chance. In fact, they may get too wild and woolly for your taste if you happen to go for the intensely showy. After the first growing season, individual flowers are a little farther apart on the stem, so they're less packed together like a bottlebrush. You might like them better this way—I'm delighted with my three-year-old planting of dark purple Dutch hyacinths this spring. The large flower stalks look colorful and appealing, and smell as fragrant as ever.

After about five years in your garden, Dutch hyacinths may begin to look sparsely delicate, resembling their wild progenitors more than the Dutch hybrids they are. That's when you might want to lift them from formal beds and replant them in a woodland or naturalistic garden, where they'll look at home. Though less showy with the passing years, Dutch hyacinths will live practically forever, but won't increase by forming offsets. With this in mind, space them closely together for the best effect and see what happens.

Time for Tulips

Tulips are among the most elegant spring flowers, with their stately stems and classic form. Unfortunately, many of these Dutch-bred masterpieces don't get better with the years. And withering tulip foliage can spoil the garden, hanging around for weeks as the broad, eye-catching basal leaves begin to yellow and finally turn bright tan before starting to dry up. (Note: Species or wild tulips are another story; see page 127.)

Some gardeners grow tulips as annuals to avoid these problems—enjoying them one year and, once the blooms are spent, ripping them out of the garden and relegating them to the compost bin. Since they might not bloom the next year anyway, this isn't as wasteful as it seems—why put up with the unsightly foliage for nothing?

If you're lucky, a new tulip planting will perform for three seasons, five at best, but don't be surprised if the second spring brings no blooms at all. In Zones 8 to 10 of the South and southern California, the most you can hope from your tulips is that they'll flower for one season, and then only if you prechill them in a refrigerator for 9 to 12 weeks before planting, or buy prechilled bulbs. (Some species tulips perform well in these warm-winter areas. See "Minor League Bulbs" on page 124.)

Repeat bloom will be yours only if you start with top-quality bulbs, planting and fertilizing them with great care. If you purchase a bag of cheap little bulbs, that's what you'll get at bloom time: cheap little blooms. And that goes for all bulbs—not just tulips.

Some tulip cultivars are more likely to be perennial than others, so choose ones from "Tenacious Tulips" on page 126 if you are aiming for repeat performance or naturalizing. My friend Claudia Scholtz planted a dozen 'Apeldoorn' plants, a Darwin hybrid tulip cultivar, over ten years ago under the dogwood tree in the cottage garden beside her kitchen door. These soft cherry red tulips have multiplied into several dozen over the years, and though their blooms aren't as large as when newly planted, they create a delightful show growing with bunches of dark blue grape hyacinths.

Most tulips are short-lived because, unlike daffodils, the mother bulb usually can't form both a flower bud and new offsets. After flowering, the large, amber-skinned tulip bulb you planted in the spring usually forms little offset bulbs, then withers up in the process of sustaining them. These offsets aren't large enough to bloom the next year but may bloom in two or three years if well-nourished. You might consider transplanting them to a nursery bed for a few years, if you want to go to all that trouble.

Research has shown that you can encourage repeat bloom in reluctant tulips with proper culture. Tulips don't like overly rich soil but do appreciate being fertilized because they take up nutrients from the time the bulbs form roots in fall until the time foliage and roots wither in summer.

In fact, Dr. Paul V. Nelson at North Carolina State University showed that if tulips were fertilized with nitrogen before flowering, they would flower again the next year. Fall or early-winter fertilizing, followed by another application in spring soon after the foliage has emerged, ought to turn your tulips into perennials. But you're still going to have to put up with the awful foliage, or figure out a way to camouflage it.

Hot summers seem to favor offset production over flower bud formation. So for flowers each year, besides fertilizing well, it helps if you choose a planting spot with full spring sunshine for photosynthesis, but with light summer shade to keep the soil cool, such as is offered by Claudia's dogwood tree. Also, deep planting—2 inches deeper than the recommended 6 to 8 inches—seems to discourage offset formation. So does a deep, cooling mulch. By breaking off spent blooms immediately after the petals fall, you can prevent energy being wasted on seed formation rather than being stored in the bulb.

Tulips, like daffodils, bloom early, in the middle, and late in the season over the span of the tulip season. The early-season hybrid tulips begin flowering in midspring about crabapple time, and the late-season tulips begin blooming in late spring when the dogwood blooms have expanded. Choose some from each group for the longest display.

The early tulip season starts with the tall Fosteriana or 'Emperor' tulips (cultivars of *Tulipa fosteriana*). Fosteriana tulips tend to be longer-lived than other tulips. Fast on their heels come the Greigii hybrids, offspring of the waterlily tulip (*T. kaufmanniana*). The Single Early tulips, with their egg-shaped blooms, and the Double Early tulips, with their double rows of petals, also bloom early, making a nice tulip show. But they lack the drama of other tulips, since stems grow only 10 to 14 inches tall.

In midseason, the tall Triumph cultivars produce large flowers on strong 12- to 14-inch stems. The Darwin hybrids (not to be confused with later-blooming Darwin tulips) arrive about a week later. Rembrandt tulips are variegated, or broken, versions of the Darwin hybrids.

Part of the class of Single Late tulips are cottage tulips, developed in English village gardens. Late spring also brings the Lily-Flowered tulips. Joining these other late tulips are the large-flowered Darwin tulips (Single Late) and the Peony-Flowered tulips (Double Late), which resemble double, 5-inch peonies. Even later in the season, we can enjoy the wildly variegated, feathery-petaled Parrot tulips and the Viridiflora tulips with their elegant flowers streaked with green.

Minor League Bulbs

Not as well-known, but equally important to creating an eye-catching spring show, the minor bulbs embellish gardens with ground-level color. Most are indeed minor in size compared to the major bulbs, but this does have its advantages: The minor bulbs often cost only pennies per bulb, compared with the cost of the hefty players, so you can afford to plant them in lavish quantity.

Two of my favorite minor bulbs—glory-of-the-snow (*Chionodoxa luciliae*) and Siberian squill (*Scilla siberica*)—are both blue-flowered beauties. Their spikes of flowers boast the rare and wonderful pure bright blue of the

Wrong

Right

How to group bulbs. *Wrong:* Spring bulbs look sparse and lonely when planted polka-dot fashion in the bare ground beneath a spring-blooming tree. It will look even more isolated after the bulbs fade.

Right: Planted in dense groups, bulbs have a big visual impact that is strengthened by a low ever-green groundcover. The groundcover will continue to add impact all year.

TENACIOUS TULIPS

The first year after planting, hybrid tulips open their extravagant blooms to a chorus of oohs and ahs. Unfortunately, many tulip cultivars diminish rapidly in subsequent years, often never blooming again. According to the Netherlands Flower Bulb Information Center, research has shown that the following tulip cultivars are most likely to persist tenaciously, putting on a pretty show for many years.

Foster Tulips: 'Candela' (yellow), 'Orange Emperor' (carrot orange), 'Princeps' (red), 'Red Emperor' (fiery red), 'Madame Lefeber' (fiery red)

Triumph Tulips: 'Don Quichotte' (rose), 'Kees Nelis' (blood red with orange rim)

Lily-Flowered Tulips: 'Aladdin' (scarlet with yellow rim), 'Ballade' (magenta with white rim), 'Maytime' (reddish violet), 'Red Shine' (deep red), 'White Triumphator' (pure white)

Darwin Hybrid Tulips: 'Apeldoorn' (cherry red), 'Apeldoorn's Elite' (red and yellow), 'Beauty of Apeldoorn' (magenta with gold rim), 'Holland's Glorie' (deep red), 'Oxford' (scarlet flushed with purple-red), 'Striped Apeldoorn' (deep red striped with yellow)

Greigii Tulips: 'Red Riding Hood' (carmine red), 'Toronto' (red tinged with vermilion)

---

color wheel—the blue of a crisp cloudless sky. Glory-of-the-snow's white-centered, star-shaped flowers appear in upward-facing clusters on 10-inch-long stems; they may also be lavender or pink. Siberian squill forms spikes of nodding flowers only about 4 inches high.

Usually beginning to bloom in late winter, these two blues may delay flowering until earliest spring in response to a cool year or a late snow. Low-growers, they form beguiling carpets of starry blue blooms beneath shrubs or naturalized in a lawn. They make great underpinnings for taller bulbs, such as daffodils and Dutch hyacinths, since the blanket of blue creates a marvelous backdrop for the bolder flowers above.

No color combination could please me more than sunny yellow daffodils set off against the brilliant blue of glory-of-the-snow or Siberian squill. Try them combined with pale blue Dutch hyacinths, or pink, or peach, or . . . well, just about any color. This shade of blue enhances almost every other flower color.

Resembling a somewhat anemic, fringed version of a Siberian squill, puschkinia (*Puschkinia scilliodes*) produces the palest blue flowers imaginable on little spikes nestled among neat leaves in early spring. Planted in mass, this extremely cold-hardy bulb (it is native to 10,000-foot-mountaintops in Eurasia) glows with an iridescent quality like milk glass. Use it like the other blue bulbs.

Depending on the species, grape hyacinths (*Muscari* spp.) begin flowering along with daffodils or tulips and produce their sweetly scented blooms for six weeks. Individual flowers resemble dainty, upside-down Grecian urns that form grapelike clusters atop the flower stalks.

Armenian grape hyacinth (*M. armeniacum*) sends up its narrow, tubular leaves in fall, and they last over winter, elongating and flopping over as the cobalt blue flower spikes appear in spring. The foliage looks a bit tattered by then, detracting from the pretty flowers, but you can clip it a bit to neaten it up if you want. This 8- to 10-inch-tall species reseeds itself with abandon, so plant it only where neatness is not a virtue.

Where neatness counts, choose the common grape hyacinth (*M. botryoides*), which blooms a bit later with more attractive, spring-emerging foliage. This is a better-behaved species with dark sky blue flowers. The white cultivar 'Alba' offers snowy white blooms. *M. azureum* bears powder blue flowers striped with dark blue amid neat leaves.

Grecian windflowers (*Anemone blanda*) will carpet the ground beneath shrubs and major bulbs with enthusiasm. Blooming in blue, pink, lavender, or white, the daisylike flowers blanket the ground above whorls of parsleylike leaves. Rapid-spreading but never invasive, this pretty plant prefers sunny sites and looks best when planted in a mass of a single color.

The checkered lily (*Fritillaria meleagris*) is an odd little thing that blooms in midspring. It bears 2-inch, bell-shaped flowers that look sort of like lamp shades in a turn-of-the-century bordello. The flowers are checkered in a light-and-dark pattern that reminds me of snakeskin. The flowers, which are usually purplish red, may be white, a color that stands out better than the purple species. Stems reach a foot or more tall and are very slender with a few long narrow leaves. Be sure to plant this one in large clumps, or the delicate flowers—especially the purple ones—will be hard to see. Unlike most bulbs, checkered lilies flourish in wet soil, as well as under normal garden conditions.

Also doing well in normal to boggy soil, the summer snowflake (*Leucojum aestivum*) actually blooms in spring with the daffodils. Bolder than many minor bulbs, summer snowflake forms tall clumps of 1½-foot-long, strap-shaped green leaves. Flowering stems bear four or more white flowers, each about an inch across. These rounded bells consist of six white petals with a green spot at each tip.

The similar spring snowflake (*L. vernum*) blooms earlier, before the daffodils, and has substantial glaucous gray leaves that form an attractive clump. Flowers resemble the summer snowflake's but are larger, with only one bloom per stem.

Also on the bigger and bolder side is the crown imperial (*Fritillaria imperialis*). The crown imperial emerges and grows rapidly in spring to flower on 3-foot-tall stalks with the midseason daffodils. A ring of tightly packed, dangling, chime-shaped flowers rests directly beneath a crown of green leaves on a bare stem. This curious plant doesn't look like anything else you've ever seen, but on close inspection it does *smell* like something you'll recognize—a skunk. Keep your distance, however, and you won't notice.

Crown imperial bulbs cost about $6 each, but they will increase in number if well-sited. Plant them in groups of three or more, and enjoy the amazement as visitors to your garden see them. The species is a soft coral color, but cultivars include brilliant yellow, red-orange, and bright orange.

Early and mid-spring bring many of the species or botanical tulips into bloom. These wildflowers of the plains and northern steppes of Iran, Turkey, Afghanistan, and Greece can't compete with hybrid tulips for flamboyant show or elegance, but they hold their own when it comes to charm. The species are considered minor bulbs, since they're so different in size, habit, and garden uses from the larger hybrids.

Many of the species tulips naturalize readily if grown in well-drained, even gravelly, soil and allowed to bake in the summer. Rock gardens or rough slopes suit these tulips better than traditional borders, where the soil is too rich and moist.

The waterlily tulip (*Tulipa kaufmanniana*) is the most readily available species tulip—its huge flowers on 3-inch stems give it the

TIPS ON GROWING SPRING BULBS

A few easy cultural techniques should keep the bulbs in your garden vigorous, making sure they bloom well year after year.

▶ Snap off faded flower heads of the major bulbs so the energy goes into increasing bulb size, not into forming seeds.

▶ Allow the minor bulbs to set seed, so they can spread themselves around your garden.

▶ Do not remove bulb foliage while it is still green, or you may weaken the plant, decreasing next year's bloom. Allow bulb foliage in a lawn to mature for at least six weeks before mowing.

▶ Fertilize bulbs every year in *fall* with nitrogen-rich organic fertilizer, so the nutrients are available in early spring when new growth begins. Fertilize again in early spring to help fuel foliage and bulb growth for the following year's bloom.

▶ Plant bulbs an inch or two deeper than recommended, but only if the soil is well-drained, to increase longevity and discourage rodents.

---

substance of a hybrid. The flowers open wide during the day and close at night, like waterlilies. Bold stripes of contrasting colors decorate the outside of the petals, and splotches of bright yellow ornament the centers. Cultivars come in shades of cream, yellow, peach, and pink. Use this low-growing species, which blooms from late winter to early spring, along a rocky path or in the front of a border.

Other species tulips, with their small flowers borne on slender stems, are more modest than the brazen waterlily tulip. The peppermint stick tulip (*T. clusiana*) reminds me of a Christmas candy cane. When closed, the outer sides of the pointed white petals display their crimson stripes, and when open, the centers display a purple blotch surrounded by prominent purple anthers. *T. clusiana* var. *chrysantha* is also two-toned, its petals crimson with a yellow edge and creamy yellow inside.

Tulipa tarda, a favorite late-spring bloomer, features glossy, bright green leaves and yellow-and-white-striped flowers borne several to a stem. Both foliage and flowers hug the ground, making a nice spring groundcover. *T. sylvestris* is also multiflowered and yellow, but with green on the outer petals. Flowers curl back curiously and are pendant in bud.

Tulipa bakeri 'Lilac Wonder' is one of my favorites, because its rosy purple blooms with yellow-splashed centers combine so well with my garden's spring color scheme. Also rosy lilac with a yellow base, *T. saxatilis* forms stolons and persists where it's happy. *T. humilis* belongs in this same color group; its magenta blooms echo the color of a 'P.J.M.' rhododendron and feature a dramatic greenish black basal blotch.

T. batalinii is perhaps the only wild tulip that looks like a miniature version of a hybrid garden tulip—its blunt-tipped petals open to cup-shaped flowers above gray-green leaves. The perfect little blooms grow on 3-inch-tall stems and are creamy yellow or peach. Several color variations have been given cultivar status: 'Bright Gem', a soft apricot; 'Red Jewel', classic red; and 'Yellow Jewel', lemon yellow with a tinge of rose.

These are only a few of the 150 species of tulips, many of which are available to gardeners. If you can't find the bulbs at your local nursery, seek them in a specialty catalog, such as McClure & Zimmerman. (See "Resources for Four-Season Landscapes" on page 328 for the address.) Southern gardeners will be successful with *T. sylvestris*, *T. bakeri* 'Lilac Wonder', *T. saxatilis,* and *T. clusiana.*

Late spring brings another blue favorite—the Spanish squill. Most recently classified as *Hyacinthoides hispanicus* but carrying around a carload of synonyms, this one might be listed in catalogs as *Scilla hispanica, S. campanulata,* or *Endymion hispanicus.* A larger-flowered version of the English bluebell, this bulb thrives in shade, blooming at the end of spring when most bulbs have finished.

Spanish squill bears dense spikes of bell-shaped blue, lavender-blue, pink, or white flowers on 15-inch-tall stems above basal clusters of glossy green leaves. The bulb readily increases and reseeds, forming pleasing patches of flowers that look right at home in a naturalistic woodland setting or under garden trees.

Other late-spring bulbs include the alliums (*Allium* spp.), which is the name we give to those onion relatives grown in gardens for their pretty flowers. The alliums are so charming because their flower clusters are—for the most part—perfect spheres held on tall stalks like scepters. Individual flowers are starlike, but they mass together to form a ball that then dries in place into a pretty, long-lasting ornament when it sets seed.

The spring-blooming species include the low-growing *A. karataviense,* whose dense lavender balls are set off by fat, gray-green leaves; and *A. aflatunense* 'Purple Sensation', with reddish purple flowers on 2-foot stems. 'Purple Sensation' makes a wonderful contrast to the shapes and sizes of other flowers also in bloom—you can be sure none of them is round like this one. Lily leek (*A. moly*) has bright yellow flowers that form loose clusters on low stems. It reseeds readily—perhaps too readily—but makes a delightful splash of color that carries on into early summer.

Groundcovers: Friends of the Bulbs

Spilling around the feet of spring-blooming shrubs and trees or somber evergreens, wide sweeps of bulbs paint a beautiful spring picture when viewed from a distance. Up close, however, the bare spring soil between plants can spoil the finery. Unless you dress up the ground with a thick mulch of wood chips or shredded leaves, your best bet is an evergreen groundcover beneath the bulbs.

Periwinkle (*Vinca minor*) makes a pretty companion for most bulbs and shrubs in a mixed border. The shiny oval evergreen leaves grow on creeping stems, which remain low enough for bulb flowers and foliage to pop right through. And the periwinkle's lavender-blue flowers add a note of gaiety to a display of yellow daffodils or pink tulips. English ivy (*Hedera helix*) and pachysandra (*Pachysandra terminalis*) do wonders to show off bulbs, too—or vice versa, come to think of it.

If your property has large, boring expanses of any of these groundcovers as a lawn replacement, don't leave them flowerless. Plant bulbs in the groundcover for a colorful spring display. Pachysandra grows about 8 inches tall, so be sure to plant tall bulbs, such as daffodils, in it since the small guys will get swallowed up.

In a perennial border, interplant bulbs with an evergreen ground-covering perennial, such as snow-in-summer (*Cerastium tomentosum*), lamb's-ears (*Stachys byzantina*), or Serbian bellflower (*Campanula poscharskyana*). Or combine bulbs with daylilies (*Hemerocallis* cultivars) and hostas (*Hosta* cultivars), which have foliage that will grow up to hide the bulbs' unsightly ripening leaves.

Ground-hugging, furry gray-green leaves of lambs'-ears may look beat up at winter's end. But if you rake out the battered and bruised parts with a light touch, as I do, velvety new foliage fills in by early or mid-spring. This bold-textured silver-gray carpet looks especially charming as a foil for tulips, which can be planted in fall in pockets dug beneath the stems of the lamb's-ears. Since both plants prefer well-drained sunny sites, they form a perfect marriage, creating a changing display throughout the year in a single garden spot.

Snow-in-summer forms a cloud of white flowers above its mat of tiny silvery leaves in early summer. But you can get a spring flower show in the same spot by interplanting bulbs such as grape hyacinths, Dutch hyacinths, or tulips beneath its aggressively creeping stems. The evergreen, or perhaps I should say evergray, foliage perks up with new growth come bulb time. And its billowy floral display swallows up dying leaves of small bulbs.

Various species of creeping thyme (*Thymus* spp.) combine especially well with miniature narcissi or botanical tulips in a rock garden. Demanding sharply drained soil, these plants form lasting friendships for four seasons of beauty.

Few perennials are making a floral display at bulb-blooming time in early or midspring, but some stalwart types can be counted on for companion plantings. These are especially important to include in a perennial border along with bulbs and evergreen types of perennials: If you leave them out, the border can look spotty and quickly goes out of bloom.

English primroses (*Primula vulgaris*) have pastel yellow clusters of bell-shaped flowers that combine well with almost any bulb. So do the pink and blue chimes of Virginia bluebells (*Mertensia virginica*). Old-fashioned bleeding heart (*Dicentra spectabilis*) starts growing early and makes obvious daily growth spurts until its 3-foot-tall clumps send out their necklaces of heart-shaped charms. Lungworts (*Pulmonaria* spp.) and Lenten roses (*Helleborus orientalis*) may begin blooming in late winter but carry on into early spring.

Evergreen candytuft (*Iberis sempervirens*) and basket-of-gold (*Aurinia saxatilis*), with their sprays of fine-textured flowers, contrast well with large, solemn tulip blooms. And these combine well with the purple and pink mats of the rock cresses (*Arabis albida* and *Aubrieta deltoides*) or moss pinks (*Phlox subulata*). By the end of spring, when all but the latest tulips and earliest alliums grace the bulb beds, flowering perennials are coming into their own. They give the garden the promise of more flowers to come as spring segues into summer.

Spring's Natural Color Scheme

The pigments you choose to paint your spring garden ought to be fresh and young—baby colors, the gay, bright, and beautiful hues that promise so much in this season of renewal and hope. If you follow nature's own color scheme at this time of year, it's difficult to go wrong in your garden.

Chartreuse Spells Spring Green

By the time the daffodil blooms have withered, the canopy of shade tree branches is beginning to color up with new growth, turning the landscape translucent. The color tinging the branches overhead usually announces the tree's flowers, though few of us ever bother to look closely enough to discover that the haze of green, yellow, or red represents clusters of tiny blooms. New leaves soon follow or join the tree flowers, suffusing the horizon with a deepening haze of chartreuse.

A soft green light bathes a wooded property by midspring as the maples, oaks, beeches, and birches catch and transmit sunlight through their translucent new leaves. These paper-thin leaves—the yellow-green color of delicate new growth—form the backdrop on which we so gleefully splash the springtime floral paint to announce winter's end.

Easter-Egg Colors

The spring bloom palette is notably lacking the hot, arresting shades of red and orange. Nature herself eschews these colors in spring—instead, she paints the forests and fields with pink, magenta, lavender, purple, blue, yellow, and white flowers—flowers that look smashing with the pastel greens of new foliage growth.

I like to think of these springtime colors as Easter-egg colors: They're the soft pastels and eggshell shades of the season of rebirth, the colors of a little girl's Sunday school dress. And these are the colors I choose for my spring borders—the flower colors that tell me spring has come to my four-season landscape.

Wine Red New Growth

Though most new foliage growth is bright light green, chartreuse, or emerald green, some new foliage surprises us with tinges of purple or wine red. Of course, the foliage of trees and shrubs like the 'Bloodgood' Japanese maple (*Acer palmatum* 'Bloodgood'), with wine red or bronze mature foliage, always emerges a bright hue. But often new foliage pops out of the bud suffused with winy red, then becomes green as it matures.

Colorful new foliage like this can play a pretty role in a mixed border. Don't overlook this delightful design element in your spring garden. Usually, these reddish tones contrast happily with the various true greens—especially the chartreuse—of surrounding foliage. And they look just fine, even downright wonderful, with most flower colors. Wine red leaves enrich the lavenders, blues, pinks, and magentas of the Easter-egg-colored flowers, and play well against pale yellow or white flowers.

I love to see cultivars of the purple-leaf plum (*Prunus cerasifera*) against the baby-green spring foliage of background trees. The rich colors pair up to paint a subtle but very colorful scene. Choose cultivars with white or pale pink flowers, rather than dark pink, since the lighter flowers show up best against dark foliage. For four-season interest, you'll be pleased with cultivars such as 'Krauter Vesuvius' and 'Thundercloud' that hold their purple color through the summer, rather than fading to green as 'Atropurpurea' will.

The new leaves of Japanese pieris (*Pieris japonica*) emerge a bronze color that quickly turns dark green. But certain cultivars of this and other pieris have been selected for their vivid red or burgundy new growth. Forming gleaming patterns above the dark green of the older leaves, this new growth puts on as eye-catching a show as any flower, and it does this about a month after the shrub's winter flowers have peaked, providing an extra season of color to catch your interest.

Two cultivars of *P. japonica*, 'Mountain Fire' and 'Scarlet O'Hara', are best-known for their spring foliage—a deep wine red that looks beautiful with pink flowers. New leaves of Chinese pieris (*Pieris forestii*) emerge a Christmas-card red.

P. × 'Forest Flame', one of the most spectacular pieris, is a hybrid between Chinese and Japanese pieris. Noted for its huge white flower clusters, 'Forest Flame' has new foliage that emerges bright red. Then, as it matures during summer, the leaves change first to pink and then to white before finally settling down to green by summer's end.

A cross between Japanese and mountain pieris (*P. floribunda*) produced another specially colored cultivar: 'Brouwer's Beauty'. As new foliage emerges, this dense evergreen plant changes into a mound of soft yellowish green leaves. Deep purplish red flower buds adorn the shrub over the winter, opening white in early spring.

Avoid Spring Color Clashes

Spring is hard to do wrong. Flowers and foliage seem so dewy-fresh and invigorating that almost anything goes. But it's possible to make mistakes—large ones—if you aren't careful. Try to plan a spring garden that traverses the three miniseasons of spring, grouping plants that bloom at the same time into perfect little pictures. You'll enjoy your garden more if you arrange plants in focal points, rather than spotting spring bloomers throughout the landscape where they remain unconnected to the garden and to each other, with only mud for a backdrop.

The Easter-egg colors of spring are soft and harmonious, and seem to combine pleasingly without much effort. Nevertheless, it takes forethought to avoid an unfortunate color clash or two in the spring garden. Magenta creeps into many of the pink colors of spring-flowering trees and shrubs, including the redbuds, rhododendrons, and azaleas. Their mauve-pinks look downright hideous next to coral-pink or fire-engine red tulips or Dutch hyacinths. But they work well with purple, lavender, or yellow bulbs.

Because the major bulbs come in such a wild array of colors, you are most likely to make a springtime mistake with them, rather than with shrubs, perennials, or more subtle minor bulbs. And even when you've tried to choose compatible colors, you may be in for a surprise if plants bloom out of sequence, creating combinations you hadn't counted on, or if they aren't the colors you expected.

This spring, I found I had made both mistakes when adding dozens of tulips to my semishaded mixed border. The border is supposed to be blue, pink, purple, and white, and it usually is. But in selecting tulip cultivars, I had not considered that the 'P.J.M.' rhododen-

drons would bloom with the early tulips. The vivid magenta of the 'P.J.M.' competed with a coral-red Greigii tulip—a cultivar that I thought was supposed to be cream and pink.

To compound the tulip problem, the dusky rose flowers of the Lenten rose (*Helleborus orientalis*) planted nearby had lingered on from their late-winter show into early spring. They also vied with the coral tulips, although they beautifully echoed the 'P.J.M.' flowers.

The other tulips I planted—pastel pink ones—looked great in this setting, along with a nearby bleeding heart and late creamy white daffodils. Out went the Greigii tulips—pretty enough to be saved, but only in another location far, far away from any magenta-flowered shrubs.

When these unfortunate surprises happen in your garden, don't sigh and resign yourself, but heft your garden spade and start rearranging things. I relocate my plants as if they were furniture, transplanting them until I find a combination that pleases me. If you dig a large rootball in spring when temperatures are still cool and soil is moist, the plants may hardly notice they've been uprooted.

Many of the mail-order bulb companies send out flashy "preseason" catalogs in spring, just about daffodil time. This clever strategy is intended to make you regret not having all those beauties flourishing right now in your very own garden—and it works. You're motivated to order scads of bulbs now at sale prices, when you don't have to think about actually planting them. All you're thinking about is how good your garden could look.

So put those catalogs to good use. Take them outside now, in spring, and use the glossy color pictures to help you match up colors of bulbs with shrubs and trees. Using this aid, I found the perfect tulips to go with my 'P.J.M.' rhododendron, Lenten roses, and bleeding hearts.

It's hard to do spring wrong if you stick strictly to the Easter-egg colors throughout the three miniseasons. Avoid any orange, red, or gold flowers, and select only pastel shades of yellow. Save the hot colors until summer, when they combine well with rich green foliage and defy the burning summer sun. If you simply can't resist those satiny scarlet 'Emperor' tulips and orange-trumpeted daffodils, choose their planting spots with care. And combine them with shrubs and trees that bloom in white or another compatible color—or later in the year!

For the same reason, be careful when choosing a crabapple or rhododendron. The hybridizers have been creating some vivid floral colors—shades of red and deep coral that may not be easy companions for the pinks, lavenders, and magentas that abound at this time of year.

Another word or two of warning about spring: Don't overdo this short season. Avid gardeners find the urge to dig and plant so irresistible that they can easily get carried away with spring bloom. Remember the rest of the year and leave room for the lesser-known summer, fall, and winter bloomers.

They're the plants that will make your garden spectacular every season of the year.

The End of Spring

Spring seems such a frantic season. Once warm weather is upon us, everything in the garden starts sprouting, growing, and blooming with extreme urgency. There's nothing patient about it. With each and every warm, sunny hour you can see measurable changes in your garden. And every day reveals a new miracle: Shoots that weren't there one day have shot up out of the earth the next. Buds fatten, suddenly unfurling petals or leaves.

When this frenetic spurt of growth finally subsides, both garden and gardener are exhausted. All the energy that fueled spring's rapid growth has dissipated—it's time to sit back and rest. The urgent, undisciplined adolescence of the year is over, and maturity has set in. As the leaves of the translucent spring landscape reach their mature size, they begin to take on more substance, thickening and becoming a richer, darker green. The landscape has become opaque: Summer is coming.

CHAPTER 4

Summer in the Four-Season Landscape

Transform the Green Season with Late Bloomers and Colorful Foliage

As spring matures into summer, the lush new foliage of April and May loses its fresh hue and deepens to the sober solidity of—I hate to say it—middle age. As the translucent leaves of spring reach their mature size, they thicken up and deepen in color, blocking rather than transmitting light. From the upper stories of my house, I feel a serene sense of coolness and privacy as the opaque curtain of summer foliage encloses my yard and garden with greenery.

If any one feature defines summer, it is this opaque leafiness. Despite summer's own alluring blooms, foliage often dominates the scene by midsummer. Summer always renews my appreciation for the color green and for foliage in general—for the forms, textures, and colors leaves have to offer.

Herbaceous perennials bring a cornucopia of colorful June flowers to fill in the garden gaps left by spent spring bulbs. Summer perennials bring new life to areas that were recently bright with spring-flowering shrubs, but now are all green. Four-season gardeners can rely on perennials for splashes of floral color. But because perennials are, for the most part, one-season plants with a short bloom season, you shouldn't rely on them totally.

Some gardeners depend on flowering annuals to provide summer flowers, especially in the South. But you should use annuals sparingly in a garden designed for year-round beauty. Annuals often look pathetic until midsummer, and they leave gaping garden holes for much of the year if you grow large masses of them instead of interplanting them with perennials.

The four-season solution is a mixed border of small trees, shrubs, perennials, ornamental grasses, *and* annuals to provide color throughout the hottest season. With careful planning and plant selection, you can design a mixed border that blooms beautifully in July and August when your neighbors' yards are barren. Choose some of the showy summer plants described in this chapter to enhance your landscape plans.

A Flowering Summer Canopy

There are enough summer-flowering trees to fill a whole garden. Unfortunately, most of them are little known and little grown. Some of these trees may even seem rare—not because they're fussy, but because they just aren't readily available. People tend to shop for plants in spring when planting fever sets in. And nursery owners know that shoppers are more likely to buy an eye-catching blooming specimen than a leafy plant quietly awaiting its turn to shine, so they rarely stock the later-blooming beauties.

If you can't find some of the wonderful trees and shrubs I describe below in your nursery or garden center, send for some of the catalogs listed in the "Resources for Four-Season Landscapes," beginning on page 328. It's worth a little effort to include these choice plants in your garden.

The Early-Summer Canopy

Perhaps the best-known of these out-of-the-ordinary late bloomers is the Kousa dogwood (*Cornus kousa*), which also answers to the names Japanese, Korean, and Chinese dogwood, reflecting its Asian origins. Beginning its long bloom period in early June in my garden, Kousa dogwood picks up where our native flowering dogwood leaves off at spring's end.

While many late-blooming trees are undeniably charming, few look as showy as the Kousa dogwood because their full-grown foliage competes with the flowers. The Kousa's creamy white blooms are borne on short stems above the horizontal branches in such profusion that it looks as if an out-of-season snowfall has settled over the layered branches. And the "snow" doesn't melt for six weeks or more.

One of the finest small trees for a four-season garden, Kousa dogwood offers handsome foliage and a display of curious red fruits in early fall, spectacular dark red foliage in late fall, and colorful patchwork bark for winter viewing pleasure. It performs better in full sun and in the heat and drought conditions of the Midwest and South than the better-known flowering dogwood. Kousa dogwood also resists the dogwood anthracnose disease that threatens its spring-blooming American cousin. Kousa dogwood cultivars of note include 'Milky Way', which flowers so profusely that the mature leaves are hardly visible, and 'Summer Stars', which retains its small but numerous flowers for more than two months.

Chinese dogwood (*Cornus kousa* var. *chinensis*), a selection raised from seed originating in China, has extremely large flowers, up to 6 inches across, as opposed to the usual 4 inches. 'National', a cultivar of the Chinese dogwood selected by the U.S. National Arboretum in Washington, D.C., grows into a graceful vase shape. Bracts of all Kousa dogwoods may flush with pink as they age or if nights are cold, but 'Rosabella' starts out with beautiful pink flowers.

I've planted 'Elizabeth Lustgarten', a weeping Kousa dogwood cultivar, in the terraced area in front of my house along the steep driveway. There, its curvaceous branches create a pretty harmony with the slope and the other weeping and creeping plants that cascade over the stone walls. Echoing this tree on the opposite, unterraced side of the driveway are two "regular" specimens. Each has grown rapidly in the partial shade.

Nurseryman Jim Cross's favorite tree for a four-season garden is Japanese snowbell (*Styrax japonicus*), which he says makes a won-

A snowbell tree. A Japanese snowbell (*Styrax japonicus*) makes a perfect tree for Conni and Jim Cross's garden. The tree's horizontal, slightly drooping branches make the patio a cool, pleasant place to sit, especially in early summer, when the snowbell bears clusters of fragrant white flowers. Conni and Jim planted pinks, Siberian iris, lavender cotton, lavender, azaleas, and peonies as colorful companions for their snowbell.

derful patio tree. He and Conni planted one outside their dining room doors, where it casts light shade on the brick patio. With horizontal, slightly pendulous branches, the tree creates a perfect canopy to sit under. Clusters of long-stemmed white flowers with flared petals dangle from the undersides of the branches in early summer after the foliage has matured.

From a distance, a snowbell tree in full bloom sparkles in a glittery green-and-white pattern. The blooms reveal themselves fully when seen from beneath, as Conni and Jim see them when walking under the tree or dining at the small patio table. With attractive striped bark and lustrous summer foliage that turns soft yellow in late fall, this little-known tree looks great beside their patio every month of the year.

If I could have only one tree in my garden, it would be an American yellowwood (*Cladrastis kentukea,* formerly *C. lutea*). Imagine a white-flowered wisteria vine transformed into a tree about the size and shape of your average maple: There you have an American yellowwood.

This low-branched, round-headed tree grows large enough to act as a shade tree. Small rounded leaflets make up the long compound leaves, giving the foliage a handsome texture throughout summer. From beneath this light-filtering abundance of grass green foliage drip long, luscious clusters of fragrant, pure white flowers in early summer. The color combination couldn't be fresher or more pleasing.

Yellowwood leaves emerge bright yellow-green in spring, change to grass green for summer, then turn hues of soft yellow or gold in autumn. After leaf drop, yellowwood's open branchwork and smooth, luminous silver-gray bark perk up the winter landscape. The common name refers to the bright yellow heartwood noticeable on freshly cut branches.

American yellowwood is a hardy tree that will grow and bloom in Minnesota and Maine,

and it does just fine in acid soil. The tree has a tendency, when grown out in the open, to branch low and form weak branch crotches, as opposed to actually being weak-wooded. Pruning and training the tree when it is young helps it develop a stronger shape. Prune yellowwood in summer only, to avoid bleeding sap.

Another summer-blooming tree that bears clusters of white, wisteria-like blooms is black locust (*Robinia pseudoacacia*), a native of the eastern United States. You can recognize black locust even out of bloom by the deep vertical fissures marking the rough bark along its trunks and by its thorny branches.

Black locusts occur in at least three distinct forms: one with a ramrod-straight trunk and short side branches that form a craggy top, another with a fan-shaped branching habit, and a third with an irregular trunk. Since the wood of all black locusts is very rot-resistant, it makes ideal material for fence posts.

Since I read that the British consider the white fringetree (*Chionanthus virginicus*) the finest native American tree introduced to their gardens, I've been wondering whether I have a sunny spot in my garden to fit one in. The fringetree is aptly named, for it covers itself with 6-inch-long panicles of bright white, honey-scented flowers that resemble the fringe edging an old-fashioned silk shawl. Inch-long, strap-shaped petals a fraction of an inch wide make up the individual blooms, which are gathered together in a fleecy cluster. The flowers seem to be in constant motion, since even the tiniest breeze sends them dancing on their threadlike stems.

A small, broadly spreading tree or large shrub native to the southern United States, fringetree performs well as far north as Maine. This late-leafing tree looks dead through much of spring, but when the flowers and lustrous, dark green leaves finally do make an appearance in early summer, they are all the more welcome.

An uncommon but choice cousin is the Chinese fringetree (*Chionanthus retusus*). This Asian plant is similar in appearance to the American version but has smaller, glossier leaves and ornamental exfoliating bark. Either fringetree makes an excellent choice for a four-season landscape, but the Chinese fringetree—if you can find it—is better because of the wonderful bark.

Fringetrees are usually either male or female, but you won't be able to tell which a tree is until it blooms. Male fringetrees have somewhat showier blooms. But female trees redeem themselves for their smaller flowers by producing wonderful sprays of dark blue berries in fall, if they have been pollinated by a male tree. Fall color is a pleasing yellow in the American version, while the Chinese fringetree holds its leaves through fall, finally losing them without much color change.

Few broadleaved evergreen trees grow north of Zone 8, but the sweet bay (*Magnolia virginiana*) performs well in Zone 5, producing its intoxicatingly fragrant white flowers in early and mid-summer. In Zone 5, the species loses its leaves in early winter, but in Zone 6 it is semi-evergreen. *M. virginiana* var. *australis* 'Henry Hicks' remains fully evergreen at the northern limits of the plant's range and is probably the best sweet bay to choose for Zones 5-7.

Because it is evergreen (or at least selected cultivars are) and thrives in shade and wet soil, you'll find that the sweet bay makes a useful and beautiful screening plant for difficult situations. It is a fairly small tree in the North, reaching 20 feet at most, but attains a much larger size in the South. I'm planning to locate several on the edge of my woodland to help enclose my property. Conifers wouldn't do well there in the shade, but I can count on the sweet bay to grow tall enough in the shady site to hide my neighbor's yard from view throughout the year.

The sweet bay doesn't put on a spectacular show like the Asian magnolias, which bloom in spring before their foliage emerges. Nevertheless, this pretty tree makes an effective display when planted near the house, where the flowers' scent can be enjoyed. The glossy green leaves have bright white undersides, giving the tree a subtle shimmery quality throughout the year.

The southern magnolia (*Magnolia grandiflora*), another southern native, blooms with tropical splendor in early summer and throughout the rest of the season. The huge, white, waxy flowers look dramatic, but since they open only a few at a time and over a long period, the overall picture is subdued rather than overpowering. The flowers' famous fragrance—incredibly sweet and lemony—doesn't pervade the garden but must be enjoyed close at hand.

The dramatic, glossy evergreen leaves make the southern magnolia a distinctive specimen. The somewhat wavy leaf margins curl up to reveal the rusty-haired undersides of the leaves. Branches can cloak the tree all the way to the bottom of the trunk, sweeping the ground if left unpruned, as they should be. Since they grow so large—to 80 feet tall and wide—and occupy both air and ground space, these are not trees to garden under, but to garden around! Give them plenty of growing space.

Since seedling-grown southern magnolias vary greatly, you'll be more satisfied with your specimen if you choose one of the cultivars. These selected forms are neater and more compact than the species, and they have extra-large flowers and handsome foliage with either rusty or pale green undersides. 'St. Mary' grows slowly and is very compact, maturing at 20 feet, while 'Samuel Sommer' has flowers a full 14 inches across and reaches 50 feet. 'Little Gem' is shrubby and suited to small gardens.

Widely planted in the Deep South and

north to Washington, D.C., southern magnolia thrives in sun or shade and moist or dry conditions. Though it isn't commonly grown north of D.C., southern magnolia will remain evergreen in coastal areas of Delaware, Maryland, New Jersey, and even Long Island. And specially selected cultivars prove that the southern magnolia doesn't have to be limited to the South, because they will survive — and even flourish — in Zone 6 and warmer parts of Zone 5!

If sited out of winter sun and wind, which can desiccate the leaves, certain cold-hardy cultivars ought to bring a touch of Dixie to the North. Some of these may lose their leaves in severe winters but will recover with new spring growth. 'Edith Bogue', which was selected from a New Jersey garden, is the most well-known cold-hardy cultivar. Magnolias in the 'Spring Grove' series, selected from Spring Grove Arboretum in Cincinnati, are extremely hardy, as is 'Bracken's Brown Beauty', named for its handsome leaves.

An outstanding tree with a shape similar to that of an apple tree, the Japanese tree lilac (*Syringa reticulata,* syn. *S. amurensis* var. *japonica*) blooms in early summer when it seems that the canopy show is over. Foot-tall, pyramidal clusters of creamy white flowers top the branch tips, lasting for several weeks. Most books describe the flowers as fragrant, but you may wonder whether the aroma, which is like a privet's, should be labeled fragrant or offensive. I don't care for the scent myself — it reminds me of old gym shoes.

Only one cultivar of Japanese tree lilac is available. 'Ivory Silk' was selected in Canada for its larger trusses of blooms, beautiful heart-shaped leaves, and more treelike shape.

Northerners appreciate Japanese tree lilac, despite its aroma, because it resists drought and is perfectly hardy to Zone 3, where other summer bloomers don't make it. The similar Manchurian tree lilac (*S. reticulata* var.

mandshurica) from China and Manchuria is made of even sturdier stuff — it's hardy in Zone 2. Both tree lilacs may need a little encouraging to set them on the path of becoming multitrunked trees rather than large shrubs. Pruning, needed only in the early years, will also reveal the lovely reddish brown bark, which shines like the bark of cherry trees.

The Midsummer Canopy

Early summer will stretch right into midsummer if you have planted *Cornus kousa* 'Summer Stars', the long-blooming cultivar of the Kousa dogwood. Of the trees that come into their own in midsummer, my favorite — one that rivals dogwoods for the longest seasonal interest — is sourwood (*Oxydendrum arboreum*). Though it's a sort of ugly duckling, leafing out only by late spring, sourwood gets showier and showier as the growing season progresses.

The tall, narrow tree produces small, bell-shaped white flowers studded along 10-inch stems. It blooms around mid-July in the Northeast and lasts into August. Before then, the creamy white flower buds catch your eye, set off against glossy green leaves. These flower sprays are often compared to lily-of-the-valley flowers, but I think they look more like the flowers of Japanese pieris (*Pieris japonica*).

After the trees have flowered, seedpods begin to form and ripen. They look just about as showy as the flowers. By the time the seedpods have dried to bright tan, the foliage begins to change to various flaming hues — one of the best fall color displays around. The seedpods hang onto the tree during winter, adding quiet interest along with the rough bark.

For a startling floral show plus midsummer shade, plant a golden-rain tree (*Koelreuteria paniculata*). The dark green canopy of deeply cut compound leaves becomes studded with loose clusters of small, golden yellow pea-

(continued on page 142)

EASY-CARE SUMMER GARDEN

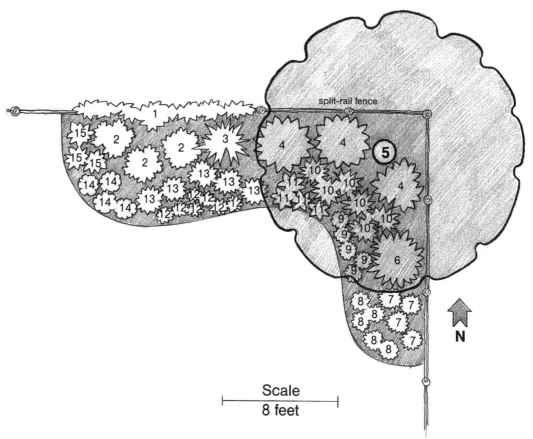

split-rail fence

N

Scale
8 feet

Plot plan for an easy-care garden. 1. *Clematis × jackmanii* (Jackman clematis) **2.** *Potentilla fruticosa* 'Goldfinger' ('Goldfinger' bush cinquefoil) **3.** *Miscanthus sinensis* 'Zebrinus' (zebra grass) **4.** *Hydrangea serrata* 'Blue Billow' ('Blue Billow' lacecap hydrangea) **5.** *Koelreuteria paniculata* (golden-rain tree) **6.** *Rhododendron carolinianum* var. *album* (white-flowered Carolina rhododendron) **7.** *Platycodon grandiflorus* var. *mariesii* (balloon flower)

8. *Hemerocallis* 'Bonanza' ('Bonanza' daylily) **9.** *Carex elata* 'Bowles Golden' ('Bowles Golden' sedge) **10.** *Hemerocallis fulva* 'Europa' (daylily) **11.** *Hosta* 'Blue Cadet' ('Blue Cadet' hosta) **12.** *Prunella × webbiana* 'Purple Loveliness' ('Purple Loveliness' self-heal) **13.** *Berberis thunbergii* 'Crimson Pygmy' ('Crimson Pygmy' purple barberry) **14.** *Coreopsis* 'Moonbeam' ('Moonbeam' coreopsis) **15.** *Asclepias tuberosa* (butterfly weed)

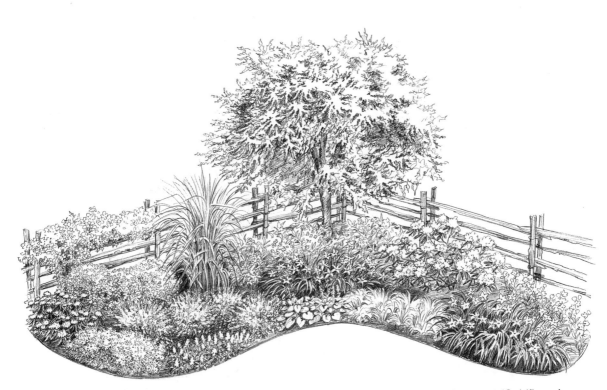

An easy-care garden. This mixed border, designed for maximum show in summer, blooms in a vivid combination of purple, blue, yellow, and orange—a color scheme that won't wither in summer's strong sunlight. The golden-rain tree's shower of bright yellow flowers is joined by two long-blooming shrubs and a vine: lacy blue hydrangeas, 'Goldfinger' cinquefoil, and purple-flowered clematis. The plum-colored leaves of 'Crimson Pygmy' barberry, chartreuse blades of 'Bowles Golden' sedge, and gold-banded swords of zebra grass add foliage interest to an assortment of long-blooming perennials.

flowers for about two weeks. Green bladder-like pods follow the flowers, and these turn reddish brown by the end of summer, creating an interesting contrast to the foliage.

But beware: Thousands of small black seeds fill those seedpods and can cause a tree seedling weed problem. Don't use this tree as a shade tree for a manicured garden or you'll be hand-pulling weedlings all spring. Instead, plant golden-rain tree in the lawn, where you can simply mow the seedlings as they sprout.

Large enough to cast appreciable shade, this round-headed tree stays fairly small as far as shade trees are concerned. Finding favor as lawn or patio trees in the Midwest because they tolerate drought, golden-rain trees ought to be more widely planted, for they certainly liven up the midsummer landscape. The cultivar 'September' blooms later than the species, usually from late August into September.

Amur maackia (*Maackia amurensis*) resembles the golden-rain tree, with deeply dissected, dark green leaves and creamy white flowers in midsummer. Flowers are borne in 8-inch-long racemes rather than the extra-large, airy panicles of the golden-rain tree, but the Amur maackia blooms in such profusion that it's a welcome sight nevertheless. Hardy to Zone 3, this small shade tree has ornamental shiny bark and is recommended for northern sites where more showy trees won't grow.

The stewartias are probably the most elegant of the summer-flowering trees. Graceful and pristine, Japanese stewartia (*Stewartia pseudocamellia*) is the most readily available species of this clan. Its 2-inch-wide, creamy white flowers with tufted centers of yellow stamens resemble small camellia blooms. The flowers don't open all at once but appear from knobby buds resembling large pearls progressively over a long period from July into August. *S. monadelpha* has white flowers with violet anthers, and the shrubby *S. ovata* has orange anthers; otherwise, the flowers are similar to those of Japanese stewartia.

The stewartias are four-season trees of special note for their off-season flowers, richly colored fall foliage, and beautiful patchwork bark. (See "Plants with Ornamental Bark" on page 38.) However, not just any site will suit a stewartia, which needs partial shade and rich, moist, humusy soil.

The Late-Summer Canopy

As summer nears its end, the leafy canopy overhead becomes a tired green. At this time of year, we're even more grateful for the few trees that offer a showy display. The premier late-summer tree is the crape myrtle (*Lagerstroemia indica*). Crape myrtle is, according to nurseryman Jim Cross, "the prettiest tree God ever created!" And I agree. Blooming for six weeks in late summer, this Indian import flourishes in southern gardens.

Crape myrtle is another southern plant that my husband, Mark, dreams of. And to his delight, breeding work at the USDA has brought us 20 new hybrid cultivars that are cold-hardy in our climate, Zone 7. We planted one of the new hybrids—an intermediate-sized cultivar named 'Osage'—beside the gate leading into our side garden. Mark lets out a sigh of relief when new leaves finally appear in mid-May, reassuring him that the late-leafing plant made it through the winter. And what a joyful sight it is when the pretty pink blooms open in August and September.

These new cultivars, introduced mostly during the 1980s, are hybrids of *L. indica* and *L. fauriei*, a tree native to Japan, and they've made the older cultivars practically obsolete. The breeders, led by the late Dr. Donald R. Egolf, set out to develop new cultivars resistant to powdery mildew, a fungal disease that often encrusts flowers and foliage. But they achieved much more: brilliant flowers in unheard-of colors, magnificent mottled bark, a longer flowering period, and improved cold-hardiness.

One or more of these wonderful trees belongs in every garden in Zone 7 and south, since no other tree displays such gorgeous color so late in the year. The clusters of pink, peach, red, lavender, purple, or white flowers rival spring-blooming trees with their abundance and brilliance. Each flower is crinkled like crepe paper, with a tuft of yellow stamens in the center. The flowers form large bunches at the branch tips of new growth. Several flushes of bloom prolong the flowering, and you can encourage rebloom by pruning off flower clusters as they fade.

You can enjoy crape myrtles even if you live in the colder parts of Zone 7. North of Baltimore, winter's cold often kills crape myrtle stems to the ground. The new hybrids are root-hardy throughout Zone 7 and into Zone 6. Though winter often kills the top growth, new stems shoot up in early summer to bear their late-season flowers, which form on the new wood anyway. In these zones, simply cut the dead stems to the ground each spring. You'll have to forfeit the beautiful bark, however, since it develops only on three- to four-year-old trunks.

One other small tree or large shrub for late-season color makes my list—the chaste tree (*Vitex agnus-castus*). Like crape myrtle, it may be killed back by a hard winter in Zone 6 and the coldest parts of Zone 7, where it attains only shrublike proportions. Where cold doesn't nip it back, chaste tree can grow into a fairly sizable tree, reaching 10 feet in the Deep South and 25 feet in the low deserts.

This heat-loving plant is a winner for its deeply cut, fine-textured leaves and fragrant, lilac-blue flowers, which appear in long, loose spikes at all the stem tips. The foliage is dark green on top and gray on the undersides. It's also aromatic, so I always get the feeling that chaste tree belongs in an herb garden.

The last of the ornamental trees to flower in the North is the Japanese pagodatree (*Sophora*

japonica), sometimes called the scholartree. It blooms in August, frosting its dark green foliage with large panicles of creamy white, pealike flowers. This large, open tree eventually reaches 50 or more feet tall.

Japanese pagodatrees grown from seed may not flower until they reach ten or more years old and are quite variable in form and growth rate. I suggest you look for the cultivar 'Regent', noted for its early bloom, rapid growth, and fine rounded to vase-shaped form. The Japanese pagodatree is a good street tree because it tolerates drought and the stresses of urban life.

Summer-Blooming Shrubs for Eye-Level Flowers

Include summer-blooming shrubs in the mixed borders and foundation plantings in your landscape, and you can keep the excitement of spring all summer. I like using flowering shrubs for summer color because compared to flowering annuals and perennials, they require very little care. Though most yards turn all-green in summer, there's a large selection of summer-blooming shrubs to choose from, as you can see from the list on page 286. In small gardens, be sure the summer bloomers you include offer year-round appeal, since some look lackluster the rest of the year.

Early-Summer Shrubs

You can enjoy spring in summer by planting late-blooming azaleas—cultivars that produce their profusion of flowers a month later than the usual types. Several groups of hybrid evergreen azaleas bloom in June in the Northeast, earlier in the South, making perfect companions beneath the spreading boughs of Kousa dogwood (*Cornus kousa*) or Japanese snowbell (*Styrax japonicus*).

WONDERFUL NEW CRAPE MYRTLES

These recently released crape myrtle cultivars are the stuff gardeners dream of. Superior four-season plants, they offer profuse late-summer flowers, mildew-resistant foliage, spectacular mottled trunk bark, and great fall color: You couldn't ask for more. They are top-hardy through Zones 7–9, root-hardy in Zone 6.

Semidwarf (5-12 feet tall)

Cultivar: 'Acoma'
Flowers: pure white, late June to September
Bark: silvery light gray
Shape: dense mound
Fall color: dark red-purple

Cultivar: 'Caddo'
Flowers: bright pink, mid-July to September
Bark: light cinnamon brown
Shape: mounding with horizontal branches
Fall color: orange-red

Cultivar: 'Hopi' (the most cold-hardy)
Flowers: clear light pink, late June to late September
Bark: gray-brown
Shape: dense globose shrub
Fall color: bright orange-red

Cultivar: 'Pecos'
Flowers: clear medium pink, early July to September
Bark: peeling dark brown
Shape: small, rounded multitrunked tree
Fall color: maroon

Cultivar: 'Tonto'
Flowers: dark fuschia, mid-July to September
Bark: cream to taupe
Shape: dense, upright
Fall color: bright red to maroon

Cultivar: 'Zuni'
Flowers: medium lavender, mid-July to September
Bark: light brown-gray
Shape: dense, multitrunked large shrub
Fall color: orange-red to dark red

Intermediate (12-20 feet tall)

Cultivar: 'Apalachee'
Flowers: light lavender, mid-July to mid-September
Bark: cinnamon to chestnut brown
Shape: upright and columnar
Fall color: orange-russet

Cultivar: 'Comanche'
Flowers: dark coral-pink, late July to mid-September
Bark: light sandalwood
Shape: dense, rounded large shrub
Fall color: purple-red

Cultivar: 'Lipan'
Flowers: medium lavender, mid-July to mid-September
Bark: near white to beige
Shape: multitrunked, upright large shrub
Fall color: orange-russet

The Satsuki and Macrantha hybrids grow about 2 to 2½ feet tall, forming low mounds blanketed by huge flowers in early summer. Flowers are usually white, pink, salmon, or coral, with streaks or flecks of contrasting colors darting through the petals. They make excellent low-maintenance plants for a foundation planting or the front of a mixed border because they stay low and shapely without pruning.

Cultivar: 'Osage'
Flowers: clear light pink, July to late September
Bark: chestnut brown
Shape: open-branched large shrub with semi-pendulous arched shape
Fall color: red

Cultivar: 'Sioux'
Flowers: intense dark pink, late July to late September
Bark: medium gray-brown
Shape: narrow, upright, with dense crown
Fall color: red-purple

Cultivar: 'Tuscarora'
Flowers: dark coral-pink, early July through September
Bark: mottled light brown
Shape: fast-growing, narrow, upright
Fall color: orange-red

Cultivar: 'Yuma'
Flowers: bicolored lavender, early July to late September
Bark: silvery gray
Shape: multitrunked with dense, irregular arching crown
Fall color: yellow-orange

Tree-Type (20-35 feet tall)

Cultivar: 'Biloxi'
Flowers: pale pink, early July to September
Bark: gray brown and dark brown
Shape: multitrunked, vase-shaped
Fall color: orange-red to dark red

Cultivar: 'Choctaw'
Flowers: clear bright pink, July through September

Bark: light to dark cinnamon brown
Shape: picturesque, multitrunked
Fall color: yellow, maroon, and bronze

Cultivar: 'Miami'
Flowers: dark coral-pink, early July to September
Bark: dark chestnut brown
Shape: multitrunked, dense oval crown
Fall color: orange to dark red-orange

Cultivar: 'Muskogee'
Flowers: prolific, light lavender, late July through September
Bark: light gray-brown
Shape: multitrunked with large, broad crown
Fall color: red

Cultivar: 'Natchez'
Flowers: pure white, late June through September
Bark: exfoliating, mottled dark cinnamon brown
Shape: sinuous trunks
Fall color: orange and red

Cultivar: 'Tuskegee'
Flowers: dark pink to red, early July to September
Bark: mottled light gray-tan
Shape: multitrunked, horizontal branches
Fall color: orange-red

Cultivar: 'Wichita'
Flowers: light magenta to lavender, early July to October
Bark: mottled dark brown
Shape: multitrunked, upright with open crown
Fall color: russet to mahogany

The Robin Hill hybrid azaleas display huge June-blooming flowers in shades of pink, rose, and white. They form low, mounded plants like the Satsukis. These American-bred hybrids, developed by Robert Gartrell in New Jersey, are more cold-hardy and heat-tolerant than the Japanese cultivars, so they do well in New England.

The North Tisbury hybrids, bred by Polly Hill of Martha's Vineyard, hug the ground, so they're at their best cascading over a rock wall or tumbling down a bank. I have several planted on the wall in front of my weeping Kousa dogwood; they bloom gloriously together in mid-June.

Several 'Sir Robert' Robin Hill azaleas nestle at the feet of a group of tall Japanese pieris (*Pieris japonica*) in the mixed border along my driveway. After the razzle-dazzle succession of spring bloom, these azaleas unexpectedly light up the area with their milky, pastel pink flowers. (See page 99 for more details on these azaleas.)

I've strategically placed several mountain laurels (*Kalmia latifolia*) with the late azaleas along my driveway and in the woodland garden at the side of my property. I've sited them where their fine evergreen foliage provides winter comfort and privacy, and their early-summer flowers can be seen to advantage.

One of the best broadleaved evergreens for four-season gardens, the native mountain laurel adorns woodlands from Louisiana to Maine, preferring moist, acid, humusy soil. Here on the North Shore of Long Island, mountain laurels fill the understory of the native oak woods with their gnarled limbs, pointed evergreen leaves, and waves of pale pink flowers.

Mountain laurel flowers are curious-looking things, especially in bud. Often darker pink than the open flowers, the crown-shaped buds are quite eye-catching. Each bud opens into a cup-shaped bloom constructed from ten fused petals with little pockets that hold the tips of the anthers. Several dozen of these dime-sized flowers group together to form a dome-shaped cluster. When in full bloom, dozens of flower clusters adorn the glossy foliage.

Wild mountain laurel flowers vary from pale pink to white, but breeders have recently brought us about 50 cultivars with intensified flower colors. Some, like 'Ostbo Red', have cherry red buds that open white or bright

pink. Others, like 'Yankee Doodle', have banded colors, and still others are pure pink or white. Plant heights range from 5 to 12 feet tall, except for the dwarf selections, which only reach 3 or 4 feet.

The new cultivars are more compact than the rangy species, which reaches almost tree-like proportions with age, so they're a better fit for today's gardens. But the cultivars are also at home in naturalistic settings, such as woodland or shade gardens, where their four-season beauty is unsurpassed. Though it tolerates fairly deep shade, mountain laurel blooms best with half a day of full sun. As with most broadleaved evergreens, morning sun is preferred to the stronger rays of afternoon.

For me, the first rose of the year signals the beginning of summer, clearly marking the end of spring and the beginning of summer's heat. One of the first four-season shrub roses to bloom is the rugosa or beach rose (*Rosa rugosa*), one of my favorites. The foliage is interesting—dark green with deep veins that give the leaves a crinkled look, as if they had been first folded into pleats, then sprung loose and left wrinkled and unironed.

The rugosa rose has rosy pink, 3-inch-wide flowers that are single with prominent yellow stamens in their centers. There are many available cultivars with single, semi-double, and double blooms that vary from white and pale pink to purplish pink. Some have a delicate fragrance. Flowering is most profuse in early summer, but sporadic blooms continue through summer. By fall, the large, glossy red rose hips are very showy, often accompanied by a scattering of flowers.

This Asian species has naturalized along many of the sandy beachfronts in the northeastern states. I've planted three rugged rugosa roses along the street at the front of our property, where the extra heat and poor soil don't faze them. I underplanted the roses with ground-

Mountain laurel and Kousa dogwood. The plants in this combination create an intense burst of easy-care, early-summer color. Kousa dogwood (*Cornus kousa*) is underplanted with mountain laurel (*Kalmia latifolia*) and late-blooming 'Sir Robert' azaleas. Ferns, hostas, and the shade-loving groundcover 'White Nancy' spotted deadnettle (*Lamium maculatum* 'White Nancy') add color and texture at ground level.

covers of catmint (*Nepeta* × *faassenii*) and snow-in-summer (*Cerastium tomentosum*), both perennials with complementary gray foliage. The groundcovers helped me solve an erosion problem, since the mulch I had covered the area with previously kept washing down the slope into the street.

Much more fragile-looking than the sturdy rugosa rose, Virginia rose (*R. virginiana*) is the epitome of a wild rose: fragrant and delicate in bloom and graceful in form. And we get vivid fall color, showy hips, and colorful twigs thrown into the bargain. Native from Newfoundland to Alabama, Virginia rose looks best planted in a naturalistic landscape where it doesn't have to compete with big, bold hybrids.

Another native shrub that deserves more attention is the Virginia sweetspire (*Itea virginica*), native from New Jersey to Alabama. In 1988, 'Henry's Garnet', a sweetspire cultivar with especially long-lasting, rich red fall color and large cascading flower spikes, was honored with a Gold Medal from the Pennsylvania Horticultural Society. Its spires of sweet-smelling white flowers open up in late June. The shrub grows well in wet soil, but also adapts to normal garden conditions in partial shade to full sun.

Midsummer Shrubs

Among the jewels of native American plants are a collection of summer-blooming deciduous azaleas—as unlike the hybrid evergreen azaleas as apples and oranges. (See "Native American Azaleas for Months of Bloom" on page 150.) These exquisite shrubs can redeem the summer garden with their profusion of graceful, honeysuckle-like flowers. Though they tolerate full sun to light shade, full sun may hasten the demise of the flowers. Choose a site lightly dappled with shade if possible, especially in hotter regions. Like other azaleas and rhododendrons, deciduous azaleas need a moist but well-drained, humusy, acid soil.

Beginning to flower in June, with various species opening throughout July and into August, these summer bloomers continue the performance started by the spring-blooming native azaleas. The petals of most of these species fuse into a tube about an inch and a half long, which flares out into a 2-inch-wide, five-pointed star. From the center of the star, the pistil and five long, curving stamens extend out past the petals.

The best selections of these shrubs release an intoxicating fragrance so intense it can perfume your entire yard, inspiring the common name "wild honeysuckle" in some parts of the country. Bob Carlson of Carlson's Gardens recommends planting pinxterbloom azalea (*Rhododendron periclymenoides*, formerly *R. nudiflorum*), roseshell azalea (*R. prinophyllum*, formerly *R. roseum*), coast azalea (*R. atlanticum*), sweet azalea (*R. arborescens*), swamp azalea (*R. viscosum*), and cultivars of *R. prunifolium* × *R. arborescens* for a sequence of fragrant shrubs from midspring through midsummer.

While white or blush pink flowers characterize most of these early- and mid-summer-blooming species, two species of note, the Cumberland azalea (*R. bakeri*) and the plumleaf azalea (*R. prunifolium*), create a fireworks display of orange-red to blood red and sometimes gold or peach flowers in mid- to late summer. The Cumberland azalea blooms here in early July, while the plumleaf azalea waits until the sultry days of late summer—July into August—before putting on its month-long display of heat-defying flowers. Unfortunately, neither species is fragrant.

Hybrids between these two hot-colored species and either the heavily scented sweet azalea or swamp azalea have brought us some stunning cultivars. (See "Native American Azaleas for Months of Bloom" on page 150.) These cultivars retain the old-fashioned qualities of sweetness and simplicity, but with a difference: They have more intense shades of pink, coral, and gold *and* a heady perfume.

Since they perform best in humus-rich, acid soil with some shade, these native beauties find the edge of a woodland garden or a shady mixed border an ideal home. But don't ask them to keep company with more voluptuous plants in a formal landscape where their delicate beauty might be overshadowed by more overblown plants.

The latest-blooming evergreen shrub in these parts is the native rosebay rhododendron (*R. maximum*), a huge, very cold-hardy species that flowers here in July. The rosebay is useful in the garden primarily for its huge proportions and fast growth—leaves can reach 8 inches long and the shrub gets to be 25 feet tall and wide. Unfortunately, the trusses of small flowers, which are rose, pale pink, or white, bloom so late that the new growth partially hides them, diminishing their impact.

Several mature rosebay specimens, which I swear are practically the size of their house, dominate the landscape at the home of my friends John and Claudia Scholtz. The shrubs fill up the view from the dining room windows, looking like massive mountains of greenery. A path winds in between them, creating a delightful feeling of seclusion. The scale of the shrubs contrasts effectively with the Scholtzes' farmhouse and cottage garden but is too large for most landscapes.

Recent hybridization by plantsman David Leach has brought gardeners a wealth of late-blooming rhododendrons with the rosebay as part of their ancestry. These hybrids grow quite tall but stay smaller than the rosebay—thank goodness—and have brilliant-colored flowers in trusses that stand above the foliage.

'Summer Glow' offers incandescent pink flowers that open from red buds. Flowers of 'Summer Snow' are pure white, in dome-shaped trusses that stand out well above the foliage. 'Summer Summit' has pink flower buds, opening to white flowers blotched with pink and spotted with olive, and 'Summer Solace' bears white, trumpet-shaped blooms with chartreuse spots. And these are just a few of the many July-blooming rhododendron cultivars.

For full-sun locations in almost all parts of the country, try Bumald spirea (*Spiraea × bumalda*) for a splash of summer color. This hybrid and its cultivars make better plants for four-season landscapes than their spring-blooming cousins because they bloom after most shrubs, and they offer fall foliage color as well.

Bumald spirea forms densely twiggy mounds that fit perfectly in foundation plantings and mixed borders. In spring, lance-shaped toothed leaves open pinkish to reddish, maturing to a fine-textured dark bluish green, and changing to red or purple in fall. The midsummer flowers form lacy, rosy red caps all over the shrub. 'Anthony Waterer' grows only 2 feet tall and wide, and 'Froebelii' tops out at a little more than 3 feet. *Spiraea albiflora* looks similar but grows larger and has white flowers. Of special note are the cultivars of Bumald and Japanese spirea (*S. japonica*) with colored leaves. (See "Sunny Yellow Foliage" on page 177 for a description.)

A number of long-blooming, yellow-flowering shrubs bring sunshine to the summer garden. Bush cinquefoil (*Potentilla fruticosa*) blooms heavily in midsummer and then intermittently through fall, making a pretty display of golden buttercup-like flowers against fine-textured foliage. Potentillas are tough plants that are especially useful for bringing color to troublesome sites: They endure drought, extremes of heat and cold, and alkaline or

NATIVE AMERICAN AZALEAS
FOR MONTHS OF BLOOM

In gardens that have acid, humusy soil, native azaleas flourish, their graceful flowers and intoxicating perfume carrying the garden from late spring through much of summer. If your soil isn't suitable, create a raised bed filled with shredded bark and peat moss for your azaleas. Native azaleas need some direct sun to flower profusely, but full sun fades the flowers. All-day high overhead shade or morning sun and afternoon shade are ideal.

Midspring

Name: *Rhododendron vaseyi* (pinkshell azalea)
Description: Profuse pink, open-faced flowers on bare branches; brilliant red to burgundy fall color; reaches 5 feet
Cultivars: Var. *album,* white flowers
Culture: Moist to wet soil; needs more shade in South; Zones 5–8

Late Spring

Name: *R. periclymenoides,* formerly *R. nudiflorum* (pinxterbloom azalea)
Description: Sweet-scented white to pale pink flowers; variable height; forms thickets
Culture: Shade-tolerant; Zones 5–8

Name: *R. prinophyllum,* formerly *R. roseum* (roseshell azalea)
Description: Intensely clove-scented, pale pink to light crimson flowers; upright to 4 to 6 feet
Cultivars: 'Marie Hoffman', true pink, very large flowers, extremely fragrant
Culture: Zones 4–8

Early Summer

Name: *R. atlanticum* (coast azalea)
Description: Highly fragrant, sugary-sweet pink to white tubular flowers; tends to form extensive thickets to 3 feet tall
Cultivars: 'Choptank River' or 'Marydel', deep pink buds open white
Culture: Tolerant of dry sites, needs more sun than most; Zones 5–9

Name: *R. calendulaceum* (flame azalea)
Description: Very showy, scentless yellow, gold, or orange flowers with emerging foliage; little color change in autumn; reaches 10 feet
Cultivars: 'Carlson's Coral Flameboyant', early-blooming, bright coral flowers
Culture: Zones 5–8

Name: *R. serrulatum* (hammock-sweet azalea)
Description: Similar to *R. viscosum,* but better in the South
Culture: Zones 7–9

Midsummer

Name: *R. arborescens* (sweet azalea)
Description: Highly fragrant, spicy-sweet white tubular flowers, often with red pistils and stamens, slightly earlier than *R. viscosum;* red fall color; reaches 10 to 15 feet
Cultivars of *R. arborescens* hybrids: 'Carlson's Pink Postscript', highly fragrant, rich pink flowers; many other fragrant cultivars
Culture: Moist woods or stream banks, but less tolerant of wet soil than *R. viscosum;* Zones 5–9

Name: *R. bakeri* (Cumberland azalea)
Description: Showy clusters of red, orange-red, or yellow flowers against mature foliage;

little fall color; variable height 4 to 8 feet with horizontal branches

Cultivars: July series reaches 3 to 4 feet tall: 'July Jester' (orange to scarlet with lighter blotch), 'July Jewel' (orange to scarlet), 'July Jingle' (rich pink), 'July Joy' (fragrant, clear pink with orange splotch), 'July Jubilation' (pale orange)

Culture: Very shade-tolerant; afternoon shade reduces flower fading; Zones 5–8

Name: R. viscosum (swamp azalea)

Description: Highly fragrant, white to pink-flushed tubular flowers slightly later than R. arborescens; dull orange fall color; reaches 8 feet

Cultivars: 'Betty Cummins' (bright pink), 'Delaware Blue' (pure white with blue-green leaves)

Cultivars of R. viscosum hybrids: 'Golden Showers' (peach-yellow, mild vanilla scent); 'Iridiscent' (silvery pink, spicy scent); 'Lemon Drop' (peach buds open yellow, lemon-scented); 'Parade' (dark pink, sweet scent); 'Pink Rocket' (red buds open pink, sweet scent); 'Pink and Sweet' (pink, spicy scent, good fall color), 'Ribbon Candy' (pink with white stripes, spicy scent, good fall color)

Culture: Moist soil; plant in hummocks in swampy sites; may form thickets and need pruning; Zones 4–8

Late Summer

Name: R. prunifolium (plumleaf azalea)

Description: Scentless bright red to orange-red or apricot tubular flowers for a month; reaches 6 to 8 feet; little fall color

Cultivars of R. prunifolium hybrids: 'Bonfire' (orange-red, fragrant); 'Garden Party' (pink with peach flare, fragrant)

Culture: Protect from afternoon sun; Zones 5–8

salty soil. 'White Gold' has soft yellow flowers; 'Katherine Dykes' has bright yellow blooms; and 'Abbotswood' bears white flowers.

Although generally not as cold-hardy as cinquefoil, St.-John's-worts (*Hypericum* spp.) tolerate heat and poor soil, blooming with abandon for several weeks in midsummer. The brilliant yellow flowers, which may be as large as silver dollars, display frilly golden yellow stamens. The semievergreen, blue-green leaves are arranged opposite each other on cinnamon brown stems, creating a pretty pattern that lingers into autumn and winter. Midwesterners whose soil and climate preclude the acid-loving azaleas and rhododendrons can rely on cinquefoil and St.-John's-wort for a blast of summer color if they can give these plants a sunny site.

Another spectacular native American shrub that can provide a lot of fanfare in either a sunny or shady spot is bottlebrush buckeye (*Aesculus parviflora*). It glows against a shaded background when in full bloom. The latest-blooming native buckeye covers itself with tall spires of delicate white flowers for several weeks in midsummer. The spreading, suckering shrub forms tiers of branches decorated with bold-textured leaves and topped with a fountain of frothy white flowers. The only drawback to this outstanding plant is its need for plenty of space.

My friend Keith Barnes, a collector of the odd and curious, harbors a fascination for a weird but lovable summer tree or shrub, the smoketree (*Cotinus coggygria*). Named for its puffy, pinkish gray fruiting panicles that rise above the tall shrublike clouds of smoke, a smoketree creates an unusual spectacle in summer.

The smoky panicles that form on female plants remain showy from June or early July through August. Plants offered for sale in nurseries are female clones, so you needn't worry about your smoketree failing to smoke. Fall color is excellent. The purple-leaved form, *C. coggygria* f. *purpureus,* and highly colored cultivars such as 'Royal Purple' are more commonly grown than the species with its bluish green leaves. (See "Wine-Dark Foliage" on page 173.)

Reminiscing about Keith and his smoketree reminds me of the trip to Atlantic City he and I took with some other plant-loving friends one Saturday in July many years ago. The little fenced yards of the quaint beach houses came alive with the colossal pink and blue sterile-flowered globes of hortensia hydrangea bushes (*Hydrangea macrophylla* var. *macrophylla,* also called bigleaf hydrangea).

These gaudy plants displayed just the right flamboyant color and voluptuous nature to match the gingerbread cottages and burn through the hazy seashore light. I usually prefer the lacecap version of these hydrangeas, with their flat lacy flower clusters, to these artificial-looking cultivars, but in certain settings their flamboyance fills the bill.

The wild version of the hortensia or florist's hydrangea (*H. macrophylla* var. *normalis*) hails from Japan and bears flat clusters of fertile flowers surrounded by a ring of sterile flowers with showy bracts. These form lacy clusters of blue flowers that paint horizontal patterns atop the branches.

Other cultivated hydrangeas have globose flowers of such large size and whiteness they're called hills-of-snow (*H. arborescens* 'Grandiflora'). This cultivar is a selected form of an American lacecap species rarely seen in cultivation. The newer cultivar 'Annabelle' displays even larger globes—up to 8 inches across—than 'Grandiflora'. Since hills-of-snow (unlike the hortensia) blooms each year on new growth, you can cut it to the ground each spring to maintain a compact size and shape without sacrificing bloom.

Hydrangea flower types. Hydrangeas produce flamboyant white, blue, or pink globes or panicles in mid- or late summer. Use the snowball types as a focal point in a cottage garden, where they contrast boldly with daintier flowers. The lacecap types and the stately oakleaf hydrangea make a more subtle statement that's perfect in a shade garden.

I always find it a bit confusing that the species name *arborescens* was given to hills-of-snow, which reaches only 3 or 4 feet tall, and not to the truly treelike panicle hydrangea (*H. paniculata*). This hydrangea tops out at about 20 or more feet, making a multiple-trunked tall shrub or small tree, though it is often trained to a single trunk. Most commonly grown is the cultivar 'Grandiflora', nicknamed the pee-gee hydrangea, which blooms in July. Other cultivars include 'Praecox', which blooms about three weeks earlier than 'Grandiflora', and 'Tardiva', which blooms in August and September.

All of these hydrangeas have coarse-textured foliage and big bold flowers that remain eye-catching even as they age. Flower arrangers covet hydrangeas for dried flower arrangements because the bracts that make up the snowballs hold tight to the stems, aging to papery panicles in shades of old rose and tan by summer's end. If you resist cutting them, these dried flowerheads will remain on the branches, often lasting through winter and providing an extended season of interest.

All hydrangeas grow well in full sun or partial shade, as long as the soil is rich and moist. The lacecaps look charming in a shade garden. But the full-blown snowball types work better if used sparingly as a focal point or in a cottage-type garden where their ostentatious flowers add boldness and texture to the tumult of other blooms. Try using a group of lacecap hydrangeas under a large, summer-blooming tree, such as golden-rain tree (*Koelreuteria paniculata*), and underplant them with drifts of daylilies or other midsummer perennials.

Although the hydrangeas mentioned above make a midsummer statement of flowers and a late-summer and fall show of dried bouquets, they don't have much to say for themselves the rest of the year. One hydrangea—I've saved the best for last—is eye-catching every season of the year, even in winter. The oakleaf hydrangea (*Hydrangea quercifolia*), native to the Deep South, is named for its phenomenal foot-long, lobed leaves, which emerge covered with silky hairs in late spring, mature to rich green, and change to brilliant wine tones in autumn. The bark peels off in long cinnamon curls.

Conical heads of both sterile and fertile white flowers tip the branches in midsummer, lasting a month or so before becoming chartreuse. The flowerheads take on an attractive antique rose color in fall and eventually become wrapping-paper brown in winter. The chartreuse stage is skipped in full-sun locations, where the florets age from white to brighter shades of raspberry and rose.

Several cultivars with all-sterile florets, such as 'Snow Queen', are available. These cultivars have larger, snow white cones that are so heavy they can weigh the branches toward the ground. All-sterile cultivars are definitely for gardeners who are into big and beautiful, since the species is a large-scale beauty in its own right.

Though it will grow in full sun, I appreciate oakleaf hydrangea for its ability to flourish and flower in shade, a challenge for most plants. I've planted several in the heavy clay soil at the back of my wooded hillside, where they are now beginning to spread via stoloniferous roots into bigger clumps. Flower buds are initiated the previous summer and may be winter-killed in the coldest part of its range (Zone 5 and northern Zone 6), but the plant's foliage looks sculptural enough to make oakleaf hydrangea desirable even without flowers.

Late-Summer Shrubs

Several late-summer bloomers display lovely flowers of elusive blue. A favorite for the misty effect of its sapphire blue blooms and gray foliage is bluebeard (*Caryopteris × clandonensis*). I see this used a lot in mixed borders, where its mounded shape and late bloom combine well with perennials like pale yellow 'Moonbeam' threadleaf coreopsis (*Coreopsis verticillata* 'Moonbeam'). Mine grows in the foreground of my ornamental grass garden, where its mounded shape contrasts well with the linear grasses. I treat it like a perennial, cutting it back almost to the ground each year in late winter to keep it compact and floriferous.

My friend Donna Bickley reports from her Maryland garden that bumblebees cover her blooming bluebeard. "You can hear the bush as well as see it!" she claims. Donna grows the cultivar 'Blue Mist', which has powder blue flowers. There are darker ones as well: 'Longwood Blue' and 'Dark Knight', which is reportedly navy blue. Bluebeard can be weedy, since many self-sown seedlings come up all over the garden, but they're easy to pull.

While bees buzz all over bluebeard, Donna attests that butterflies literally cover her butterfly bush (*Buddleia davidii*). This dependable cottage-garden plant attracts moths and butterflies like a magnet. While the species is gangly, with an open, leggy shape, there are many improved cultivars. The cultivars produce more substantial flower spikes in an assortment of colors, and they stay more compact, making much better garden additions.

I've seen innovative designers include butterfly bushes in mixed borders, perennial borders, and even in wildflower meadows. They look great with ornamental grasses, as the colorful flowers wave on their long, flexible stems with the same nonchalant grace as the grasses' plumes.

Donna planted a 'Nanho Blue' butterfly bush in her fragrance garden behind a teak bench. She likes this cultivar for its compact size and clear blue color. Under the shrub she grows gold-leaved marjoram (*Origanum vulgare* 'Aureum'), and behind it, in back of the bench, two renegade wild mulleins (*Verbascum* spp.), which she enjoys for the majesty of their size and the prettiness of their sparse but striking blooms.

Next to the butterfly bush, Donna grows another fragrant August bloomer: summersweet (*Clethra alnifolia*). This native shrub, sometimes called sweet pepperbush after its peppercorn-like fruiting capsules, has pretty spires of white blooms, which complement the blue and contrast with the yellow of her bench garden. I've planted the pink-flowered cultivar of summersweet (*C. alnifolia* 'Rosea') in a semishaded spot of moist soil in my native plant garden. There its month-long blooms are among the last flowers of the growing season, and they perfume the garden with their spicy-sweet scent.

If it's late pink color you want, you can't go wrong with glossy abelia (*Abelia* × *grandiflora*). This fine-textured shrub forms a loose globe of glossy dark green leaves and begins blooming in August, continuing through fall. The small, bell-shaped, pink-tinged white flowers rest in a dark pink calyx. The calyx persists after the individual flowers drop, so the overall floral effect is a pink-and-white mist.

Glossy abelia leaves are dark green with a highly polished surface, but they take on a gleaming dark purplish bronze hue in cold weather. The purplish foliage enhances the pink of the flowers. In my climate, most of the outer leaves remain on the shrub through winter, while the inner foliage drops. This semi-evergreen nature means that the plant doesn't have enough substance to perform the role of a true evergreen. For example, I had to transplant mine from the foundation planting because they looked too flimsy in January.

Fine Foliage

Although summer's blooms are sought-after, once any plant has finished flowering—usually in a fleeting two weeks out of the year's 52—its chief attraction is its leaves. For longer-lasting color excitement, I like to include a few trees, shrubs, perennials, and groundcovers with colorful or variegated leaves.

Colorful leaves—blue-green, purple-bronze, and golden yellow ones—can sustain your garden for months, while blooms come

(continued on page 171)

Summer

Fill summer's sultry days with a serene display of flowers and foliage when you plan a mixed border of easy-care flowering shrubs and perennials. Designed to unfold in a continual sequence of bloom, the garden never tires.

This late-summer scene at the New York Botanic Garden features an effective mix of shrubs and perennials. The purple smoketree and barberries really set off the astilbes, garden phlox, Russian sage, bee balm, and inula (*Inula helenium*). Garden design: Lynden B. Miller.

155

Late summer brings another striking picture in Angela Garguila's garden, which was designed for year-round beauty. Plants include a crabapple (*Malus* cv.), hortensia hydrangea (*H. macrophylla*), 'Autumn Joy' sedum, 'Montgomery' blue spruce, maiden grass (*Miscanthus sinensis* 'Gracillimus'), and Chinese astilbe (*Astilbe chinensis* var. *pumila*). Garden design: Conni Cross.

▲ Unlike most flower gardens, which seem to have reached an exhausted finale by late summer, this mixed border overflows with wonderful flowers and foliage. Shrubs, including oakleaf hydrangea (*H. quercifolia*), butterfly bush (*Buddleia davidii*), and 'Royal Purple' smokebush (*Cotinus coggygria* 'Royal Purple'), form a framework to set off the grasses and perennials. Garden design: Lynden B. Miller.

▶ Thriving in poor soil and hot sun, this orange-flowered cultivar of common yarrow (*Achillea millefolium* 'Fire King') will bloom all summer if you keep removing the faded flowers.

▲ Butterfly bush (*Buddleia davidii*) is an old-fashioned shrub that's now available in compact cultivars with purple, lavender, pink, or white flowers. It blooms from late summer into fall. Shown bordering the walk is catmint (*Nepeta × faassenii*), which blooms from spring through fall, with Queen-Anne's-lace, a charming roadside weed. All attract flocks of butterflies.

◄ Grown primarily for its foliage, redleaf rose (*Rosa glauca*) is a plant for all seasons. Late spring through early summer brings a flush of abundant but tiny bright pink flowers set against purple foliage. Leaves mature to a romantic, dusky blue-gray in summer. Autumn brings a wonderful display of cranberry-like fruits, which persist on the thorny, bare stems through winter.

A summer garden that relies on foliage requires little care but can look as exciting as any flower garden. Here, maiden grass (*Miscanthus sinensis* 'Gracillimus') arches in front of a 'Royal Purple' smokebush (*Cotinus coggygria* 'Royal Purple') for an electrifying contrast of foliage form and color.

Vines are one of the secrets of successful four-season gardeners because they bring color and form to narrow spaces. Here, Jackman clematis (*Clematis × jackmanii*), one of the most vigorous clematis hybrids, decorates a fence with midsummer flowers, which will be followed in autumn by silky seedpods.

▲ Designed for ease of care, Angela Garguila's lawnless side-yard garden relies on shrubs for structure and color. Shrubs and trees include, from front to back: 'Goldmound' Bumald Spirea (*Spiraea × bumalda* 'Goldmound'), fountain leucothoe (*Leucothoe fontanesiana*), 'Hetzii' Japanese holly (*Ilex crenata* 'Hetzii'), 'Blue Pyramid' Arizona cypress (*Cupressus arizonica* 'Blue Pyramid'), and white spruce (*Picea glauca*), with 'Karagusawa' Japanese maple (*Acer palmatum* 'Karagusawa'), hills-of-snow hydrangea (*Hydrangea arborescens*), and chastetree (*Vitex agnus-castus*) behind the fence. Garden design: Conni Cross.

▶ Carolina lupine (*Thermopsis caroliniana*), a native of the southeastern states, produces tall spires of yellow flowers in early summer. Use this perennial where a dramatic vertical accent will contrast with rounder shapes.

▲ Summersweet (*Clethra alnifolia*), a native shrub, produces fragrant white flowers in mid- to late summer. Russian sage (*Perovskia atriplicifolia*) and a sterile cultivar of loosestrife (*Lythrum* 'Morden Pink') add foreground color. Garden design: Conni Cross.

◀ Disease-free and cold-hardy, rugosa rose (*Rosa rugosa*) excels all year with showy summer flowers, heavily textured dark green leaves, golden orange fall color, and gleaming red fruits that persist in winter.

▶ A mixed border of shrubs, perennials, and grasses looks stunning all year. From front to back: blue oat grass (*Helictotrichon sempervirens*), 'Autumn Joy' sedum, Stokes' aster (*Stokesia laevis*), Russian sage (*Perovskia atriplicifolia*), and oakleaf hydrangea (*Hydrangea quercifolia*). Garden design: Lynden B. Miller.

Stunning when blooming in late summer, these two tall perennials make an excellent foliage contrast when not in flower. The jagged-edged, heart-shaped leaves of *Ligularia* 'The Rocket' look all the more effective beside the ferny leaves of fall astilbe (*Astilbe taquettii* 'Superba').

◄ A study in contrasting scale and texture, this combination of early-summer perennials features bold, dark red peonies (*Paeonia lactiflora*), delicate blue flax (*Linum perenne*), and silver-leaved lamb's-ears (*Stachys byzantina*). Even after flowers fade, the foliage combination carries on to create an equally pretty picture. Garden design: Conni Cross.

▼ An outstanding native shrub, oakleaf hydrangea (*Hydrangea quercifolia*) blooms in mid- to late summer. The creamy white flowers open lime green and fade to old rose. The dramatic leaves have silky white undersides; leaves turn gorgeous shades of red in fall.

▲ Combine flowers of different shapes to make a border sizzle with excitement. Here, garden phlox (*Phlox paniculata* 'Bright Eyes'), speedwell (*Veronica longifolia* 'Blue Charm'), annual flowering tobacco (*Nicotiana alata*), and lamb's-ears (*Stachys byzantina*) bloom with 'Rosy Glow' barberry and oakleaf hydrangea.

▲ Chaste tree (*Vitex agnus-castus*) shim-
mers with lavender-blue flowers in late
summer, combining effectively with leadwort
(*Ceratostigma plumbaginoides*) and long-
blooming 'Goldsturm' black-eyed Susans
(*Rudbeckia fulgida* 'Goldsturm'). Garden
design: Conni Cross.

▶ The latest-blooming of the native
azaleas, plumleaf azalea (*Rhododendron
prunifolium*) literally glows with blooms in
hot shades of orange or scarlet in July or
August. It combines perfectly with summer's color scheme.

◀ The Kousa dogwood (*Cornus kousa*)
produces long-lasting, star-shaped white
flowers in early summer and has magnificent red fall color. Here the tree stands out
against a barn wall in a groundcover of
climbing hydrangea (*H. anomala* subsp.
petiolaris) and ferns.

◄ Silver-edged lilyturf (*Liriope muscari* 'Variegata') marks the bend of a path.

▶ Elwood false cypress (*Chamaecyparis lawsoniana* 'Elwoodii') makes a strong vertical accent in this mixed border. Its blue-green needles echo the blue Lyme grass (*Elymus arenarius* 'Glaucus'), which contrasts with the hardy geranium (*Geranium platypetalum*) and garden phlox (*Phlox paniculata* 'Bright Eyes'). In back are zebra grass (*Miscanthus sinensis* 'Zebrinus') and a variegated lacecap hydrangea. Garden design: Lynden B. Miller.

▼ This midsummer border brims with flowers. Lacecap hydrangeas (*H. macrophylla* var. *serrata*) are flanked by towering lilies. A purple-leaved Japanese maple (*Acer palmatum* 'Atropurpureum') creates background color. Garden: Wave Hill.

▲ Arranged informally in a naturalistic drift, these easy-care perennials create an abundance of midsummer color year after year and require no staking or special care. Pictured are a dwarf daylily (*Hemerocallis* 'Corky'), a compact form of gayfeather (*Liatris spicata* 'Kobold'), and a compact balloon flower (*Platycodon grandiflorus* var. *mariesii*). Garden: Wave Hill.

◄ Fabulous plants for shady spots, the hundreds of hostas available offer a wide range of foliage colors and textures. *Hosta* 'Frances Williams' is noted for both attractive foliage and flowers, featuring heavily corrugated, blue-green leaves edged with yellow-green and tall stalks of white flowers.

A summer plant combination. Two fragrant summer-blooming shrubs, butterfly bush (*Buddleia davidii*) and summersweet (*Clethra alnifolia*), perfume my friend Donna's garden in August while attracting butterflies like magnets. She planted a carpet of golden oregano (*Origanum vulgare* var. *aureus*) to add a jazzy fragrance when she walks on it toward the bench. The upright mulleins appeared on their own, making a nice contrast with the rounded shrubs.

and go. Although I try to choose summer bloomers with good flowers *and* good foliage, it sometimes makes sense to select plants for their fine foliage alone.

Blue-Green and Gray-Green Foliage

Blue-green leaves occur most often in conifers such as the well-known Colorado blue spruce (*Picea pungens* 'Glauca'), but a number of deciduous shrubs and perennials also feature blue-green foliage. In describing plants with foliage colors in the cool range, the terms blue-green and gray-green are used inconsistently and often interchangeably.

Technically, blue-green comes from a generous supply of blue pigments inside a leaf, while a white waxy skin or a powdery bloom on the leaf surface gives the leaf a gray cast. Often a white wax covers a leaf that is already on the blue side of green, giving it a rich blue-gray or steel blue color.

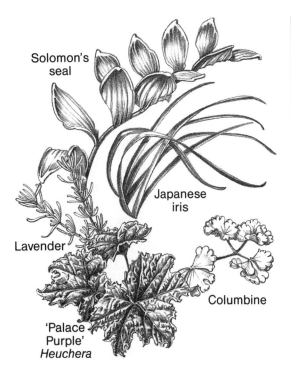

Solomon's seal

Japanese iris

Lavender

Columbine

'Palace Purple' *Heuchera*

Perennial leaves. When choosing flowering perennials, remember that the flowers will adorn your garden for only a few weeks, while you'll see the foliage for months. Choose perennials with beautiful blooms *and* textured or colorful leaves, and your garden will shine from spring through fall, no matter what's in bloom.

My favorite plants for bringing lovely blues—as well as other foliage colors—to a summer garden are hostas (*Hosta* spp.). So many cultivars of these magnificent foliage plants abound that I cringe at even trying to select a few to mention here—there are just too many enticing hostas to choose from.

The blue hostas I have in my garden are fairly common cultivars, but they're all beautiful. They include *H. sieboldiana* 'Elegans', with heavily waxed, blue leaves that mature at about the size of a shovel blade and are arranged in a symmetrical swirl, forming a 3-foot-wide mound. On a smaller scale is 'Blue Cadet',

noted for its spikes of pale lavender flowers that arise in midsummer above low clusters of heart-shaped leaves. 'Krossa Regal' is more gray-green, and its leaves stand almost upright, creating an arching vase of slightly twisted leaves about 3 feet tall. Above this leafy sculpture, stalks of lavender flowers rise as high as 5 feet.

Blue-green and gray-green foliage looks simply smashing planted near white or cool-colored flowers such as dark purple or blue Siberian iris (*Iris sibirica*) or deep mauve or pink garden phlox (*Phlox paniculata*). I like to combine blue-leaved hostas with pink- and white-flowered astilbes (*Astilbe* cultivars) in a shady garden. The flower colors of astilbe enhance the glaucous color of the hosta leaves, while their fine-textured dark green leaves play up the hostas' handsome, flat planes.

Foliage Forged of Silver

Silver and gray leaves get their color from the fine hairs that cover their surfaces. This downy coat is actually a survival technique the plant uses to shade itself and prevent leaf scorch and dehydration. As you might expect, silver- and gray-leaved plants are often adapted to hot sun, dry soil, wind, and even salty or alkaline soil.

Try silver- and gray-foliaged plants in the hotter parts of your garden. In cooler areas, amend your cherished garden loam with sand in the planting pocket where you place these drought-tolerant plants, because if their diet is too rich and moist, they are apt to rot. It pays to experiment, however, because some of these sun-lovers may surprise you with their adaptability and tolerance of partial shade as long as the soil drains sharply. Soggy soil is certainly the ruination of gray plants. Most silvery things languish during the humid summers of the South, while flourishing in the dry western states.

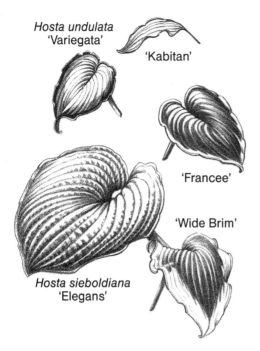

Hosta undulata 'Variegata'

'Kabitan'

'Francee'

'Wide Brim'

Hosta sieboldiana 'Elegans'

Hosta foliage types. Shade-loving hostas come in an astonishing assortment of leaf sizes, textures, and colorful patterns. Green and blue-gray hostas can tolerate more sun than chartreuse, golden, or heavily variegated types, which thrive in deep to dappled shade.

You can use silver and gray foliage with just about any other landscape color. The light-reflecting silvery grays and the duller grays or greenish grays can be compared to sterling silver and pewter: The silver creates more contrast between neighbors, while the pewter does a better job of blending and harmonizing.

Mixing silver- and gray-foliaged plants with white, blue, and purple flowers is a classic combination, because the gray gives these somewhat weak colors much stronger impact. I find that silvery leaves make pastel pink and yellow blooms look even softer, and they tone down red and magenta flowers without diminishing their vibrancy.

One of the easiest-to-grow gray-leaved perennials (and also one of my favorites) is lamb's-ears (*Stachys byzantina*), with thick felty leaves that make me want to reach out and pet them each time I pass. I like to use lamb's-ears along the front of a border where it meets the lawn. The contrast between emerald green grass and plush silver-white foliage defines the border's edge in no uncertain terms.

Another favorite of mine is silvermound artemisia (*Artemisia schmidtiana* 'Nana', also sold as 'Silver Mound'). This popular plant's fine-textured, silvery green leaves form an airy cushion that looks like sea foam when massed in front of shrubs or flowing around upright, green-leaved perennials. Used this way, silvermound artemisia tames bright floral colors that might otherwise seem garish.

Unfortunately, high heat and humidity cause the mound to flop open, a frequent occurrence in southern gardens. When this happens, cut the stems back to the ground and new growth will quickly return, or search out the taller and harder-to-find cultivar 'Powis Castle', which performs better under adverse conditions.

Silver-leaved shrubs and trees, including those such as poplar (*Populus* spp.) with leaves that are green on top but silvery beneath, add brightness and light to a landscape. When the silver leaves of a Russian olive (*Elaeagnus angustifolia*) are caught and twisted by an evening breeze or the gusts of wind preceding a summer thunderstorm, they reflect light like mirrors suspended from the branches. You can use these plants to create a silvery background or accent.

Wine-Dark Foliage

The foliage color gardeners call "purple" hardly resembles the purple of the color wheel. Nor do bronze and copper leaves closely imitate the metals used to describe them. Purple, bronze, and copper foliage are really reddish

TOP-RATED HOSTAS
FOR FOLIAGE AND FLOWERS

The craze for hosta breeding makes choosing among the 500 or so available cultivars a toss-up for most gardeners. You'll find that the following list of the top 25 hostas will help guide you through the variegations. This assortment of hostas features those that are readily available, not too expensive, and just as stunning as the high-priced new cultivars.

Dwarf (to 10 inches tall)

Name: *Hosta* 'Gold Edger'
Foliage: gold, heart-shaped
Flowers: pale lavender, midsummer
Comments: needs some sun to color up; forms neat mounds

Name: *H. sieboldii* 'Kabitan'
Foliage: lance-shaped, ruffled, light yellow with green margins
Flowers: deep purple, midsummer
Comments: excellent groundcover; needs shade

Name: *H. venusta*
Foliage: green, heart-shaped
Flowers: lilac, midsummer
Comments: excellent groundcover

Small (10-15 inches tall)

Name: *H.* 'Birchwood Parky's Gold'
Foliage: gold-green
Flowers: lavender, on tall stalks, midsummer
Comments: not sun-tolerant, but needs bright shade to color up; forms dense clumps

Name: *H.* 'Blue Cadet'
Foliage: heart-shaped, blue-green
Flowers: dark lavender, midsummer
Comments: excellent edger; forms dense clumps

Name: *H.* 'Ginko Craig'
Foliage: dark green, lance-shaped with distinct white edge
Flowers: purple, on tall stalks, late summer
Comments: shade to full sun

Name: *Hosta* 'Hadspen Blue'
Foliage: glaucous blue
Flowers: lavender, on low stalks, late summer
Comments: slug-resistant; one of the bluest

Medium (15-22 inches tall)

Name: *H.* 'August Moon'
Foliage: pale green to gold, large, puckered, round
Flowers: pale lavender to white, midsummer
Comments: deepens to gold in dappled shade

Name: *H. fortunei* 'Albo-Marginata'
Foliage: clear green, irregular white margins
Flowers: lavender
Comments: needs moist shade

Name: *H.* 'Francee'
Foliage: forest green, narrow white margins, heart-shaped
Flowers: pale lavender, midsummer
Comments: full sun to shade; margins don't burn

Name: *H. lancifolia*
Foliage: dark green, lance-shaped
Flowers: lilac-blue, late summer to fall
Comments: quickly forms thick clump; tolerates drought

Name: *H.* × *tardiana* 'Halcyon'
Foliage: spear-shaped, heavily ribbed, blue
Flowers: abundant lilac-blue, midsummer
Comments: very blue in shade

Name: *H. undulata* (*H.* 'Variegata', *H.* 'Medio-Picta')
Foliage: white with green wavy edges
Flowers: lilac, on tall stalks, midsummer
Comments: old-fashioned favorite

Large (22 inches or taller)

Name: *H. fortunei* 'Aureo-Marginata'
Foliage: medium green, rich yellow borders
Flowers: lilac, on tall stalks, midsummer
Comments: forms huge upright clump; tolerates sun if soil is moist

Name: *H.* 'Krossa Regal'
Foliage: frosty blue, slightly twisted
Flowers: orchid-lavender, on 5-foot stalks
Comments: forms 3-foot vase-shaped clump; slug-resistant

Name: *H. plantaginea* (August lily)
Foliage: large, oval, light green
Flowers: beautiful, fragrant, white, late summer
Comments: 'Honeybells' is similar, with pale lavender flowers

Name: *H. sieboldiana* 'Elegans'
Foliage: large, blue-gray, round, puckered
Flowers: white with slight lavender cast, early to mid-summer
Comments: forms huge mound; slug-resistant

Name: *H. sieboldiana* 'Frances Williams'
Foliage: blue-green, puckered, wide dark yellow borders, round
Flowers: nearly white, early to mid-summer
Comments: spectacular specimen

Name: *H.* 'Sum & Substance'
Foliage: glossy, chartreuse to gold, huge, puckered
Flowers: lavender, late summer
Comments: forms huge, upright clump; needs some sun to color up; tolerates sun if soil is moist; slug-proof

Name: *H. tokudama*
Foliage: large, cupped, blue-green, heavily puckered
Flowers: white, early to mid-summer
Comments: needs moist shade

Name: *H.* 'Wide Brim'
Foliage: blue-green with irregular, wide, creamy margins
Flowers: pale lavender, midsummer
Comments: forms huge upright stand; best in dappled shade

or purplish brown. Usually, the term "purple" refers to hues with more blue, while the reddish brown tones are called copper or bronze.

Purple foliage by whatever name can be gorgeous stuff when used correctly. These rich dark hues combine with almost any color, enriching them all and harmonizing well. I especially love wine-colored foliage plants in combination with pastel pink- or blue-flowering perennials. For a jazzier and more daring combination, try purple foliage with yellow, gold, or coal-hot orange flowers.

One of the best purple-leaved plants for four-season landscapes is 'Notcutt's Variety' purple smoketree (*Cotinus coggygria* 'Notcutt's Variety'). The leaves of purple smoketree are the translucent color of a ripe plum. Plant one where light strikes it from the side or back to light up the leaves. To keep the color intense and the size in bounds for a mixed border, some gardeners prune smoketree severely—almost to the ground—each spring to keep it about 4 feet tall. Such drastic pruning means the plant won't flower, but the wine red foliage certainly makes up for that.

Jane Owens, a landscape architect and nursery owner practicing in New York's Adirondack Mountains, has a lot of fun using purple-leaved trees in her designs. She uses the eye-catching contrasting foliage to bring attention to something in the landscape rather than putting up a man-made sign. She might use a 'Bloodgood' Japanese maple (*Acer palmatum* 'Bloodgood') to mark the front entrance of a building or the place to turn from the street onto the driveway.

Jane recommends using purple-leaved canopy trees, such as 'Bloodgood' Japanese maple, as a contrast to their surroundings, rather than mass-planting them. The dark, brooding color can be overpowering if there's too much of it, but it works effectively when used as an accent or to enhance smaller purple-leaved plants set at a distance from one another.

Making the most of purple foliage. Purple foliage looks gloomy if it's mass-planted; it works best as a contrast to green leaves. Here, the eye-catching 'Bloodgood' Japanese maple brings attention to the gate in the garden wall, marking the entrance better than a sign. A shrubby leucothoe echoes its fountaining shape. The 'Crimson Pygmy' Japanese barberry at the other side of the gate echoes the purple foliage color, creating an exciting color pattern, while an arborvitae adds structural balance. Blooms are provided by clematis (on the wall), feathery astilbes, and columbines, all growing in a groundcover of ajuga.

If you can, position purple-foliaged plants—and this includes perennials as well as shrubs and trees—where the sun shines on them from behind. This seems to light up the leaves from within, giving them brilliant shimmery red lights. This technique works best for the lighter and redder hues of purple foliage. Darker foliage doesn't light up well and looks best if sun strikes it from the front.

One of my best combinations is low-spreading, blue-foliaged 'Blue Star' junipers (*Juniperus squamata* 'Blue Star') in front of 'Crimson Pygmy' Japanese barberries (*Berberis thunbergii* var. *atropurpurea* 'Crimson Pygmy'). The intense steel blue of the juniper needles enriches the wine tones of the barberry.

I used this combination in my foundation planting. I added 'Purple Loveliness' prunella (*Prunella* × *webbiana* 'Purple Loveliness'), a mat-forming, purple-flowered perennial with green leaves, to weave between the shrubs. All this stands in front of several glossy abelias (*Abelia* × *grandiflora*), which have dark green foliage, reddish stems, and pale pink flowers in late summer and autumn. I love these colors against my gray-shingled house.

Purple-foliaged groundcovers or low perennials, such as 'Palace Purple' heuchera (*Heuchera micrantha* 'Palace Purple'), need careful siting or they'll seem to disappear into the brown earth or mulch beneath them. I think the gray of gravel or stones sets them off best, but they'll do just fine rising from a green mat of even lower plants.

Sunny Yellow Foliage

Golden, yellow, and yellow-green foliage retains a springlike freshness throughout the summer, bringing dramatic light to a dark area. Dark green becomes less somber when contrasted with chartreuse or lime green, while the golden hues are intensified by a dark background, especially in sun.

Be careful when using gold-leaved plants—they're even harder to use than purples. Gold and chartreuse don't go with everything, and some people think yellow foliage looks sick, bleached and yellowed from malnutrition. However, when combined carefully with compatible plants and given a dark green background, these sunny leaf colors provide four-season gardens with cheerful summer color.

Because yellow-hued foliage lacks the chlorophyll content of green leaves, it's usually slow-growing and easily burned by strong sun. These plants do best in shade, either in the fairly dense shadows under trees, where they'll create the effect of sun shining under the dark overhead branches, or in the half-shade of morning sun. The open shade on the north side of a building glows with imitation sunlight when you grow golden-foliaged plants there. The blue light in a shade garden tones down some of the brashness of golden foliage.

Two of my favorite yellow-foliaged plants are spireas. The fine-textured, bright chartreuse foliage and rounded shape of *Spiraea* × *bumalda* 'Limemound' creates an eye-catching accent. The similar 'Goldmound' spirea (*Spiraea* 'Goldmound') has coppery new growth that matures to a golden green. Both shrubs are useful for their long season of colorful foliage.

I grow many plants with lime green or chartreuse leaves in the dappled light beneath several tall black locust trees. The tallest is the golden fullmoon maple (*Acer japonicum* 'Aureum'), with chartreuse leaves that glow like the full moon, but certainly with a greener light. Great clumps of 'Gold Edger' hostas repeat the color of the maple.

I used gold-and-green variegated lilyturf (*Liriope muscari* 'Variegata') to echo the chartreuse but add a linear shape that contrasts with the flat planes of the hosta and maple leaves. And I added darker green foliage from white-flowered astilbes, Christmas ferns, creeping phlox (*Phlox stolonifera*), and crested iris (*Iris cristata*), as well as a background of rhododendron foliage, to keep the chartreuse looking springlike instead of sickly.

Bicolored and Tricolored Leaves

Variegated foliage, with its streaks, stripes, spots, and patches of color, delights the eye— sometimes. Variegated foliage can be lovely, introducing points of light and enticing patterns to the garden. On the other hand, some of the most hideous plants I've seen are variegated. It's a struggle to use these sometimes-gaudy plants well. If in doubt, I always err on the conservative side, choosing plants with subtle rather than bold patterns.

Plants with only a narrow band or dainty edge of cream or white variegation are the easiest to use. When viewed from a distance, you may not even realize that these plants are multicolored. The lovely variegated Japanese kerria (*Kerria japonica* 'Variegata', also sold as 'Picta') appears gray-green from a distance. The creamy edges of its deeply cut leaves and glaucous waxy coating dull the normally deep green leaves to a mellow shade.

Use large variegated plants such as trees and shrubs individually as an accent against a darker background. Use them sparingly to echo or repeat a color in a neighboring plant. This is also the best way to use large showy perennials, such as *Hosta* 'Frances Williams' with its bold, heavily corrugated blue-green leaves and broad creamy edges. Try one of these spectacular hostas as a specimen plant in your shade garden.

You can use groundcovers and perennials with refined variegations in larger clumps or expanses—they aren't overpowering as long as they look unvariegated when viewed from afar. In a group, these plants form a single eye-catching mass, similar in substance to a single tree or shrub.

But whether you're using large variegated specimens or subtle groundcovers, don't get carried away. Overdo variegated plants and you'll find they no longer act as eye-catching accents but create a discordant jumble. Gardens with too many striped, speckled, and blotched leaves lose their coherence, making the viewer feel uncomfortable and restless.

Be warned that you may need to help variegated plants hold their own in your garden. Because they lack chlorophyll in the white or gold areas of their leaves, variegated plants aren't usually as vigorous as their green counterparts. Be prepared to feed these plants and weed out encroaching neighbors. Variegated plants also may be more susceptible to insect attack, according to Dr. Charles S. Sadoff, an entomologist at Purdue University.

Highly variegated plants, especially the yellow-green and gold ones, need protection from strong sun. In most cases, leaves with gold marginal variegation can withstand a lot of sun, while foliage with large gold centers needs light shade to keep it from scorching. Full sun may not damage plants with white marginal variegation, but it will almost certainly scorch plants with white centers.

Perennials and Bulbs for Summer

The usual way we get our rush of summer flowers is with an elaborate perennial border designed to be in continuous bloom for three or four months of the year, or with stiff beds of soldierly annuals. But these flowers-only gardens lie lifeless for much of the year, leaving a mudflat in winter in the prominent location where you've sited the bed. I've learned

Using variegated plants. Variegated Japanese silver grass (*Miscanthus sinensis* 'Variegatus') glints like sunstruck silver swords against the dark shadows between mature rhododendron and juniper bushes. The white-striped grass stands out against the greenery, a silvery beacon in summer, a tawny fountain in fall and winter. A mixed groundcover of periwinkle (*Vinca minor*) and impatiens adds texture and flowers.

to rely more on the woody plants of my land-scape for flowers, foliage, and special features all year.

That doesn't mean I've given up on per-ennials, though. I just use my flowering perennials as companions to the shrubs. Perennials and bulbs used artfully in a mixed border provide glorious color and fragrance to enhance the shrubs and small trees. When choosing perennials for your mixed border, consider time of bloom and flower color so you can keep the summer on a continuous roll of advancing flowers.

The form and shape of your perennials are even more important than their flowers. The shapes of the perennials you choose must complement the shrubs and trees they grow with. Choose sprawling, spreading types to frolic at the feet of vase-shaped shrubs; billowing, massing types to fill in between groups of upright shrubs; and tall spires to rise up behind rounded shrubs.

Summer in the Mixed Border

Summer, the opaque foliage season, is anything but monotonous green in a gar-den designed for four seasons of pleasure and beauty. You can enjoy a kaleidoscope of blooms by seeking out rare and unusual summer-flowering trees and shrubs to add to your mixed border.

Weave summer-flowering perennials in and out of groups of evergreens and spring-blooming shrubs to add seasonal color. Choose plants with silvery, golden, and purple foliage to enrich the garden. With so much diversity to choose from, you may find that summer has become your favorite garden season!

CHAPTER 5

Autumn in the Four-Season Landscape

Enhance the Golden Season's Blaze of Foliage with Colorful Flowers and Fruits

As summer moves into autumn, the lush foliage surrounding my yard and garden begins to thin, imperceptibly at first. Throughout the autumn months, I watch the trees surrounding my second-story office windows change as they color up and then gradually shed their leaves. The red maples (*Acer rubrum*) turn vivid red in October, suffusing the upstairs rooms with the glow of an autumnal bonfire. Once the foliage drops, flooding the patio and lawn with ankle-deep waves of red, light streams into the upstairs windows for the first time in months.

I know that autumn has arrived, however, well before the maples' dramatic display, when I notice that the crabapple tree—my barometer of the seasons—has cycled into its early-fall garb. The summer-green fruits now begin to show a tinge of gold, as they slowly ripen to deep gold and apricot. The leaves gradually yellow and, when they drop to the ground, the branches are revealed with their great clusters of colorful crabapples.

In early autumn, the sunny border that fills part of my view has begun to look a bit tattered, too, although plenty of flowers still decorate the garden. The semidouble white Japanese anemones (*Anemone* × *hybrida* 'Avalanche') are my favorites, with their elegant clusters of furry-sepaled blooms held above clumps of large, maplelike leaves.

The anemones' white flowers are echoed by the billowing clouds of boltonia (*Boltonia asteroides*) at the back of the border and the tall spires of 'White Pearl' Kamchatka bugbane (*Cimicifuga simplex* 'White Pearl'), which wave like tall fairy wands casting a benevolent spell on the garden. Mums (*Chrysanthemum* × *morifolium*) planted near the saucer magnolia bloom in a blaze of autumn foliage colors—gold, yellow, russet, and burgundy. And rosy pink and purple asters shout with color.

Labor Day Parade

Here on Long Island, Labor Day marks the end of summer and the beginning of autumn's parade of flowers and foliage. Just about when summer vacations come to an end and school days begin, a decided change comes over the weather.

I am always struck by summer's end, when the humidity lifts suddenly and the air seems as crisp and clean as a soda cracker. By September, the sun's rays strike from a lower angle, delivering far less heat than the full sun of summer. Rarely is a sunny day actually hot in autumn, and the low angle of the sun means that the house stays cool even when it's pleasantly warm outdoors.

Indian Summer

Of course, this relief from the dog days of summer is not entirely reliable. Autumn's mounting chill is often disrupted by the lovely warm, sunny days—or sometimes hot, muggy days—that we call Indian summer. If you live in a climate where an early frost routinely precedes a lengthy Indian summer, use frost-tolerant plants for ongoing beauty in your autumn garden.

Many garden annuals—those mainstays of showy but short-lived summer displays—are tender plants that blacken and perish overnight when hit by frost. Many perennials also succumb in part to fall's frosts, dying back to the ground to await the following spring. Some perennials and hardy annuals, however, bloom unscathed right through a frost. Requiring a real freeze to make them give up for the season, these cold-hardy plants have the staying power to help your fall garden reach its fullest potential. Rely on these plants—including mums, asters, goldenrods, and sedums—to keep your garden going.

Autumn's Color Scheme

The hot colors of autumn's spectrum are the opposite of spring's cool tones. The ruby red, burnt orange, burnished gold, and canary yellow typical of the season derive more from the foliage of deciduous plants than from flowers. Because of the brilliant colors and sheer volume of leaves, autumn foliage defines the season. Not that autumn doesn't have its own flowers—it does. But the fiery foliage of maples and birches—the spectacle of the New England landscape—comes to mind first when we conjure up a fall scene.

These flaming foliage colors seem hot and vibrant, intense and exciting after the overwhelming greenness of late summer. And when they are set off against an Indian summer sky of purest blue, no painter could devise a more exciting color scheme.

Goldenrods and Asters

The mighty composite family comes into its flowering glory in autumn, dominating the roadsides and meadows with goldenrods, asters, and sunflowers. These flowers of the fields mirror the colors of autumn's larger landscape, blooming in the reds, golds, and yellows of the sugar maple and the white, blue, and purple of a cloud-filled autumn sky.

Nature's gold-and-purple floral display, punctuated by bursts of white, influences my fall garden palette. I concentrate on these vibrant colors when choosing fall garden flowers and stay away from soft pastels, which remind me of spring. Large splashes of blue and purple asters enrich the ruddy ruby and burgundy fall foliage of nearby shrubs and trees. These cool colors temper the heat of autumn's more fiery colors, keeping the hot colors from overpowering the garden.

Fall wildflowers. These native wildflowers make a great combination in a flower bed or meadow garden. Place 'October Glory' shining coneflower (*Rudbeckia nitida* 'October Glory') in back, 'Red-Gold Hybrid' sneezeweed (*Helenium autumnale* 'Red-Gold Hybrid') in the middle, and 'Crown of Rays' Canada goldenrod (*Solidago canadensis* 'Crown of Rays') in the front for three golden tiers of flowers.

A Blaze of Foliage

The intensity of any year's changing fall foliage—the grand paint of the autumn garden—depends on many factors, most of them under Mother Nature's control. Superb red and scarlet autumnal displays don't occur every year because weather strongly influences the intensity of red pigments. Yellow pigments are usually more predictable and less influenced by weather.

The best red displays—the kind that make New England a tourist mecca in September and October—happen during years of abundant moisture when fall days are warm and sunny and nights are cold (below 45°F). Moisture from summer and early-fall rains prevents the aging leaves from drying up and dropping prematurely, before they change color. Bright sunshine encourages leaves to manufacture plenty of sugars. Normally, sugars are transported to roots for storage, but cold nights trap them in the leaves, where they are transformed into brilliant red pigments.

The best fall foliage displays appear in regions where rainfall occurs evenly throughout the year, and where autumn nights are cold. In North America, this includes New England and the Northeast, the southern Appalachian Mountains, and high-elevation areas of the West. The farther south you go, the poorer the fall color, even in tree species that color beautifully in the North.

Some trees and shrubs, such as the tupelo (*Nyssa sylvatica*) and staghorn sumac (*Rhus typhina*), color up early, turning scarlet by late September hereabouts. Others, such as river birch (*Betula nigra*), remain green throughout October and into November but go out in a blaze of golden yellow glory about Thanksgiving time. The color transformation in my garden is usually a pleasantly drawn-out process. But, as with spring, the pleasure and beauty of the season never last quite long enough!

While you can't control weather variations from year to year, you *can* maximize your garden's fall color. Start by choosing trees and

MAXIMIZING FALL COLOR

While Mother Nature has the greatest influence over how showy a plant will be each year, you, the gardener, can help her along. First, choose plants known for their brilliant autumn displays, then take care to:

▶ Locate plants with showy fall foliage in a south- or west-facing location where afternoon sun is abundant.

▶ Locate plants with showy fall foliage in a frost pocket or a low-lying spot in the garden where cold air accumulates at night.

▶ Irrigate deciduous woody plants in summer and autumn if natural rainfall is scarce.

shrubs known for outstanding fall color, then enhance their displays by planting them in sites that receive at least six hours of full sun a day in autumn. Remember that the changing angle of the sun means that shadows lengthen as the days get shorter. Building and tree shadows may shift enough at this time of year to cast unwelcome shade on some garden beds that were sun-filled in summer.

West- or south-facing locations are usually best for fall color—you'll find that the brightest red colors of a sugar maple, for instance, appear on its west side. A burning bush (*Euonymus alata*) changes to blood red in full sun, but becomes a deep rosy pink when grown in shade. If you can, design your fall garden so that you'll be looking at the west-facing sides of those shrubs and trees you choose for fall foliage.

In years of drought, or even in years when late-summer and fall rains are sparse, irrigating the trees and shrubs in your garden not only helps prepare them for winter dormancy, but also encourages a better color display. So don't put your hose away on Labor Day; keep it handy through fall. And remember—water thoroughly, or don't water at all.

If you aren't sure what color a tree or shrub will turn in autumn, you can base an educated guess on the color of its summer leaves. I've observed that trees with summer foliage on the yellow side of green tend to turn yellow or gold in autumn. Those with bluish green foliage are most likely to become red or purple.

Trees for Fall Foliage

I can't think of any maple—be it the famous sugar maple, the fiery red maple, or the stunning Japanese maple—that doesn't exhibit remarkably attractive fall colors. Most maple species are capable of putting on a spectacular display, although some are more colorful than others.

The sugar maple (*Acer saccharum*) is undoubtedly the most famous tree in the world when it comes to fall color. Flourishing from Canada through the upper South, this stout-trunked, low-branched tree has wide-reaching upcurved branches and makes a lovely woodland or shade tree.

Although individual trees vary and weather certainly plays a role, sugar maples usually put on a stunning autumn show. Individual leaves on a tree vary in color, making the display all the more alluring. In the best years, the outer leaves, especially those facing the sun, become scarlet—the color of flames—while leaves in the tree's interior vary from pure orange to gold and bright yellow.

Several outstanding sugar maple cultivars have been selected to put on a more predictable or uniform display. Maples don't usually color well in neutral or alkaline soils, but the cultivar 'Bonfire' gives a great red performance even in the slightly alkaline conditions of the Midwest. 'Green Mountain' also tolerates the Midwest's heat and drought, but turns brilliant golden yellow in alkaline soils rather than the red it attains in acid soils.

The red maple (*Acer rubrum*), native to the east coast of North America from Canada to the Gulf Coast, is famous for its fall color. In early October, the small, three-lobed leaves turn deep, glowing red. The silvery bark makes a pretty sight in the dead of winter, while late winter or early spring brings a haze of red blooms, which, though small, are showy against the bare branches.

Like sugar maples, not all red maple specimens turn glorious shades of red in fall. Seek out named cultivars known for their autumn color. 'October Glory' turns deep crimson late in fall, retaining its colorful foliage about three weeks later than other maples. This cultivar is not quite as cold-hardy as the species but makes the most colorful selection for southern gardens. 'Red Sunset' turns red and orange-red in both northern and southern climates. 'Autumn Flame' colors up earlier than any other cultivar, turning brilliant red, and holds its colorful leaves for several weeks. 'Northwood' endures the cold of Minnesota and has glittering gold fall foliage.

Japanese maples (*Acer palmatum*) look their finest in autumn, though their foliage texture gives the graceful small trees a lovely delicacy from spring through fall. Depending on the cultivar, the leaves become almost phosphorescent shades of blood red, glowing gold, or vivid orange, changing color very late in the season and lengthening autumn's display almost to winter.

A Japanese maple's leaves give quiet serenity to a garden, for their texture can be as intricate as a spider's web. Summer sunlight passing through the foliage creates a tracery of delicate shadows on the ground beneath tall specimens. When lit from behind by the autumn sun, a Japanese maple dressed in its fall colors glows like a brightly colored paper lantern.

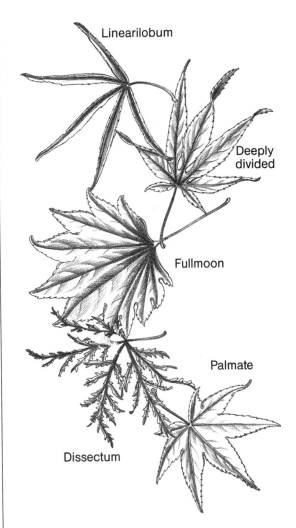

Japanese maple leaf types. The hundreds of Japanese maple (*Acer palmatum* and *A. japonicum*) cultivars feature a variety of leaf shapes, ranging from wide fans to deeply dissected lacelike patterns. The more deeply cut the foliage, the more sensitive the tree is to hot sun and dry soil.

Japanese maples are available in an assortment of leaf shapes and forms. The starlike leaves of the species and its cultivars are palmately lobed into seven to nine segments, forming the rounded outline of a hand with the fingers spread. Deeply divided palmate leaves appear more fine-textured, with the fingers of the hand cut almost to the leaf base and with shallowly cut teeth along the margins.

The laceleaved or dissected cultivars (*A. palmatum* 'Dissectum' and related cultivars) feature leaves that are deeply dissected to the base, with jagged toothed or doubly dissected margins. These delicate leaves give the trees a feathery, ethereal look. Still more fragile-looking are the threadleaved cultivars; they have deeply divided leaves with very narrow, almost threadlike sections.

There are about 250 Japanese maple cultivars, many of them rare collectors' items. Just as there are many leaf shapes, plant form varies from waterfall-like mounds to upright and vase-shaped to round and bushy. Some cultivars, such as 'Aoyagi' and 'Sango Kaku', offer brightly colored bark that becomes even more intense in winter.

There's an array of leaf colors, too; green- and purple-leaved cultivars are available in all leaf types. Some cultivars, such as 'Bonfire', exhibit brilliantly colored new foliage that matures to summer green and then undergoes another dramatic metamorphosis as it takes on flamboyant fall colors. And a few cultivars exhibit lovely chartreuse or yellow-green foliage that brings sunshine to the garden throughout the growing season.

Palmate cultivars most frequently grow into vaselike small trees with age, while thread-leaved cultivars grow more upright and round-headed. Those in the deeply divided group form wide-spreading, often multitrunked trees with cascading branches. Unless grafted high, most laceleaved cultivars form mounding shrubs with cascading foliage. If grafted onto a 3- to 4-foot-tall understock, a laceleaved Japanese maple eventually becomes a waterfall of weeping branches, forming a 12- to 15-foot-tall tree as it matures.

Laceleaved and threadleaved types need as much coddling as their delicate looks imply, being easily desiccated by strong wind and sun. If you provide them with protection from the elements and good garden loam, they will thrive. Palmate and deeply divided types suffer less from adverse weather, but nevertheless perform best with a bit of protection.

All Japanese maples thrive in partial or light filtered shade, especially in the South and Midwest, where protection from summer's hot afternoon sun prevents leaf scorch. Golden- and purple-foliaged cultivars can lose their beautiful coloration in too much shade, but too much sun will sunburn or bleach them out. Finding just the right exposure is the key to having the best-looking specimen. Green-leaved types take full sun better than purple-leaved types.

Because the color and texture of these trees add interest and excitement to almost any setting, nurseryman Jim Cross recommends that you plant many Japanese maple cultivars. Use them as stunning focal points throughout your year-round garden. Japanese maples combine beautifully with evergreen azaleas and rhododendrons, which need similar growing conditions, and with other Japanese maples.

Try situating a vase-shaped, palmate-leaved cultivar so that it fans out above and behind a cultivar that forms a low cascading mound of finely dissected foliage. With just these two plants, you can begin to create a lovely contrast of form and foliage color that changes throughout the year. "Best Japanese Maples for Four-Season Landscapes" on page 188 includes some of the most attractive and readily available Japanese maple cultivars.

Less familiar than the Japanese maple, but just as arresting in its fall finery, is the Amur maple (*Acer ginnala*). This tough, cold-hardy tree deserves a prominent place in small gardens in northern climates where the Japanese maple can't tough it out. Small and tidy, the Amur maple makes a lovely display throughout the year when planted in a mixed border. You'll enjoy a progression of attractive features, beginning with fragrant spring flowers. These are followed by clusters of showy red samaras (winged seeds), which contrast prettily with summer's tidy, fine-textured green leaves.

Like sugar maples, several other trees exhibit an assortment of electrifying hues when their foliage begins to change. Cultivars of callery pear (*Pyrus calleryana*) turn vibrant shades of pumpkin orange, old gold, wine red, and eggplant purple. A single tree may display all these colors, with the reddest leaves on the exterior set off against a golden interior. Color develops late and remains showy for several weeks as the glossy, leathery leaves—as highly polished as those of any broadleaved evergreen—persist until late in the season.

Sweet gum (*Liquidambar styraciflua*) is at least as colorful, and it shows its colors earlier in fall. The exquisite star-shaped leaves are particularly noteworthy in fall, because the red and purple leaves stand out against the dense, lighter-colored orange or golden ones on the tree's interior. Individual specimens of this native tree vary greatly in fall color, so try to choose a cultivar known to produce a good display.

You can't go wrong by planting a sourwood (*Oxydendrum arboreum*)—whether as a tall tree in small landscapes, or as an understory tree beneath mighty shade trees. Truly a tree for four seasons, in autumn sourwood becomes a tower of deep, glossy red to maroon leaves decorated by straw-colored seedpods. The foliage turns in midautumn and persists until fall passes into winter.

The best tree for fall color in the Deep South and southern Midwest is the Chinese pistache (*Pistacia chinensis*). In these areas, the fine-textured foliage becomes as gorgeous an orange-red or blood red as the sugar maple's

does in the North. Female trees also produce showy clusters of red to purple berries in fall when the foliage changes.

For pure golden yellow hues, nothing brings light and warmth to the autumn landscape better than a ginkgo tree (*Ginkgo biloba*). This ancient tree species has no equal. The unique fan-shaped leaves cling to spurlike side branches along the outstretched main branches. A ginkgo creates a particularly pretty sight in autumn, with its yellow leaves against a sharp blue sky. But make sure you buy a male clone—fruits produced by female trees smell like an uncleaned kennel.

Many other trees besides those described here will create a sensation in the fall garden. "Plants with Outstanding Fall Color" on page 190 includes the best four-season trees for fall color.

Shrubs for Fall Foliage

Several of my favorite spring-flowering shrubs put on magnificent displays of foliage in autumn. Red-vein enkianthus (*Enkianthus campanulatus*), a member of the heath family, turns an almost iridescent shade of orange-red. The tidy rounded leaves grow in whorls on slender gray stems, making a colorful, fine-textured statement.

I planted two of these shrubs in the border along the lower part of my steep driveway, where they color up magnificently even in the partial shade. With the deep green evergreen foliage of pachysandra swirling around their feet and rhododendron and pieris foliage for a backdrop, these two shrubs glow like hot, slow-burning embers when they change color in October.

Witch hazels (*Hamamelis* spp.), best known for the mophead-like blooms that bring light to dreary winter landscapes, also brighten the fall garden with golden yellow or rich orange leaves. *H.* × *intermedia* 'Diane', with copper-

BEST JAPANESE MAPLES
FOR FOUR-SEASON LANDSCAPES

Specimens of the highly variable Japanese maple (*Acer palmatum*) beautify a four-season landscape every day of the year, contributing their exquisite silhouettes, fine-textured foliage, and glorious fall colors. The following cultivars are just a few of the fine selections of this small tree. Use them to create year-round landscape interest.

Name: 'Aoyagi' (green-bark maple)
Winter: brilliant pea green branches and twigs, upright to 9 feet tall
Spring: pale green new growth
Summer: bright green palmate leaves
Autumn: clear yellow fall foliage

Name: 'Aureum' (golden Japanese maple)
Winter: upright to 12 feet tall, bright red twigs
Spring: new growth yellow tinged with red
Summer: light yellow-green palmate leaves with red petioles
Autumn: brilliant clear yellow fall color

Name: 'Bloodgood'
Winter: round-headed tree to 30 feet
Spring: new growth bright red
Summer: deep reddish purple palmate leaves, red seedpods
Autumn: excellent clear red fall color

Name: 'Bonfire'
Winter: small, upright tree to 15 feet
Spring: new growth bright crimson
Summer: palmate, slightly toothed leaves bronze changing to green
Autumn: outstanding flame red fall color

Name: 'Butterfly'
Winter: small, bushy tree to 10 feet tall
Spring: new growth pale green with pink
Summer: finely toothed palmate leaves variegated pale green and white
Autumn: white variegation turns bright pink

Name: 'Crimson Queen'
Winter: cascading silhouette to 9 feet tall
Spring: bright crimson new growth
Summer: deep red dissected leaves all summer
Autumn: bright scarlet fall color

Name: 'Filigree'
Winter: rounded cascading mound, 6 feet tall by 9 feet wide
Spring: new growth light yellow-green
Summer: light green, deeply dissected leaves, flecked with cream and pale gold
Autumn: rich gold, long-lasting fall color

Name: 'Hogyoku'
Winter: round-headed to 20 feet tall
Spring: green new growth
Summer: rich deep green broadly palmate leaves
Autumn: outstanding pumpkin orange fall color

Name: 'Oshio-beni'
Winter: round-topped, to 15 feet tall
Spring: new growth vibrant orange-red
Summer: bronze to greenish red palmate leaves
Autumn: rich scarlet fall color

Name: 'Red Filigree Lace'
Winter: silvery branches form dome-shaped mound to 6 feet tall
Spring: wine red new growth
Summer: deep wine red leaves, doubly dissected into a tracery
Autumn: bright crimson fall color

Name: 'Red Pygmy'
Winter: upright with broad top, to 7 feet tall
Spring: bright red new growth
Summer: bright red-maroon threadleaved foliage
Autumn: brilliant golden yellow fall color

Name: 'Sango Kaku' (also 'Sen Kaki') (coral-bark maple)
Winter: bright coral-red young trunks and branches, vase-shaped to 25 feet
Spring: reddish-tinged new growth
Summer: bright green palmate leaves
Autumn: fall color yellow-gold with red cast

Name: 'Seiryu'
Winter: upright to 12 feet tall; unique shape for dissected cultivar
Spring: bright green new growth
Summer: light green dissected leaves tipped with red
Autumn: spectacular yellow, gold, and crimson fall color

Name: 'Sekimori'
Winter: weeping to 15 feet tall, white stripes on green trunk bark
Spring: bright green new growth
Summer: deep green dissected leaves
Autumn: magnificent yellow and gold fall color

Name: 'Sherwood Flame'
Winter: round-topped small tree to 15 feet tall
Spring: rich burgundy-red new growth
Summer: deeply divided burgundy leaves all summer
Autumn: bright red fall color

Name: 'Viridis'
Winter: cascading and wide-spreading, to 15 feet tall if grafted
Spring: new growth bright chartreuse
Summer: light green, dissected leaves
Autumn: gold fall foliage with splashes of red

Name: *A. japonicum* 'Aureum' (fullmoon maple)
Winter: round-topped small tree to 8 feet tall
Spring: pale yellow-green new growth
Summer: chartreuse shallowly lobed, rounded leaves
Autumn: beautiful golden leaves tipped with crimson

red, spidery flowers from January through March, has the best fall color of the witch hazels, turning shades that rival the maples. Witch hazels' leaf texture makes exciting contrasts, too. Much coarser than red-vein enkianthus, the leaves have prominent veins, giving them the appearance of rough-hewn wood.

Dwarf fothergilla (*Fothergilla gardenii*), a member of the witch hazel family, creates more of a fall foliage sensation than other family members. In October, the leaves of this native shrub present a spectrum of passionate sunset colors. Although fothergilla grows in sun or shade, the best orange-red and burnished gold foliage develops in full-sun locations. In shade, autumn leaves turn brilliant golden yellow.

Virginia sweetspire (*Itea virginica*) is a native shrub noted for both summer flowers and fall foliage. Some think the cultivar 'Henry's Garnet' is best, because its leaves become a deeper jewel red than the species, but others prefer the brighter yellows and golds of the species. This shrub performs in shade or sun, as long as the soil stays moist.

Perhaps the most widely planted shrub for red autumn foliage is the burning bush or winged euonymus (*Euonymus alata*). A plant for four seasons, burning bush's spring flowers aren't particularly showy, but they suffuse the branches with a lovely lime green mist before spring's new leaves emerge. Summer foliage grows dense and makes a serviceable screen, but autumn brings the shrub into its prime. When grown in full sun, burning bush does appear to be burning with a pure, clear red fire. When leafless in winter, the odd corky wings edging the branches make a curious sight and act as snow-catchers.

The deciduous barberries (*Berberis* spp.), so useful for creating impenetrable barriers, turn unpredictable shades of orange, scarlet, and reddish purple in autumn. To me, they appear most stunning when the fine-textured

(continued on page 192)

PLANTS WITH OUTSTANDING FALL COLOR

Like colorful paints, the changing hues of deciduous plants can transform the autumn landscape into a blaze of glory. The following plants put on the best, most reliable performance.

Small Deciduous Trees
RED TO BURGUNDY FALL FOLIAGE
Acer ginnala (Amur maple), Zones 3–6
A. japonicum (fullmoon maple), Zones 6–8
A. palmatum (Japanese maple), Zones 5–8
A. palmatum 'Dissectum' (cutleaf Japanese maple), Zones 5–8
Cornus florida (flowering dogwood), Zones 5–9
C. kousa (Kousa dogwood), Zones 5–7
Cotinus coggygria (smoketree), Zones 5–7
Franklinia alatamaha (franklinia), Zones 6–8
Lagerstroemia indica × *L. fauriei* (hybrid crape myrtle), Zones 7–9
Rhus spp. (sumacs), Zones 3–9

YELLOW TO GOLD FALL FOLIAGE
Acer japonicum 'Aureum' (golden fullmoon maple), Zones 6–8
A. palmatum 'Aureum' (golden Japanese maple), Zones 5–8
A. palmatum 'Sango Kaku' (coral-bark maple), Zones 5–8
Cercis spp. (redbuds), Zones 5–9
Chionanthus virginicus (American fringetree), Zones 5–9
Prunus sargentii (Sargent cherry), Zones 5–9

ORANGE TO GOLD FALL FOLIAGE
Lagerstroemia indica × *L. fauriei* (hybrid crape myrtle), Zones 7–9
Parrotia persica (Persian parrotia), Zones 6–9
Prunus serrulata 'Kwanzan' ('Kwanzan' Japanese flowering cherry), Zones 5–8

Tall Deciduous Trees
RED TO BURGUNDY FALL FOLIAGE
Acer rubrum 'October Glory', 'Morgan', 'Red Sunset' (red maples), Zones 3–9
Amelanchier arborea (downy serviceberry), Zones 3–8

Liquidambar styraciflua (sweet gum), Zones 5–9
Nyssa sylvatica (black gum, tupelo), Zones 5–9
Oxydendrum arboreum (sourwood), Zones 5–9
Pyrus calleryana (callery pear), Zones 5–9
Quercus coccinea (scarlet oak), Zones 5–9
Sorbus rufoferruginea 'Longwood Sunset' ('Longwood Sunset' mountain ash), Zones 4–7

YELLOW TO GOLD FALL FOLIAGE
Acer capillipes (snakebark maple), Zones 5–7
A. davidii (David maple), Zones 7–9
A. pensylvanicum (striped-bark maple), Zones 3–7
Betula spp. (birches), Zones 2–9
Cercidiphyllum japonicum (Katsura tree), Zones 5–9
Cladrastis lutea (American yellowwood), Zones 4–8
Ginkgo biloba (ginkgo, maidenhair tree), Zones 4–8
Liriodendron tulipifera (tulip tree), Zones 4–9
Zelkova serrata 'Green Vase' ('Green Vase' Japanese zelkova), Zones 5–9

ORANGE, SCARLET, OR GOLD FALL FOLIAGE
Acer saccharum (sugar maple), Zones 3–7
Liquidambar styraciflua (sweet gum), Zones 5–9
Pistacia chinensis (Chinese pistache), Zones 6–9
Sorbus alnifolia (Korean mountain ash), Zones 4–7

Deciduous Shrubs
RED OR BURGUNDY FALL FOLIAGE
Aronia melanocarpa var. *elata* (black chokeberry), Zones 3–7
Cornus sericea, syn. *C. stolonifera* (red-osier dogwood), Zones 3–8
Deutzia gracilis 'Nikko' (dwarf slender deutzia), Zones 5–8
Euonymus alata (burning bush), Zones 4–8
Hydrangea quercifolia (oakleaf hydrangea), Zones 5–9
Itea virginica 'Henry's Garnet' ('Henry's Garnet' Virginia sweetspire), Zones 6–9

Rhododendron arborescens (sweet azalea), Zones 5-9

R. schlippenbachii (royal azalea), Zones 5-8

R. vaseyi (pinkshell azalea), Zones 5-8

R. yedoense var. *poukhanense* (Korean azalea), Zones 5-8

Rosa setigera (prairie rose), Zones 4-9

Vaccinium corymbosum (highbush blueberry), Zones 4-9

Viburnum carlesii (Koreanspice viburnum), Zones 4-8

V. dilatatum (linden viburnum), Zones 5-8

V. plicatum var. *tomentosum* (doublefile viburnum), Zones 5-8

V. setigerum (tea viburnum), Zones 6-8

V. trilobum (American cranberrybush viburnum), Zones 2-8

YELLOW OR GOLD FALL FOLIAGE

Callicarpa japonica (Japanese beautyberry), Zones 5-8

Clethra alnifolia (sweet pepperbush), Zones 4-9

Fothergilla spp. (fothergillas), Zones 5-9

Hamamelis spp. (witch hazels), Zones 4-9

Ilex verticillata (winterberry), Zones 4-9

Kerria japonica (Japanese kerria), Zones 5-9

Rhododendron mucronulatum (Korean azalea), Zones 5-8

R. viscosum (swamp azalea), Zones 4-9

Rosa rugosa (rugosa rose), Zones 3-7

R. virginiana (Virginia rose), Zones 5-8

ORANGE, SCARLET, OR GOLD FALL FOLIAGE

Aronia arbutifolia (red chokeberry), Zones 4-9

Berberis thunbergii (Japanese barberry), Zones 4-9

Enkianthus campanulatus (red-vein enkianthus), Zones 5-8

Viburnum dilatatum 'Catskill' and 'Oneida', Zones 5-8

Vines and Groundcovers
RED TO BURGUNDY FALL FOLIAGE

Ceratostigma plumbaginoides (leadwort), Zones 5-9

Parthenocissus quinquefolia (Virginia creeper), Zones 3-9

P. tricuspidata (Boston ivy), Zones 4-8

YELLOW TO GOLD FALL FOLIAGE

Celastrus spp. (bittersweets), Zones 3-8

Wisteria spp. (wisterias), Zones 5-9

Perennials
RED TO BURGUNDY FALL FOLIAGE

Bergenia spp. (bergenias), Zones 3-9

Heuchera spp. (coral bells), Zones 3-9

Paeonia spp. (peonies), Zones 2-8

YELLOW TO GOLD FALL FOLIAGE

Aconitum spp. (monkshoods), Zones 3-8

Amsonia tabernaemontana (willow blue star), Zones 3-9

Aquilegia × *hybrida* (hybrid columbine), Zones 3-9

Boltonia asteroides (boltonia), Zones 3-9

Hosta spp. (hostas), Zones 3-9

Platycodon grandiflorus (balloon flower), Zones 3-8

Ornamental Grasses
RED TO BURGUNDY FALL FOLIAGE

Erianthus ravennae (plume grass), Zones 6-10

Imperata cylindrica 'Red Baron' (Japanese bloodgrass), Zones 6-9

Miscanthus sinensis 'Purpurascens' (flame grass) Zones 7-8

Panicum virgatum 'Rotstrahlbusch' and 'Rehbraum' (red switch grasses) Zones 5-9

Schizachyrium scoparium (little bluestem), Zones 3-10

YELLOW TO GOLD FALL FOLIAGE

Chasmanthium latifolium (northern sea oats), Zones 5-9

Hakonechloa macra 'Aureola' (golden variegated hakone grass), Zones 7-9

Panicum virgatum 'Heavy Metal' and 'Strictum' (switch grasses), Zones 5-9

Pennisetum alopecuroides (fountain grass), Zones 6-9

leaves are glowing orange, which sets off the multitude of red berries. The best barberries for year-round appeal are the purple-foliaged cultivars; these turn scarlet in October. *Berberis thunbergii* 'Aurea', noted for fine chartreuse summer foliage, becomes canary yellow in autumn.

I've described only a few of the wonderful deciduous shrubs that can bring your garden to life with their autumnal foliage. "Plants with Outstanding Fall Color" on page 190 presents more outstanding choices. Keep in mind that evergreen shrubs play an important role in the autumn garden, too, primarily as a neutral background for autumn's star performers.

Some of the small-leaved dwarf and compact rhododendrons rival deciduous plants for outstanding fall color. In preparation for winter, their permanent foliage takes on the deep glowing tones of a French wine, while the dying inner foliage becomes vibrant with brighter colors. (See "Getting Into the Chameleon Act" on page 29 for details on the best rhododendrons for fall color.)

Berried Beauties

Along with the drama of changing foliage colors, the end of the year brings a cornucopia of bright berries on many ornamental trees and shrubs. Clusters of glistening red, orange, or yellow add a wonderful radiance to even the dullest autumn day.

Not every berry is a seasonal showstopper. Some, like those of privets (*Ligustrum* spp.), ripen to a barely visible black, while others are hidden behind foliage or fall quickly to the ground. Truly eye-catching berries tend to attract hungry birds that can quickly decimate an autumnal display. For tips on fending them off—at least for a while—see "Berry-Saving Tactics" on page 45.

However, many ornamental plants bear fruits guaranteed to add a tantalizing touch to your autumn garden, if only for a few weeks. In Chapter 2, I discussed plants with berries that persist from fall well into winter, adorning bare branches with unexpected sparks of color. (See "Plants with Showy Winter Berries" on page 46.) Often set against contrasting foliage, berries of most of these winter-interest plants also look spectacular in autumn.

Shrubs for Bright Berries

A number of shrubs with noteworthy fall fruit belong to the vast *Viburnum* genus. Viburnums offer several seasons of substantial interest: charming, often fragrant flowers in winter or spring; handsome, heavily textured summer foliage; cheerful fall color; and the best berry display of any genus. I discussed the finest spring-blooming viburnums in Chapter 3 (see pages 101-102) but saved those with the most magnificent berry displays for this chapter.

Four-season gardeners can choose from some very special viburnums, thanks to the work of the late Dr. Donald Egolf, a breeder of woody plants at the U.S. National Arboretum. Dr. Egolf's goal was to create compact, disease-resistant viburnums with better blooms and more persistent fruits. His viburnum cultivars are excellent ornamentals for four-season gardens. The very best of these selections are described in "Dr. Egolf's Best Viburnums" on page 194.

Linden viburnum (*Viburnum dilatatum*) displays magnificent flat clusters of shiny red berries from September until Christmas. Usually a very large, lanky shrub, this viburnum has been tamed a bit at the National Arboretum. Cultivars selected for excellent flowering, fruiting, fall color, and a dense habit include 'Iroquois' and 'Oneida' and the dwarves 'Erie' and 'Catskill', which grow to 5 feet tall, about half the size of the others. Yellow-gold berries flushed with orange adorn 'Xanthocarpum', an attractive but hard-to-find cultivar.

These linden viburnum cultivars bear lacy, flat-topped clusters of white flowers, which transform the tall shrub into a snowlike mountain in late spring. (Some people do not like the flowers' musky fragrance, so you might choose to plant linden viburnum away from the house.) Planting several cultivars together assures cross-pollination and heavy fruit set.

European cranberrybush viburnum (*V. opulus*) produces flat clusters of lacy spring flowers, each surrounded by a collar of sterile flowers that gives the inflorescence a substantial ornamental character. The fruits, as the shrub's name implies, resemble cranberries in size and shape but are more translucent, shimmering like red glass beads when struck by the low rays of the sun. These edible berries hang on well into winter.

The cultivar 'Compactum' flowers and fruits prolifically, and grows dense while staying below 5 feet tall. Yellow-fruited cultivars are also available. European cranberrybush's three-lobed maplelike foliage turns a rich russet as the fruits ripen in fall.

The less commonly grown American cranberrybush viburnum (*Viburnum trilobum*) resembles its European cousin in almost every respect and may actually be a variety of the European species. Its berries, however, are said to be tastier and its foliage is a more attractive red in autumn.

Planted amid low-mounding shrubs to mask its sparse knees, the vase-shaped tea viburnum (*Viburnum setigerum*) will electrify a mixed border in September and October with its luscious berry display. Individual berries measure only about one-half inch long but form in such abundance that the clusters actu-

ally weigh down the branches. Their orange-red to orange-gold color shows up well from a distance, especially when displayed against the dark ruddy tones of the shrub's arrow-shaped fall leaves.

One of the marvels in my fall garden are the berries of the purple beautyberry (*Callicarpa bodinieri* 'Profusion') when they ripen from green to intense violet. These glossy little fruits possess a color unique among berried plants and add an element of surprise to the fall garden with their unexpected hue.

Although the arching branches show off frothy lavender flowers in midsummer, the shrub's true merit is revealed in the abundant clusters of berries that encircle the stems in autumn and winter. Ripening in midautumn, when the foliage is still green, the berries look really spectacular in late fall when the leaves turn pinkish purple. Even after leaf-fall, the berries linger and remain rich and colorful well into winter, since birds don't eat them.

Since beautyberry flowers and fruits on new wood, it's easy to keep this otherwise large shrub in scale by cutting it back to the ground in spring every three years or so. It's supposed to grow and fruit even better if you give it this harsh treatment.

Birds will devour the true-blue berries of sapphireberry (*Symplocos paniculata*), but while they last, the berries adorn the large treelike shrub like magnificent ornaments. Spring flowers permeate the garden with the fragrance of honeysuckle; they need cross-pollination to set berries. This somewhat rangy shrub looks best planted in the back of a shrub border or in a naturalistic setting, where it can reside in obscurity until autumn brings it into its prime.

Native plant enthusiasts and berry connoisseurs claim that the fruit of red chokeberry (*Aronia arbutifolia*) is as showy in autumn and winter as the better-known winterberry

DR. EGOLF'S BEST VIBURNUMS

The late Dr. Donald Egolf, one of the country's leading woody plant breeders, introduced a number of excellent viburnum cultivars. The following baker's dozen are the most outstanding for four-season landscapes, offering spring flowers, fall berries, and either vivid fall foliage color or heavily textured evergreen leaves.

Name: 'Catskill' (*V. dilatatum*)
Flowers: numerous lacy, creamy white clusters of fertile flowers in late spring
Foliage: small rounded leaves with good yellow, orange, and red fall color
Fruits: dark red, in abundant clusters
Comments: compact and slow-growing compared to species; reaches 5 feet tall and 8 feet wide; needs cross-pollination for fruiting; Zones 5–8

Name: 'Cayuga' (*V. carlesii* × *V.* × *carlcephalum*)
Flowers: pink buds open to abundant, fragrant white, medium-sized, snowball-type flower clusters; midspring
Foliage: dark green leaves; finer texture than *V. carlcephalum;* red fall color
Fruits: dull red ripening to black, not showy
Comments: resistant to leaf spot and mildew; compact and spreading to 5 feet tall; Zones 5–8

Name: 'Chippewa' (*V. japonicum* × *V. dilatatum* 'Catskill') and 'Huron' (*V. lobophyllum* × *V. japonicum*)
Flowers: huge, flat, lacy, white clusters
Foliage: leathery, dark glossy green leaves; semi-evergreen, turning bright red to maroon in autumn
Fruits: dark red; late summer into winter
Comments: dense, very large, and multi-stemmed; perform well in the South; plant together for best fruit; Zones 5–8

Name: 'Conoy' (*V. utile* × *V.* × *burkwoodii* 'Park Farm Hybrid')
Flowers: small balls of dark red buds open creamy white, slightly fragrant; midspring
Foliage: dark, glossy green, evergreen to semi-evergreen leaves with pale undersides; tinged maroon in winter

Fruits: remain red for many weeks before ripening to black in late fall
Comments: outstanding dense, spreading shrub; Zones 6–8; evergreen to Zone 7

Name: 'Erie' (*V. dilatatum*)
Flowers: white, in lacy, flat-topped, 6-inch clusters; late spring
Foliage: dark green, turns yellow, red, and orange in fall
Fruits: abundant bright red and orange; turn coral-pink after frost and persist
Comments: rounded, taller than wide; disease-resistant; Styer Award winner; Zones 5–8

Name: 'Eskimo' (*V.* 'Cayuga' × *V. utile*)
Flowers: large snowballs composed of pale cream, pink-tinged buds opening pure white; not fragrant; midspring
Foliage: lustrous dark green, semi-evergreen
Fruits: dull red ripening to black
Comments: dense and compact, to 4 feet; Styer Award winner; Zones 6–8

Name: 'Mohawk' (*V.* × *burkwoodii* × *V. carlesii*)
Flowers: dark red flower buds highly ornamental for several weeks before opening to white petals with red reverse; spicy clove scent; early to mid-spring
Foliage: dark glossy green leaves; turns brilliant orange-red in fall
Fruits: not showy; summer
Comments: compact growth; resistant to bacterial leaf spot and mildew; Styer Award winner; Zones 5–9

Name: 'Mohican' (*V. lantana*)
Flowers: creamy white, lacy, somewhat rounded, 5-inch clusters in midspring
Foliage: wrinkled, leathery, dark green with felty white undersides
Fruits: large clusters, brilliant orange-red for a month in fall before turning black
Comments: dense shrub, to 8 feet tall by 10 feet wide; showier fruit than the species; performs well in Midwest and North, poorly in South; resistant to leaf spot; Zones 4–7

Name: 'Oneida' (*V. dilatatum* × *V. lobophyllum*)

Flowers: lacy, white, flat-topped clusters in mid-spring, with sporadic flowering in summer

Foliage: thinner and of finer texture than most viburnums; pale yellow and orange-red in autumn

Fruits: abundant, glossy, cardinal red; persist until mid- or late winter

Comments: upright and wide-spreading; good in Midwest and North; Zones 5–8

Name: 'Onondaga' (*V. sargentii*)

Flowers: red buds open to pink-tinged creamy white, flat-topped, 5-inch clusters surrounded by ring of showy sterile flowers in summer

Foliage: fine-textured and three-lobed; velvety dark maroon new growth; maroon-tinged when mature; red fall color

Fruits: glossy red in autumn; persist into winter

Comments: rounded shrub; performs well in North; Zones 4–7; 'Susquehanna' similar, performs better in South (to Zone 8)

Name: 'Shasta' (*V. plicatum* var. *tomentosum*)

Flowers: enormous double rows of flat-topped clusters with showy, pure white sterile flowers in outer ring; late spring

Foliage: dark green with heavy texture, turning velvety red in autumn

Fruits: bright red, changing to black in midsummer; showy if not eaten by birds

Comments: 6 feet tall, twice as wide; striking gray horizontal branching in winter; Styer Award winner; Zones 6–8

Name: 'Shoshoni' (seedling of *V. plicatum* var. *tomentosum* 'Shasta')

Flowers: profuse double rows of flat-topped white clusters with very showy sterile outer ring; late spring

Foliage: dark green, turning reddish purple in autumn

Fruits: glossy red, abundant in midsummer

Comments: compact, smaller than parent, to 4 feet tall and 8 feet wide; excellent horizontal branching in winter; needs shade in South; Zones 5–8

(*Ilex verticillata*), described in Chapter 2. Red chokeberry, however, is a leggier plant that spreads by suckers to form thickets. Relegate it to a naturalistic landscape or wildlife garden where it will form a sea of red for several months late in the year. The cultivar 'Brilliantissima' has much larger and showier berries than the species. With its dazzling berries and rich red or purplish fall foliage, this chokeberry outdoes just about any plant in the fall garden.

As a group, the cotoneasters (*Cotoneaster* spp.) provide dependable year-round texture and color to a four-season landscape. Almost all of the many species and cultivars create a significant berry display for several months in autumn, but two species outshine all the others for the sheer abundance of their red fruits.

Cranberry cotoneaster (*C. apiculatus*) develops a heavy display of cranberry red pomes, which resemble miniature apples lined up along the mounded shrubs' herringbone-patterned stems. Deep purplish fall leaves create a contrasting backdrop that sets off the tapestry of berries. Very similar in appearance but lower-growing, creeping cotoneaster (*C. adpressus*) decks its ground-hugging branches with dark red berries. The variety *praecox* grows taller, reaching 3 feet tall and twice as wide.

While cotoneaster berries create a display best enjoyed from nearby, the berries of scarlet firethorn or pyracantha (*Pyracantha coccinea*) form spectacular clusters that engage your attention even from across the garden. The fruits may occur in such quantities as to almost obscure firethorn's semi-evergreen foliage.

Cultivars of this drought- and heat-resistant shrub abound. You can choose cultivars with berries of lustrous red, orange, or golden yellow on either upright or mounding plants. Upright cultivars, such as 'Lalandei', can be trained to grow up a pillar or lamppost. Or you can fan

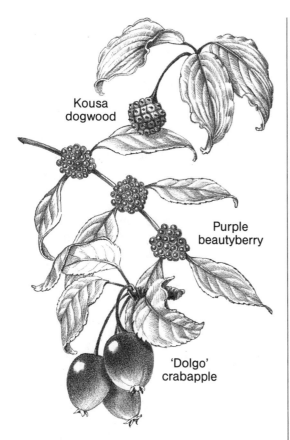

Kousa
dogwood

Purple
beautyberry

'Dolgo'
crabapple

Showy fall fruits. Much of autumn's excitement comes from ripening fruits and berries. For outstanding color in your fall garden, make sure you include the rosy pink strawberry-like fruits of Kousa dogwood (*Cornus kousa*), the bright lavender clusters of Chinese beautyberry (*Callicarpa dichotoma*), and the red or gold fruits of a crabapple, such as the 'Dolgo' crab shown here (*Malus* 'Dolgo').

them out along a fence or wall, where the berries really show off their stuff for months in fall and winter. Use shrubby types as barrier plantings, where their sharp thorns discourage even the most intrepid invaders.

Like many other rose family members, firethorn falls prey to fire blight and scab, both of which may disfigure or diminish the fruits. The best cultivars resist these ailments, so choose wisely or your garden will be berryless.

Trees for Bright Berries

Hawthorns (*Crataegus* spp.) look rather like cotoneasters turned into trees, with their little red fruits dangling in pretty clusters throughout the canopy. One cultivar of the many available outshines all the others when it comes to landscaping for year-round beauty. This is the magnificent *C. viridis* 'Winter King', with orange-red fall and winter berries that are so persistent and prolific, they paint a wash of red all over the branches for months on end. (See "The Bright Berries of Winter" on page 43 and "The Late-Spring Canopy" on page 89 for more about hawthorns.)

If hawthorns resemble cotoneasters, then mountain ashes (*Sorbus* spp.) remind me of firethorns grown into trees. The berry clusters of both plants are about the same size, creating heavy masses of intense color that can weigh the branches toward the ground.

The most readily available mountain ash is the European mountain ash (*S. aucuparia*). It's a tough, cold-hardy tree that prospers in New England, the West, and the upper Midwest, but languishes in the South and lower Midwest. If borers pose a problem in your area, however, a European mountain ash is not a good choice. Instead, choose the equally attractive and insect-resistant Korean mountain ash (*S. alnifolia*).

Either tree will delight you with white spring flowers that resemble Queen-Anne's-lace and rich bundles of berries. The Korean species' leaves develop richer fall colors, and its bloom clusters are larger. While you'll recognize the many European mountain ash cultivars right away because of their characteristic compound leaves, the Korean species masquerades as a beech with simple, crisp beechlike leaves and smooth silvery gray bark.

Red to orange-red berries of both species can almost conceal the foliage in a good year, but squirrels and birds can eat them all up in the space of a few weeks. Each year I watch with delight as the berries on the trees at the foot of my neighbor's driveway ripen to Sunkist orange in late summer. But birds and squirrels start feasting and quickly strip away the berries. Not a single fruit remains after a week or two.

If no hungry wildlife devours mountain ash berries, they will last through autumn and well into winter. The showy berries of 'Brilliant Yellow', a yellow-berried cultivar of European mountain ash, may successfully escape bird depredations and linger into autumn and beyond because birds often ignore yellow fruits.

Sorbus rufoferruginea 'Longwood Sunset' may be hard to come by but is worth seeking out. Almost indistinguishable from European mountain ash, 'Longwood Sunset' excels over both European and Korean mountain ashes in hot, humid climates. Unlike the other two species, it takes stressful summers in stride without defoliating or losing its berries to scab fungus. Fall foliage color and berries are both cardinal red.

Two white-berried mountain ashes (*S. cashmiriana* and *S. forrestii*) make spectacular and unusual fall statements. They can be mail-ordered from Forestfarm Nursery in Oregon. (See "Resources for Four-Season Landscapes" on page 328.)

Crabapples (*Malus* cultivars) adorn the fall scene with red, orange, or gold fruits, which color up before the foliage, creating a pretty contrast of bright fruit and green leaves. Leaves of some cultivars later develop attractive shades of orange or gold, but most change to an undistinguished yellowish green before dropping. Nevertheless, the combination of gleaming fruits set against changing foliage paints a stimulating fall scene.

As with most fruiting trees, feasting wildlife can strip away this show. But more often, birds and squirrels nibble at crabapples throughout fall and winter rather than devastating the fruits seemingly overnight. Some older crabapple cultivars drop fruits early, creating a mess, but newer, improved cultivars hold onto theirs well into winter.

"Choosing a Crabapple for Four-Season Display" on page 86 lists some of the best disease-resistant crabapple cultivars for four-season landscapes. These choice trees go about their business undaunted by the disfiguring scab and leaf spot fungi that plague many older crabapple cultivars. They'll provide four seasons of distinguished service in your garden with their gorgeous spring flowers, fine summer foliage, colorful fall foliage, and showy fruits that persist well into winter.

Autumn's Flowers

Fall flowering is a chancy business for a plant. The season is short and can be cruel. Flowers may not have enough time to set seed before frost cuts them down. Few woody plants flower in fall, engaged as they are in hardening off summer's growth in preparation for the coming winter. However, each of autumn's flowers is all the more cherished in this season when flowers are rare.

Many of fall's flowering trees, shrubs, and perennials—perhaps the majority of them—are late-summer bloomers that keep on flowering well into autumn, sometimes right up until frost. You can often extend perennials' end-of-summer bloom into fall by deadheading flowers as they fade.

LANDSCAPE PLANTS WITH SHOWY FALL BERRIES

Huge clusters of ripening berries can be as colorful as any flowers. The following plants put on a stunning display of attractive berries at the end of the year. See "Plants with Showy Winter Berries" on page 46 for other plants with fall berries that linger well into winter.

Deciduous Trees

RED BERRIES
Crataegus spp. (hawthorns), Zones 3–9
Malus cultivars (crabapples), Zones 3–8
Pistacia chinensis (Chinese pistache), Zones 6–9
Sorbus alnifolia (Korean mountain ash), Zones 4–7
S. aucuparia 'Cardinal Royal' ('Cardinal Royal' European mountain ash), Zones 3–7
S. rufoferruginea 'Longwood Sunset' ('Longwood Sunset' mountain ash), Zones 4–7

YELLOW TO GOLD BERRIES
Malus cultivars (crabapples), Zones 3–8
Poncirus trifoliata (hardy orange), Zones 6–9
Sorbus aucuparia 'Brilliant Yellow' ('Brilliant Yellow' European mountain ash), Zones 3–7

ORANGE BERRIES
Malus cultivars (crabapples), Zones 3–8
Sorbus aucuparia (European mountain ash), Zones 3–7

WHITE BERRIES
Sorbus cashmiriana (Kashmir mountain ash), Zones 4–7

Deciduous Shrubs

RED BERRIES
Aronia arbutifolia (red chokeberry), Zones 4–9
Berberis spp. (barberries), Zones 3–9
Cotoneaster spp. (cotoneasters), Zones 2–9
Ilex verticillata (winterberry), Zones 4–9
Rhus spp. (sumacs), Zones 3–9
Rosa moyesii (Moyes rose), Zones 5–7
R. rubrifolia (formerly *R. glauca*) (redleaf rose), Zones 2–8
R. rugosa (rugosa rose), Zones 3–7
R. virginiana (Virginia rose), Zones 5–8
Viburnum dilatatum (linden viburnum), Zones 5–8
V. opulus (European cranberrybush viburnum), Zones 3–8
V. setigerum (tea viburnum), Zones 6–8
V. trilobum (American cranberrybush viburnum), Zones 2–8

ORANGE BERRIES
Ilex verticillata 'Aurantiaca' (orange-berried winterberry), Zones 4–9
Rosa eglanteria (sweetbriar, eglantine), Zones 6–9
Viburnum setigerum 'Aurantiacum' (orange-berried tea viburnum), Zones 6–8

YELLOW TO GOLD BERRIES
Ilex laevigata 'Hervey Robinson' ('Hervey Robinson' smooth winterberry), Zones 4–7
I. verticillata 'Chrysocarpa' (yellow-berried winterberry), Zones 4–9
Viburnum dilatatum 'Xanthocarpum' (yellow-berried linden viburnum), Zones 5–8
V. opulus 'Xanthocarpum' (yellow-berried European cranberrybush viburnum), Zones 3–8

BLUE TO PURPLE BERRIES
Aronia prunifolia (purple chokeberry), Zones 4–9
Callicarpa spp. (beautyberries), Zones 5–8
Symplocos paniculata (sapphireberry), Zones 6–8

BLACK BERRIES
Aronia melanocarpa var. *elata* (black chokeberry), Zones 3–7

Evergreen Shrubs
RED BERRIES
Aucuba japonica (Japanese aucuba), Zones 7–9
Cotoneaster salicifolius (willowleaf cotoneaster), Zones 6–9
Ilex aquifolium (English holly), Zones 7–9
I. cornuta 'Burfordii' (Burford holly), Zones 7–9
I. × *meserveae* (blue holly), Zones 5–8
Nandina domestica (heavenly bamboo), Zones 7–9
Pyracantha 'Apache' ('Apache' firethorn), Zones 5–9
Sarcococca ruscifolia (sweet box), Zones 7–9
Skimmia japonica (Japanese skimmia), Zones 7–8

ORANGE BERRIES
Pyracantha coccinea 'Kasan' and 'Lalandei' ('Kasan' and 'Lalandei' firethorns), Zones 5–9
P. 'Mohave' ('Mohave' firethorn), Zones 5–9

YELLOW TO GOLD BERRIES
Ilex aquifolium 'Bacciflava' (yellow-berried English holly), Zones 7–9
I. aquifolium var. *xanthocarpum* (yellow-fruited English holly), Zones 7–9
I. × *meserveae* 'Golden Girl' ('Golden Girl' blue holly), Zones 5–8
I. opaca 'Xanthocarpa' (yellow-berried American holly), Zones 6–9
Pyracantha 'Shawnee' ('Shawnee' firethorn), Zones 5–9
P. 'Teton' ('Teton' firethorn), Zones 6–9

BLUE TO PURPLE BERRIES
Viburnum davidii (David viburnum), Zones 7–9
V. tinus (laurustinus), Zones 8–9

Groundcovers
RED BERRIES
Gaultheria procumbens (wintergreen), Zones 3–7
Mitchella repens (partridgeberry), Zones 3–9

Fall-Blooming Trees

One of fall's most special trees, franklinia, or Franklin tree (*Franklinia alatamaha*), begins blooming in late August but carries on throughout autumn. The tree's sumptuous fall foliage colors join the exquisite flowers in late September and October. Franklinia bears white camellia-like flowers, measuring 3 inches across, in August, throughout September, and often until frost. Blooms unfurl from knobby buds that resemble large pearls. Leaves change from glossy dark green to dark shades of orange, red, and burgundy in autumn. Winter reveals the tree's smooth gray bark and graceful branching habit.

Plant franklinia in loamy soil near a patio or in a mixed border where you can enjoy it close at hand; its flowers arrive with restraint, not with the abandon of spring bloomers. I especially love the franklinia in the mixed border of my side yard during the several weeks in October and November when both rich fall foliage and creamy white blooms decorate the tree.

Crape myrtles (*Lagerstroemia indica*) begin flowering in late summer, but many cultivars, especially those introduced by the National Arboretum, bloom through September and into October. (See "Wonderful New Crape Myrtles" on page 144.) The clusters of intricate crinkled flowers may be hot pink, lavender, purple, or white, and work well in a fall garden. The long, tapered, lavender bloom clusters of 'Yuma' echo fall's asters, while playing up the golds and reds of the season. After flowering, these spectacular four-season plants develop gorgeous fall foliage colors.

For a bit of spring in October, plant the autumn-flowering cherry (*Prunus subhirtella* 'Autumnalis'). The semidouble, almond-scented flowers open pinkish white from pink buds for an overall pale pink effect. Flowers open sporadically over a long period in both

(continued on page 202)

AUTUMN COLOR GARDEN

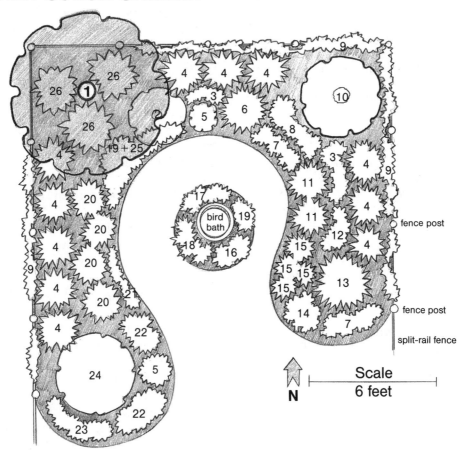

Plot plan for a color garden. 1. *Oxydendrum arboreum* (sourwood) **2.** *Callicarpa bodinieri* 'Profusion' ('Profusion' Bodinier beautyberry) **3.** *Anemone vitifolia* 'Robustissima' ('Robustissima' grapeleaf anemone) **4.** *Thuja occidentalis* 'Emerald' ('Emerald' American arborvitae) **5.** Sedum 'Autumn Joy' **6.** *Pennisetum setaceum* 'Rubrum' (purple fountain grass) **7.** *Sedum* 'Vera Jameson' ('Vera Jameson' sedum) **8.** *Aster tataricus* (Tartarian aster) **9.** *Clematis maximowicziana* (sweet autumn clematis) **10.** *Viburnum plicatum* var. *tomentosum* 'Shoshone' ('Shoshone' doublefile viburnum) **11.** *Pennisetum alopecuroides* 'Hameln' ('Hameln' fountain grass) and *Narcissus* spp. (daffodils) **12.** *Rudbeckia nitida* 'Autumn Glory' ('Autumn Glory' shining coneflower) **13.** *Miscanthus sinensis* 'Gracillimus' (maiden grass)

14. *Chrysanthemum* × *morifolium* 'Mei-Kyo' ('Mei-Kyo' garden mum) **15.** *Festuca cinerea* 'Elijah Blue' ('Elijah Blue' fescue) **16.** *Sedum cauticola* **17.** *Chrysanthemum zawadskii* var. *latilobum* 'Clara Curtis' ('Clara Curtis' hardy garden chrysanthemum) **18.** *Juniperus conferta* 'Silver Mist' ('Silver Mist' shore juniper) **19.** *Ceratostigma plumbaginoides* (leadwort) **20.** *Panicum virgatum* (switch grass) and *Narcissus* spp. (daffodils) **21.** *Imperata cylindrica* 'Red Baron' ('Red Baron' bloodgrass) **22.** *Aster* × *frikartii* 'Monch' ('Monch' Frikart's aster) **23.** *Eupatorium colestinum* (hardy ageratum) **24.** *Viburnum* 'Oneida' ('Oneida' viburnum) **25.** *Colchicum byzantinum* (autumn crocus) **26.** *Fothergilla gardenii* 'Blue Mist' (Blue Mist dwarf fothergilla)

Color garden. Leaves of the sourwood, viburnum, and fothergilla smolder red, scarlet, gold, and orange in this autumn garden. Their colors are made even more intense by the contrasting emerald green of the arborvitae. Ripe berries and fall-blooming ornamental grasses, perennials, and vines add to the season's drama. Although the garden was designed for autumn impact, its good bone structure holds its own all year: Winter features evergreens and red and purple berries; spring displays flowering shrubs and daffodils; and summer shows off the blooming sourwood, along with beautifully textured green, purple, and blue foliage.

late fall and very early spring. Warm days in autumn and even winter bring out the blooms; trees have been known to bloom for five months straight during mild winters in the South.

During especially cold autumns, however, an autumn-flowering cherry may not bloom at all until the end of winter. Catalogs usually exaggerate the fall floral show, which is surpassed by spring's display, but nevertheless this oddball cherry creates quite a stir when it does bloom in fall.

Fall's Shrubs and Vines

Very few shrubs begin to bloom in autumn; most of fall's blooming shrubbery consists of late-summer holdovers. Late-blooming hydrangea flowers often remain creamy white or age to shades of old rose or bright tan. Glossy abelia continues to bloom and show off its deep pink flower calyxes where petals once grew, and bluebeards and buddleias carry summer's blues into early fall.

The native Virginia witch hazel (*Hamamelis virginiana*) blooms in October and November, sometimes as the leaves flare up deep gold and sometimes after the golden foliage drops off the branches. Since the flowers are inconspicuous when the foliage is present, you're better off planting a cultivar of this shrub or small tree that blooms after leaf-fall. The flowers—typical of witch hazel—form little yellow mopheads held close to the branches and emit a sweet perfume that can lead you to a blooming shrub growing in the woods.

The rosy purple flower clusters of bush clover (*Lespedeza thunbergii*) are so heavy that they bend the branches into graceful arches. Undoubtedly one of the showiest fall-blooming shrubs, this Japanese species looks wonderful combined with purple-foliaged plants such as smoketree and purple barberry. Japanese bush clover (*L. japonica*) bears pure white flowers. In cold climates these shrubs may die back to the ground in winter, but their new growth will bloom in autumn and can reach 6 feet in a single growing season.

While many of the large-flowered clematis rebloom in fall, one outstanding species waits until fall to bloom. This fragrant vine is the sweet autumn clematis (*Clematis maximowicziana,* formerly *C. paniculata*), a rampant grower that covers itself with a snow shower of tiny white blooms for more than a month in early to mid-autumn. Use this showstopper on trees, fences, or walls to bring autumn flowers to eye level and above. Tame it by cutting the stems to the ground each spring, if necessary.

Surprise of Fall Bulbs

Spring doesn't have a monopoly on flowering bulbs, even though it certainly seems that way in April and May. A number of bulbs bloom in September and October, even November, waking up after summer dormancy to push their way through the fallen leaves strewn across the garden floor.

Most autumn-blooming bulbs produce flowers that are pink, blue, mauve, or lavender— cool colors that blend beautifully with the hot reds and yellows of fall foliage. The main exception to the cool rule is winter daffodil or lily-of-the-field (*Sternbergia lutea*) with its yellow blooms.

I planted several dozen winter daffodils along my driveway several years ago, interplanting them with blue-flowered leadwort (*Ceratostigma plumbaginoides*). In late September, when cobalt blue blooms still cover the leadwort, the crocuslike canary yellow flowers of winter daffodils join them. They remain showy for almost a month, as red maple leaves drop all around.

A pair of glossy green leaves resembling daffodil foliage flanks each bloom, staying low until the flowers fade, then elongating to almost a foot. These leaves remain green throughout winter, finally withering in midspring.

(continued on page 219)

Autumn

The crisp days of autumn come alive with blazing foliage colors. Stretch the display right to the edge of winter by including ornamental grasses and fall's own flowers and bright berries in your garden.

Saffron crocus (*Crocus sativus*) blooms in autumn when tree leaves are starting to color and drop. Its lavender flowers with their startling red stigmas look pretty combined with the pink, fall-blooming *Sedum sieboldii,* which marks the dormant bulbs' location during summer.

▲ Even evergreen plants can exhibit outstanding fall color. The leathery leaves of *Rhododendron* 'Aglo', a pink-flowered dwarf, turn brilliant shades of red in fall before becoming dark purple for winter.

▶ The russet and gold fall color of cinnamon fern (*Osmunda cinnamomea*) warms the forest floor like a sunbeam. Use this fern in a naturalistic shade garden among blooming wildflowers, where its feathery fronds bring a quiet elegance.

◀ Known for its magnificent fall berry and foliage show, linden viburnum (*Viburnum dilatatum*) makes an excellent large shrub for a four-season landscape. Lacy white flowers bloom in late spring, and the foliage is handsomely textured with prominent veins.

▲ Asters are one of the best fall flowers, adding abundant pink, lavender, purple, or white daisy flowers to the garden. Here their fine texture contrasts nicely with the bold swords of a yucca (*Yucca filamentosa*).

▶ Narrow silver bands edge the fine-textured leaves of late-blooming 'Morning Light' Japanese silver grass (*Miscanthus sinensis* 'Morning Light'), creating a subtle glowing effect. 'Monch' Frikart's aster (*Aster × frikartii* 'Monch') and Japanese anemones (*Anemone tomentosa* 'Robustissima') nestle up to the fountain of grass leaves to create a lovely early-fall combination. Garden: Brookside Gardens.

◀ Selected for its outstanding silvery plumes, silver feather maiden grass (*Miscanthus sinensis* 'Silberfeder') can reach 6 to 9 feet by autumn, making a magnificent specimen for a large-scale garden.

▲ The late-summer garden on page 156 is seen here in early autumn. Red fruits now ornament the crabapple, chrysanthemums bloom where the astilbe flowered, and the green flowers of 'Autumn Joy' sedum have developed a rich rose color. Garden design: Conni Cross.

▶ 'Autumn Glory' shining coneflower (*Rudbeckia nitida* 'Autumn Glory'), a cultivar of a coneflower native to the American prairie, blooms on tall stems from early through late fall. Combine it with ornamental grasses for a great naturalistic effect.

◀ Producing a succession of yellow flowers from early through late fall, winter daffodil (*Sternbergia lutea*) blooms here in a leaf-strewn garden. Once harvested from the wild in Iran, the plant is now endangered and banned from export; be sure you purchase nursery-propagated bulbs.

▲ The feathery plumes of fountain grass (*Pennisetum alopecuroides*) sparkle in autumn's clear light and look beautiful in winter, too, when they look like a dried flower arrangement. Fall-blooming perennials include 'Moonbeam' coreopsis, which begins bloom in midsummer, 'Autumn Joy' sedum, 'Victoria' mealycup sage (*Salvia farinacea* 'Victoria'), and *Verbena bonariensis.* Garden design: Conni Cross.

◀ Flowering dogwood (*Cornus florida*) is transformed from its sedate summer green in midautumn, when its showy, bird-attracting berries ripen and its leaves turn crimson.

▶ Developing vivid fall colors even in shady sites, red-vein enkianthus (*Enkianthus campanulatus*) is one of autumn's most outstanding specimens.

Hardy chrysanthemum (*Chrysanthemum* × *morifolium*), with its musk-
scented flowers and leaves, is one of autumn's traditional perennials. You
can set these plants out each year and treat them like annuals, but they
will have a looser, more natural appeal if you establish cold-hardy cultivars
in the garden.

▶ The unique fruits of Kousa dogwood (*Cornus kousa*) resemble round strawberries suspended from the tree. Ripening in early fall, the decorative fruits are enjoyed by migrating birds.

▼ A perennial border can bloom from spring through fall if you choose plants carefully, with bloom sequence in mind. Here, 'Vera Jameson' sedum, 'Huntington' artemisia, blue fescue (*Festuca cinerea*), 'Zagreb' coreopsis, 'Valerie Finnis' artemisia, obedient plant (*Physostegia virginiana*), asters, and 'Morning Light' Japanese silver grass add to the autumn show. The vine on the wall is sweet autumn clematis (*Clematis maximowicziana*). Garden: Brookside Gardens.

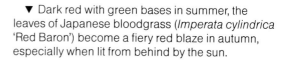

▼ Dark red with green bases in summer, the leaves of Japanese bloodgrass (*Imperata cylindrica* 'Red Baron') become a fiery red blaze in autumn, especially when lit from behind by the sun.

▲ Sneezeweed (*Helenium autumnale*) begins blooming in late summer and continues well into fall, bridging the gap between seasons with golden flowers. Pinch in early summer to promote prolific flowering. Its name notwithstanding, this plant won't make you sneeze.

◄ Creating an interesting mosaic of changing flowers and foliage colors, this heath and heather garden is located outside a dining room window, where it can be admired every day of the year. Shown in bloom in the foreground is 'E. F. Brown', a late-blooming heather that blooms in early autumn. The patch of golden foliage in the background is 'Gold Haze'. The evergreen heaths bloom in winter. Garden design: Conni Cross.

Sugar maples (*Acer saccharum*), native up and down the East Coast, are world-renowned for their flaming scarlet and gold fall color. In the Midwest and South, choose improved cultivars for reliable color.

The most useful perennials for a four-season garden have long-lasting foliage or floral interest. Here, 'Vera Jameson' sedum shows off succulent purple leaves and pink flowers against a filigree of silver 'Valerie Finnis' artemisia leaves and yellow 'Zagreb' coreopsis flowers.

▲ New England asters (*Aster novae-angliae*) and *Sedum* 'Autumn Joy', which has ripened to its final shade of rusty pink, predominate in this Connecticut garden in early October. Sweet alyssum (*Lobularia maritima*), a cool-season annual, flourishes in the crisp weather, creating a soft foreground of purple flowers. Garden design: Barbara Damrosch.

▶ Flame grass (*Miscanthus sinensis* 'Purpurascens') changes from summer green to vivid autumn hues with the arrival of cool weather. This specimen has apricot-colored leaves because it grows in half-shade. Blooming in mid- to late summer, flame grass is relatively small for a *Miscanthus,* reaching only 3 to 4 feet.

▲ Developing their distinctive lilac-purple color in midautumn, the fruits of 'Profusion' beautyberry (*Callicarpa bodinieri* 'Profusion') stand out against the foliage, which remains green until late fall. The berries cling to the stems through most of winter. To encourage lavish flowering and fruiting, prune the shrub severely in late winter to stimulate new growth.

◄ Shown here blooming in late October, even while the leaves have taken on their rich fall color, franklinia (*Franklinia alatamaha*) makes a startlingly beautiful specimen for a four-season landscape. Flowers begin appearing in late summer and continue until frost. The tree has sinuous trunks with smooth gray bark.

FALL-BLOOMING WOODY PLANTS

Because fall-blooming plants have only a short time to flower, get themselves pollinated, set seed, and harden up before frost, few woody plants choose this time of year to blossom. The following list features the best of these rare bloomers, all of which will add great dimension to your year-round garden.

Trees

Franklinia alatamaha (franklinia), Zones 6–8*
Lagerstroemia indica (crape myrtle), Zones 7–9*
Prunus subhirtella 'Autumnalis' (autumn-flowering cherry), Zones 6–8

Shrubs

Abelia × *grandiflora* (glossy abelia), Zones 6–9*
Buddleia davidii (butterfly bush), Zones 4–7*
Caryopteris × *clandonensis* (bluebeard), Zones 4–8*
Fuchsia magellanica (hardy fuchsia), Zones 7–8*
Hamamelis virginiana (Virginia witch hazel), Zones 4–9
Hebe 'Autumn Glory' ('Autumn Glory' hebe), Zones 6–9
Hydrangea paniculata 'Tardiva' (late-flowering panicle hydrangea), Zones 4–8*

Hypericum patulum 'Hidcote' ('Hidcote' St.-John's-wort), Zones 6–9*
Lespedeza bicolor (shrub bush clover), Zones 5–7
L. japonica (Japanese bush clover), Zones 6–8
L. thunbergii 'Gibraltar' ('Gibraltar' bush clover), Zones 6–8

Vines and Groundcovers

Calluna vulgaris (heather), Zones 5–7*
Ceratostigma plumbaginoides (leadwort), Zones 5–9*
Chrysanthemum pacificum (gold-and-silver chrysanthemum), Zones 5–9
Clematis 'Duchess of Edinburgh', Zones 3–9*
C. 'Lady Betty Balfour', Zones 3–9
C. 'Mme. Baron Veillard', Zones 3–9
C. maximowicziana, syn. *C. paniculata* (sweet autumn clematis), Zones 5–9
C. 'Nelly Moser', Zones 3–9*
C. viticella (Purple virgin's bower), Zones 3–9*
Hosta lancifolia (lance-leaved hosta), Zones 3–8
Polygonum aubertii (silverlace vine), Zones 5–9

Begins blooming in late summer but continues well into fall.

While a number of little-known crocus species bloom in fall, the common name "autumn crocus" ironically applies to a member of the genus *Colchicum*. Autumn crocuses do look like long-stalked crocuses without leaves, but you can tell the difference by counting stamens: *Colchicum* has six, while *Crocus* has three. The blooms of autumn crocus form chalice-shaped cups 4 to 6 inches tall. Blooms, which may be delicate rosy lilac, raspberry pink, or pure white, usually appear in succession over an extended period in early to mid-autumn.

The most readily available autumn crocuses are *Colchicum autumnale* and *C. byzantinum,* which bloom in September or October, and *C. speciosum,* which blooms a few weeks later. Double-flowered cultivars such as 'Waterlily' will make you do a double take because they bear an uncanny resemblance to miniature waterlilies. And 'Autumn Queen' is a bizarre cultivar with petals that sport purple checks on a paler background. (See "Resources for Four-Season Landscapes" on page 328 for nurseries that offer a selection of autumn crocus species and cultivars.)

A fall combination. Create a bright and unexpected combination by interplanting fall bulbs—such as saffron crocus (*Crocus sativus*), autumn crocus (*Colchicum autumnale*), or the winter daffodil (*Sternbergia lutea*), shown here—with leadwort (*Ceratostigma plumbaginoides*), which produces cobalt blue flowers in autumn.

Planting autumn crocus corms offers instant gratification for children and impatient gardeners. The flower buds are often bursting from the corms when you purchase them in August, and flowers appear quite speedily after planting in fall. In fact, autumn crocuses are so anxious to bloom that the fist-sized corms will bloom in the paper bag where you've stored them if you delay planting.

While I feel quite comfortable saying that a well-grown autumn crocus bloom looks about as beautiful as a flower can, I feel equally comfortable saying that autumn crocus foliage looks about as ugly as foliage can. The leaves appear in spring, and you'll find yourself wondering what the heck the ugly stuff is, as I did the first time I grew autumn crocuses.

Tall, coarse-textured, and slowly yellowing and dying in June, the leaves can't be successfully camouflaged because they need to ripen in sun. Suzanne Bales, bulb expert

for W. Atlee Burpee's catalog, recommends just looking the other way when passing by autumn crocus foliage in your garden. Because the foliage has died by the time the flowers appear, they look best when planted in a groundcover or among low-growing perennials.

One widely sold September-blooming true crocus is the lilac-blue *Crocus speciosus*. It adapts to most garden sites with vigor and spreads happily if well sited. Deeper-colored veins feather the satiny petals, set off by the brightness of golden anthers and scarlet stigma. The elegant pure white form reminds me of a ghostly lady clad in a diaphanous gown. *C. pulchellus* looks similar but flowers a month later, so plant the two together to prolong the display. I have also grown *C. goulimyi,* which produces successive lavender-pink blooms over two months.

My resident squirrel family, which totally obliterated 300 spring crocus corms in a single season, ignores these autumn beauties. Be sure to plant autumn crocus corms deep enough (about 4 inches), because their flowers tend to topple over otherwise. The crocus leaves appear in autumn, with or soon after the flowers, and shrivel quickly in spring.

Saffron crocus (*C. sativus*) electrifies the garden floor in autumn with its blocky but intensely colored flowers, which open up into flat stars and don't reclose like other crocuses. Dark veins form a contrasting network across the deep rosy lilac or lavender petals. Satiny scarlet, the pistil's prominent stigma grows large and divides itself into three long tips, which extend from the bloom's center like the forked tongue of a snake. Yellow anthers form a charming wreath around the pistil's base. *C. medius* looks similar, but opens and closes with the October sun.

The red stigmas of saffron crocus are the source of saffron, that expensive condiment. I don't recommend harvesting the stigmas from your saffron crocuses, however—once dried, the threadlike stigmas won't go very far in a recipe. I prefer to enjoy mine for the color drama they create in the garden.

I planted saffron crocuses with the fall-flowering *Sedum cauticola,* which has ruby flowers and dusky blue foliage that complement the lavender blooms perfectly. This arrangement looks especially delightful when showered with red and yellow maple leaves. Saffron crocuses's grasslike foliage emerges in autumn, overwinters, and elongates in spring before dying back. The corms proliferate best when planted in spots that bake in summer sun.

Allium thunbergii opens its heads of plum-colored blooms in mid-October, even in Vermont. A dainty thing with glaucous foliage, this ornamental onion finds a perfect home tucked into or on top of a sunny rock wall, where its dried flower heads retain their color well into winter.

Although these bulbs offer only one season of beauty, their unique fall flowers add an important facet to a landscape designed for year-round color. You'll find some of the best autumn-flowering bulbs in "Fall-Blooming Perennials and Bulbs" on page 223.

Border Blooms

Whenever I encounter the scent of chrysanthemums (*Chrysanthemum* × *morifolium*), the mood of autumn almost overpowers me. Even when I'm pinching the stems in late spring, or brushing against the aromatic foliage as I walk through the garden in summer, the scent evokes the crispness of an October breeze, and I expect to hear fallen leaves crunch beneath my feet.

Chrysanthemums dominate the autumn floral scene. Their warm lavender, russet, and gold colors perfectly mirror the season's grand palette. Pot-grown mums abound at nurseries and farm stands in September, and it's easy to succumb to the temptation to pop them into bare spaces in your garden. But these perfectly rounded mounds of dense flowers look stiff and unnatural when inserted in the border this way.

It's better to purchase small mum plants or cuttings in spring, and tame them a bit with pinching to promote branching and denser bloom. Pinching is also necessary, especially in the South, to prevent the short days of spring from triggering premature bloom. When grown this way, chrysanthemums form taller, more open plants with sprays of long-lasting flowers that appear much more casual and at home.

When purchasing a potted chrysanthemum, be sure it is a *hardy* mum, not a florist's mum, which cannot tolerate winter's cold. Hardy types will return year after year if you meet their needs. You can tell which type of chrysanthemum you have as winter approaches, because hardy mums form a rosette of over-wintering leaves at their crowns.

Another drawback of pot-grown mums is their bloom schedule. Chosen mainly for their adaptability to pot production and reliable early-fall bloom, the cultivars you'll find at the nursery aren't necessarily the best for a four-season garden. Because they bloom in early fall, pot mums make good choices where freezes come early, but not necessarily where they come late.

In the North, look for early bloomers, such as 'Minn Gold', from the University of Minnesota's 'Minn' series. Where autumn stretches through November and freezes don't typically occur until December, it pays to seek out the harder-to-find late-blooming mums. These super-hardy cultivars, which bloom in late October and November, are available from mail-order nurseries. They may still be in bloom even after all your trees have lost their foliage—late enough to decorate your Thanksgiving table.

A favorite of mine is 'Mei Kyo', with double, rich lavender yellow-centered blooms on tall stems. Flowering from late October into November, and cold-hardy only into Zone 6, this is a mum for mild-winter areas. 'Bronze Elegance' looks similar but has pale red-sandstone blooms.

Another late-blooming chrysanthemum with yellow-eyed daisy flowers is *Chrysanthemum weyrichii*, represented in gardens by the enchanting creamy white 'White Bomb' and rosy pink 'Pink Bomb'. Growing about a foot tall and spreading by stolons, this is probably the latest bloomer of all the chrysanthemums. Flowers of this very cold-hardy mum successfully fend off fall frosts until a hard freeze finally spells their inevitable demise.

Flowering earlier than the other hybrid chrysanthemums, *Chrysanthemum zawadskii* var. *latilobum* (also sold as *C.* × *rubellum*),

with big daisylike flowers, begins blooming in mid- to late summer and doesn't stop until late fall. Garden designers and writers Joe Eck and Wayne Winterrowd report from southern Vermont that these flowers are highly frost-tolerant. They recommend 'Mary Stoker' for its butter yellow blooms that age to apricot, and 'Clara Curtis' for its bright cerise earlier blooms.

Eck and Winterrowd also grow blue-flowered *Gentiana scabra* in their fall garden, relying on its ability to weather frost unscathed. But hardy ageratum (*Eupatorium coelestinum*), with its misty lavender-blue flowers, fares less well in their unpredictable climate, though it spreads enthusiastically here on Long Island.

Asters (*Aster* spp.) are everywhere in the fields and roadsides this time of year. Their wonderful, cool lavender-blues, purples, and rose-pinks perfectly offset the warmer hues of chrysanthemums. Asters are called Michaelmas daisies by the British, because they are in bloom around the feast of St. Michael, September 29. Hybrids of New York asters (*A. novi-belgii*), New England asters (*A. novae-angliae*), and several other species bloom for six weeks in September and October, with billowing clouds of fine-textured, daisylike flowers.

Often called fall-blooming asters in garden catalogs, these hybrids are sometimes separated into New England and New York types based on height, with the New England asters being taller and the New York ones lower. Such categorizing is for convenience only, because the exact parentage of these hybrids is lost to history. Hybrid asters vary from 2 to 6 feet tall; tall types need careful placement, and you must stake and divide them every other year. Susceptible to mildew, they need even moisture, rich soil, and full sun to ward off the disease.

Because asters grow tall and lanky with small nondescript leaves, they aren't much to look at when out of bloom. Use them in combi-

FALL-BLOOMING PERENNIALS AND BULBS

Bringing a final flowering to the garden floor, these autumn-blooming perennials and bulbs usually tolerate a few degrees of frost. In fact, they'll continue to bloom even in frosty weather, creating a stunning color contrast to autumn foliage.

Perennials

Aconitum carmichaelii (azure monkshood), Zones 3–7*

Anaphalis cinnamomea (pearly everlasting), Zones 3–8*

Anemone hupehensis (Chinese anemone), Zones 5–9

A. × hybrida, syn. *A. japonica* (Japanese anemone), Zones 4–8

A. tomentosa 'Robustissima', syn. *A. vitifolia* 'Robustissima' (grapeleaf anemone), Zones 3–8*

Aster × frikartii (Frikart's aster), Zones 5–8*

A. novae-angliae (New England aster), Zones 3–8

A. novi-belgii (New York aster), Zones 3–8

A. tataricus (Tartarian aster), Zones 2–8

Begonia grandis (hardy begonia), Zones 6–10

Chrysanthemum arcticum (Arctic daisy), Zones 2–9

C. × morifolium (garden mum), Zones 4–9

C. nipponicum (Nippon daisy), Zones 5–8

C. weyrichii, Zones 3–9

C. zawadskii var. *latilobum* 'Clara Curtis', also sold as *C. × rubellum* 'Clara Curtis' ('Clara Curtis' hardy garden chrysanthemum), Zones 4–9*

Cimicifuga simplex 'White Pearl', also sold as 'The Pearl' ('White Pearl' Kamchatka bugbane), Zones 3–8

Corydalis lutea (yellow corydalis), Zones 5–8*

Eupatorium coelestinum (hardy ageratum), Zones 6–10

E. fistulosum (Joe-Pye weed), Zones 4–9

Gentiana scabra (rough gentian), Zones 5–8

Hosta montana 'Aurea-Marginata', Zones 3–8

H. tardiflora (late-flowering hosta), Zones 3–8

Liriope muscari (blue lilyturf), Zones 6–9*

Perovskia atriplicifolia (Russian sage), Zones 4–9*

Rudbeckia fulgida var. *sullivantii* 'Goldsturm' ('Goldsturm' black-eyed Susan), Zones 3–9*

R. nitida 'Autumn Glory' ('Autumn Glory' shining coneflower), Zones 4–9*

Salvia azurea (azure sage), Zones 5–9

Sedum 'Autumn Joy' ('Autumn Joy' sedum), Zones 3–10

S. cauticolum, Zones 5–9

S. maximum var. *atropurpureum* 'Honeysong' ('Honeysong' purple-leaved stonecrop), Zones 3–8

S. 'Vera Jameson' ('Vera Jameson' sedum), Zones 5–9

Bulbs

Allium senescens 'Glaucum' (formerly *A. glaucum*), Zones 3–9

A. stellatum (prairie onion), Zones 4–8

A. thunbergii (formerly *A. japonicum*), Zones 4–8

Colchicum autumnale (meadow saffron), Zones 3–9

C. cilicicum, Zones 5–9

C. speciosum, Zones 3–9

Crocus goulimyi, Zones 7–9

C. medius, Zones 6–9

C. ochroleucus, Zones 5–9

C. sativus (saffron crocus), Zones 5–9

C. speciosus (showy crocus), Zones 5–9

Cyclamen hederifolium, formerly *C. neapolitanum* (hardy cyclamen), Zones 5–9

Galanthus nivalis subsp. *reginae-olgae* (autumn snowdrop), Zones 3–7

Leucojum autumnale (autumn snowflake), Zones 5–9

Lycoris radiata (red spider lily), Zones 7–10*

Nerine bowdenii, Zones 9–10

Sternbergia lutea (winter daffodil), Zones 6–9

*Begins blooming in late summer but continues well into fall.

nation with earlier-blooming plants that draw your attention away from the asters until it's their turn to shine. Pinching asters early in the growing season encourages denser, more floriferous plants.

Some cultivars bloom later than the species, carrying on well into November in freeze-free areas. 'Our Latest One', with medium violet-blue flowers on 3-foot stems, blooms throughout October in North Carolina and November farther north. 'Fanny's Aster' is a late-blooming aster, displaying darker flowers than 'Our Latest One'.

Cushion forms of aster are derived from the species *A. dumosus*. Their small lilac-blue flowers bring vivacious blooms to the front of a mixed border. These low growers combine well with a background of grasses or Japanese anemones (*Anemone* × *hybrida*). *Aster* × *frikartii*, a hybrid of two European asters, bears large, daisylike flowers that display a frill of lavender-blue ray petals surrounding a prominent yellow disc. Blooms start appearing in July and keep right on bearing through October. This desirable hybrid resists mildew, which can disfigure other asters. The cultivar 'Monch' boasts the bluest flowers of any aster, while 'Wonder of Staffa' features darker lavender-blue flowers.

If you wish to draw on nature for garden inspiration, grow some goldenrods (*Solidago* spp.) with your asters. Their golden yellow flower clusters form long, arching feathers. The color and form of the goldenrods create the perfect contrast to the asters' cool-colored clouds. This much-maligned roadside wildflower does not cause hay fever, as is so commonly believed, but happens to bloom at the same time as the inconspicuous real culprit: ragweed.

European-bred cultivars of goldenrod are now becoming more readily available. Since it's another favorite wildflower of my husband's,

I planted a well-behaved, 2-foot-tall cultivar of *S. canadensis* named 'Crown of Rays' in front of several 5-foot-tall plants of sneezeweed (*Helenium autumnale* 'Red-Gold Hybrid'). Beside these I set some 6-foot-tall *Rudbeckia nitida* 'Autumn Glory' for a hot-colored early-fall combination.

Asters may not be much to look at until September, but *Sedum* 'Autumn Joy' earns its fine reputation by being the single most showy perennial you can use in a four-season landscape. I enjoy its changing form and color every season of the year. Starting out in spring as a rosette of fleshy jade green leaves, 'Autumn Joy' grows into a substantial mound topped by pale green, cauliflower-like buds in summer. These gradually turn light pink, then deep rosy pink, and finally rusty red as autumn progresses.

Winter forces the leaves of 'Autumn Joy' to drop, but the bare stems remain, holding aloft the reddish brown dried flower heads. The whole arrangement resembles a rusted metal sculpture that attracts attention throughout winter. The flower heads' changing colors succeed well with a number of plants, but I like them planted with red-leaved Japanese barberries (*Berberis thunbergii* var. *atropurpurea*) and ornamental grasses.

Another of my can't-do-without fall-blooming perennials is a Kamchatka bugbane cultivar, *Cimicifuga simplex* 'White Pearl' (also sold as 'The Pearl'). Thriving in semishade, this October-blooming selection of a native wildflower produces tall wands of light-catching, fluffy white flowers above handsome clumps of deeply divided foliage. You can create a sensation in autumn by grouping a dozen of these tall plants on the edge of a woodland or behind or between low shrubs. The numerous bottlebrush flower stalks all arch the same direction, creating a windswept look even in still air.

The flowers of fall. By choosing perennials with autumn bloom in mind, your flower borders can be as bright in fall as in spring. Some of the best include blue-flowering azure monkshood (*Aconitum carmichaelii*), pink, white or lavender New England asters (*Aster novae-angliae*), and the pearly white wands of 'White Pearl' Kamchatka bugbane (*Cimicifuga simplex* 'White Pearl').

The fall-blooming azure monkshood (*Aconitum carmichaelii*) flourishes in light shade beneath trees. Contributing handsome, bold-textured, deeply divided leaves throughout the growing season, monkshood enriches the garden in September and October with tall stalks of dark blue flowers. The spires bear helmet- or hood-shaped flowers reminiscent of a secretive monk with his cloak pulled down low to conceal his face.

Cultivars of this blue beauty can grow 4 to 6 feet tall. So, use monkshoods boldly, allowing the spires to rise up behind or between low shrubs. Or try them behind clumps of hostas and ferns beneath high-branched trees. While the species tends to lean a bit and benefits from staking, the cultivar 'Arendsii' grows strong and sturdy without support.

It looks like a begonia, and it feels like a begonia, but the hardy begonia (*Begonia grandis*) overwinters as far north as Boston and New York. I first observed this plant on an early October day, where its quiet beauty stood sentry over a shady walk. Hardy begonias produce reddish pink stems decked with sprays of pretty pink flowers from mid-September until frost, bringing welcome color to shady garden sites.

Even before blooming, however, hardy begonias are attractive. As with many begonias, the heart-shaped leaves are shiny and somewhat succulent, with ruby red backs and red veins. When lit from behind by the sun, the plant gleams.

My fall garden wouldn't be complete without sturdy clumps of elegant Japanese anemones (*Anemone × hybrida*). I first fell in love with these flowers when at Cornell. They grew in a protected courtyard at the Plant Science Building and bloomed there with abandon during the fall semester, when the cobalt blue flowers of leadwort (*Ceratostigma plumbaginoides*) formed a pretty carpet at their feet.

These anemones form nice clumps of dark green, lobed leaves that look handsome all summer. In early autumn, tall, wiry flower stems topped with clusters of blooms flutter high above the foliage. The flowers are actually petal-less, consisting of showy bracts surrounding a central crown of golden stamens. Bracts may be pinkish mauve, rose, or white, and a darker shade usually tints the backs of pink sepals. The wiry stems and flower buds often sport a silky fur coat that sparkles in sunlight like the fine hair of a newborn baby.

The grapeleaf anemone (*A. vitifolia*, formerly *A. tomentosa*) begins blooming in August, a month earlier than the hybrids—a reliable clue to its identity. Blooms of this floriferous plant keep opening throughout September. 'Robustissima' is a truly superb plant, with silvery pink blooms that stand on graceful tall stems well above the foliage.

Of the hybrid cultivars, my favorite— perhaps because it has performed so well in my garden—is 3-foot-tall 'Avalanche', a semi-double white form. The petal-like bracts form a ruffly frame like a starched white collar surrounding the yellow stamens.

Fully double hybrid anemone flowers, such as the mauve 'Margarete', tend to camouflage the stamens—a real failing, in my opinion. And, at least in my garden, the weight of all those extra flower parts bends the stems into a dejected slouch. I prefer the single, silvery pink 'September Charm' over double pinks. 'Honorine Jobert', the oldest white-flowered cultivar and still top-rated today, grows into an impressive 4-foot-tall clump of small but numerous single white flowers.

Japanese anemones form happy alliances with shrubs and other fall flowers. Use white anemones with any of the hot-colored flowers of fall, and give them an evergreen background. Save the pink and mauve ones to complement the blues and lavenders of asters and monkshoods or the blue-green needles of dwarf conifers and junipers.

Many other fall-flowering perennials can turn this often-neglected season into a time of enduring interest. See "Fall-Blooming Perennials and Bulbs" on page 223.

Glorious Grasses

Throughout the summer months, ornamental grasses grow steadily and surreptitiously, becoming ever larger and taller, their long streamers of leaves eventually achieving a volume that you could hardly imagine in April. By September, the maiden grass (*Miscanthus sinensis* 'Gracillimus') along the street in front of my house has sprouted from the few shoots of spring into an immense sheaf arching above my head and reaching wider than my outstretched arms.

Lower-growing, but still substantial, fountain grass (*Pennisetum alopecuroides*) fills up its allocated space with a chest-high hummock. Other grasses become more upright or vase-shaped, and some reach only knee-high but spread by stolons to form wonderful masses.

Late summer and autumn bring many of the warm-season grasses into flower, adding to their magnificence. Flowers are usually feathery affairs taking the form of foxtails or bottlebrushes, open fans, or upright sheaves. The flowers, attractive enough in their own right, mature into seedheads that are even more glorious. Bristles or hairs often decorate the seeds, turning them into light-catching silken tassels that gleam when the autumn sun strikes them.

Japanese silver grass (*Miscanthus sinensis*) and its many cultivars send up fan-shaped

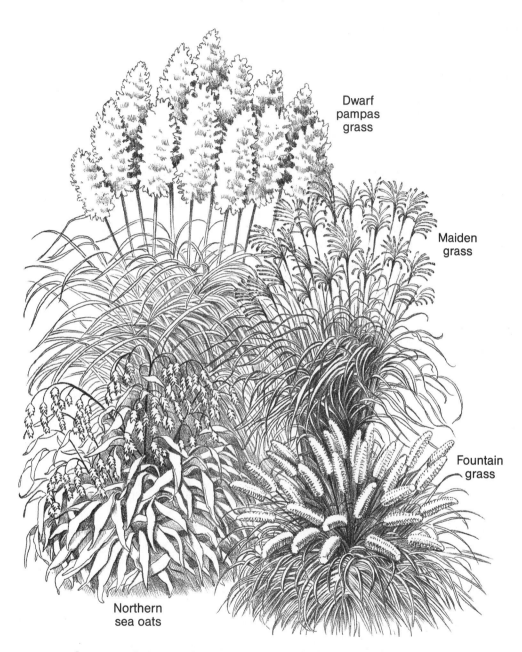

Dwarf
pampas
grass

Maiden
grass

Fountain
grass

Northern
sea oats

Ornamental grasses. Ornamental grasses come into their own in
autumn, when they produce feathery flowers and seedheads. The exciting
grasses shown here dry into handsome "flower arrangements" that add
color and structure to the winter garden.

FALL-BLOOMING ORNAMENTAL GRASSES

Having reached their mature height and produced billowing plumes of feathery flowers and seedheads, the following grasses become the stars of the autumn garden. Leave them to dry in place over winter; they'll look handsome all season.

Calamagrostis arundinacea var. *brachytricha* (fall-blooming reed grass), Zones 5–9
Cortaderia selloana (pampas grass), Zones 8–10
Erianthus ravennae (ravenna grass), Zones 6–10
Miscanthus sinensis cultivars (Japanese silver grass), Zones 5–9
Molinia caerulea (moor grass), Zones 4–9
Panicum virgatum (switch grass), Zones 5–9
Pennisetum alopecuroides (fountain grass), Zones 6–9
P. orientale (oriental fountain grass), Zones 7–9*

*Begins blooming in late summer but continues well into fall.

inflorescences that bloom in taupe or rusty brown and turn into silver-white feathers. More plumelike, the impressive flowers of the huge ravenna grass (*Erianthus ravennae*) remind me of cotton candy. A more tender version of ravenna grass popular in the South, pampas grass (*Cortaderia selloana*) grows into an immense specimen notable for its tropical-looking, white feather-duster plumes. These can be pale pink in some cultivars. On the fine-textured side, switch grass (*Panicum virgatum*) and moor grass (*Molinia caerulea*) form an airy mist of tan flowers that create soft contrasts to fall's bolder blooms.

Of the many ornamental grasses, fountain grasses probably fit most easily into mixed borders because, though voluminous, they're not massive like many other species. Fountain grass produces graceful, arching stems of buff foxtails that take on a pink or maroon cast with age.

I fell in love with black-flowering pennisetum (*Pennisetum alopecuroides* 'Moudry') when I saw it planted beside Jim and Conni Crosses' pond. A smaller and later-blooming grass than the species, 'Moudry' has long foxtails that look like black-bristled bottle-brushes. Perennial fountain grass's tender cousin, purple fountain grass (*P. setaceum* 'Rubrum'), blooms in purple, maturing to pink, while the tassels of the small, rounded oriental fountain grass (*P. orientale*) appear earlier and possess a lovely pink, cottony texture.

Cool-season feather reed grass (*Calamagrostis acutiflora* 'Stricta'), a summer bloomer, ripens into the richness of a sheaf of grain by midsummer but holds its attractive coppery seedheads through fall and winter. Whether planted in a single clump or in a mass, this grass makes a strong vertical statement. The dainty sprays of dangling, flattened green flowers of northern sea oats (*Chasmanthium latifolium*) turn into almond-colored grains so much like oats that you'd expect to see them decorating a box of oatmeal.

Fall in the Mixed Border

Although autumn is the time of year when the garden winds down and eventually calls it quits, I don't like to compare this season to death and decay, as so many writers do. Even though its finale brings the end of the growing season and the onset of dormancy, autumn is a bountiful season, with plentiful seedheads and berries suggesting harvest and ripeness.

The mixed border offers the grandest way to bring together all of autumn's bounty—a place to contrast and combine vibrant foliage, dancing flowers, brilliant berries, and silvery grasses with the stabilizing influence of evergreen leaves. Your garden can be at its richest and most colorful at this time of year, achieving a crescendo of hot colors that autumn's soft light burnishes to a warm glow.

CHAPTER 6

Designing a Year-Round Landscape

Create a Garden to Enjoy Every Day of the Year

Have you ever looked at your garden and felt that it just didn't make it? Something was wrong. The garden should have been pretty—the individual plants were nice, but for some unfathomable reason, the combination didn't hold together. It might have even left you feeling unnerved or bored, but you couldn't put your finger on exactly what was wrong.

This feeling that things aren't right can happen when a garden lacks structure. It can also happen when basic design principles are ignored: when either color or texture are used badly, when the garden contains too much or too little contrast, when the elements clash, or when the garden lacks a strong focal point.

Artists know that first they must learn the basic rules of good design and then, once mastered, they can break the rules to create surprising effects. An artist uses color, line, form, scale, and texture to create the mood and message of a painting, leading your eye, stimulating your senses, and capturing your imagination. You can do the same thing with your home's landscape once you become familiar with some basic guidelines.

Terrific Textures

Foliage texture—the visual fineness or coarseness of a plant's leaves—dramatically affects your garden's mood. Small-leaved plants such as Japanese holly (*Ilex crenata*) or Bumald spirea (*Spiraea* × *bumalda*) have a fine texture and an airy, weightless quality. So do plants with compound leaves or deeply cut leaf margins, such as maidenhair fern (*Adiantum pedatum*) or cutleaf maple (*Acer palmatum* 'Dissectum'). Fine-textured plants seem to recede from view and may look smaller than they really are, making a small area look bigger and more restful.

Plants with large, solid leaves, such as saucer magnolia (*Magnolia* × *soulangiana*) and the large blue-leaved hostas (like *Hosta sieboldiana* 'Elegans'), display a bold texture that

CREATING SEASONAL PLANTINGS

The easiest way to begin transforming your property into a landscape with year-round interest is to plan small seasonal plantings in various parts of your yard, rather than trying to design every area at once. You might want to concentrate on a different season in each planting.

If you design these plantings so that they possess a good bone structure as well as a strong seasonal impact, they'll look good, if not exciting, even during their off-seasons. Combined in a landscape, these seasonal plantings create a larger garden picture, offering something to catch your attention day after day as the focus shifts from one area to the next.

In selecting sites for seasonal plantings, think about how you use your property during the year. Choose locations that allow you to enjoy each seasonal garden at its peak of interest. Try planting a winter garden along your driveway or near the walk to your front door so you can enjoy it as you dash to the car. Emphasize summer flowers around outdoor sitting areas—a terrace, patio, or swimming pool.

This plan makes a lot of sense for most regions, except those where you can enjoy outdoor living most of the year. In warm climates, design your entire landscape for maximum year-round interest.

Turn parts of the yard that you see every day into four-season plantings. Choose trees and shrubs that offer year-round interest for the most prominent positions, and then add an assortment of bulbs and perennials that bloom at different seasons. Create plantings with year-round interest for sites you see every day from indoors—say, from your kitchen or dining room. Give yourself a captivating view from every picture window in your home.

But they make eye-catching focal points when properly placed, and can reduce visual distances in a large garden when used in quantity. Most plants fall between these texture extremes, bearing medium-textured leaves.

Working with Texture

How you use fine-, bold-, and medium-textured plants determines your garden's visual impact. Texture can give the garden a pleasantly stimulating quality; it can also make it boring or disturbingly jumbled and busy. You can learn a lot about using foliage texture by analyzing any garden you like or dislike to see how the use of textures influences its look. Use your imagination to replace a small-leaved plant with a large-leaved one, and vice versa, then evaluate the result.

Too many fine-textured plants grouped together create a boring combination. The plants lack individuality and meld into a busy-looking whole. I distinctly remember the terrible effect my former neighbors created when they renovated their landscape. Though they wisely extended the foundation planting into a border that swept away from the house and around the side of the property, the plants they chose were monotonous.

Evergreen azaleas backed the planting area and provided spring flowers, while Bumald spireas grew in front for summer bloom. Both of these plants have fine-textured leaves and round or spreading shapes. While there's nothing wrong with either plant, grouped together in quantity they became a boring sea of busy leaves. Even the addition of a few bold-textured rhododendrons would have provided some visual relief.

A collection of too many different plants will look just as bad as one where all the plants look the same. When each plant contrasts too much with its neighbor, the effect becomes jarring, a tangle of contradictory

jumps forward and grabs your attention. Bold-textured plants usually seem weighty and heavy, and can look coarse and overpowering if overused, especially in small spaces.

Texture contrasts. Since a perennial's leaves last from spring through fall but the plant flowers for only a few weeks, the best plant combinations rely on contrasting foliage textures. Here, a hosta's bold broad leaves make an effective combination with sweet woodruff's fine whorled foliage.

messages. A well-designed planting relies on a gradual transition from fine-textured to bold-textured plants and back again, with a majority of plants with medium-textured leaves.

By occasionally placing a single bold-textured plant within a fine- or medium-textured mass, you can create an exciting focal point. In my shade garden, sweet woodruff (*Galium odoratum*) carpets the floor with whorls of tiny leaves; into this fine-textured carpet I have added plants with bold textures, including the striking *Hosta sieboldiana* 'Elegans'. Combinations like these are what makes great gardens—gardens that leave lasting impressions.

Other factors besides foliage contribute to a plant's texture, especially with deciduous plants. When the leaves drop in autumn, a shrub or tree may be transformed from a fine-textured specimen into a bold-textured one or vice versa. A cutleaf smooth sumac (*Rhus typhina* 'Laciniata'), for instance, has lacy leaves during the growing season, but in winter the bare, sparsely branched, thick trunks and limbs appear coarse and rough. The foliage of Bumald spirea (*Spiraea × bumalda*) is a refined mass of scallop-edged leaves. The shrub retains this fragile look even when leafless, emerging as a twiggy mound of extremely slender branches.

Like leaves and stems, flowers have a fine, medium, or bold texture. A plant's visual character may change dramatically during its flowering period. But since most plants bloom for a short time compared to their out-of-flower state, consider a plant's leaves and branches as its primary textures when designing your garden.

Balancing Mass and Weight

A plant's mass—the space it takes up in your garden—is only one of several factors that contribute to its visual weight in the landscape. Texture, color, and density also influence how you perceive a plant's visual weight. These characteristics interact to determine how commanding a plant's presence is in your garden. A heavy or weighty plant claims your attention, seeming to move forward, while a more lightweight plant seems to recede and is easier to overlook.

Leaf density and color influence a plant's appearance and its weight in the garden. A dark-leaved plant such as a yew looks heavier, and thus more weighty, than a blue juniper of the same size. Densely branched and needled, a Colorado blue spruce (*Picea pungens* 'Glauca') looks heavier than a loose-needled, open-branched eastern white pine (*Pinus strobus*), even if both are about the same size and shape.

A shrub's or tree's weight becomes most apparent and important in winter. Evergreens carry the garden's structure through the winter, since they remain solid and commanding, while deciduous plants become transparent and insubstantial. Give deciduous shrubs an evergreen backdrop to anchor them to the landscape during the leafless winter months.

Your landscape's weighty plants—generally the large, dark-colored, or dense evergreens—form the major part of the garden's bone structure. You can arrange groups of heavyweight and lightweight plants throughout your landscape to create a rhythmic pattern and visual excitement that last through the seasons. But the pattern must be balanced or the garden will seem out of kilter.

Striking a Balance

Balancing the design does not mean that plants must be placed symmetrically, with identically shaped shrubs and trees situated opposite each other. It does mean, however, that the combined weights of plants on each side of a planting must equal out.

Pretend that you are balancing a seesaw with plants rather than with children teetering in the balance. A single, tall, pyramidal Japanese yew (*Taxus cuspidata*) placed at one end balances three rounded dwarf Japanese hollies (*Ilex crenata* 'Compacta') placed at the other end, because their collective volumes add up to equal visual weights.

In practice, this means that you could place the yew on one side of your front door and the Japanese hollies on the other side for a balanced but asymmetrical look. If you substitute a more open and airy plant of equal size, such as heavenly bamboo (*Nandina domestica*), for the Japanese hollies, you'll need more of them to balance the yew. If you like symmetry, place a yew on each side of the door.

Tree and Shrub Shapes

Another key element of good garden design is plant shape, especially as it relates to trees and shrubs. Trees and shrubs are the essential elements of a four-season landscape, since they remain highly visible all year. Their shapes will still dominate the landscape long after perennials, bulbs, and annuals have disappeared from view.

Along with texture and mass, plant form or shape contributes to the design and mood of your garden. There are seven basic shape classifications: columnar (also called fastigiate), pyramidal or conical, round, spreading or horizontal, vase-shaped, weeping, and irregular.

Columnar forms are narrow, upright shapes that point skyward, attracting attention like a church steeple in a village of roofs. The steeple leads your eye upward, creating an uplifting feeling. Use this strong form cautiously,

Symmetrical balance. These evergreen and deciduous shrubs are arranged in identical groups on each side of the bench, creating a visually balanced design because of their symmetrical arrangement.

Asymmetrical balance. The halves of this design don't form a mirror image, but it still appears balanced because the visually weighty evergreens on the left side of the bench are offset by a large mass of deciduous shrubs on the right side.

because it acts as a dominant focal point. Using a columnar plant like a false cypress (*Chamaecyparis* sp.) or red cedar (*Juniperus virginiana*) is like adding an exclamation point to your garden.

A garden with too many columnar plants feels disturbing and looks overdone, especially if they are scattered around. And a line of columnar plants looks very formal and stiff. Use a single columnar shrub to punctuate lower rounded or spreading plants, and you'll give the planting just the right degree of excitement.

Pyramidal or conical plants, such as spruce and fir trees, have broad bases and narrow or pointed tops. Like columnar plants, pyramidal shapes point upward but look less severe. Because of their formal shape and visual heaviness, use pyramidal plants sparingly as accents, rather than in a mass planting. The sloping lines of a pyramidal evergreen nicely echo the sloping roof lines of many architectural styles, especially Victorian and Tudor houses with their many peaks and gables.

Rounded plants, like winged euonymus (*Euonymus alata*) and red oak (*Quercus rubra*), may be almost perfectly spherical or simply curved on top. Since this shape is fairly neutral and easy to get along with, rounded shrubs and trees make good fillers, working well with most other plant shapes. Use them as the mainstay of your garden's design.

Trees, shrubs, and shrubby groundcovers with spreading horizontal shapes include flowering dogwood (*Cornus florida*), doublefile viburnum (*Viburnum plicatum* var. *tomentosum*), and the many prostrate or spreading junipers. Spreading plants usually grow wider than they are tall and feature horizontal or nearly horizontal branches. Use them to emphasize other horizontal lines in your landscape, carrying your eye quickly across a design to create the illusion that an area is wider than it is. Spread-ing forms make excellent companions for columnar or pyramidal shapes.

With a narrow bottom and an arching top, a vase-shaped plant makes a graceful contribution to a garden's design. Trees with vase shapes, such as Japanese zelkova (*Zelkova serrata*) and 'Kwanzan' Japanese flowering cherry (*Prunus serrulata* 'Kwanzan'), allow plenty of space beneath their high branches, making good street and garden trees.

Use weeping plants, like golden weeping willow (*Salix alba* 'Tristis') and weeping European beech (*Fagus sylvatica* 'Pendula'), on slopes and hillsides where they can spill down the sides, creating a fluid feeling. In fact, hills and walls practically demand a few weeping trees and shrubs, with their smooth waterfall of branches, to add interest.

Irregular plants, such as atlas cedar (*Cedrus atlantica*), grow into picturesque, craggy specimens with tiers of uneven branches. Their informal shapes and rugged personalities are well suited to naturalistic sites, where they make spectacular specimens when silhouetted against the sky or a light background.

Getting in Shape

From this abundance of shapes, you, the gardener, must put together a jigsaw puzzle of different pieces to make a harmonious garden. Fortunately, this isn't as difficult as it seems. Your goal should be to keep the shapes of large, dominant trees and shrubs uncluttered by nearby competing or interfering shapes. Give a weeping Higan cherry (*Prunus subhirtilla* var. *pendula*), for instance, plenty of elbow room so you can appreciate its graceful silhouette. Keep surrounding plants low and horizontal to contrast with the downcast lines of the weeping branches.

Don't make the design mistake of placing a large vase-shaped shrub, such as a weigela (*Weigela florida*), beneath the weeping cherry:

The branches would physically interfere with each other, and their lines would visually cancel each other out, creating a shapeless blob. And don't put another tree too close to the cherry, since it would clutter up the cherry's outline.

Whatever shape you choose for the tallest plant in a planting, allow it to stand alone as a focal point and surround it with lower plants of a different but complementary shape. Tuck rounded shrubs, for instance, under the arching branches of a vase-shaped tree, where they will act as fillers without competing physically or visually with the tree's shape.

Finally, don't be afraid to move a plant if it looks wrong where it is. One spring, I planted a vase-shaped coral-bark maple (*Acer palmatum* 'Sango Kaku') in a terraced area of my garden. Though this small tree has four-season interest, the result didn't satisfy me. On the advice of my friend Conni Cross, I replaced the maple with a weeping Kousa dogwood (*Cornus kousa* 'Elizabeth Lustgarten'), transforming the discordant scene into a pleasing one. Who would have guessed how important a single shape could be to a design?

Creating Contrast

Using contrast effectively in the landscape is like using seasonings when cooking: Add just enough pepper and you'll excite the taste buds, enhancing the flavors of the dish, but add too much and you'll overpower the other ingredients.

Save spicy contrasts for occasional use as accents or focal points that draw your attention. Use more subtle contrasts as staples to add interest and relieve sameness. A dark green tree flanked by light green trees, for instance, stands out effectively but with less force than a purple-leaved tree in the same place. Which

you choose depends on how strong an effect you wish to create.

You won't have any trouble choosing a contrasting partner for any plant in your garden if you really allow yourself to get to know the plant. Take a few minutes to study it. Really look at it. Decide what its most significant characteristic is: Is it weight, form, texture, or color? Then choose another plant to respond to this characteristic. For instance, contrast a strong horizontally branched mass of shrubs with a single tall pinnacle.

To keep contrast from becoming jarring and overpowering the garden, you also need a strong element of repetition. By repeating the same plant or group of plants throughout the garden, you will give rhythm to the design. You might plant five hostas together to form an impressive clump, then repeat the plant as a single specimen farther down the border to link the areas while developing an exciting rhythm.

Making Echoes

If you're clever, you can incorporate enough contrast into your design to bring the garden to life without anyone identifying the ingredients of your recipe. The secret is to use contrasting plants that possess some similarity—plants that echo each other.

For example, grasses and conifers differ markedly in form and texture, creating a sharp contrast. But you can keep the contrast from being too assertive by choosing cultivars with similar colors. The steel blue needles of *Cupressus arizonica* 'Blue Pyramid' match the color of the swordlike leaves of blue lyme grass (*Elymus arenarius* 'Glaucus'). Their contrasting form and texture combines with the striking color they have in common to make them great garden companions.

Instead of echoing color, you can echo shape, repeating a weeping habit, for example, but contrasting scale, color, or texture. For example, plant a white-barked weeping European birch (*Betula pendula* 'Youngii') on top of an incline. Beneath it, place a weeping dwarf hemlock (*Tsuga canadensis* 'Cappy's Choice'). By echoing the weeping form from the upper layer of the garden to the lower layer, you establish a unifying link while still providing a contrasting note.

Background and Accent

In a well-designed garden, foliage usually functions either as background or as accent. When the leaves of neighboring plants blend together visually to form a restful, opaque curtain of greenery, you've got a background. The tall maples and oaks of my woodland, the screen of white pines and rhododendrons along the street, and the hedge bordering my property all work to create a green background.

But a background is just that—a quiet, unassuming backdrop. Without some excitement in the foreground, the effect can be extremely dull. This is where an accent plant can come to the rescue. For example, my pine and rhododendron screen didn't offer much to look at once spring's lavender rhododendron flowers faded. Because the planting was mature, there wasn't much space for additional planting. I finally created the visual excitement the view needed with a single accent plant: a white-variegated ornamental grass (*Miscanthus sinensis* 'Variegatus').

I located the 5-foot-tall, vase-shaped grass in a curve between a 10-foot-tall rhododendron and a huge spreading juniper. This grass grows opposite the front of my house, and it grabs my attention like a magnet whenever I pass through the door. The arching leaves with their bold white stripes glint like sunlit silver swords before the shrubs' dark shadows.

A Paintbox of Colors

Many beginning gardeners don't think much about planning for color other than that they know they want a lot of it—the more the better. But you'll be happier with your plant choices and your landscape's appearance if you plan your garden's color scheme carefully. Don't let yourself be intimidated by working with color—if you think about it, you'll realize that you already do it all the time.

After all, you think about a color scheme when decorating your home or choosing your clothes, and more likely than not you do a pretty good job of it. But when it comes to garden colors, even those of us who dress beautifully often create chaos, combining colors we would never dream of wearing together.

Begin to think of your garden in terms of color schemes and combinations rather than in terms of color quantity. By planning a color scheme for your garden, you can compose a rich pageant of colors that combine to make a satisfying picture. This is easy to do once you've reviewed a little basic color theory.

Free-Wheeling Color

Few colors in nature exist as the pure colors of the color wheel. But you'll feel more comfortable using color in your garden if you start with an understanding of the wheel's 12 colors. Red, yellow, and blue are the *primary colors*. These pure vibrant hues, when mixed, create all the other colors of the color wheel.

The *secondary colors* are half-and-half mixtures of these 3 colors: equal portions of red and yellow create orange, blue and yellow yields green, and red combined with blue becomes violet. Mix equal portions of a primary with a neighboring secondary color and you get the *intermediate colors:* red-orange, yellow-orange, yellow-green, blue-green, blue-

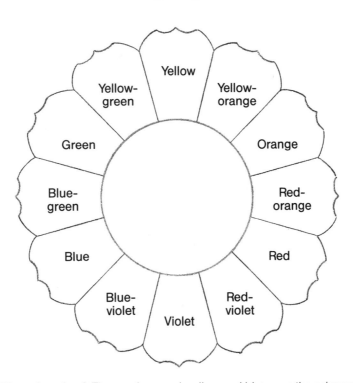

The color wheel. Three colors—red, yellow, and blue—are the *primary colors.* Half-and-half mixes of two primary colors create the *secondary colors*—orange, green, and violet. Equal portions of a primary and a neighboring secondary color produce the *intermediate colors:* red-orange, yellow-orange, yellow-green, blue-green, blue-violet, and red-violet. You can use these color relationships to design effective plant combinations.

violet, and red-violet. These 12 colors make up the palette of a basic color wheel.

Picture the six primary and secondary colors spaced out around a circle like six slices of a pie, beginning with red and swinging around in the following order: orange, yellow, green, blue, and violet. Then expand the color wheel so that the six intermediate colors lie between the two colors that compose them, to create a complete color wheel of 12 hues.

More sophisticated color wheels rely on more intermediary colors and may indicate gradations in lightness and darkness of any of these colors. Any color mixed with white is called a *tint,* a pastel version of that color. Mix in some black and you get a darker color, a *shade.* Add both white and black (essentially gray) and the result becomes a *tone.* Garden flowers, more often than not, are tints, shades, and tones of intermediary colors—rarely do they match up perfectly with the hues on the color wheel.

Opposite each primary color you'll find a secondary color. These paired colors are called *complementary colors.* They look good together, forming vibrant but pleasing high-contrast combinations: yellow and violet, red and green, and blue and orange. If you find these combinations too strong, use them only in small quantities. Or dilute the effect by using tints and tones rather than pure hues, such as peach with blue, or lavender with pale yellow.

Colors adjacent to each other on the color wheel are called *analogous colors.* These colors, such as red-violet, violet, and blue-violet, form soothing and harmonious combinations when woven together in a garden design. Contrasts appear soft and subtle, soothing and peaceful. A color scheme based on analogous colors and their tints and shades reaches a level of sophistication and beauty that primary and complementary color schemes cannot.

Moody Blues and Cheerful Yellows

Colors and their combinations evoke an emotional response from their viewers. In fact, we use colors in everyday speech to describe emotions: "seeing red" for someone who is angry, or "feeling blue" for someone who feels sad. When you plan a color scheme for your garden, you'll want to choose colors that you like and that match the mood you wish to create.

Blues and lavenders in the garden give it a romantic, cool, misty feeling. Yellow brings a feeling of sunshine and warmth, especially welcome on a cold day. Cool colors, such as violet and blue, recede, seeming to be farther away than they are. If you plant them at a distance, cool colors may seem weak and are difficult to see. Hot colors, such as yellow and orange, advance, seeming closer than they are. They are easier to see from afar.

Keep in mind, too, that colors change with the light striking them. Overcast days intensify colors, allowing pastels and light colors to glow without darkening, while brilliant sunshine may wash out pastels. Intense colors can compete with brilliant sun, glowing into richness without fading. In shadow, pastel pinks, lavenders, and yellows stand out, while dark shades such as burgundy or purple become gloomy and shadowy.

Colors affect each other and may change according to the colors placed beside them. Yellow-green looks sallow placed next to blue but glows with a healthy warmth next to orange. If you want to use clashing colors in your garden, it's best to separate them with neutrals. Time-honored peacekeepers include cream and white flowers, but gray or silver foliage, and even grass green foliage, can help to end a color war.

Taking Your Garden's Temperature

One of the easiest—and most visually pleasing—ways to plan color in your four-season garden is to choose plants with primarily cool or warm colors. This gives the garden a sense of harmony, while allowing you a lot of leeway in choosing colors.

Every color has its warm and cool variants, based on how much yellow (warm) or blue (cool) it contains. Take red, for example: Scarlet is an orange-red based on adding a little yellow to red, which makes it a hot color. Magenta contains red and a little blue, making it a cool color.

The hot and cool versions of a primary color rarely look good together—imagine a scarlet blouse with a magenta skirt! You know that combination clashes, so why place scarlet zinnias next to magenta phlox? Plant lavender-pink zinnias with the phlox instead; both are cool hues.

If you're mail-ordering plants, color catalogs can help a lot. Although colors are hard to reproduce exactly, you should be able to judge whether the flower or foliage is warm or cool. Trust your eyes, not catalog descriptions, because what one catalog calls red you may swear is magenta, and it probably is.

You can elaborate on your cool and warm themes with berries, bark, and flowers. The orange-red berries of winterberry (*Ilex verticillata*) look stunning set off against golden-hued evergreens, while the lavender berries of a beautyberry (*Callicarpa* spp.) brighten the winter landscape when planted near the steel blue needles of 'Montgomery' Colorado spruce (*Picea pungens* 'Montgomery').

In your warm or cool color scheme, don't strive for strict color separation. You can include a few plants of the opposite "temperature" to add some variety, as long as you don't go to extremes. Even when you focus on warm or cool colors, there are other ways to feature the full color spectrum in your four-season garden. You can use a vibrant complementary color scheme or the quieter, more sophisticated appeal of analogous hues.

Seeing Green

In popular use, the term "garden color" almost always refers to *flower* color. For some reason, green, the color of foliage, gets overlooked. It's thought of as a throwaway color, the canvas we paint the "real" color on. If you really look at the various greens in your garden, you'll discover that green is an important color, too. Used wisely and well, green stands on its own and enhances all the other colors in your garden.

Keep the basic principle of segregating cool and warm colors in mind even when combining foliage. Evergreens play an especially important role in a four-season garden, particularly in winter when their foliage becomes a major source of color in the landscape. You can combine them beautifully by grouping the cool greens and blue-greens in one plant-

ing and the warm greens and golden greens in another, then separating the two with a mass of primary green.

True green, provided by rhododendrons, Japanese pieris (*Pieris japonica*), and Japanese holly (*Ilex crenata*), combines well with both the warm and cool versions of green. Choose plants such as cultivars of Colorado spruce (*Picea pungens*), creeping juniper (*Juniperus horizontalis*), and blue holly (*Ilex* × *meserveae*) for cool or blue-greens. For warm or golden greens, select plants like Scotch pine (*Pinus sylvestris*), American holly (*Ilex opaca*), and 'Golden Mop' Sawara false cypress (*Chamaecyparis pisifera* 'Golden Mop').

Even in summer, the coolness or warmth of foliage color manipulates the garden's other colors. Take as much time to consider the leaf colors of the deciduous shrubs and trees in your landscape as you do the evergreens, and group them accordingly.

Don't forget variegation when you're planning foliage combinations. Plants with white- or silver-variegated foliage harmonize with a cool color scheme while standing out as lively accents. Yellow- or gold-variegated plants look best in warm color schemes.

A Mixed Border for Four Seasons

All of the design elements we've talked about—bone structure, texture, balance, and color—come together in the showpiece of the four-season landscape, the mixed border. The mixed border relies on trees and shrubs to form the garden's structure, while herbaceous plants add seasonal color. Such a diverse garden offers both exciting variety and continual change to delight you throughout the year.

Because a mixed border relies on so many kinds of plants, it's all too easy for the form to

(continued on page 242)

FOUR-SEASON FRONT YARD

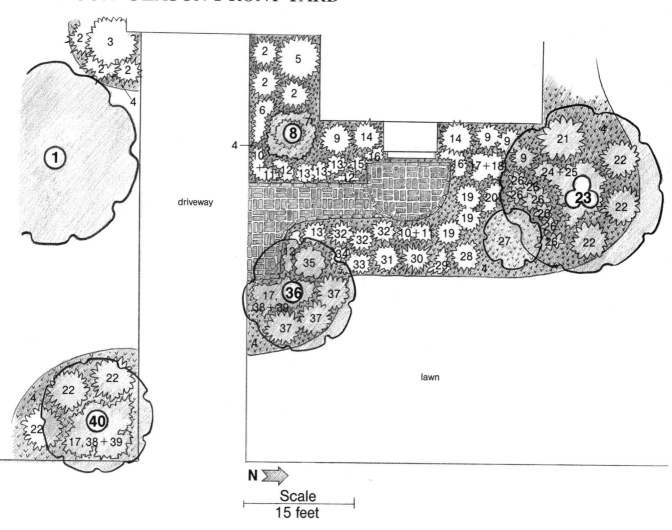

driveway

lawn

N

Scale
15 feet

Plot plan for a front yard. 1. *Koelreuteria paniculata* (golden-rain tree) **2.** *Taxus baccata* 'Repandens' (spreading English yew) **3.** *Corylopsis pauciflora* (buttercup winterhazel) **4.** *Vinca minor* (periwinkle) **5.** *Hamamelis* × *intermedia* (hybrid witch hazel) **6.** *Campanula garganica* (Gargano bellflower) **7.** *Scilla siberica* (Siberian squill) **8.** *Acer palmatum* var. *dissectum* 'Crimson Queen' ('Crimson Queen' cutleaf Japanese maple) **9.** *Rhododendron* 'Aglo' ('Aglo' rhododendron) **10.** *Tulipa* × *hybrida* (tulips) **11.** *Stachys byzantina* (lamb's-ears)

12. *Phlox subulata* (moss pink) **13.** *Leucothoe fontanesiana* 'Scarletta' ('Scarletta' fountain leucothoe) **14.** *Picea glauca* 'Conica' (dwarf Alberta spruce) **15.** *Pinus mugo* (mugo pine) **16.** *Iberis sempervirens* (perennial candytuft) **17.** *Narcissus* 'Thalia' ('Thalia' narcissus) **18.** *Hemerocallis* 'Hyperion' ('Hyperion' daylily) **19.** *Spiraea* × *bumalda* 'Limemound' ('Limemound' Bumald spirea) **20.** *Aster* × *frikartii* 'Monch' ('Monch' Frikart's aster) **21.** *Hydrangea quercifolia* (oakleaf hydrangea) **22.** *Rhododendron* 'Delaware Valley White' ('Delaware Valley White' azalea) **23.** *Betula nigra* 'Heritage' ('Heritage' river birch) **24.** *Narcissus* 'February Gold' ('February Gold' narcissus) **25.** *Ceratostigma plumbaginoides* (leadwort) **26.** *Hosta* 'Hadspen Blue' ('Hadspen Blue' hosta) **27.** *Viburnum dilatatum* 'Erie' ('Erie' viburnum) **28.** *Caryopteris* × *clandonensis* (bluebeard) **29.** *Anemone* × *hybrida* (Japanese anemone) **30.** *Miscanthus sinensis* 'Moonlight' ('Moonlight' Japanese silver grass) **31.** *Picea pungens* var. *glauca* 'Nana Pendula' (weeping blue spruce) **32.** *Deutzia*

gracilis 'Nikko' ('Nikko' slender deutzia) **33.** *Coreopsis* 'Moonbeam' ('Moonbeam' coreopsis) **34.** *Sedum* 'Autumn Joy' ('Autumn Joy' sedum) **35.** *Pieris japonica* 'Dorothy Wycoff' ('Dorothy Wycoff' Japanese pieris) **36.** *Cornus kousa* (Kousa dogwood) **37.** *Rhododendron* 'Sir Robert' ('Sir Robert' Robin Hill azalea) **38.** *Dicentra eximia* (fringed bleeding heart) **39.** *Crocus* Dutch hybrids (Dutch hybrid crocuses) **40.** *Malus* 'Indian Summer' ('Indian Summer' crabapple)

Front yard. This year-round design relies on easy-care evergreen and deciduous trees and shrubs for its structure and for many of its flowers. Groups of trees and shrubs bloom in winter, spring, and summer, while the autumn focus is on colorful tree and shrub foliage. Spring bulbs and summer- and fall-blooming perennials add to the changing display. A fine-textured evergreen groundcover ties all the elements together, adding the necessary bit of formality that makes this an exciting and appropriate landscape for the front of a house.

be lost and the colors to blur. To keep your garden from becoming a formless jungle, follow these guidelines:

▶ Create vertical layers in your garden with informal groups of culturally compatible trees, shrubs, and groundcovers.

▶ Arrange woody plants informally according to size in the background, midground, and foreground of each group. Consider compatibility of texture, form, color, and seasonal interest as you position the plants.

▶ Place deciduous trees and shrubs in front of taller evergreens.

▶ Place low evergreen or deciduous shrubs and groundcovers as an edging along the front of the border.

▶ Link the clusters of trees and shrubs with generous drifts of perennials and bulbs in the lower and middle levels.

Remember the planting pyramid I discussed in Chapter 1? Your best plan of attack in developing your garden's bone structure is to begin at the top of an imaginary planting pyramid. (See "Planting Pyramids" on page 14.) Choose trees for the top layer of the garden, and then fill in with smaller trees and shrubs in the lower layers. Put this permanent framework in place over several years, if you can't do all the work at once, and add groundcovers, perennials, bulbs, and vines later. "Steps to Building a Mixed Border" on this page provides step-by-step instructions.

Focus on Winter First

Your garden's structure will be most apparent—and most important—during winter, so begin your design with that in mind. (You don't have to actually plan your landscape during winter, but at least try to visualize what it would look like then.) Remember that deciduous trees and shrubs will have

---

STEPS TO BUILDING A MIXED BORDER

If your site already has mature shade trees, follow these steps, in this order, to create a beautiful mixed border:

1. Select a single medium-height or small deciduous tree or conifer to grow near the existing tall trees and form a focal point.

2. Situate groups of evergreen shrubs around this tree.

3. Situate groups of deciduous shrubs around the tree and evergreen shrubs.

4. Site walls, fences, and background hedges or screen plantings.

5. Add groundcovers to fill in the border beneath the trees and shrubs.

6. Plant groups of perennials in the groundcover in front of and between shrub groups.

7. Plant bulbs in the groundcover under deciduous shrubs.

8. Add vines to drape over fences and grow up into trees and shrubs.

9. Plant annuals each season.

---

a very different effect in the garden when they've dropped their leaves. (For more on plant weight and how it works in landscape design, see "Balancing Mass and Weight" on page 232.)

Evergreens play a central role in a mixed border, so choose and place them carefully. In the South, you'll rely more on broadleaved evergreens and in the North on conifers to form the strong bones of your design. A mixture of both creates lovely textural contrasts, especially noticeable in winter. See "Guidelines for Placing Evergreens" on page 244 for some helpful guidelines on choosing and using evergreens.

Wrong

Right

Placing evergreens. *Wrong:* The lovely bark and graceful outline of this tree are hidden by a foreground planting of evergreen shrubs. *Right:* This deciduous tree's textured bark and silhouette stand out against a dark background of evergreens.

GUIDELINES FOR PLACING EVERGREENS

When selecting the backbone evergreen trees and shrubs for your landscape and mixed borders, imagine how they will look every season. Consider the following guidelines when deciding where and how to place them:

▶ Isolate a dramatic evergreen tree, such as a pine, against the open sky where its dark silhouette can be enjoyed against a colorful sunset or sunrise.

▶ Locate tall evergreens where their shadows will fall away from the house and walkways in winter.

▶ Group several rounded or spreading evergreen shrubs together to create an effective mass.

▶ Use a single upright or conical evergreen shrub or tree as an accent in a group of rounded or spreading shrubs.

▶ Most broadleaved evergreens appreciate some shade, especially in the South; most conifers need full sun.

▶ Golden and yellow-green evergreens look good with dark or bright green evergreens, as do blue-gray and blue-green ones, but separate the golds from the blues.

▶ Use a formal or informal evergreen hedge as a backdrop for deciduous shrubs and flowering perennials.

▶ Rather than planting a uniform row of evergreens for a privacy screen or to block unattractive views, try a mixed planting of tall evergreens in groups of three and five with medium-height shrubs in front.

▶ Plant deciduous shrubs in front of, not behind, evergreen shrubs and trees.

Influential Trees

The tallest trees are extremely important in creating your landscape's overall scale and mood. By their size, trees tell you whether the garden is small or large, and by their distribution, whether the garden is open and formal or woodsy and informal.

A tree's shape and placement play such an important—and permanent—role in your garden's design that you should choose each tree for your landscape very carefully. Consider its ultimate size and shape, the degree of shade it casts, and how aggressive its roots are. Figure out where its shadow will fall and what views it will block or frame, so that you place it perfectly. If you make a mistake, you may live with it for a long time.

Trees, because of their tall, straight trunks and great height, form accent points in your landscape. Don't use too many of them scattered around the lawn. A lot of disconnected trees break up the landscape design with exclamation points. It's better to create a pleasing blend, with plants of various heights dominated by a few tall punctuation marks.

Spheres of Influence

A tree in an open garden dominates the area of the landscape where it grows—this is the tree's sphere of influence. You can usually assume this is an area of ground space equal in width to twice the tree's height. Remember that the tree's height will change as it grows: Plan your design using the tree's ultimate height during your landscape's lifetime. This might be its expected height after 10 to 15 years—not its mature height at 100 years. You'll probably have to redesign and renovate your landscape several times before the tree grows that large and old!

Position trees in your landscape so their spheres of influence do not overlap, or the effect becomes jumbled. You can, however, group similar trees into a fairly dense grove with a united canopy so they create a single sphere of influence and a woodsy, informal effect. Most suburban lots won't have room for more than a few tall shade trees, though you

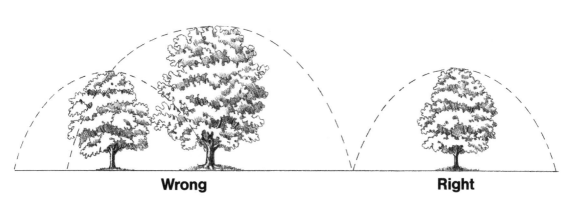

Wrong   **Right**

Spheres of influence. A tree dominates the area of the landscape where it grows. This area is called the tree's sphere of influence, and it usually covers ground space equal in width to twice the tree's height. Your landscape will look best if you position its trees so their spheres of influence don't overlap, thus avoiding a jumbled appearance.

might be able to use a dozen or so small flowering trees.

Select shrubs and other plants that are in scale with the tree for the lower rungs of your planting pyramid. Place them so they fill up the space in the tree's sphere of influence. This means your border's width and length should be at least two-thirds of the dominant tree's height.

If you are lucky enough to have a mature, stately shade tree on your property, you can plant an understory of one or several small flowering trees within the shade tree's sphere of influence without disrupting its dominance. Since you can only plant a limited number of trees in your landscape, make sure each offers several seasons of beauty, and site them for maximum impact.

Shrubs for Structure

All too often, shrubs are used in unattractive ways in a landscape. They're lined up in rows to form a flat-walled hedge. Or they're scattered around the lawn, regardless of shape or size, as if they were so many traffic signs. The way to use shrubs so that they come into

their own is to combine them with other plants in a mixed border. In fact, the bulk of the plants in your four-season mixed border should be shrubs.

An underplanting of shrubs will unite the trees in your yard into a harmonious landscape. Large shrubs, which can grow as tall as small trees, differ from trees because they feature multiple trunks with leafy branches all the way to the ground. These can fill up the background and frame the border, or be used in seasonal-interest clusters. Medium-height shrubs add volume and bulk to the planting, while lower ones act as edging, defining the front of the border and separating it from the lawn.

I love the large selection of deciduous shrubs I can choose for mixed borders. Because of their changeable nature, deciduous shrubs, with a shifting show of flowers, foliage, and textures, offer a lot of excitement and variety for your money. Evergreen shrubs usually take more of a backseat, changing only modestly throughout the seasons. But evergreens create vital green islands in otherwise barren winter landscapes.

Group several evergreens, choosing one plant as the centerpiece and adding others to complement its color, texture, and form. Repeat the same grouping or plan another one farther down the border. Between the two evergreen groups, plant deciduous shrubs and perennials, showcasing one or two with outstanding winter interest, such as winterberry (*Ilex verticillata*) with its sparkling red berries. Space the shrubs irregularly so they're not lined up in rows, and you'll have a flowing structure that will hold up throughout the seasons.

Gifted Groundcovers

Groundcovers—those ground-hugging plants that flow along the ground or form low-spreading masses a foot or so tall—knit the parts of a design together. Groundcovers are beautiful in their own right, decorating the base of your planting pyramid with gorgeous foliage, flowers, and even berries. But they serve many practical purposes, too. A groundcover helps to crowd out or smother weeds, keeps the soil shaded and cool, and, if evergreen, provides a foil for early-spring bulbs that would otherwise bloom in bare soil.

A single type of groundcover—such as the commonly grown Japanese pachysandra (*Pachysandra terminalis*) or periwinkle (*Vinca minor*)—suits more formal landscapes. It creates a uniform blanket that blends different areas together. The groundcover gives the landscape a sense of continuity, linking all the plants into a coherent design.

Informal and naturalistic designs don't need this uniform carpet. Instead, you can use a wide variety of deciduous and evergreen groundcovers to add interest. You can include small clumps of plants with flowers, foliage color, or texture that would be overpowering when used in great quantity.

I prefer to use bugleweed (*Ajuga reptans*) in patches, like throw rugs, rather than as

THE LAYERED LOOK

After visiting my garden one day last spring, my friend Stephanie commented that she now realized what was wrong with her own garden—there wasn't enough stuff in it. Stephanie's garden looks like an elegant country estate on a small suburban lot, and it has many choice plants. But she had put her finger on its one shortcoming.

I wouldn't exactly call her garden's problem a lack of "stuff"—it's really a lack of layering. In Chapter 1, I described how to plan your garden by thinking of the plants as forming a planting pyramid, with the tallest shade trees at the pyramid's top and the groundcovers at the bottom.

A garden designed like a pyramid has at least three layers—a top layer composed of trees and tall shrubs, a middle layer of midsized shrubs and perennials, and a bottom layer of low perennials and small shrubs, annuals, groundcovers, and bulbs. Stephanie needs to add a few flowering trees behind her shrubs and include a wider variety of perennials and groundcovers.

Stephanie's garden got in trouble because she succumbed to plant collector's syndrome—she looked at plants as isolated individuals rather than as part of a garden community. She could avoid the syndrome by asking herself a critical question whenever she selects a plant for her garden: What am I going to plant *with* this?

This question should be uppermost in your mind when you go plant shopping, too, whether you're purchasing a single plant or a truckload. No matter how beautiful a plant is, you won't be viewing it in isolation, but in combination with the other plants in your landscape. Creating successful combinations in your mixed border—on both a small and a grand scale—is the true art of the garden designer.

wall-to-wall carpet. When in full bloom, the spikes of purple flowers can literally obliterate the foliage, creating too overwhelming a sight for a large planting. But the effect is wonderful used in a generous, eye-catching patch.

Another good choice is the shade-loving 'White Nancy' spotted deadnettle (*Lamium maculatum* 'White Nancy'). I use it around the bases of hostas with blue or gray foliage, such as 'Krossa Regal'. I also enjoy 'White Nancy' planted near white-flowered azaleas and rhododendrons. Its silver-splashed leaves and little whorls of pure white flowers weave around the bases of these plants, echoing their gray foliage or white flowers.

Be forewarned, however, that useful as they are, groundcovers do have one drawback: Most grow aggressively, or they wouldn't do a good job creating a ground-covering blanket. Choose wisely, using the descriptions in Chapter 7 as your guide. But be prepared for corrective weeding, or some of these otherwise lovable plants will romp all over your garden.

Prized Perennials

From late spring through summer and into early fall, perennials take the spotlight in the mixed border. The woody framework of your border may almost disappear behind the wealth of perennial flowers.

When carefully designed with clusters of evergreen and deciduous shrubs and trees, the outlines of your mixed border will contain unstructured bays between the islands of shrubs. These bays provide the perfect place to grow flowering perennials interplanted with spring bulbs. Here, their flowers and foliage can reach full glory, but when they fade and pass into winter dormancy, their absence leaves no void.

Here, you'll need to put your artistic eye to the test again. Choose perennials for their seasonal flowers and colors, but also consider each plant's form and its foliage texture and color. Flowers are fleeting compared to foliage, which is on display until it dies back in fall.

You'll want to create both harmony and contrast within these concentrations of perennials. Don't overindulge in the rounded, mounding form of perennial—the predominant perennial plant shape. Instead, juxtapose different shapes and textures. For example, contrast the filigreed, silvery gray leaves of silvermound artemisia (*Artemisia schmidtiana*) with the smooth vertical swords of Adam's-needle (*Yucca filamentosa*).

In large landscapes, your mixed border may have spacious planting bays. If so, you can group perennials of the same kind into effective masses, using bold architectural plants such as featherleaf rodgersia (*Rodgersia pinnata*) as single focal points. Where space is more limited, you may need only one plant of a kind to give you enough impact. But don't overdo variety at the expense of continuity, or your garden will have a spotty look.

Keep in mind, too, that the woody plants in your garden represent a long-term investment in your garden's structure. Don't overcrowd young shrubs and trees with perennials—you may set them back or do them permanent harm. Shrubs and trees need plenty of light, moisture, and nutrients, so don't allow tall, vigorous perennials to rob them. Evergreens may suffer permanent damage if nearby perennials shade out their foliage. Give every plant the space it needs, and your mixed border will flourish.

Fine Vines

Vines are often overlooked in American gardens, but they add the finishing touch to a mixed border. They link the garden's layers with their twining stems and showy flowers. Vines grow upward with twining stems or tendrils, or with specialized suction cups or rootlets that hold them fast to their supports.

We most often think of training vines to climb over garden structures such as fences,

(continued on page 250)

FOUR-SEASON SHADE GARDEN

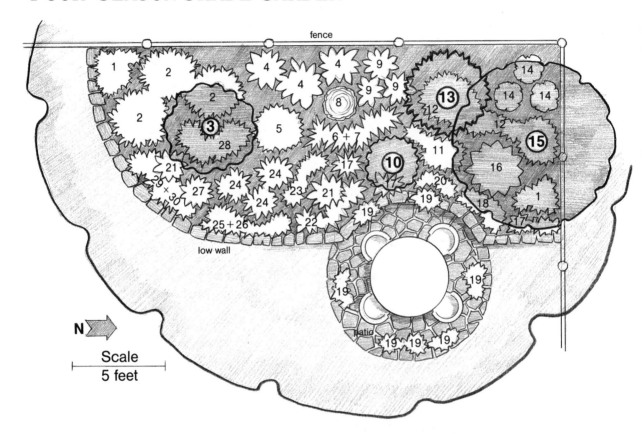

Plot plan for a shade garden. 1. *Epimedium* ×
versicolor var. *sulphureum* (bicolor barrenwort)
2. *Rhododendron carolinianum* var. *album* (white-
flowered Carolina rhododendron) **3.** *Acer japonicum*
'Aureum' (golden fullmoon maple) **4.** *Hosta fortunei*
'Aureo-Marginata' (variegated Fortune's hosta) **5.** *Ilex
crenata* 'Golden Gem' ('Golden Gem' Japanese
holly) **6.** *Narcissus* 'Thalia' ('Thalia' narcissus)
7. *Liriope muscari* (big blue lilyturf) **8.** *Quercus rubra*
(red oak) **9.** *Hosta* 'August Moon' ('August Moon'
hosta) **10.** *Fothergilla gardenii* (dwarf fothergilla)
11. *Cimicifuga simplex* 'White Pearl' ('White Pearl'
Kamchatka bugbane) **12.** *Scilla siberica* (Siberian
squill) **13.** *Enkianthus campanulatus* (red-vein
enkianthus) **14.** *Osmunda cinnamomea* (cinnamon fern) **15.** *Cornus* × *rutgersenensis* 'Aurora'

('Aurora' stellar dogwood) **16.** *Taxus baccata* 'Aurea'
(golden English yew) **17.** *Iris cristata* (crested iris)
18. *Hakonechloa macra* 'Aureola' (golden variegated hakone grass) **19.** *Corydalis lutea* (yellow
corydalis) **20.** *Chrysogonum virginianum* (green-
and-gold) **21.** *Hosta plantaginea* (August lily)
22. *Hosta sieboldii* 'Kabitan' ('Kabitan' seersucker
hosta) **23.** *Phlox stolonifera* 'Bruce's White' ('Bruce's
White' creeping phlox) **24.** *Rhododendron yakusimanum* (Yako rhododendron) **25.** *Hemerocallis* 'Stella
d'Oro' ('Stella d'Oro' daylily) **26.** *Narcissus* 'February
Gold' ('February Gold' narcissus) **27.** *Helleborus
orientalis* (Lenten rose) **28.** *Liriope muscari* 'Gold
Banded' ('Gold Banded' blue lilyturf) **29.** *Crocus
tomasinianus* (Tomasini's crocus) **30.** *Hosta* 'Gold
Edger' ('Gold Edger' hosta)

Shade garden. This design's warm color scheme lights the shady spot beneath a mature red oak tree like a beam of sunlight touching the ground. Easy-care shade-loving trees, shrubs, and perennials open their white or yellow flowers in spring and summer. Foliage plants with deep green, gold, chartreuse, or variegated leaves join them to carry the garden through the seasons. In winter, the deep green leaves of the small rhododendrons make a dark background to set off the gold-variegated holly and yew.

walls, and trellises. But the best way to use vines in the mixed border is to train them to grow over shrubs and into trees. Pair a flowering vine with any tree or shrub that needs a little decoration, remembering to match the strength of the supporting plant to the weight of the vine.

Some vines are too heavy for any but a very large tree like a mature oak. The weight of a massive vine such as a wisteria (*Wisteria* spp.) or climbing hydrangea (*Hydrangea anomala* subsp. *petiolaris*) can pull down a small tree, and its thick foliage can smother the plant beneath.

Choose more delicate vines, such as clematis (*Clematis* spp.) or trumpet honeysuckle (*Lonicera sempervirens*), to twist their way through deciduous trees or shrubs. Neither of these vines is too aggressive or dense to coexist with a healthy shrub. And you can always tame the vine by administering the pruning shears on an as-needed basis.

Just as you can create a succession of bloom by interplanting bulbs and perennials, you can create two seasons of bloom by growing summer-blooming vines among spring-blooming shrubs. Try threading a Jackman clematis (*Clematis* × *jackmanii*) through the branches of a Korean azalea (*Rhododendron mucronulatum*). You'll have a summer display of deep purple clematis after the lavender-pink azalea flowers in late winter. Or allow a sweet autumn clematis (*Clematis maximowicziana*) to spill over the top of a privet hedge at the back of your mixed border, turning the hedge into a sweet-smelling cloud of white flowers in September.

One of my favorite vines is the vanilla-scented anemone clematis (*C. montana*), which produces masses of some of the prettiest flowers I've ever seen. The wide-open four-petaled blooms with crowns of yellow stamens resemble small dogwood flowers. There's also a variety, *C. montana* var. *rubens,* with soft blush pink flowers. The rich colors and eye-catching size of the large-flowered clematis hybrids also make a spectacular show. As with most clematis, these are followed by showy, long-lasting seedpods that resemble satin pinwheels.

Another good two-for-one way to use vines is to plant two vines with different bloom seasons on the same fence. (Keep in mind that both should grow at the same pace so one won't take over, and their combined weight mustn't be great enough to topple the fence.) For instance, you might train the spring-flowering Carolina jessamine (*Gelsemium sempervirens*) to spill down a fence in a waterfall of yellow blooms in April, and combine it with summer-flowering goldflame honeysuckle (*Lonicera* × *heckrottii*), named for its carmine-and-yellow flowers.

Better Ways with Bulbs

Bulbs should be the last plants you add to your mixed border, because their yearly disappearing act means you'll invariably forget where you planted them. You'll find yourself spearing a dormant hyacinth or unearthing and wounding a dozen innocent crocuses, when you were only trying to plant a couple of astilbes. Better to wait until the trees, shrubs, and perennials are in place and *then* install the bulbs in your mixed border, tucking them under and around other plants.

Plant the earliest-blooming bulbs, such as Siberian squill (*Scilla siberica*) and common snowdrops (*Galanthus nivalis*), under deciduous shrubs, where they can carpet the ground with bloom and then disappear from view once the shrubs' spring foliage matures. Or naturalize minor bulbs such as crocuses, snowdrops, glory-of-the-snow (*Chionodoxa luciliae*), and Siberian squill in a lawn for late-winter color. As long as you wait at least six weeks after the bulbs bloom before mowing the lawn, minor bulbs will thrive and spread, forming ever-increasing clusters.

Bulbs with taller and larger flowers and foliage, such as tulips and daffodils, bloom later and work best in a mixed border. Interplant them with annuals or perennials to hide their yellowing leaves and cover up the bare spots they leave behind.

When grown with evergreen groundcovers, early-emerging perennials, or cool-season annuals and biennials, bulbs paint a charming garden picture and aren't left with nothing but soil to set them off. If you have bulbs planted in a spot without companion plants, at least dress the ground with a pretty mulch of wood chips, shredded leaves, or pine needles.

Planted in an evergreen groundcover, such as pachysandra, English ivy, or periwinkle, bulbs seem dressed for a party and won't get mud on their feet or faces. If your yard already features large expanses of these groundcovers, enliven the monotonous green expanse with crowds of spring-flowering bulbs. Just make sure the bulbs you choose are tall enough to grow above the groundcover's foliage.

Suzanne Bales, bulb expert for W. Atlee Burpee's catalog, likes to sow seeds of blue-flowered forget-me-not (*Myosotis sylvatica*) in fall around a planting of tulips or white grape hyacinths. The biennial forget-me-not germinates in early spring and blooms with the bulbs. Other cool-season companions that flower at the same time as spring bulbs are annual pansies (*Viola* × *wittrockiana*) and perennial violas (*V. cornuta*).

Two winning combinations of bulbs and perennials are hostas and daylilies with any of the minor or major bulbs. Daylilies work especially well with daffodils or other grassy-leaved bulbs: The similar foliage blends together and the yellowing bulb leaves go unnoticed among the taller green daylily foliage. The daylilies flower in the summer, giving you a second season of bloom in the same spot where spring bulbs bloomed earlier.

Some hostas, such as *H. undulata* 'Variegata', emerge early, while others, such as the blue-leaved *H. sieboldiana* 'Elegans', appear later. But in either case, their fast-growing, round leaves swallow up aging bulb foliage, keeping the garden lush and gorgeous for an extended season.

One of my favorite combinations is pastel pink or creamy yellow tulips and lamb's-ears (*Stachys byzantina*). Although the furry gray foliage of lamb's-ears overwinters, it may get bedraggled by season's end. Clean it up as early as possible by gently "combing" the tattered leaves with a bamboo rake. The new growth will develop in time to accompany midseason tulips. Unfortunately, the leaves won't camouflage unsightly tulip foliage. You'll have to either live with it or treat the tulips as annuals and cut them off at ground level when blooms fade, as I do.

Most bulbs are practically foolproof, and they increase and spread, making fuller, more attractive plantings year after year. (Hybrid tulips and hyacinths are the only exceptions.) However, many gardeners forget to cluster bulbs for impact.

All too often, I see daffodils, tulips, hyacinths, and grape hyacinths (*Muscari* spp.) set out so far apart they stand lost and waiflike. Bulb flowers look best when clustered together. This goes especially for the little bulbs, many of which bloom in late winter. Suzanne thinks that small-flowered types such as grape hyacinths and snowflakes (*Leucojum* spp.) need to be planted in a generous sweep of up to 100 or more to really catch your eye.

Designing a Succession of Bulbs

When it comes to bulbs, Suzanne has taken interplanting and succession planting to ultimate heights. She's planted an area

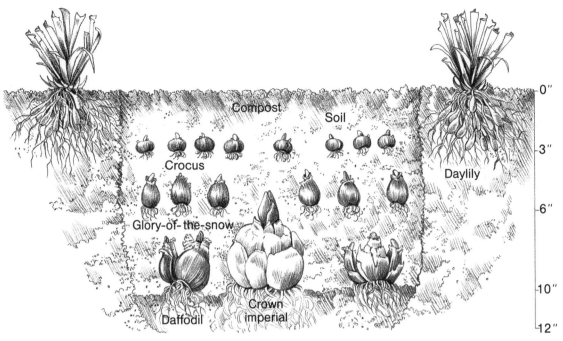

Layering bulbs. Don't waste the space between large perennials! Get more bloom in the same space by interplanting your perennials with bulbs that are layered to bloom over time. The crocuses will bloom first, followed by the daffodils, then the crown imperials—all before the daylilies have filled in.

beneath a dozen or so high-branched trees with mind-boggling quantities of bulbs that bloom in succession from late winter to late spring. And she's added shade-loving perennials to follow them with beautiful foliage and summer flowers.

Suzanne's planting techniques make the scheme work. You can adapt her clever ways to almost any size of garden. First, she advises, throw away your bulb planter and replace it with a garden spade. Dig a 10-inch-deep hole the size of a dinner plate and put 2 inches of topsoil in the bottom.

Press 6 daffodil bulbs at equal distances around the edge in the bottom of the hole, and place 1 crown imperial (*Fritillaria imperialis*) in the center. Add 2 more inches of soil, then plant 12 bulbs of glory-of-the snow (*Chionodoxa luciliae*) or another late-winter or early-spring bulb. Add 2 more inches of soil, then plant 2 dozen snowdrops or crocuses. Finally, completely fill in the hole.

Layering the bulbs in the soil produces a magnificent succession of bloom in a small space. And all the bulbs are happy—they aren't crowded, since each occupies its preferred soil level.

To continue a succession of bloom and foliage, plant three hostas, three astilbes, or three daylilies in a circle surrounding the bulbs. Be sure to space the perennials according to their ultimate size—some hostas can form magnificent clumps 3 feet across, while others are 3-inch dwarfs. Repeat this combination side by side as many times as you like to fill up a naturalistic garden. Or modify the technique, planting a river of bulbs and perennials to line a path or filling in the bays between groups of shrubs in a mixed border.

Appealing Annuals

Annuals wouldn't seem to have much future in a garden designed for year-round beauty, since they live only a few months. But annuals earn a place in the four-season landscape because of their steady bloom through summer and into fall. I find the constant bloom boring in an all-annual garden, but it works in a mixed border to tie disparate areas of the garden together.

For about a month after you transplant them, annuals look sparse. But once they fill in, they usually bloom nonstop until frost, though summer's heat may slow down some types. The reliable flowering of annuals provides a source of dependable blooms that will carry the garden between the perennials and summer-flowering shrubs.

I avoid most of the common annuals, such as African marigolds, red salvia, petunias, and wax begonias, since I find their oversized blooms and gaudy colors hard to use. One exception is impatiens. Though they're almost as ubiquitous as marigolds, I use them in shady gardens where their billowing masses of flowers light up a shadowy spot with pastel colors.

Instead of the usual bedding plants, I like to use more airy, natural-looking annuals, such as cosmos (*Cosmos bipinnatus*), cleome (*Cleome hasslerana*), browallia (*Browallia speciosa*), annual larkspur (*Consolida ambigua*), and *Zinnia angustifolia* (also sold as *Z. linearis*). Start these from seed in your sunniest window, since you're not likely to find them at your nursery.

Annuals that stall out in midsummer's heat reach their peak performance in autumn, relishing cool nights and sunny days. Sweet alyssum (*Lobularia maritima*), Swan River daisy (*Brachycome iberidifolia*), edging lobelia (*Lobelia erinus*), and garden verbena (*Verbena × hybrida*) may still be blooming furiously in November and into December here on Long Island, well after most fall-blooming perennials have passed.

Putting It All Together

When you've planned your design carefully with year-round interest as the priority, your four-season landscape will possess a beauty that won't succumb to summer's heat or winter's frost. Its enduring appeal lies in its intricate layering of plants, in its well-defined structure, and in its changing textures and colors. Each day brings new surprises and a chance to revisit old friends. You'll find—as I have—that your landscape becomes a source of pleasure every day of the year.

CHAPTER 7

An Encyclopedia of Four-Season Plants

In this encyclopedia, I've included over 300 of the best evergreen and deciduous trees and shrubs and herbaceous plants for four-season landscapes. The encyclopedia contains only those woody plants that, because of their flowers, foliage, berries, bark, or silhouettes, offer at least two seasons of interest. Most are easy-care plants that will have a significant impact in your garden throughout the year.

The herbaceous plants for mixed borders I've chosen for this encyclopedia include perennials, ornamental grasses, vines, and groundcovers. Even though bulbs, especially winter- and spring-flowering ones, play a significant role in a year-round garden, I haven't included them here because they offer only one season of interest. But don't overlook them in your garden—their single season of bloom is unforgettably showy. I've also omitted flowering annuals because they don't contribute to a permanent show.

I *have* included 50 of the best flowering perennials, however. They are all long-blooming, easy-care plants with attractive foliage through-out the growing season. The 15 ornamental grasses in the encyclopedia are the best for year-round interest. And the groundcovers and vines I've included can't be beat for multiseason ornamental value.

You'll find these four-season plants listed alphabetically by botanical name, with common names given in capital letters so they're easy to find. Plants have been separated into categories according to plant type—all the evergreen shrubs are listed together, the grasses are together, and so on—to make it easy for you to compare them. And I've included a simple key with each entry so you can see at a glance how much light, soil moisture, and soil fertility each plant needs. I've added hardiness zones, descriptions, and comments for each entry, with the best cultivars listed for each species. And I've called out each plant's best seasonal features to help you decide which ones meet your needs.

I've tried to make this encyclopedia fun to read, easy to use, and information-packed. I hope you'll enjoy it and turn to it again and again as you plan your four-season landscape.

Evergreen Trees
for Four-Season Landscapes

Arbutus unedo
STRAWBERRY TREE
Zones 7-9 ☼-☀ ◐-◊ ▲-△

Winter: Shredding bark reveals bright red inner bark on gnarled trunk and branches.
Summer: Lustrous dark green leaves; red petioles.
Autumn: Small, white to pinkish urn-shaped flowers and year-old orange fruits.
Description: Round-headed to irregular, broadleaved evergreen; 15'-30' tall.
Comments: Salt-tolerant. 'Compacta' forms a 6' shrub at maturity.

CULTURE KEY

✹	✷	✸	☼
Full shade	Light shade	Half sun, half shade	Full sun

⬨	⬤	◖	◊
Tolerates wet soil	Moist soil	Average–dry soil	Drought-tolerant

▲	◮	△
Rich soil	Average soil	Poor soil

Key symbols. These symbols appear at the beginning of each plant entry to tell you, at a glance, the plant's preferred conditions. Four are for preferred light exposure (full sun, half sun/half shade, light shade, and full shade); four are for soil moisture preference or tolerance (moist soil, average to dry soil, drought-tolerant, and wet soil-tolerant); and three are for preferred soil fertility (rich humusy soil, average soil, and poor soil). Compare these symbols to your garden's conditions for the best plant matches.

Cedrus atlantica
ATLAS CEDAR
Zones 7-9 ☼-☀ ◐-◖ ▲-◮

Winter–Autumn: Showy green to purple cones; horizontal branching; fine-textured, bright green needles.
Description: Wide-spreading pyramidal conifer with horizontal, somewhat weeping branches; reaches 60' tall and 40' wide.
Comments: Withstands heat of the South. *C. atlantica* 'Glauca', blue atlas cedar, features powder blue needles and cones. Stake weeping 'Glauca Pendula' or train it as an espalier on a wall or fence. 'Aurea' is narrowly pyramidal with golden foliage; 'Fastigiata' is narrowly pyramidal with bluish needles. *C. libani*, cedar-of-Lebanon, Zones 5-9, is a denser plant with dark green needles; 'Pendula' is a weeping selection. *C. deodara*, deodar cedar, Zones 7-9, is a pyramidal small tree with light green needles on somewhat pendulous branches; 'Kashmir', hardy to Zone 6.

Chamaecyparis nootkatensis 'Pendula'
WEEPING NOOTKA
FALSE CYPRESS
Zones 5-7 ☼ ◐ ▲

Winter–Autumn: Picturesque, irregular spire with graceful, pendulous branches and flattened sprays of dark green, scalelike needles.
Description: Conifer; 50' tall, 15' wide.
Comments: Native tree. Best in cool, moist areas. Excellent specimen or accent in mixed border. *C. nootkatensis* 'Aurea', gold-tinged new growth; 'Glauca', blue-green foliage.

Cryptomeria japonica
JAPANESE CRYPTOMERIA
Zones 6-9 ☼-☒ ◗ ▲

Winter: Evergreen foliage turns bronze in winter. Reddish brown, shredding trunk bark.
Spring–Autumn: Soft-textured, glossy, blue-green needles.
Description: Dense, pyramidal tree with branches to the ground; reaches 50′ tall.
Comments: Best with light shade in the North, full sun in coastal areas. Dwarf cultivars: 'Jindai-sugi', conical to 5′ tall, light green year-round; 'Sekkan-sugi', upright, with cream and gold new growth, to 8′ tall.

Cupressus arizonica 'Blue Pyramid'
'BLUE PYRAMID' ARIZONA CYPRESS
Zones 7-9 ☼ ◗-◊ ▲-△

Winter–Autumn: Bright blue-gray, soft-textured needles on strongly upright plant.
Description: Conifer; narrowly conical to 15′-40′ tall.
Comments: Needs well-drained soil. Excellent year-round blue color for mixed border or foundation.

Ilex aquifolium
ENGLISH HOLLY
Zones 7-9 ☼-☒ ◗-◊ ▲-△

Winter: Highly polished, dark green spiny leaves; bright red berries; strong pyramidal shape.
Spring–Autumn: Dense, glossy dark green foliage.
Description: Broadleaved evergreen with branches to the ground; broadly columnar to 20′.
Comments: Needs acid soil, shade in the South; protect from winter wind and sun. Berries only on female plants; locate male nearby for pollination. 'Silver King', 'Silver Queen', 'Argenteo-marginata', creamy white leaf margins; 'Golden King', 'Golden Queen', 'Aureo-marginata', golden yellow leaf margins; 'Bacciflava', yellow fruits.

Ilex opaca
AMERICAN HOLLY
Zones 6-9 ☼-☒ ◗-◊ ▲-△

Winter: Evergreen spiny leaves may be glossy dark green or white-edged in cultivars; showy red berries; pyramidal to open shape.
Spring–Autumn: Dense, glossy dark green foliage.
Description: Broadleaved evergreen with dense foliage; pyramidal, branching to ground; 15′-50′ tall and 10′-40′ wide.
Comments: Native tree. Prefers acid soil; protect from winter wind and sun. Leaves may be disfigured by leaf miners. Berries only on female plants; plant 1 male for every 2 to 3 females for pollination. 'Stewart's Silver Crown', creamy white leaf margins; 'Amy', 'Jersey Princess', 'Merry Christmas', glossy dark foliage and abundant red berries; 'Goldie', 'Canary', yellow berries; 'Jersey Knight', glossy-leaved male.

CULTURE KEY

✹	✖	✖	☼
Full shade	Light shade	Half sun, half shade	Full sun
⚘	●	◗	◊
Tolerates wet soil	Moist soil	Average–dry soil	Drought-tolerant
▲	◮	△	
Rich soil	Average soil	Poor soil	

Juniperus scopulorum
ROCKY MOUNTAIN JUNIPER, COLORADO RED CEDAR
Zones 4-7 ☼ ◕-◔ ▲-△

Winter: Foliage often striking blue or blue-green; reddish brown or gray shredding bark.
Spring: Light green to silvery new growth.
Summer–Autumn: Dark green, blue-green, or light green aromatic scalelike needles; small dark blue fruits.
Description: Narrow pyramidal conifer; may be multitrunked; reaches 30'-40' tall and 3'-15' wide.
Comments: Native tree, good for hedges, screens, and background plantings. Excellent for Midwest. 'Blue Heaven', striking blue foliage and heavy fruiting; pyramidal to 20'. 'Gray Gleam', silver-gray foliage, pyramidal, slow-growing; 15'-20' tall. 'Green Ice', sea green foliage matures gray-green, broadly pyramidal.

Juniperus virginiana
EASTERN RED CEDAR
Zones 3-9 ☼ ◕-◔ ▲-△

Winter: Needles turn brownish to bronze; strong pyramidal shape; reddish brown shredding bark.
Spring: Bright green new growth.
Summer–Autumn: Dark green to blue-green, scalelike needles; small blue-green fruits.
Description: Pyramidal conifer; reaches 50' tall and 20' wide.
Comments: Native tree. 'Hillspire', rich green all year; tightly columnar to 20'. 'Idyllwild', dark green, pyramidal; 20' tall, 3'-4' wide. 'Skyrocket', silvery blue-green needles, very narrowly columnar to 15' tall, 1½' wide.

Magnolia grandiflora
SOUTHERN MAGNOLIA
Zones 6-9 ☼-◉ ◕-◔ ▲-▲

Winter: Bold-textured, glossy green leaves with rusty undersides; pyramidal shape.
Spring: Huge, fragrant creamy white flowers.
Summer: Flowers appear sporadically.
Autumn: Rusty brown fruits split to reveal red berries.
Description: Broadleaved pyramidal evergreen with branches to the ground; reaches 60'-80' tall and 30'-50' wide.
Comments: Protect from winter sun and wind in the North. 'St. Mary', slow and compact to 20'; 'Samuel Sommer', 14" flowers, 50' tall; 'Little Gem', shrubby. Cold-hardy in Zone 6: 'Edith Bogue', tightly pyramidal; 'Spring Grove' series; 'Bracken's Brown Beauty', compact to 30'.

Magnolia virginiana
SWEET BAY
Zones 5-9 ◉-☀ ◔-◕ ▲

Winter: Glossy evergreen to semi-evergreen bold-textured leaves, bright green on top, white beneath; green twigs on deciduous plants.
Spring: Silky-haired new foliage.
Summer: Fragrant, waxy, white, 3" flowers.
Autumn: Orange-red fruits in dark red cucumber-like pods.
Description: Evergreen to semi-evergreen, open-branched, multistemmed tree; reaches 40' tall and wide in South, 20' in North.
Comments: Excellent native tree. Needs acid soil. Floral show is subtle, not spectacular. Deciduous in Zones 5-6, but *M. virginiana* var. *australis* 'Henry Hicks' is completely evergreen in North.

Picea omorika
SERBIAN SPRUCE
Zones 4-8

Winter–Autumn: Dark green undersides and silvery tops give sharp-pointed needles a bicolored look.
Description: Narrowly columnar conifer with pendulous branches; 50'-60' tall, 20'-25' wide.
Comments: A graceful and beautiful tree better suited to smaller spaces than Colorado spruce. Acid or alkaline conditions. Similar *P. orientalis* (oriental spruce), Zones 5-8, tolerates poor gravelly soil in Midwest.

Picea pungens
COLORADO SPRUCE
Zones 3-7

Winter–Autumn: Gray-green to silvery blue rigid needles.
Description: Stiffly pyramidal conifer with horizontal branches to the ground; grows 30'-50' tall.
Comments: Native tree. 'Fat Albert', very dense and blue, slow-growing to 15'-20'; 'Hoopsii', bright silvery blue, to 12'-18'; 'Iseli Fastigiata', columnar to 8'-15' tall, 2'-3' wide. 'Green Spire', green form of 'Fat Albert'. 'Pendula', very blue weeping form, needs staking.

Pinus bungeana
LACEBARK PINE
Zones 5-9

Winter–Autumn: Extremely colorful patchwork bark of green, yellow, gray, and reddish tan. Glossy green needles.
Description: Open-branched conifer, rounded to irregular and flat-topped; reaches 30'-50' tall and 20'-35' wide.
Comments: Slow-growing. Bark develops white patches and becomes more beautiful with age.

Pinus densiflora
JAPANESE RED PINE
Zones 5-7

Winter–Autumn: Peeling, brilliant orange-red bark on trunk and branches. Horizontal branches and irregular silhouette. Bright green or golden variegated needles.
Description: Conifer, irregular to flat-topped with twisted trunk; to 40'-60' tall and wide.
Comments: Magnificent specimen. 'Oculus-Draconis' (dragon's-eye pine), dwarf to 30', needles ringed with bands of gold and green, needs a protected location in dappled light. 'Watts Golden', green in summer, bright golden yellow in winter.

Pinus nigra
AUSTRIAN PINE
Zones 4-8

Winter–Autumn: Dense, stiff, dark green needles. Bark marked with cream, beige, pink, and gray; ridged with deep black furrows.
Description: Dense and pyramidal when young, irregular and flat-topped with age; to 50'-60' tall, 20'-40' wide.
Comments: Tolerates heat, drought, and a variety of soil conditions.

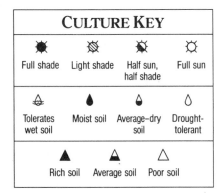

CULTURE KEY			
Full shade	Light shade	Half sun, half shade	Full sun
Tolerates wet soil	Moist soil	Average–dry soil	Drought-tolerant
Rich soil	Average soil	Poor soil	

Pinus strobus
WHITE PINE
Zones 3-9 ☼ ◦-◦ ▲-△

Winter–Autumn: Soft-textured, gray-green to bright green needles.
Description: Pyramidal conifer with graceful horizontal to slightly pendulous branches; reaches 50'-80' tall, 20'-40' wide.
Comments: Native tree. 'Contorta' has twisted branches, densely tufted needles; 'Fastigiata', narrowly columnar; 'Nana', mounded shrub; 'Pendula', weeping tree when trained to central leader.

Pinus sylvestris
SCOTCH PINE
Zones 3-8 ☼ ◦-◦ ▲-△

Winter–Autumn: Blue-green, stiff, slightly twisted needles. Horizontal branches. Orange-red bark.
Description: Irregular, openly pyramidal conifer; to 30'-60' tall and 30'-40' wide.
Comments: Picturesque tree. Twig blight may be serious in humid climates. 'French Blue', bright blue-green needles. 'Aurea,' yellow-green needles turn yellow-gold in winter. 'Hillside Creeper', prostrate form spreading to 15'.

Pseudotsuga menziesii
DOUGLAS FIR
Zones 3-6 ☼ ◦ ▲

Winter–Autumn: Deep green to blue-green needles. Deeply furrowed bark.
Description: Conical to pyramidal conifer with branches to the ground; to 40'-80' tall.
Comments: Native tree. From the Rocky Mountains, var. *glauca* is most blue-green and cold-hardy. Coastal trees are green and hardy only to Zone 5. 'Pendula', weeping; 'Fastigiata', gray-green needles, narrow spire.

Sciadopitys verticillata
UMBRELLA PINE
Zones 6-8 ☼-◐ ◦ ▲

Winter–Autumn: Long, glossy, spirally arranged, deep black-green needles.
Description: Dense, pyramidal conifer that has branches to the ground; 20'-30' tall, 15'-20' wide.
Comments: Needs acid soil. Protect from winter wind and full sun in coldest areas; part shade in hot summer areas. Very slow-growing. A striking, bold-textured specimen for a mixed border.

Tsuga canadensis
CANADA HEMLOCK
Zones 3-8 ☼-◐ ◦ ▲

Winter–Autumn: Dark green, small flattened needles with gray-green undersides.
Description: Gracefully pyramidal, fine-textured conifer with slightly pendulous branches; reaches 40'-75' tall and 25'-35' wide.
Comments: Native tree. Needs acid soil. Best in cool moist sites. Beautiful background tree. Woolly adelgids are a serious pest in Northeast; control with soap and oil sprays. 'Pendula' ('Sargentii'), weeping form for specimen use, slow-growing to 6' tall and twice as wide. In the South, *T. caroliniana* (Carolina hemlock), Zones 5-8.

Tsuga caroliniana
CAROLINA HEMLOCK
Zones 5-8 ◐-◐ ◦ ▲-△

Winter–Autumn: Small, glossy, dark green needles with gray-green undersides, borne bottlebrush-style around the stems; clusters of 1"-1½" attractive brown cones.
Description: Pyramidal, fine-textured conifer with slightly pendulous branches; more compact than *T. canadensis;* reaches 45'-60' tall and 20'-25' wide.
Comments: Native tree. Better city tree than *T. canadensis,* but still needs sheltered site and moist soil. More resistant to woolly adelgids than *T. canadensis.* 'Arnold Pyramid', dense, 25'-35' tall.

Evergreen Shrubs
for Four-Season Landscapes

Abelia × grandiflora
GLOSSY ABELIA
Zones 6-9 ☼ - ☒ ◐ ▲

Winter: Bronze-purple, semi-evergreen foliage.
Spring: Glossy dark green, fine-textured foliage.
Summer: Late-summer clusters of small, bell-shaped white flowers with pink calyxes.
Autumn: Bloom continues until frost; foliage darkens with cold.
Description: Open, rounded, broadleaved; to 6' tall and wide.
Comments: Makes excellent hedge or background for mixed border. 'Edward Goucher', darker pink flowers but less attractive plant. 'Francis Mason', leaves yellow to yellow-green. 'Sherwoodii', excellent dwarf to 3'.

Aucuba japonica
JAPANESE AUCUBA
Zones 7-9 ☒ - ☀ ◐ - ◐ ▲

Winter: Showy red berries all winter; glossy, bold-textured leaves.
Summer: Dark olive green or variegated, bold-textured leaves.
Autumn: Red berries.
Description: Upright, broadleaved; 8'-10' tall.
Comments: Thrives in shade. Only female plants produce berries; place male plant nearby for pollination. 'Picturata', large gold spot in leaf centers; 'Variegata', female with gold flecks on dark green leaves.

Berberis julianae
WINTERGREEN BARBERRY
Zones 6-9 ☒ - ☒ ◐ - ◐ ▲ - △

Winter: Evergreen leaves may turn wine red.
Spring: Showy yellow flowers, midspring; bright green new leaves.
Summer: Glossy dark green, medium-textured spiny leaves; blue-black fruits.
Autumn: Fruits may still be showy.
Description: Dense, thorny, mounding, broadleaved; 6'-8' tall.
Comments: Excellent evergreen barrier or hedge. Needs some protection from winter sun.

CULTURE KEY			
☀	☒	☒	☼
Full shade	Light shade	Half sun, half shade	Full sun
⬩	◐	◑	◊
Tolerates wet soil	Moist soil	Average–dry soil	Drought-tolerant
▲	△	△	
Rich soil	Average soil	Poor soil	

Buxus sempervirens
COMMON BOXWOOD
Zones 6-8   ☼-☒   ◐-◓   ▲-△

Winter: Fine-textured, glossy green leaves.
Spring: Bright green new growth.
Summer–Autumn: Dark green leaves with yellowish undersides.
Description: Dense, rounded, broadleaved shrub; to 15'-20', but easily pruned.
Comments: Needs acid soil and some shade in winter, especially in the North. Excellent hedge or background plant. 'Elegantissima', compact mound with creamy white-edged leaves. Cultivars hardy in Zone 5: 'Northland', 'Vardar Valley'. *B. microphylla* var. *koreana* (Korean boxwood), Zones 5-8; 3'-4' tall and wide; very tiny leaves.

Camellia japonica
COMMON CAMELLIA
Zones 7-9   ☒-☒   ◐   ▲

Winter: Red, rose, pink, or white 3"-5" flowers all winter.
Spring: Flowering may continue into midspring.
Summer–Autumn: Lustrous dark green, medium-textured leaves with hairy undersides.
Description: Upright to pyramidal, broadleaved; to 10'-15' tall.
Comments: Somewhat stiff and formal-looking. Cold weather turns open flowers brown; remove brown flowers for best appearance. Keep mulched. Numerous cultivars, some more cold-hardy than others. Plant in protected location.

Camellia sasanqua
SASANQUA CAMELLIA
Zones 7-9   ☒-☒   ◐   ▲

Winter: Flowering continues from autumn; evergreen foliage.
Summer: Lustrous dark green leaves; medium- to fine-textured, hairy stems.

Autumn: Pink, red, rose, or white 2"-3" flowers.
Description: Pyramidal, broadleaved; to 6'-10' tall.
Comments: More open and cold-hardy than *C. japonica*. Keep mulched. Many cultivars.

Cedrus deodara 'Snow Sprite'
'SNOW SPRITE' DEODAR CEDAR
Zones 7-9   ☼-☒   ◐   ▲

Winter–Autumn: Fine-textured, white-variegated needles.
Description: Mound-shaped dwarf conifer; to 3' tall and 4' wide.
Comments: Excellent specimen in a mixed border.

Chamaecyparis obtusa
HINOKI FALSE CYPRESS
Zones 5-8   ☼-☒   ◐   ▲

Winter–Autumn: Architectural plants with glossy dark green to gold needles in flattened to fernlike fans, depending upon cultivar.
Description: Dwarf cultivars vary from pyramidal to rounded and from 3'-25' tall.
Comments: Best in humid climates and when protected from wind. Dark green: 'Filicoides', long branches with pendulous clusters of green, fernlike needles; 'Nana', rounded to 3', with twisted sprays and stems, striking silhouette; 'Nana Gracilis', similar but is compactly pyramidal to 6'. Golden: 'Crippsii', pyramidal to 25' with spreading branches, rich golden yellow new growth fading to dark green within; 'Fernspray Gold', golden pyramid with fernlike foliage; 'Golden Drop', pale gold globe; 'Golden Sprite', tiny golden mound; 'Lynn's Golden', slow-growing golden pyramid; 'Nana Aurea', twisted sprays and branches with golden tips and green interior, to 6'; 'Tetragona Aurea', golden pyramid to 25', fernlike gold foliage.

Chamaecyparis pisifera
SAWARA FALSE CYPRESS
Zones 5-8 ☼-☒ ● ▲

Winter–Autumn: Bright green to blue-green to golden, fine-textured needles.
Description: Pyramidal; dwarf cultivars to 5'-25' tall. Leaves may be of the 'Filifera' type with fine, stringy threadlike texture; the 'Plumosa' type with feathery, fine-textured sprays of needles; or the 'Squarrosa' type with soft mosslike foliage.
Comments: Best in relatively moist and humid climates. Green: 'Filifera' (threadleaf cypress), bright green, densely rounded pyramid to 3'. Blue: 'Boulevard' (blue moss Sawara false cypress), steel blue, pyramidal to 6'; 'Squarrosa Intermedia', blue-green, threadlike pyramid to 3' tall. Gold: 'Filifera Aurea Nana' (dwarf golden threadleaf Sawara false cypress), bright yellow-green threadleaf, weeping, to 1' tall and 3' wide; 'Golden Mop', bright gold mound, 1½' tall and 2' wide.

Cotoneaster salicifolius
WILLOWLEAF COTONEASTER
Zones 6-9 ☼-☒ ● ▲

Winter: Semi-evergreen, purplish plum leaves. Bright red berries.
Spring: Light green new leaves.

CULTURE KEY			
☀	☒	☽	☼
Full shade	Light shade	Half sun, half shade	Full sun
⬟	●	◑	◊
Tolerates wet soil	Moist soil	Average–dry soil	Drought-tolerant
▲	△	△	
Rich soil	Average soil	Poor soil	

Summer: Inconspicuous, small white flowers, early summer. Willowy, leathery leaves, dark green on top, white underneath.
Autumn: Reddish fall color. Numerous small, bright red berries.
Description: Arching, broadleaved; 10'-15' tall.
Comments: Does better in the South than other cotoneasters. Evergreen in Zones 8-9. Cultivars with ground-covering habit available.

Daphne × burkwoodii 'Carol Mackie'
'CAROL MACKIE' BURKWOOD DAPHNE
Zones 4-7 ☒-☒ ● ▲

Winter: Semi-evergreen; may drop inner foliage in northern zones, while leaves at stem tips persist.
Spring: Fragrant, light pink flower clusters at stem tips in late spring.
Summer–Autumn: Fine-textured, green leaves with creamy leaf margins.
Description: Round, broadleaved shrub to 3'-4' tall.
Comments: Elegant variegated plant useful for mixed borders.

Daphne cneorum
ROSE DAPHNE, GARLAND DAPHNE
Zones 4-7 ☼-☒ ● ▲

Winter: Small, glossy evergreen leaves.
Spring: Bountiful, fragrant pink flowers.
Autumn: May rebloom.
Description: Spreading with ascending branches, broadleaved; to 1' tall and 3' wide.
Comments: Perfect for edging paths or borders. Mulch soil to keep cool. Do not fertilize. *D. mezureum* (February daphne), Zones 3-7; semi-evergreen; rosy purple flowers in early spring; bright red, poisonous berries in late summer. *D. odora* (winter daphne), Zones 8-10; evergreen; deep crimson flower buds open to fragrant white flowers from late winter into early spring.

Fatsia japonica
JAPANESE FATSIA
Zones 7-9

Winter: Blue or purple berries.
Spring: New foliage.
Summer: Large, glossy, palmately lobed, dark green leaves.
Autumn: Large clusters of greenish white flowers.
Description: Open, rounded, broadleaved evergreen; keep pruned to 6' tall.
Comments: Protect from wind and winter sunshine. An exotic-looking foliage plant useful against a shady wall.

Ilex cornuta
CHINESE HOLLY
Zones 7-9

Winter: Long-lasting clusters of red berries.
Spring: Inconspicuous flowers; new foliage.
Summer: Glossy dark green, spiny, medium-textured leaves.
Autumn: Foliage and colorful berries.
Description: Compact, rounded, broadleaved; to 10' tall and 12' wide.
Comments: Needs acid soil. 'Burfordii' (Burford holly), only 1 terminal spine per leaf; upright to 15'; heavy fruit set without pollination. 'Rotunda', densely compact mound to 4' tall and 6' wide; spiny leaves.

Ilex crenata
JAPANESE HOLLY
Zones 6-9

Winter–Autumn: Fine-textured, oval, glossy dark green leaves.
Description: Dense, rounded, broadleaved evergreen; to 5'-10' tall and wide.
Comments: Needs acid soil. Inconspicuous black berries. Excellent hedge or background plant. Use

dwarf cultivars in mixed borders and foundations. 'Compacta', to 6'; 'Convexa', convex leaves, hardy to Zone 4, to 10'; 'Golden Gem', low-spreading plant with golden leaves; 'Helleri', dwarf and mounded, tiny leaves, slow-growing to 3'-4'; 'Hetzii', similar to 'Convexa' but to 8'. *I. glabra* (inkberry), 6'-8' tall and 8'-10' wide with larger leaves and more open habit than Japanese holly; needs moist to wet, acid soil; Zones 5-9.

Ilex × meserveae
BLUE HOLLY
Zones 4-8

Winter: Thick clusters of gleaming red, orange, or yellow berries. Highly polished, spiny leaves become purplish.
Spring: Bright green new growth.
Summer: Dark blue-green foliage.
Autumn: Berries take on color.
Description: Pyramidal broadleaved evergreen, reaching 15'-20' tall.
Comments: Hybrid of *I. aquifolium* and *I. rugosa*. Needs acid soil. Berry-forming female plants need 'Blue Stallion', a spineless form, nearby for pollination. 'Blue Princess' has heavy set of red berries. 'Blue Angel', Zones 7-8. 'Golden Girl', rich yellow berries. Hybrids of *I. cornuta* and *I. rugosa*, 'China Girl' and 'China Boy' are compact and rounded with glossy green foliage; 'China Girl' produces abundant bright red fruits.

Juniperus chinensis
CHINESE JUNIPER
Zones 4-9

Winter: Retains summer foliage color.
Spring: Bright green new growth.
Summer–Autumn: Olive green to blue-green needlelike (juvenile) and scalelike (adult) foliage.
Description: Species a pyramidal tree to 100' tall, but rarely cultivated. Cultivars vary from dwarf pyramids to vase-shaped shrubs to spreading groundcovers, all with an array of foliage colors.

Comments: 'Hetzii', vigorous, vase-shaped to 15'; 'Hetzii Glauca', light frosty blue fountain; 'Kaizuka Variegated', spiraled branches on conical plant with white-tipped leaves; 'Pfitzeriana Aurea', gray-green with gold-tipped new growth, semi-erect; 'Pfitzeriana Glauca', silvery blue, large spreading shrub. 'Gold Coast', graceful and compact; new growth remains golden all year.

Juniperus squamata 'Blue Star'
'BLUE STAR' JUNIPER
Zones 5-8

Winter–Autumn: Steel blue, soft-textured needles.
Description: Mounded; 3' tall and 5' wide.
Comments: Does poorly in heat and humidity of Southeast. Excellent for color contrast in mixed border or foundation plantings. *J. squamata* 'Blue Carpet' is a groundcover. 'Meyeri' is bushy and dense to 5'-8'.

Kalmia latifolia
MOUNTAIN LAUREL
Zones 5-9

Winter: Glossy, dark green foliage; flower buds.
Spring: Showy flower buds; new growth of some varieties tinted bright maroon or red.

CULTURE KEY

✸	⊗	☀	☼
Full shade	Light shade	Half sun, half shade	Full sun
⬩	⬤	◗	◊
Tolerates wet soil	Moist soil	Average-dry soil	Drought-tolerant
▲	◮	△	
Rich soil	Average soil	Poor soil	

Summer: Clusters of white, pale pink, deep pink, or bright reddish pink blossoms, early summer.
Autumn: Clusters of flower buds form.
Description: Medium-textured, broadleaved. Species' habit is loose, open, to 15' tall; select improved cultivars for slower, compact growth, 4'-6'.
Comments: Native shrub. Needs acid soil. 'Bay State', coral blossoms; 'Candy', dark-striped pink flowers; 'Olympic Fire', red buds opening to pale pink; 'Ostbo Red', deep red buds opening to pink; 'Sarah', red buds and flowers, bright maroon new growth and stems.

Leucothoe fontanesiana 'Scarletta'
'SCARLETTA' FOUNTAIN LEUCOTHOE
Zones 5-9

Winter: Dark green leaves turn rich burgundy.
Spring: Bright red new growth; clusters of creamy white flowers at branch tips in late spring.
Summer: Leaves mature to dark green.
Autumn: Foliage begins to redden.
Description: Dwarf broadleaved evergreen; spreading to 2' tall and wide with double rows of sharp-pointed leaves.
Comments: Needs acid soil. *L. fontanesiana* 'Rainbow' ('Rainbow' leucothoe), green leaves irregularly variegated with creamy yellow and pink. *L. keiskei* (Keisk's leucothoe), Zones 6-9, dark purple winter foliage on ground-hugging plant.

Mahonia aquifolium
OREGON GRAPE HOLLY
Zones 5-9

Winter: Spiny, bold-textured evergreen foliage turns bronze to claret red.
Spring: Clusters of bright yellow flowers in mid-spring; coppery new growth in some cultivars.
Summer: Dark green leaves; showy clusters of edible, waxy blue berries.
Autumn: Foliage begins to turn bronze.

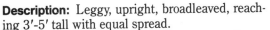

Description: Leggy, upright, broadleaved, reaching 3'-5' tall with equal spread.
Comments: Protect from strong winter sun. Prune out stems in spring to encourage new compact growth. 'Compacta' has small leaves, grows to 3' tall and 5' wide, but bears few fruits. 'Orange Flame', coppery new growth, red in winter.

Mahonia bealei
LEATHERLEAF MAHONIA
Zones 6-9 � ☀ 🌢-◊ ▲-△

Winter: Upright spikes of fragrant yellow flowers in late winter against dark blue-green foliage.
Spring: Bright green new leaves.
Summer-Autumn: Dense, bold-textured, compound leaves; robin's-egg blue berries, midsummer.
Description: Upright, broadleaved evergreen to 6'-10' tall.
Comments: Birds eat berries. Protect from winter wind and sun. Prune to reduce legginess.

Nandina domestica
HEAVENLY BAMBOO
Zones 7-9 ☼-☀ 🌢-◊ ▲-△

Winter: Large clusters of bright red berries; evergreen to semi-evergreen leathery leaves.
Spring: Bronze or red new foliage; lacy clusters of white flowers in late spring.
Summer: Medium-textured, glossy, dark green compound leaves.
Autumn: Leaves and berries redden with frost.
Description: Open, leggy, flat-topped shrub with many upright unbranched stems, giving graceful bamboolike effect; 6'-10' tall.
Comments: Tough plant able to withstand soil extremes. Prune out older branches annually to prevent legginess. 'Alba', striking white berries; 'Harbour Dwarf', graceful 2'-3' tall mound; 'Nana Purpurea', bright reddish purple winter color, stiff mound to 2'; 'Wood's Dwarf', intense crimson winter color, stiff mound to 2'.

Picea glauca 'Conica'
DWARF ALBERTA SPRUCE
Zones 5-7 ☼-☒ 🌢-◊ ▲-△

Winter-Autumn: Dense, bright green, very fine-textured needles.
Description: Forms a perfect cone; very slow-growing, eventually reaching 10'-12' tall.
Comments: Useful upright accent for mixed border or foundation. Protect from winter dehydration.

Picea orientalis 'Aurea Compacta'
COMPACT GOLDEN ORIENTAL SPRUCE
Zones 5-8 ☼-☒ 🌢-◊ ▲-△

Winter-Autumn: Very short, stiff, golden needles.
Description: Dwarf conifer; broadly pyramidal mound to 4' tall and 3' wide.
Comments: Tolerant of poor gravelly soil. Provide some shade to prevent needles from burning. Excellent for color contrast in mixed border.

Picea pungens 'Montgomery'
'MONTGOMERY' DWARF BLUE SPRUCE
Zones 3-7 ☼ 🌢-◊ ▲

Winter-Autumn: Stiff, vivid blue needles.
Description: Dwarf conifer; dense spreading pyramid to 2' tall and wide.
Comments: Excellent year-round color accent for mixed border or foundation planting. *P. pungens* 'Glauca Globosa', rounded to 2'; 'Glauca Procumbens', prostrate, mounding to 18'.

Pieris floribunda
MOUNTAIN PIERIS
Zones 5-8

Winter: Attractive green flower buds; evergreen foliage.
Spring: Upright clusters of showy white flowers in earliest spring.
Summer–Autumn: Lustrous, dark green leaves.
Description: Neat, mound-shaped shrub, medium-textured and broadleaved; 1½' tall and 5' wide.
Comments: Native shrub. Tolerates higher soil pH than other pieris. Excellent foreground or woodland plant.

Pieris japonica
JAPANESE PIERIS
Zones 5-9

Winter: Attractive evergreen foliage; prominent clusters of tan, pink, or red flower buds.
Spring: Dangling, long-lasting clusters of bell-shaped white, pink, or deep rose flowers bloom for 6-8 weeks beginning in earliest spring.
Summer: Evergreen foliage; dried seedpods.
Autumn: Flower buds form; evergreen foliage may take on rich colors.
Description: Species is leggy, broadleaved, reaching 15' tall and half as wide. Many cultivars offer

desirable traits such as a compact habit, burgundy winter foliage, and brilliant red new growth.
Comments: Needs acid soil. 'Dorothy Wycoff' and 'Mountain Fire', red new growth and white flowers. 'Red Mill', deep bright red new foliage, white flowers, good winter color. 'Snowbells', snowy white blossoms. 'Variegata', bright white leaf margins, white flowers, pink to red new growth, slow-growing. 'Flamingo', large deep pink buds and flowers; 'Valley Valentine', deep rose-red buds and long-lasting pink flowers. *P. formosa* var. *forestii* 'Wakehurst', Zones 8-9, exceptionally bright red new growth, fading to pink then pale green before becoming dark green. *P.* × 'Forest Flame', similar to 'Wakehurst' but more compact.

Pinus mugo var. *mugo*
DWARF MUGO PINE
Zones 3-7

Winter–Autumn: Dark green, fine-textured needles.
Description: Slow-growing conifer, broad-spreading to mounding; size varies, to 2'-8' tall and wide.
Comments: 'Aurea', light green needles turn bright gold in winter, to 3'. 'Gold Spire', gold new growth matures to green, to 3'.

Pyracantha coccinea
SCARLET FIRETHORN
Zones 5-9

Winter: Huge clusters of brilliant red to orange berries; dark green to brownish leaves.
Spring: Lacy white flower clusters, midspring.
Summer: Glossy green, medium-textured leaves.
Autumn: Berries ripen, early to mid-fall.
Description: Semi-evergreen, thorny shrub; 6'-18' tall and wide unless pruned.
Comments: Often espaliered or trained to grow on posts or fences. Prune to keep in bounds and for good air circulation. Susceptible to fire blight and leaf scab. Hybrids of *P. coccinea* and other species offer varying levels of disease resistance. Orange-red fruits: 'Kasan', 'Lalandei', 'Mohave'. Yellow fruits: 'Shawnee' (disease-resistant), 'Teton'. Bright red

CULTURE KEY			
☀	☼	☀	☼
Full shade	Light shade	Half sun, half shade	Full sun
⬙	⬥	⬦	◊
Tolerates wet soil	Moist soil	Average-dry soil	Drought-tolerant
▲	▲	△	
Rich soil	Average soil	Poor soil	

fruits: 'Apache' (disease-resistant). *P. angustifolia* (narrow-leaf firethorn) and *P. atalantioides* (Gibbs firethorn), both Zones 7-9, similar with persistent fruits.

Rhododendron carolinianum
CAROLINA RHODODENDRON
Zones 5-7   ✿-◐   ◆   ▲

Winter: Dark green leaves curl during cold.
Spring: Pale pink, rosy purple, or white flowers, midspring.
Summer–Autumn: Leathery dark green leaves with brown undersides.
Description: Rounded, medium-textured, broad-leaved evergreen; to 6' tall and wide.
Comments: Native shrub. Needs acid soil. Remove faded flowers to encourage next year's bloom. *R. carolinianum* var. *album,* lovely white flowers.

Rhododendron catawbiense
CATAWBA RHODODENDRON
Zones 5-8   ✿-☀   ◆   ▲

Winter: Bold-textured, leathery, yellow-green to dark green leaves curl with the cold.
Spring: Huge clusters of pink, rose, or white flowers, late spring. Light green new growth.
Summer–Autumn: Leathery dark green leaves.
Description: Dense, rounded, broadleaved; 6'-10' tall and wide.
Comments: Native shrub. Needs acid soil. Parent of many modern-day hybrids. *R. catawbiense* var. *album,* a beautiful white-flowered variety.

Rhododendron dauricum hybrids
DWARF RHODODENDRON CULTIVARS
Zones 5-7   ✿-☀   ◆   ▲

Winter: Leaves often take on purplish tones.
Spring: Clusters of pink, rose, lavender, purple, magenta, or white flowers in early spring. Light green new growth.
Summer: Neat dark green foliage.
Autumn: Inner leaves often take on bright colors before dropping.
Description: Upright to mounded, broadleaved evergreens; 3'-4' tall and wide. Species is semi-evergreen to deciduous.
Comments: Need acid soil. Numerous cultivars and hybrids, including the 'P.J.M.' series. Need little maintenance. Excellent in mixed borders and naturalistic plantings.

Rhododendron × indicum
EVERGREEN AZALEA HYBRIDS
Zones 6-9   ✿-☀   ◆   ▲

See "Sorting Out the Evergreen Azaleas" on page 99.

Rhododendron maximum and cultivars
ROSEBAY RHODODENDRON
Zones 4-7   ✿-☀   ◆   ▲

Winter: Coarse-textured, dark green leaves.
Spring: Light green new growth.
Summer: Huge clusters of pink or rose flowers, early to mid-summer, partly obscured by new foliage in the South.
Autumn: Leathery, evergreen leaves.
Description: Rounded, broadleaved evergreen; to 15'-30' tall and wide.
Comments: Native shrub. Used in hybridizing summer-blooming rhododendrons.

Rhododendron yakusimanum
YAKO RHODODENDRON
Zones 6-8 ☀ ● ▲

Spring: Gorgeous clusters of bright rose flower buds open to white or pale pink, midspring.
Summer–Winter: Neat mound of bold-textured dark green leaves with felty brown undersides.
Description: Densely mounded broadleaved evergreen; to 3′ tall and wide.
Comments: Outstanding in both foliage and flower.

Sarcococca ruscifolia
SWEET BOX, FRAGRANT SARCOCOCCA
Zones 7-9 ✖-☀ ●-◐ ▲-△

Winter–Summer: Dense, medium-textured, glossy dark green, pointed leaves; red berries.
Autumn: Inconspicuous, but highly fragrant flowers followed by red berries.
Description: Spreading, stoloniferous, broadleaved; to 2′ tall.
Comments: Native plant. Best in acid soil. Excellent evergreen groundcover for woodland situations. *S. hookerana* var. *humilis* (sweet box) blooms in late winter; black fruits follow in late fall and winter.

Skimmia japonica
JAPANESE SKIMMIA
Zones 7-8 ✖-☀ ●-◐ ▲

Winter: Showy red flower buds; rich green foliage; brilliant red berries.
Spring: Creamy white flower clusters, mid- to late spring; bright green new growth.
Summer: Rich, deep green, medium-textured foliage.
Autumn: Berries ripen to red.
Description: Low-mounded, medium-textured, broadleaved; 3′-4′ tall and 6′ wide.
Comments: Needs acid soil. Protect from winter sun. Compact; never needs pruning. Berries on female plants; locate male nearby for pollination.

Taxus species
YEWS
Zones 3-9 ☼-☀ ●-◐ ▲-△

Winter: Glossy dark green, fine-textured needles.
Spring–Summer: Several flushes of light green new growth maturing to dark green.
Autumn: Dark green needles; attractive red fruits in some cultivars.
Description: The species grow into pyramidal trees 40′ tall; shrub-sized cultivars vary in shape from spreading to round to columnar.
Comments: Avoid waterlogged soil and winter wind and sun in harsh winter areas. Excellent year-round green color for border, background, or foundation; unfortunately overused as sheared hedges and formal shrubs. Respond readily to pruning; thinning recommended over shearing to retain graceful appearance. *T. baccata* (English yew), Zones 6-8: black-green needles with yellow-green undersides; 'Aurea', golden new growth matures to green; 'Nana', dwarf pyramid to 3′; 'Repandens', dwarf, spreading to 3′ tall and 12′ wide, hardy in Zone 5; 'Standishii', columnar with yellow needles. *T. cuspidata* (Japanese yew), Zones 4-7: dark green needles with pale green undersides; 'Aurescens', new growth deep yellow, very low and compact; 'Capitata', pyramidal tree, lower with pruning; 'Densa', very

---

CULTURE KEY

☀	✖	☀	☼
Full shade	Light shade	Half sun, half shade	Full sun
⬥	●	◐	◊
Tolerates wet soil	Moist soil	Average–dry soil	Drought-tolerant
▲	△	△	
Rich soil	Average soil	Poor soil	

dense, rounded, and low; 'Nana', spreading wider than tall. *T.* × *media* (Anglojapanese yew), Zones 5-7: dark green needles with pale undersides, olive green branches; 'Brownii', densely rounded; 'Densiformis', dense, taller than wide; 'Wardii', flat-topped and wide-spreading.

Thuja occidentalis
AMERICAN ARBORVITAE
Zones 3-7 ☼-☀ ◗-◍ ▲-△

Winter: Evergreen needles may turn brownish.
Spring: Light green new growth.
Summer–Autumn: Dark green, bright green, or golden fans of scalelike needles, depending on cultivar.
Description: Dense conical tree in species; cultivars form pyramidal to rounded shrubs.
Comments: Protect from full sun in harsh winter areas. Multiple leader forms may suffer damage from weight of snow. 'Emerald', narrowly pyramidal to 10'-15', bright green year-round; 'Ericoides', rounded to 3', sharp needles are yellow-green in summer and bronze in winter; 'Hetz Midget', 3' globe, rich green needles; 'Lutea', pyramidal to 30', golden yellow; 'Rheingold', conical to 5', rich deep gold needles.

Thuja orientalis 'Juniperoides'
ORIENTAL ARBORVITAE
Zones 6-8 ☼-☀ ◗-◍ ▲-△

Winter: Purplish plum needles.
Spring–Autumn: Sharply pointed blue-gray needles.
Description: Feathery textured dwarf conifer; roundly columnar to 4'.
Comments: Excellent for color contrast in mixed border. *T. orientalis* 'Meldensis', similar but smaller and more formal-looking; 'Golden Ball', soft gold in summer, orange-brown in winter.

Tsuga canadensis cultivars
DWARF CANADA HEMLOCKS
Zones 3-8 ☼-☀ ◗ ▲

Autumn–Winter: Soft-textured dark green needles.
Spring: Light green new growth, golden- or white-tipped in cultivars.
Description: Species is a loosely pyramidal conifer to 75'; cultivars vary from weeping to prostrate to rounded to dwarf pyramids.
Comments: Need acid soil. Use soap and oil sprays to control woolly adelgids in Northeast. Graceful soft-textured shrubs for mixed border, foundation, or hedge. 'Albospica', columnar to 6', white-tipped new growth; 'Aurea Compacta', columnar to 3', golden; 'Bennett', weeping mound to 3'; 'Cole's Prostrate', ground-hugging mound to 1' tall and 3' wide; 'Geneva', globe-shaped to 3'; 'Gentsch White', flattened globe to 4', silvery white-tipped new growth.

Viburnum tinus
LAURUSTINUS VIBURNUM
Zones 8-9 ☼-☀ ◗-◌ ▲-△

Winter: Pink flower buds; glossy dark green leaves.
Spring: Fragrant, white blossoms in late winter or earliest spring.
Summer: Clusters of bright blue berries.
Autumn: Glossy green foliage.
Description: Dense, rounded, broadleaved evergreen; to 9' tall and wide.
Comments: Tolerates salt spray and shade. 'Spring Bouquet', a dwarf variety, grows in Zone 7. *V. davidii* (David viburnum), Zones 7-9, 3'-5' tall.

Deciduous Trees
for Four-Season Landscapes

Acer capillipes
SNAKEBARK MAPLE
Zones 5-7 ◐-☀ ◗ ▲-△

Winter: In youth, dark green trunk and branches vertically striped with white. Mature bark ridged and grayish brown.
Spring: Bright coral new growth.
Summer: Green leaves with red petioles.
Autumn: Good yellow fall color.
Description: Bold beautiful tree, to 35′ tall.
Comments: Most sun-tolerant of the striped maples. Similar trees: *A. pensylvanicum* (striped-bark maple, moosewood), young trunks have clear white stripes and green bark, Zones 3-7. *A. tegmentosum* (Manchurian snakebark maple), smooth rich green to purple-green bark with vertical white stripes, Zones 5-7. *A. davidii* (David maple), striking green-and-white-striped bark, Zones 7-9.

Acer ginnala
AMUR MAPLE
Zones 3-6 ☼-⊗ ◗-◖ △

Spring: Pale yellow, fragrant flowers.
Summer: Fine-textured dark green leaves; showy bright red fruits.
Autumn: Brilliant scarlet to deep red foliage.
Description: Small, rounded, dense tree, reaching 20′ tall and wide.
Comments: Very cold-hardy, best in northern areas. Use as focal point for fall color in small garden or as hedge or screen. 'Flame' colors better than the species. 'Red Rhapsody', upright and bushy, excellent fall color.

Acer griseum
PAPERBARK MAPLE
Zones 5-7 ☼ ◗-◖ △

Winter: Cinnamon or reddish brown bark on trunk and branches peels in large curls. Highly ornamental.
Spring: New growth light green; contrasts with shiny bark.
Summer: Bluish green, deeply cut 3-lobed leaves. Prune lower branches to reveal showy bark on trunk.
Autumn: Foliage turns red to reddish green; can be spectacular. Colors develop late.
Description: Small tree, reaching 25′-30′ tall.
Comments: Bark begins to peel when branches reach ½″-1″ in diameter. Does well in clay soil.

CULTURE KEY			
☀	⊗	◐	☼
Full shade	Light shade	Half sun, half shade	Full sun
⚶	◗	◖	◇
Tolerates wet soil	Moist soil	Average–dry soil	Drought-tolerant
▲	◮	△	
Rich soil	Average soil	Poor soil	

Acer japonicum
FULLMOON MAPLE
Zones 6-8   ☼-☀   ◐   ▲

Winter: Rounded silhouette.
Spring: Light green new growth.
Summer: Bright green or golden green ('Aureum') circular leaves with shallow lobes. Ornamental gold to orange-red seed capsules dangle beneath foliage.
Autumn: Outstanding orange to gold fall foliage.
Description: Small tree, to 20'.
Comments: *A. japonicum* 'Aureum' (syn. *A. shirawasanum* 'Aureum'), golden fullmoon maple, has striking golden green foliage and gold fall color.

Acer palmatum 'Bloodgood'
'BLOODGOOD' JAPANESE MAPLE
Zones 5-8   ☼-☀   ◐-◑   ▲

Winter: Dark red twigs; smooth gray branches and trunk bark.
Spring: Hazy red flowers before rosy red new foliage emerges.
Summer: Palmately lobed foliage matures to deep wine red.
Autumn: Brilliant red fall color.
Description: Reaches 25' tall and wide.
Comments: Retains red summer foliage better than 'Atropurpureum'. Many other cultivars abound with various foliage shapes and colors; see "Best Japanese Maples for Four-Season Landscapes" on page 188. Grow in rich, fertile, moist soil in full to part sun and protect from wind.

Acer palmatum var. *dissectum*
CUTLEAF JAPANESE MAPLE
Zones 5-8   ☼-☀   ◐-◑   ▲

Winter: Smooth gray branches in weeping mound.
Spring: Beautiful translucent new foliage.
Summer: Deeply dissected, lacelike foliage.

Autumn: Brilliant red or gold fall color.
Description: Deciduous shrub or small tree; 12' tall if grafted high.
Comments: Protect from wind. *A. palmatum* var. *dissectum* 'Atropurpureum', purple dissected foliage.

Acer palmatum 'Sango Kaku', syn. 'Sen Kaki'
CORAL-BARK MAPLE
Zones 6-9   ☼-☀   ◐-◑   ▲

Winter: Twigs brilliant coral-red.
Spring: Emerging foliage lime green.
Summer: Light green foliage.
Autumn: Brilliant yellow fall color.
Description: Reaches 10'-15' tall and wide.
Comments: Effective against an evergreen background in winter.

Acer rubrum
RED MAPLE, SWAMP MAPLE
Zones 3-9   ☼   ◐-◑   ▲-△

Winter: Silvery gray bark.
Spring: Clusters of red flowers, before foliage.
Summer: Dark green leaves, whitish undersides, on red petioles.
Autumn: Often brilliant red, yellow, or orange fall color.
Description: Broadly oval tree, to 60' tall and 45' wide.
Comments: Tolerates damp or wet soil and air pollution; needs acid soil. Surface roots make it difficult to grow grass underneath. Avoid planting near walks and driveways. 'Northwood', selected by the University of Minnesota for cold-hardiness and red, orange, and yellow fall color. 'Autumn Flame', early and long-lasting, brilliant red fall color. 'Armstrong', very narrow shape. 'October Glory', deep crimson, late-coloring fall foliage; performs well in the South. 'Red Sunset', brilliant orange to red fall color.

Acer saccharum
SUGAR MAPLE
Zones 3-7 ☼-☒ ♦-♦ ▲-△

Winter: Distinctive oval silhouette; rough bark.
Spring: Pale yellow flowers before new foliage.
Summer: Dark green leaves.
Autumn: Brilliant red to golden orange and yellow foliage.
Description: Large shade tree with oval shape; 65'-80' tall.
Comments: Best in well-drained, fertile, somewhat acid soil. Sensitive to road salt, dry compacted soil, and urban stress. Use as shade tree in lawn or garden. 'Green Mountain' tolerates hot, dry, midwestern conditions; colors golden yellow. 'Bonfire', brilliant red fall color in alkaline soils of Midwest. 'Endowment', columnar. 'Goldspire', narrow, heat-tolerant.

Acer triflorum
THREE-FLOWER MAPLE
Zones 5-7 ☼-☒ ♦ ▲-△

Winter: Shaggy outer bark peels back to reveal creamy white inner bark.
Summer: Dark green, 3-lobed leaves.
Autumn: Combination of brilliant yellow and red foliage appears orange.

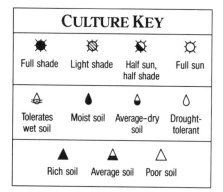

CULTURE KEY			
☀	☒	☒	☼
Full shade	Light shade	Half sun, half shade	Full sun
⚍	♦	♦	◊
Tolerates wet soil	Moist soil	Average–dry soil	Drought-tolerant
▲	△	△	
Rich soil	Average soil	Poor soil	

Description: Graceful, upright small tree, to 30' tall.
Comments: Needs acid soil. A gorgeous small tree.

Aesculus × carnea
RED HORSE CHESTNUT
Zones 5-8 ☼ ♦ ▲

Spring: Deep pink to red upright flower clusters stand like candles at branch tips in late spring.
Summer: Dark green, coarsely compound foliage.
Autumn: Glossy brown nuts in spiny husks.
Description: Shade tree, to 45' tall.
Comments: Highly adaptable, rugged tree. Less susceptible to leaf disease than *A. hippocastanum* (horse chestnut). More compact than other horse chestnuts. Somewhat drought-tolerant. Leaf and nut litter may be messy. 'Briotii', to 40' with bright red flowers.

Amelanchier arborea, syn. *A. canadensis*
SHADBLOW, DOWNY SERVICEBERRY
Zones 3-8 ☼-☒ ♦ ▲

Winter: Beautiful shape; silvery gray bark with subtle dark stripes.
Spring: Lacy clouds of white flowers in early spring before or with leaves.
Summer: Fine-textured green leaves. Red edible fruits attract birds.
Autumn: Excellent red-orange or russet early-fall foliage color.
Description: Rounded, often multitrunked flowering tree, to 15'-25' tall.
Comments: Native American tree. Best in acid soil. Excellent for naturalistic plantings. Many cultivars and hybrids available. *A. laevis* (serviceberry) similar, with bronze-red new foliage.

Betula jacquemontii
WHITE-BARK HIMALAYAN BIRCH
Zones 5-7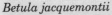

Winter: Pure white, exfoliating bark.
Spring: Light green new growth.
Summer: Dark green leaves.
Autumn: Yellow fall color.
Description: Pyramidal to oval tree, to 25′ tall.
Comments: White bark appears on very young trees. Resists leaf miners; may be borer-resistant. Perhaps the best white-barked birch.

Betula nigra 'Heritage'
'HERITAGE' RIVER BIRCH
Zones 4-9

Winter: Highly ornamental tan, pink, and salmon peeling bark on trunk and branches. Older trunks reveal creamy white inner bark.
Spring: Bright green foliage and tan catkins.
Summer: Medium green foliage.
Autumn: Clear bright yellow fall color.
Description: Pyramidal, often multitrunked, shade tree, to 45′ tall.
Comments: Fast-growing. Casts dappled shade. Resistant to bronze birch borers, which trouble many other birches. Styer Award winner 1990. 'Little King' dwarf, 10′. *B. albo-sinensis* (Chinese paper birch), similar, Zones 6-8; 'Septentrionalis' has buff-pink underbark.

Betula papyrifera
CANOE BIRCH, PAPER BIRCH, WHITE BIRCH
Zones 2-7

Winter: Brilliant white, exfoliating bark.
Spring: Brown catkins; soft green new foliage.
Summer: Rich green leaves.

Autumn: Excellent clear yellow fall color; often forms multitrunked clumps.
Description: Rounded shade tree, to 50′-70′ tall.
Comments: Trunks slow to turn white. Native American tree. Much more resistant to bronze birch borers than *B. pendula* and better in the Midwest. May be troubled by leaf miners.

Betula pendula (syn. *B. alba*) 'Tristis' and 'Youngii'
WEEPING EUROPEAN BIRCHES
Zones 3-5

Winter: Bright chalky white, peeling bark on trunk and branches; strong weeping outline.
Spring: Leaf out early.
Summer: Lustrous dark green leaves.
Autumn: Leaves remain green late, change to yellow.
Description: 'Tristis' has central leader and weeping branches, to 35′ tall. 'Youngii', strongly pendulous branches; grafted to 25′ tall.
Comments: White trunk at young age but lower trunk turning black with age. Leaf miner and bronze birch borer are serious pests if trees are drought-stressed.

Betula platyphylla var. *japonica* 'Whitespire'
'WHITESPIRE' BIRCH
Zones 5-7

Winter: Bright chalky white bark on trunk and branches.
Spring: Light green new growth.
Summer: Fine-textured dark green leaves.
Autumn: Yellow fall foliage.
Description: Narrowly pyramidal, to 40′-50′ tall; single-stemmed or clump-forming.
Comments: The cultivar—not the species—is highly resistant to birch borers, which trouble other white birches. The most heat-tolerant white birch; best white birch for Midwest. Bark slow to turn white. Preferred over European birch (*B. pendula*), which suffers from borers and leaf miners.

Carpinus betulus 'Pendula'
WEEPING EUROPEAN HORNBEAM
Zones 5-7 ☼-☀ ♦-◊ ▲-△

Winter: Smooth dark gray bark and muscular trunk, with graceful weeping shape.
Spring: Light green leaves.
Summer: Dark green, crisp-textured foliage.
Autumn: Leaves remain green very late, turning yellowish.
Description: Small weeping shade tree, to 50'.
Comments: Extremely attractive, trouble-free, and adaptable. Good tree for Midwest. Tolerant of acid to alkaline soil and difficult sites. 'Columnaris', narrowly upright.

Cercidiphyllum japonicum
KATSURA TREE
Zones 5-9 ☼ ♦ ▲

Winter: Handsome silhouette with shaggy bark.
Spring: New foliage striking reddish purple.
Summer: Lovely, dark bluish green rounded leaves.
Autumn: Excellent yellow to apricot fall foliage, smelling of caramel.
Description: Pyramidal to spreading, often multi-trunked shade tree, to 60' tall.
Comments: Needs partial shade in the South. 'Pendula', a weeping form.

Cercis spp.
REDBUDS
Zones 5-9 ☼-☀ ♦-◊ ▲-△

Winter: Smooth gray trunks and branches.
Spring: Rosy pink to magenta pea-shaped flowers in clusters along the bare branches in early spring; white-flowered cultivars.
Summer: Large heart-shaped matte green leaves are bold-textured in eastern and Chinese redbuds; smaller and high-gloss green in Texas and Mexican species.
Autumn: Yellow fall foliage.
Description: Small flowering trees. *C. canadensis* (eastern redbud) reaches 20'-40' tall with multiple trunks, or prune to a single stem. *C. chinensis* (Chinese redbud) more shrubby, to 15', with more profuse, larger, deeper pink flowers. *C. occidentalis* (western redbud), to 12'; *C. mexicana* (Mexican redbud) and *C. reniformis*/*C. texensis* (Texas redbud), to 20', hardy to Zone 7.
Comments: Eastern redbud needs summer heat to develop cold-hardiness. In the Pacific Northwest, grow western redbud, which tolerates alkaline soil, and Chinese redbud. Canker disease may strike old or marginally hardy redbuds in Mid-Atlantic states. *C. canadensis* (Zones 4-9 with local selections); *C. chinensis* (Zones 6-9); *C. mexicana* (Zones 7-9); *C. occidentalis* (Zones 7-9); *C. reniformis* (Zones 8-9; 'Oklahoma', Zones 6-9). *C. canadensis* 'Forest Pansy', vivid red-purple spring foliage, which remains colorful with cool summer nights but fades to green with hot summer nights; 'Alba', white flowers; 'Silver Cloud', white variegated foliage, sparse flowers. *C. reniformis* 'Oklahoma', extremely showy foliage and deep magenta flowers; 'Texas White', white-flowered, showy foliage. *C. chinensis* 'Avondale', extremely profuse flowers; does well in the Northwest. Redbuds usually look best planted with a dark background to show off early bloom; normally live 20-25 years.

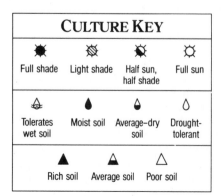

CULTURE KEY			
☀	�star	☀	☼
Full shade	Light shade	Half sun, half shade	Full sun
⚎	♦	♦	◊
Tolerates wet soil	Moist soil	Average–dry soil	Drought-tolerant
▲	▲	△	
Rich soil	Average soil	Poor soil	

Chionanthus spp.
FRINGE TREES
Zones 5-9 ☼-☒ ◑ ▲

Winter: Ridged, furrowed, and exfoliating gray-brown bark on trunk is highly ornamental on *C. retusus*. Unremarkable bark on *C. virginicus*.
Spring: Egg-shaped dark green leaves appear late.
Summer: Clusters of fragrant, snow white, 4-petaled flowers cover tree in early summer.
Autumn: Ornamental sprays of dark blue fruits on female trees; eaten by birds. Leaves remain late into fall without much color change on *C. retusus*; turn yellow on *C. virginicus*.
Description: Round-headed, small flowering trees, to 15'-20' tall and 20'-30' wide. Grow as single-trunked trees or multitrunked large shrubs.
Comments: Need acid soil. *C. retusus* (Chinese fringetree), Zones 6-9; *C. virginicus* (American fringetree), Zones 5-9. Difficult to propagate, so not readily available but worth seeking.

Cladrastis kentukea, formerly *C. lutea*
AMERICAN YELLOWWOOD
Zones 4-8 ☼ ◑-◔ ▲

Winter: Ornamental silver bark resembles that of beech tree.
Spring: Bright yellow-green compound leaves.
Summer: Long clusters of white wisteria-like flowers in early summer; grass green foliage.
Autumn: Soft yellow fall color.
Description: Slow-growing round-headed flowering shade tree, to 30'-50' tall with broader spread.
Comments: Remarkably disease-free. Endangered species native to the southeastern United States; easy to propagate. May bloom in alternate years.

Clethra barbinervis
JAPANESE TREE CLETHRA
Zones 6-9 ☼-☒ ◑-◑ ▲-△

Winter: Spectacular polished, multicolored bark on older trunks; softly mottled blend of pink, green, cream, and terra-cotta.
Spring: Whorled clusters of lustrous green leaves.
Summer: Long-lasting, dangling, fragrant white flowers in late summer.
Autumn: Yellow foliage.
Description: Multistemmed bushy tree, to 18' tall.
Comments: Needs shade in the South. Flowers attract butterflies. Great in the winter landscape. *C. acuminata* (American clethra) more shrublike with peeling cinnamon brown bark.

Cornus alternifolia
PAGODA DOGWOOD
Zones 4-7 ☽-☒ ◑ ▲

Winter: Striking tiered branches; green twigs.
Spring: Fuzzy clusters of creamy white flowers in late spring.
Summer: Neat green alternate leaves on layered branches; variegated cultivar available; blue-black fruits on red stems.
Autumn: Reddish purple fall color.
Description: Small flowering tree with outstanding horizontal branching pattern, to 35' tall and wide.
Comments: Needs cool, moist acid soil. 'Argentea' has striking white-edged leaves. The Japanese species, giant dogwood (*C. controversa*), is similar but grows larger and 'Variegata' has beautiful creamy white variegated leaves; Zones 6-8.

Cornus florida
FLOWERING DOGWOOD
Zones 5-9 ☽-☒ ◑-◑ ▲-▲

Winter: Horizontal branches with undulating pattern makes effective silhouette.

Spring: Showy creamy white flower bracts emerge in midspring and mature to pure white blooms. Pink cultivars available.
Summer: Medium green leaves.
Autumn: Red to maroon fall foliage and orange-red berries.
Description: Small flowering tree with gently layered branches, to 25′ tall and wide.
Comments: Anthracnose leaf disease serious in Northeast; do not wet foliage; borers troublesome on stressed trees; plant in excellent soil, and keep moist and partially shaded. 'Cloud 9', extremely dense-flowering and compact. Recently released 'Spring Grove', very floriferous, heavy berry set, may resist anthracnose. 'Cherokee Chief', deep pink flowers, called red, and red new growth. 'Cherokee Sunset', ruby flowers, foliage variegated with rose, yellow, and green. 'Gold Nugget', gold-splashed foliage. 'Pendula', weeping. 'Rubra', pink flowers.

Cornus kousa
KOUSA DOGWOOD
Zones 5-7 ☼ ◖ ▲-△

Winter: Smooth ornamental patchwork bark on trunks mottled with gray, tan, and maroon; more striking with age. Horizontal branching pattern.
Spring: Tiers of flat, starlike white flowers for 4 or more weeks in late spring.
Summer: Flower bracts may continue to be showy, often aging to pink. Attractive green foliage.

Autumn: Large strawberry-like rose-pink fruits appear late summer and fall. Excellent scarlet to dark red fall color.
Description: Vase-shaped to spreading, small flowering tree, to 25′-30′ tall and wide.
Comments: Keep soil mulched. Prune lower branches to reveal trunk. Plant more than one tree for heavy fruiting. 'Milky Way' flowers heavily. 'Summer Stars' features numerous small flowers that remain showy all summer. Var. *chinensis* blooms longer than the species. 'Elizabeth Lustgarten' and 'Lustgarten Weeping', weeping forms.

Cornus mas
CORNELIAN CHERRY
Zones 5-8 ☼-☒ ◖ ▲

Winter: Mottled, flaking gray and tan bark. Hazy yellow flowers cover tree in late winter and early spring before leaves appear.
Spring: Bright green emerging foliage.
Summer: Dark green, crisp foliage. Bright red glossy berries resembling cherries in late summer; eaten by birds.
Autumn: Foliage remains green well into autumn, may turn red late.
Description: Small, rounded flowering tree, to 20′ tall and wide.
Comments: Native tree. A pleasing harbinger of spring. Locate with dark background. *C. officinalis* (Japanese cornel) similar but more open habit and more ornamental exfoliating bark in patchwork of gray, tan, and creamy white.

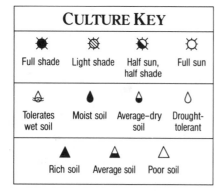

CULTURE KEY			
✹	⊘	☒	☼
Full shade	Light shade	Half sun, half shade	Full sun
⚘	◖	◗	◊
Tolerates wet soil	Moist soil	Average–dry soil	Drought-tolerant
▲	◮	△	
Rich soil	Average soil	Poor soil	

Cornus × rutgersenensis
STELLAR DOGWOOD
Zones 5-8 ☒-☒ ◖ ▲

Winter: Silhouette varies from horizontal to rounded to vase-shaped, depending on the cultivar.
Spring: Large white or pink blooms with pointed bract tips in late spring.
Summer: Glossy green foliage.
Autumn: Brilliant red foliage.

Description: Narrow to rounded small flowering tree, to 25' tall and wide.
Comments: Recently released hybrid between Kousa dogwood and flowering dogwood, with bloom time exactly in between. Highly resistant to anthracnose and borers. White flower bracts of 'Aurora' large and rounded, overlapping to form magnificently showy blooms. White bracts of 'Constellation' remain more separate, creating a delicate show; a narrow tree, perfect for tight spaces. 'Stellar Pink', brightly blushed pink inflorescences on rounded tree.

Cotinus coggygria f. *purpureus*
PURPLE SMOKETREE
Zones 5-7 ☼ ◐-◊ ▲-△

Spring: Purple new leaves.
Summer: Small flowers and seeds held in cloudlike pink panicles from mid- to late summer; blue-green rounded leaves, purple in cultivars.
Autumn: Orange-red fall color.
Description: Multitrunked tree or large shrub, to 15' tall and wide, unless pruned.
Comments: 'Royal Purple', excellent dark purple foliage. 'Notcutt's Variety', bright maroon-purple leaves. Plants can be pruned to ground level each spring to maintain shrublike proportions for foliage interest in mixed border.

Crataegus viridis 'Winter King'
'WINTER KING' HAWTHORN
Zones 4-9 ☼ ◐ ▲

Winter: Flat-topped horizontal shape. Extremely showy, orange-red berries all winter. Silvery bark flakes to reveal orange patches.
Spring: Showy clusters of small white flowers in late spring and early summer.
Summer: Fine-textured, glossy green foliage.
Autumn: Little foliage color change; showy orange-red berries.
Description: Flowering small tree, to 30' tall and wide.

Comments: Cultivar of native American tree. Extremely tolerant of tough growing conditions and air pollution. Larger fruit size than most hawthorns. Insect- and disease-resistant, unlike most other hawthorns. Styer Award winner in 1992.

Fagus sylvatica
EUROPEAN BEECH
Zones 5-9 ☼ ◐ ▲

Winter: Dramatic silhouette. Smooth, silvery gray bark and massive trunks with branches to the ground.
Spring: Late-emerging foliage is a beautiful fresh green; pink or red in purple-leaved forms.
Summer: Purple-leaved cultivars make stunning summer appearance.
Autumn: Green-leaved cultivars turn beautiful coppery yellow.
Description: Pyramidal tree, to 90' tall and wide; weeping cultivars available.
Comments: Best in well-drained, slightly acid soil with good moisture; more tolerant of urban conditions than American beech (*F. grandifolia*). Consider ultimate size when choosing a site. Low branches and surface roots preclude all but the toughest groundcovers. 'Pendula' (weeping green beech). 'Purpurea' (purple beech), deep burgundy-black foliage. 'Purpurea-Pendula' (weeping purple beech). 'Cuprea' (copper beech), lighter color than purple beech. 'Riversii', deep purple foliage holds well all summer. 'Rohan', purple, fern-leaf foliage. 'Tricolor', white, rose, and green variegated foliage, very slow-growing. 'Rosea-Marginata', purple leaves edged with pink. 'Asplenifolia', deeply cut green leaves.

Franklinia alatamaha
FRANKLINIA, FRANKLIN TREE
Zones 6-7 ☼-◈ ◐ ▲

Winter: Smooth dark gray sinuous trunk striped with light gray.
Spring: Very late-emerging foliage, shiny green.
Summer: Clusters of pearl-like flower buds at branch tips open to white, camellia-like blooms in late summer.

Autumn: Scattered bloom until frost, standing out against dark red and plum fall foliage.
Description: Open-branched, oval tree, to 20′ tall.
Comments: Needs acid soil; keep well-mulched. Native to the Southeast; now extinct in the wild. Elegant specimen for small gardens.

Ginkgo biloba
GINKGO, MAIDENHAIR TREE
Zones 4-8 ☼ ◐-◊ ▲-△

Winter: Open horizontal branching and spurlike side shoots make interesting picture.
Summer: Unusual fan-shaped, bright green leaves.
Autumn: Brilliant golden yellow in late fall.
Description: Open-branched shade tree, to 50′-80′ tall, variable spread.
Comments: Tough, stress-tolerant tree free of insect and disease problems. Avoid female trees; fruit drop is messy and very malodorous. 'Princeton Sentry', male form with a columnar habit. 'Autumn Gold', male with full form and outstanding yellow fall color.

CULTURE KEY			
☀	⊗	⊛	☼
Full shade	Light shade	Half sun, half shade	Full sun
⊿	◆	◑	◊
Tolerates wet soil	Moist soil	Average–dry soil	Drought-tolerant
▲	△	△	
Rich soil	Average soil	Poor soil	

Halesia carolina
CAROLINA SILVERBELL
Zones 5-9 ☼-⊗ ◆ ▲

Winter: Round, spreading form with smooth gray, lightly furrowed bark.
Spring: Beautiful white, bell-shaped flowers dangle from undersides of branches in midspring with emerging foliage.
Summer: Neat green foliage.
Autumn: Soft yellow fall color.
Description: Reaches 30′ tall and wide; spreading branches form a round-headed tree.
Comments: Needs acid soil. Native to the Southeast. Use as a woodland or understory tree in a naturalistic landscape. Good patio or border tree.

Koelreuteria paniculata
GOLDEN-RAIN TREE
Zones 5-9 ☼ ◐-◊ ▲-△

Winter: Rounded silhouette, brown Japanese lantern-shaped seedpods.
Spring: Purplish new growth matures to airy, grass green, deeply cut leaves.
Summer: Panicles of pealike yellow flowers showy in midsummer. Prominent papery seedpods follow, ripening from green to yellow to cinnamon brown.
Description: Globular, to 30′-40′ tall and as wide.
Comments: An excellent lawn or patio tree; tolerates tough sites. Seedlings may cause weed problem. 'September' blooms late summer or early fall.

Laburnum × watereri 'Vossii'
'VOSSII' GOLDEN-CHAIN TREE
Zones 6-8 ⊗ ◆ ▲

Winter: Bright green bark on vase-shaped trunks and branches.
Spring: Clusters of golden yellow, wisteria-like blooms dangle from the branches in late spring, against 3-parted green leaves.
Autumn: Soft yellow fall color.

Description: Small flowering tree, to 15'-20' tall.
Comments: Protect from strong wind, which can burn foliage and snap the weak wood. Water during drought. Unusual yellow color beautiful in spring garden. Seeds in conspicuous seedpods are deadly poisonous, as are all the plant's parts.

Lagerstroemia indica
CRAPE MYRTLE
Zones 6-9 ☼ ◑-◐ ▲

See "Wonderful New Crape Myrtles" on page 144.

Larix decidua
EUROPEAN LARCH
Zones 4-6 ☼ ◑ ▲

Winter: Striking bare-branched, pyramidal silhouette.
Spring: Pale green new needles.
Summer: Dark green needles.
Autumn: Gorgeous ocher yellow needles in late fall.
Description: Deciduous conifer, pyramidal with horizontal branches, to 75' tall.
Comments: Sensitive to air pollution. 'Pendula', weeping form. *Pseudolarix kaempferi* (golden larch), Zones 6-8, similar but branches more pendulous.

Liquidambar styraciflua
SWEET GUM
Zones 5-9 ☼ ◑-◐ ▲-△

Winter: Symmetrical pyramidal shape and horizontal branches; small branches silvery gray edged with unusual corky wings.
Summer: Deep green, glossy, star-shaped leaves.
Autumn: Unsurpassed red, orange, and purple fall color; spiky ball-like fruits.
Description: Shade tree, to 60' tall.

Comments: Trouble-free native tree. Best in acid soil. Fruits may be a cleanup nuisance. 'Corky', slender, extremely corky twigs, fruitless, excellent fall color. 'Burgundy', wine red fall color. 'Festival', pink, peach, and yellow fall color. 'Palo Alto', uniform growth, orange-red fall color.

Liriodendron tulipifera
TULIP TREE, TULIP POPLAR
Zones 4-9 ☼ ◑-◐ ▲-△

Winter: Striped gray bark on striking tall, straight, polelike trunks.
Spring: Tulip-shaped pale green 2" flowers with showy orange bases, held upright at the ends of branches.
Summer: Handsome glossy green leaves with distinctive square shape.
Fall: Yellow fall foliage color; conelike tan fruits made of overlapping scales; fruits persist into winter.
Description: Shade or specimen tree, to 100' tall; very upright form.
Comments: Native tree requiring good soil and lots of room; relatively trouble-free where adapted.

Maackia amurensis
AMUR MAACKIA
Zones 5-7 ☼ ◑-◐ ▲

Winter: Rich, shining brown bark, peeling as it matures.
Spring: Grayish green compound leaves.
Summer: Dark green foliage and white pealike flowers in 8" racemes.
Description: Round-headed, to 25'-30' tall and wide.
Comments: Acid or alkaline soil. Widely adapted and trouble-free. Flowers long-lasting if tree is not water-stressed.

Magnolia × loebneri
LOEBNER MAGNOLIA
Zones 5-9 ☼ ◑ △

Winter: Pyramidal outline; smooth gray bark; furry flower buds.
Spring: Magnificent 12-petaled white or pink-flushed, fragrant flowers in early spring before foliage.
Summer: Dense green foliage.
Autumn: Little color change; leaves drop late.
Description: Rounded, to 30' tall and wide.
Comments: Perhaps the most beautiful magnolia. A hybrid of *M. kobus* and *M. stellata*; resembles Kobus magnolia but blooms at a much earlier age. 'Spring Snow' blooms a bit later in season, so may be a better choice in frost-prone areas.

Magnolia × soulangiana
SAUCER MAGNOLIA
Zones 5-9 ☼ ◑ △

Winter: Furry buds and smooth gray bark.
Spring: Large, chalice-shaped, white, pink, or bi-colored white-and-purple blooms in early spring before foliage.
Summer: Lustrous, bold-textured green foliage.
Autumn: Leaves drop late with little color change.
Description: Round, multitrunked, with low branches to 25' tall and wide.

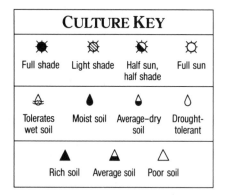

CULTURE KEY			
✹	⊘	☀	☼
Full shade	Light shade	Half sun, half shade	Full sun
⬭	◐	◔	◌
Tolerates wet soil	Moist soil	Average–dry soil	Drought-tolerant
▲	△	△	
Rich soil	Average soil	Poor soil	

Comments: Hybridized 150 years ago, from the Yulan magnolia (*M. heptapeta*, syn. *M. denudata*) with fragrant, tulip-shaped, ivory blooms in profusion in late winter or very early spring, and the lily magnolia (*M. quinquepeta*, syn. *M. liliflora*), which blooms a full month later; bloom time intermediate between the two. 'Brozzonii', pink-flushed blooms. 'Amabilis', pure white. 'Alexandrina', bicolored. Where frost is a problem, plant a late-blooming (midspring) cultivar such as 'Lennei', deep purple with white; 'Speciosa', ivory white; or 'Verbanica', rosy pink.

Magnolia stellata
STAR MAGNOLIA
Zones 5-9 ☼ ◑-◑ ▲

Winter: Smooth gray bark; furry buds.
Spring: Very early, many-petaled, fragrant white blossoms on bare branches; pink in some cultivars.
Summer: Green foliage.
Autumn: Yellow to bronze fall color.
Description: Multitrunked small tree or large shrub, 15'-20' tall.
Comments: Flowers may be blackened by late frost. Selected cultivars of star magnolia offer a choice of larger or double blossoms, shades of pink or rose, bushier shapes, and even later-blooming dates. 'Centennial', spectacular double white flowers tinged with pink on the outside. 'Leonard Messel', dark pink flowers. 'Rosea', pale pink. *M. kobus* similar but larger, to 40'.

Malus species and cultivars
CRABAPPLES
Zones 3-9 ☼ ◑-◑ △

See "Choosing a Crabapple for Four-Season Display" on page 86.

Metasequoia glyptostroboides
DAWN REDWOOD
Zones 5-9 ☼-❀ ⬙-◗ ▲-△

Winter: Horizontal branches; neat pyramidal form with massive tapered trunk and shredding bark.
Spring: Fresh green lacy foliage.
Summer: Dark green feathery foliage.
Autumn: Apricot-gold to tan fall color.
Description: Deciduous conifer. Rapid-growing to 50′ in 25 years; ultimately 100′.
Comments: Will grow in wet soil. Native to China and once almost extinct in the wild. Similar to bald cypress (*Taxodium distichum*) of southern United States.

Nyssa sylvatica
BLACK GUM, BLACK TUPELO
Zones 5-9 ☼-❀ ⬙-◗ ▲-△

Winter: Pyramidal silhouette with horizontal, slightly pendulous branches; blocky, gray bark.
Summer: Glossy dark green, oval leaves.
Autumn: Blazing gold to scarlet fall color. Dark blue cherrylike fruits eaten by birds.
Description: Pyramidal shade tree, to 50′ tall.
Comments: Widely adapted tree; tolerates swampy and seashore conditions. Needs acid soil. Native to the East Coast. Best to purchase locally grown specimens.

Oxydendrum arboreum
SOURWOOD, SORREL TREE
Zones 5-9 ☼-❀ ◗-◗ ▲-△

Winter: Strong upright to pyramidal shape; blocky ridged bark on older trees; dried seedpods.
Spring: Rich green emerging foliage.
Summer: Pendulous clusters of lily-of-the-valley-like blossoms drip from branch tips in midsummer. Lustrous dark green leaves.

Autumn: Outstanding rose-red, purple, deep scarlet, or orange-gold fall color often on same tree. Tan seedpods stand out against the foliage.
Description: Narrowly pyramidal tree, to 25′-30′ tall and half as wide; may reach 50′ tall with age.
Comments: Needs acid soil; intolerant of dry sites or drought. Native to southeastern United States. Good woodland or specimen tree.

Parrotia persica
PERSIAN PARROTIA
Zones 6-9 ☼-❀ ◗-◗ ▲-△

Winter: Dark reddish brown bark flakes off to reveal creamy patches.
Spring: Subtle ruby red flowers in late winter or early spring. Reddish purple new leaves.
Summer: Lustrous, medium-textured green leaves.
Autumn: Leaves bright orange, yellow, and scarlet.
Description: Single-stemmed tree or multitrunked shrub, 20′-40′ tall.
Comments: Tolerant and problem-free. Beautiful specimen; should be more widely used.

Pistacia chinensis
CHINESE PISTACHE
Zones 6-9 ☼ ◗-◊ ▲-△

Winter: Scaly gray bark flakes to reveal salmon to orange inner bark.
Summer: Rich green compound leaves.
Autumn: Red to golden orange leaves, late fall.
Description: Oval to vase-shaped, to 35′ tall.
Comments: Tolerates alkaline soil. Most reliable and outstanding fall color for the South.

Prunus cerasifera 'Krauter Vesuvius'
'KRAUTER VESUVIUS' PURPLE-LEAF PLUM
Zones 5-9 ☼ ◗ ▲

Winter: Oval-shaped silhouette; dark bark.
Spring: Clouds of single pink flowers before ruby red young leaves.
Summer: Dark purple foliage.
Description: Shrubby tree, to 15′-20′ tall and wide.
Comments: Best cultivar for season-long purple foliage. 'Thundercloud' also has good color. Performs well in Midwest. *P.* × *blireana* (double-pink purple-leaf plum), Zones 6-9, has double-pink flowers. *P.* × *cistena* (purple-leaf sand cherry), Zones 3-8, shrublike to 6′ tall.

Prunus maackii
AMUR CHOKECHERRY
Zones 3-7 ☼ ◗ ▲

Winter: Outstanding, peeling cinnamon brown bark with metallic sheen on trunk and branches.
Spring: Small racemes of small white flowers add interest in late spring.
Summer: Glossy green foliage; bird-attracting black berries.
Description: Round, multitrunked or single-trunked tree, to 30′ tall.
Comments: Relatively trouble-free.

Prunus 'Okame' (*P. incisa* × *P. campanulata*)
'OKAME' CHERRY
Zones 5-8 ☼ ◗ ▲

Winter: Small, pink, long-lasting blooms for about 3 weeks in late winter.
Spring: Flowers may last into early spring.
Summer: Fine-textured foliage.
Autumn: Bright orange and yellow fall foliage.
Description: Rounded, to 25′ tall and wide.
Comments: Earliest-blooming cherry. Winner of the Styer Award in 1988. *P. mume* (Japanese apricot), Zones 7-9, also blooms in late winter.

Prunus serrulata
JAPANESE FLOWERING CHERRY
Zones 6-8 ☼ ◗ ▲

Winter: Lustrous deep reddish brown bark with prominent light brown horizontal bands. Wide-spreading, flat-topped silhouette.
Spring: Gorgeous white or pink double or single blooms in midspring with bronze new leaves.
Summer: Deep green coarse-textured leaves.
Autumn: Bronze to red fall foliage.
Description: Cultivars usually wide-spreading, to 18′ tall and 24′ wide.
Comments: Some serious pests, but rarely cause problems. 'Shirotae' (syn. 'Mt. Fuji'), fragrant pure white double flowers. 'Shogetsu' and 'Shirofugen', clouds of blush pink blooms fading to white. *P. yedoensis* (Yoshino or Potomac cherry) similar, with extremely showy single, fragrant flowers. 'Kwanzan', strong vase shape; huge clusters of brilliant pink double flowers. *P. sargentii* (Sargent cherry), Zones 5-9, similar with excellent pink single flowers, fall color, lustrous bark. *P. serrula* (paperbark cherry), Zones 5-8; outstanding, metallic, mahogany-red bark with horizontal tan bands peeling off in thin strips and pretty white flowers in early spring.

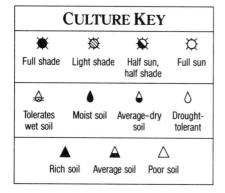

CULTURE KEY

✸	⊘	✷	☼
Full shade	Light shade	Half sun, half shade	Full sun
⟁	◗	◗	◊
Tolerates wet soil	Moist soil	Average–dry soil	Drought-tolerant
▲	△	△	
Rich soil	Average soil	Poor soil	

Prunus subhirtella var. *pendula*
WEEPING HIGAN CHERRY
Zones 6-8 ☼ ◖ △

Winter: Dramatic weeping outline; gray-brown bark.
Spring: Single pink flowers before foliage.
Summer: Lustrous dark green leaves.
Description: Usually grafted to 6′ understock; reaches 20′-40′ tall and almost as wide.
Comments: Cold-, heat-, and stress-tolerant. Rapid-growing and long-lived compared to other cherries. 'Wayside Pendula', extra hardy, Zones 4-8. Blooms last longer on double-flowered cultivars.

Pyrus calleryana
ORNAMENTAL PEAR, CALLERY PEAR
Zones 5-9 ☼ ◖ △-△

Winter: Strongly pyramidal silhouette.
Spring: Covered with a cloud of lacy white flowers in early spring before foliage emerges. New leaves bronze-tinged.
Summer: Glossy, dark green, heart-shaped leaves.
Autumn: Leaves change late to beautiful shades of dark red, purple, orange, and gold.
Description: Oval, eventually reaching 50′ tall and 35′ wide.
Comments: Uniform shape makes ornamental pear suitable for formal settings. Tolerates city conditions. 'Bradford', most common cultivar, no longer recommended due to weak structure. 'Chanticleer', oval shape with stronger branching structure than 'Bradford'. 'Faurei', dwarf form to 25′ tall. 'Whitehouse', a narrow columnar form.

Pyrus salicifolia 'Silver Frost'
'SILVER FROST' WEEPING PEAR
Zones 5-8 ☼ ◖ △

Winter: Graceful, long pendulous branches.
Spring: Clouds of white flowers bloom with emerging foliage.
Summer: Narrow silvery gray leaves.
Autumn: Maintains silvery gray foliage color.
Description: Weeping, to 15′-25′ tall and 15′ wide.
Comments: Useful as a fine-textured specimen in a small garden.

Salix alba 'Tristis'
GOLDEN WEEPING WILLOW
Zones 4-9 ☼ -◖ △

Winter: Bright yellow twigs and young branches on graceful pendulous branches.
Spring: Yellowish catkins with gold bark and light green new growth.
Summer: Narrow olive green leaves with whitish undersides.
Description: Weeping, round-headed tree, to 50′-70′.
Comments: Gorgeous tree, but constant litter from leaves and twigs a maintenance problem; situate in naturalistic location away from sewer lines, which roots can invade. 'Vitellina', less common, with brighter bark. *S. babylonica* (Babylon weeping willow), Zones 7-9, most pendulous of all weeping willows, but lacks golden twig color.

Salix matsudana 'Tortuosa'
CORKSCREW WILLOW
Zones 5-9 ☼ ◖ △

Winter: Striking contorted twigs and gnarled branches; yellow to olive green bark on young growth.
Spring: Catkins with the new bright green leaves.
Summer: Twisted, narrow dark green leaves.

Autumn: Yellow-green fall color.
Description: Rounded, to 20'-30' tall.
Comments: May be pruned severely to maintain as a shrub. 'Golden Curls', golden bark and twisted branches and leaves.

Sophora japonica
PAGODATREE, SCHOLARTREE
Zones 6-9 ☼ ◐-◊ ▲

Winter: Olive green twigs on young branches; rough bark on mature trunks.
Spring: Feathery light green leaves.
Summer: Dark green foliage. Attractive airy panicles of creamy, fragrant, late-summer flowers.
Autumn: Leaves remain green late. Ornamental yellow-green seedpods resemble string of beads.
Description: Rounded, to 50'-70' tall and wide.
Comments: Drops flowers, fruit, twigs all year, but withstands heat, drought, and air pollution. 'Regent', fast-growing; flowers at a younger age.

Sorbus alnifolia
KOREAN MOUNTAIN ASH
Zones 4-7 ☼ ◐ ▲

Winter: Upright, pyramidal shape with silvery bark; persistent berries.
Spring: Extra-large clusters of white flowers.

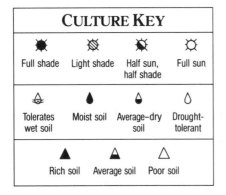

CULTURE KEY			
☀	◍	◐	☼
Full shade	Light shade	Half sun, half shade	Full sun
⚰	◐	◐	◊
Tolerates wet soil	Moist soil	Average–dry soil	Drought-tolerant
▲	△	△	
Rich soil	Average soil	Poor soil	

Summer: Bright green oval leaves.
Autumn: Gleaming cherrylike berries in huge clusters; excellent red and gold fall color.
Description: Reaches 40' tall.
Comments: Resistant to borers, which plague *S. aucuparia* (European mountain ash) in East but not in Northwest; scab and fire blight can be serious on both in hot, humid areas (Zones 3-7). *S. rufoferruginea* 'Longwood Sunset' resembles European mountain ash but is highly disease-resistant; features white flowers, excellent burgundy fall foliage, and orange berries (Zones 4-7).

Stewartia pseudocamellia
JAPANESE STEWARTIA
Zones 6-8 ◐-◍ ◐ ▲

Winter: Colorful apricot, reddish orange, and tan patchwork bark on sinuous trunks.
Spring: Rich green foliage.
Summer: 2″ white camellia-like flowers with yellow anthers, midsummer.
Autumn: Magnificent golden, rich red, or dark purple fall color.
Description: Open-branched, oval to vase-shaped tree, to 30' tall.
Comments: Requires acid soil. Excellent for border or naturalizing. *S. koreana* (Korean stewartia) very similar and may be the same species; 'Korean Splendor' has larger flowers. *S. monadelpha* (Hime-Sayara stewartia), Zones 6-8, metallic orange bark, 1″ flowers with violet anthers. *S. ovata* (mountain stewartia) native to southern Appalachians, Zones 7-8, lacks multicolored bark.

Styrax japonicus
JAPANESE SNOWBELL
Zones 6-8 ☼-◐ ◐ ▲

Winter: Dark gray-brown bark with orange stripes.
Summer: Bell-shaped white flowers dangle from undersides of branches in early summer. Lustrous deep green leaves.
Autumn: Yellowish to rusty red foliage in late fall.

Description: Rounded with low horizontal branches, to 25' tall.
Comments: Needs acid soil. Train to tree shape. Excellent patio or border tree. 'Pink Chimes', pendulous branches with pale pink blooms aging to dark pink. 'Carillon', weeping shrub to 7' tall.

Styrax obassia
FRAGRANT SNOWBELL
Zones 6-8 ☀-☼ ◉ ▲

Winter: Gray-brown bark with orange stripes.
Spring: New foliage velvety silver-green.
Summer: Large, round, dark green leaves covered with silver-green velvety hairs on undersides. Small, white, bell-shaped flowers in early summer.
Description: Pyramidal to round, to 25' tall.
Comments: Needs acid soil. Protect from late-spring frost.

Syringa reticulata, syn. *S. amurensis* var. *japonica*
JAPANESE TREE LILAC
Zones 3-7 ☀ ◉ ▲

Winter: Attractive, shiny, reddish brown bark.
Summer: Early-summer, foot-long panicles of creamy white flowers with aroma of privet.
Autumn: Yellow foliage.
Description: Rounded, to 40' tall and wide.
Comments: Highly valued flowering tree in cold climates; fragrance may not please. 'Ivory Silk', larger flowers. Manchurian tree lilac (*S. reticulata* var. *mandshurica*), hardy to Zone 2.

Ulmus parvifolia 'Emerald Vase'
'EMERALD VASE' LACEBARK ELM
Zones 5-9 ☀ ◉-◇ ▲-△

Winter: Fine-textured mottled tan and brown bark on striking vase-shaped silhouette.
Summer: Deep green, neat leaves.
Autumn: Evergreen in mild climates; purplish leaves late in cold climates before dropping.
Description: Vase-shaped, to 70' tall and 40' wide.
Comments: Adaptable tree; withstands city conditions. Suggested American elm replacement because of similar shape and with good resistance to Dutch elm disease. 'Golden Rey' ('Golden Rey' elm), Zones 6-9, new cultivar with lovely gold-tipped foliage.

Zelkova serrata 'Green Vase'
'GREEN VASE' JAPANESE ZELKOVA
Zones 6-9 ☀ ◉-◇ ▲-△

Winter: Striking vase-shaped silhouette; mottled brown and tan bark.
Summer: Deep green foliage.
Autumn: Rusty red fall color.
Description: Vase-shaped, to 70' tall.
Comments: Best American elm replacement, because highly resistant to Dutch elm disease and elm leaf beetles, and possesses distinctive silhouette. Styer Award winner 1988. 'Village Green' also a superior cultivar, grows more slowly, wine red fall color. *Z. sinica* (Chinese zelkova) similar, with striking orange-, gray-, and brown-mottled bark.

Deciduous Shrubs for Four-Season Landscapes

Abeliophyllum distichum
WHITE FORSYTHIA
Zones 4-7 ☼ ◉ ▲

Winter: Brown stems with prominent ridges.
Spring: Fragrant white flowers in late winter or very early spring before foliage.
Summer: Medium to dark green foliage
Autumn: No color change.
Description: Rounded shrub with arching stems, to 5′ tall and wide.
Comments: Prune severely immediately after flowering every few years. Valued for early bloom.

Aesculus parviflora
BOTTLEBRUSH BUCKEYE
Zones 5-9 ☼-◈ ◉-◊ ▲-△

Winter: Attractive bold-textured mound of stems.
Spring: New yellow-green foliage emerges early.
Summer: 12″ tall, white flower panicles at stem tips in midsummer; medium green, bold-textured leaves with red stems.

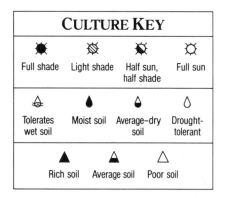

CULTURE KEY			
✸	✺	✹	☼
Full shade	Light shade	Half sun, half shade	Full sun
⬇	◉	◊	◊
Tolerates wet soil	Moist soil	Average–dry soil	Drought-tolerant
▲	△	△	
Rich soil	Average soil	Poor soil	

Autumn: Yellow fall color; glossy brown nuts.
Description: Multistemmed, 8′-12′ tall and spreading 8′-15′ with extensive suckering.
Comments: Tough plant; excellent large specimen for the Midwest. Disease-free. Less coarse-looking than other *Aesculus* species.

Aronia arbutifolia
RED CHOKEBERRY
Zones 4-9 ☼-✺ ◉-◊ ▲-△

Winter: Brilliant red berries persist to early or mid-winter.
Spring: Profuse dense clusters of small white flowers with showy red stamens.
Summer: Glossy dark green to gray-green foliage.
Autumn: Consistent bright red fall foliage.
Description: Upright and thicket-forming, to 10′ tall, spreading by suckers.
Comments: Native to eastern North America. Useful for mass-planting in naturalistic landscape. 'Brilliantissima', exceptionally glossy, showy berries. *A. melanocarpa* var. *elata* (black chokecherry), Zones 3-7, black fruits. *A. prunifolia* (purple chokecherry), Zones 4-9, tall shrub with brilliant purple berries; use in background.

Berberis koreana
KOREAN BARBERRY
Zones 3-8 ☼-✺ ◉-◊ ▲-△

Winter: Egg-shaped red berries cover twiggy, reddish stems with fine-textured thorns.
Spring: Showy yellow flower clusters, midspring.
Summer: Medium green, fine-textured leaves.
Autumn: Deep reddish purple foliage, late fall; showy bright red berries.

Description: Dense, rounded shrub, to 7' tall.
Comments: Attractive year-round when mass-planted as barrier hedge.

Berberis thunbergii var. *atropurpurea*
RED-LEAVED JAPANESE BARBERRY
Zones 4-8 ☼ ◐-◊ ▲-△

Winter: Teardrop-shaped red berries cover thorny, red-brown stems.
Spring: Yellow flowers in midspring. Bright burgundy new leaves emerge early.
Summer: Purplish red, fine-textured leaves.
Autumn: Fluorescent orange, red, and purple fall color; bright red berries.
Description: Dense, rounded shrub, to 6' tall.
Comments: Excellent in mixed border for foliage contrast and winter interest. 'Crimson Pygmy' ('Atropurpurea Nana'), dwarf 2' tall and 3' wide; 'Rose Glow', foliage rose-pink, mottled deep purple, to 5' tall; 'Aurea' (golden barberry), vivid yellow to chartreuse foliage, to 5' tall.

Buddleia alternifolia 'Argentea'
FOUNTAIN BUTTERFLY BUSH
Zones 4-7 ☼ ◐-◊ ▲-△

Winter: Arching stems form graceful fountain.
Spring: Profuse small clusters of lilac flowers in late spring.
Summer: Silvery gray, fine-textured leaves.
Description: Vase-shaped, to 12' tall and 15' wide.
Comments: Beautiful in flower and leaf. Thin out old branches every few years immediately after flowering. Trouble-free.

Buddleia davidii
BUTTERFLY BUSH
Zones 5-9 ☼ ◐-◊ ▲

Winter: Fountain of long stems.
Spring: Cut back to ground.
Summer: Long spikes of blue, lavender, purple, pink, or white fragrant flowers, late summer. Green leaves with gray undersides appear gray-green.
Autumn: Flowers appear until frost. Leaves remain green late, then drop.
Description: Fountain-shaped, open shrub to 10' tall; dwarf cultivars 3'-6' tall.
Comments: Excellent plant for late-summer and fall color in mixed border. Attracts hordes of butterflies. Tolerates heat and drought. Mulch heavily to prevent root damage in winter. Tops winterkilled in Zones 5-6; cut back to ground in late winter in all zones for best form and flowering. 'Royal Red', 12" long, purple-red flower clusters; 'Black Knight', dark purple flowers; 'Empire Blue', 12" long pure blue flower clusters; 'Fascination', large vivid pink clusters; 'White Profusion', white; 'Nanho Blue', pure blue flowers on compact plants; 'Nanho Purple', purple flowers on compact plants. *B.* × *weyeriana* 'Sungold' has yellow flowers flushed with pink and mauve.

Callicarpa bodinieri 'Profusion'
'PROFUSION' BODINIER BEAUTYBERRY
Zones 5-7 ☼-☀ ◊ ▲

Winter: Abundant clusters of gorgeous, glossy lilac-purple berries on bare brown stems; white berries on some cultivars.
Summer: Misty, lavender-pink flowers along stems in midsummer; coarse-textured, light green leaves.
Autumn: Lilac-purple berries showy from mid-autumn on. Holds leaves late; may turn pinkish purple.
Description: Vase-shaped with erect branches, to 8' tall and 5' wide. Blooms on new growth; can cut to ground every few years in late winter to renew growth and maintain shape.

Comments: Avoid overly fertile soil. Best cultivar of Chinese beautyberry; produces huge quantities of berries; not widely available. *C. americana* (American beautyberry), Zones 7-9, *C. dichotoma* (Chinese beautyberry), Zones 5-8, and *C. japonica* (Japanese beautyberry), Zones 5-8, are similar but more rounded and bushy. All species have white-berried forms.

Caryopoteris × clandonensis
BLUEBEARD, BLUE SPIREA
Zones 4-8 ☼ ◐-◊ ▲-△

Winter: White twiggy mound.
Summer: Clusters of tiny, bright blue flowers in late summer; grayish green fine-textured leaves.
Autumn: May flower until frost. Leaves remain late, drop without color change.
Description: Rounded mound, 2'-3' tall and wide.
Comments: Fertile soil causes rampant, weak growth. Drought-tolerant. Tops winter-killed in Zones 4-6, sometimes in 7-8; best to cut to ground in spring for compact growth. 'Blue Mist', powder blue flowers; 'Heavenly Blue', compact plant, dark blue; 'Longwood Blue', brilliant blue.

CULTURE KEY

☀	⊘	☼	☼
Full shade	Light shade	Half sun, half shade	Full sun
⚑	●	◐	◊
Tolerates wet soil	Moist soil	Average–dry soil	Drought-tolerant
▲	△	△	
Rich soil	Average soil	Poor soil	

Cephalanthus occidentalis
BUTTONBUSH
Zones 4-9 ☼-⊘ ⚑-● ▲

Winter: Gray to reddish brown, coarse-textured bark.
Summer: Spherical white flower clusters in mid-summer; bright green leaves with white undersides.
Autumn: Little foliage color change; red gum-ball-like seedheads turn brown.
Description: Rounded and loose; 3'-6' tall.
Comments: Cut back to renew if gangly. Grows in wet locations, even standing water. Native to much of North America. Attracts bees.

Chimonanthus praecox
WINTERSWEET
Zones 7-9 ☼-⊘ ⚑-● ▲-△

Winter: Fragrant yellow flowers with purple centers, mid- to late winter. Shiny gray-green bark.
Summer: Shiny dark green, rough-textured leaves.
Autumn: Foliage changes late to yellow-green.
Description: Fountain-shaped, to 10'-15' tall and 8'-12' wide; shorter in the North.
Comments: Provides light shade in South. Prune to ground in late winter after flowering to rejuvenate if becomes leggy. Locate where winter fragrance can be enjoyed.

Clethra alnifolia
SUMMERSWEET, SWEET PEPPERBUSH
Zones 4-9 ☼-⊘ ⚑-● ▲

Winter: Light brown stems and delicate seedpods.
Summer: Fuzzy spires of white or pink fragrant flowers for 6-8 weeks in mid- to late summer.
Autumn: Long-lasting golden yellow fall color and interesting dry seedpods.
Description: Upright, to 3'-8' tall and 4'-6' wide; forms colonies by underground stems.

Comments: Native to East Coast. Best in moist, acid soil, but adapts to clay, somewhat alkaline or seashore conditions. Excellent for summer color. Attracts bees. 'Rosea' has pink flowers.

Cornus alba
TARTARIAN DOGWOOD
Zones 3-8 ☼-☀ ◗-◑ ▲-△

Winter: Stems and branches brilliant to dark red or deep coral, becoming redder through winter.
Spring: Yellow-green new foliage and flattened clusters of lacy white flowers in late spring.
Summer: Bark greenish. Dense, dark green leaves; variegated in cultivars. White, late-summer fruits.
Autumn: Dull to rich red fall foliage.
Description: Upright, sparsely branched, to 8'-10' tall, 5'-8' wide.
Comments: Native shrub. 'Elegantissima' ('Argenteo-Marginata'), beautiful creamy white and gray-green variegated leaves; 'Variegata', creamy white and green variegated leaves; 'Spaethii', yellow-edged leaves. Variegated forms effective in mixed border. *C. sericea*, syn. *C. stolonifera* (red osier dogwood), similar but spreads quickly through underground stems; 'Isanti', dwarf form with good bark color.

Cornus sericea (syn. C. stolonifera) 'Flaviramea'
GOLDEN-TWIG DOGWOOD
Zones 3-8 ☼-☀ ◗-◑ ▲-△

Winter: Gleaming golden yellow branches and stems.
Spring: Yellow-green new leaves; lacy white flowers in late spring.
Summer: Medium-textured green leaves; variegated in cultivars. White berries, late summer. Bark greenish.
Autumn: Fall foliage may be purplish red.
Description: Rounded and loose, spreading vigorously by stolons, to 7'-9' tall and 10' or more wide.
Comments: Native shrub. Species has red stems. Prune out older stems at ground level each spring

to encourage new, bright gold-stemmed growth. Also listed as 'Aurea' or 'Lutea'. 'Silver & Gold', creamy white leaf margins, bright gold winter stems; 1990 Styer Award winner.

Corylopsis pauciflora
BUTTERCUP WINTERHAZEL
Zones 6-9 ☼-☀ ◗-◑ ▲-△

Winter: Zigzagged, light brown, horizontal branches.
Spring: Pastel yellow, fragrant flowers in dangling racemes before foliage in early spring.
Summer: Heart-shaped, blue-green leaves with fuzzy undersides.
Autumn: Golden brown fall foliage.
Description: Open and spreading. *C. pauciflora*, 4'- 6' tall and wide; *C. glabrescens* (Zones 5-9), 8'-15' tall and wide.
Comments: Needs acid soil and plenty of space to mature. Protect from late-spring frost.

Corylus avellana 'Contorta'
CORKSCREW HAZEL, HARRY LAUDER'S WALKING STICK
Zones 4-8 ☼-☀ ◗-◊ △

Winter: Curious twisted, corkscrew branches and twigs. Prominent catkins all winter open to fuzzy yellow in late winter.
Summer: Coarse, dark green, twisted leaves.
Autumn: Yellow fall color.
Description: Rounded to upright, 7' tall and wide. Grows in sun or light shade.
Comments: Locate where it can be appreciated from indoors in winter. Prune suckers regularly from understock to maintain form. Cut branches useful in arrangements.

Corylus maxima 'Purpurea'
PURPLE-LEAF HAZEL
Zones 5-8 ☼-☀ ◗-◊ ▲

Winter: Showy purplish male catkins.
Spring: Deep purple foliage, early spring.
Summer: Large heart-shaped leaves change to green.
Description: Upright shrub, to 20' tall.
Comments: Edible hazelnuts (filberts).

Cotoneaster horizontalis
ROCKSPRAY COTONEASTER
Zones 5-8 ☼ ◗ ▲

Winter: Interesting herringbone branching pattern and red berries on low-spreading plants.
Spring: Tiny, pink flowers line stems along with new foliage.
Summer: Tidy, dark green, fine-textured leaves and strong branching pattern. Variegated cultivar.
Autumn: Leaves remain green late, change to red before falling, accompanied by bright red berries.
Description: Low, dense, and spreading with tiers of layered branches; 2'-3' tall and 5'-8' wide.
Comments: Useful for draping over walls or in foreground of mixed border. 'Variegata' with white-edged leaves adds sparkle to summer garden. Fire blight serious in the South. Showier fruit: *C.*

apiculatus (cranberry cotoneaster), less distinct branching pattern, best for the Midwest; and *C. adpressus* (creeping cotoneaster), prostrate, 1'-1½' tall.

Cytisus × *praecox*
WARMINSTER BROOM
Zones 6-9 ☼ ◗-◊ ▲-△

Winter: Green to olive green stems and branches.
Spring: Sulfur yellow flowers in midspring before foliage.
Summer: Sparse, very fine-textured, silky-haired leaves; green stems conspicuous.
Description: Dense and rounded with fountain of branches, to 5' tall and 7' wide.
Comments: Tolerates infertile and alkaline soil. 'Hollandia', salmon-pink flowers.

Deutzia gracilis 'Nikko'
'NIKKO' SLENDER DEUTZIA
Zones 5-8 ☼-☀ ◗ ▲-▲

Spring: Pink buds open to white, starlike flowers in late spring.
Summer: Fine-textured, light green foliage with maroon tinges.
Autumn: Deep burgundy foliage, late fall.
Description: Low and spreading, to 2' tall and 5' wide, rooting as it spreads.
Comments: Needs light shade in the South. Use as a groundcover or foreground of border, or to cascade over a wall. Recipient of Styer Award in 1989.

Elaeagnus angustifolia
RUSSIAN OLIVE
Zones 3-7 ☼ ◗-◊ ▲-△

Winter: Silvery, thorny young branches; brown trunk bark.

CULTURE KEY			
☀	⊘	☀	☼
Full shade	Light shade	Half sun, half shade	Full sun
⬥	◗	◊	◊
Tolerates wet soil	Moist soil	Average-dry soil	Drought-tolerant
▲	◮	△	
Rich soil	Average soil	Poor soil	

Spring: Silvery new foliage. Small, very fragrant yellow flowers, late spring to early summer.
Summer: Fine-textured, silvery green leaves.
Autumn: Holds summer color until late fall. Silvery scaled fruits can be showy.
Description: Large, rounded shrub or small tree, to 20' or more.
Comments: Tolerates seashore and alkaline conditions; excellent in dry climates. Very effective for silver-gray foliage effect. *E. commutata* (silverberry), Zones 2-6, showier silver leaves. *E. × ebbengei*, Zones 7-9, green leaves with flashing silver undersides, lacks thorns, semi- to fully evergreen, fragrant fall flowers; 'Gilt Edge' has dramatic soft yellow-margined light green leaves.

Elsholtzia stauntonii
MINT SHRUB
Zones 5-7   ☼   ♦   ▲

Winter: Rounded stems in spreading mound.
Spring: Cut back to ground.
Summer: Large, fluffy, lavender-pink spikes in late summer; coarse-textured, lance-shaped, mint-scented leaves.
Autumn: Flowers continue to appear until frost.
Description: Loose mound, to 3'-5' tall and wide.
Comments: Cut back to ground in late winter or early spring to encourage profuse bloom and retain compact shape.

Enkianthus campanulatus
RED-VEIN ENKIANTHUS
Zones 5-8   ☼-◫   ♦   ▲-△

Winter: Graceful, whorled branching structure.
Spring: Clusters of small bell-shaped creamy yellow flowers marked with red veins as leaves emerge in midspring.
Summer: Fine- to medium-textured, blue-green leaves with red petioles.
Autumn: Brilliant scarlet, orange, and gold fall color.
Description: Upright shrub or small tree, to 6'-8' tall and wide; old specimens to 20'.
Comments: Needs acid soil.

Euonymus alata
WINGED EUONYMUS, BURNING BUSH
Zones 4-8   ☼-◫   ♦-◊   ▲-△

Winter: Curious twigs and branches with prominent corky wings, intriguing when holding snow.
Spring: Yellow-green blossoms and new foliage create a pleasing haze of color.
Summer: Green, medium-textured foliage.
Autumn: Spectacular red fall color. Showy red fruits.
Description: Rounded to horizontal shrub to small tree, 15'-20' tall and wide.
Comments: Excellent fall color even in South and Midwest; may be deep pink in light shade. 'Compactus', 6' tall and 4' wide but lacks good display of corky twigs. 'Monstrosa', extremely corky branches.

Fothergilla gardenii
DWARF FOTHERGILLA
Zones 5-9   ☼-◫   ♦   ▲

Spring: Creamy white, honey-scented bottlebrush flowers in early spring before or with foliage.
Summer: Neat heart-shaped, leathery, green leaves; 'Blue Mist' has blue-green foliage.
Autumn: Gorgeous red and golden orange fall color.
Description: Upright to rounded, 3' tall and wide.
Comments: Needs humusy acid soil. Best flowering and fall color in full sun. Trouble-free. Needs no pruning. Excellent in naturalistic plantings and mixed borders. 'Blue Mist', beautiful deep blue-green leaves, Styer Award winner 1990. *F. major* (large fothergilla), 8' tall and wide. *F. monticola* (Alabama fothergilla), 6' tall, spreads very wide.

Hamamelis × intermedia
HYBRID WITCH HAZEL
Zones 5-9   ☼-◫   ♦   ▲

Winter: Fuzzy flower buds open to mopheads of fragrant yellow or coppery flowers, lasting from midwinter until spring. Vase-shaped silhouette.

Summer: Gray-green, bold-textured foliage.
Autumn: Brilliant orange or gold fall color.
Description: Vase-shaped, to 15'-20' tall.
Comments: Needs fertile acid soil. 'Diane', coppery-colored blossoms. 'Jelena', orange-pink flowers; plant close to house to enjoy winter bloom. 'Arnold Promise', large primrose yellow blossoms show up well from a distance. *H. mollis* (Chinese witch hazel), to 30' tall; 'Pallida', a Styer Award winner, showy primrose yellow flowers with dark centers. *H. vernalis* (vernal witch hazel), native shrub, Zones 4-8, yellow flowers less showy but bloom early.

Hamamelis virginiana
VIRGINIA WITCH HAZEL
Zones 4-9   ☼-☒   ●-◐   ▲

Winter: Attractive branching.
Summer: Dark green, bold-textured, toothed leaves.
Autumn: Fragrant yellow flowers; yellow foliage.
Description: Rounded and open, to 10'-15' tall.
Comments: Native shrub; use in naturalistic planting. Flowers often masked by foliage; showier after leaf drop in late fall.

CULTURE KEY			
☀	☒	☒	☼
Full shade	Light shade	Half sun, half shade	Full sun
⬦	●	◐	◇
Tolerates wet soil	Moist soil	Average–dry soil	Drought-tolerant
▲	△	△	
Rich soil	Average soil	Poor soil	

Hibiscus syriacus
ROSE-OF-SHARON
Zones 5-9   ☼-☒   ●-◐   ▲-△

Winter: Upright trunks.
Spring: Leafs out late.
Summer: Large, funnel-shaped, white, pink, red, or lavender flowers for 1-2 months in late summer. Glossy lobed leaves.
Autumn: Holds green color late, then drops without much change.
Description: Tall, vase-shaped shrub to 12' tall.
Comments: Adaptable plant; pH-tolerant. Prune heavily in early spring. May cause seedling weed problem. Does well at the seashore and in heat and humidity of South and Midwest. 'Diana', Gold Medal Award winner from the Pennsylvania Horticultural Society; has large, white flowers that stay open at night; blooms mid- through late summer and doesn't set seed.

Hydrangea arborescens 'Grandiflora'
HILLS-OF-SNOW HYDRANGEA
Zones 4-9   ☼-☒   ●-◐   ▲-△

Winter: Unbranched, stout, shreddy-barked brown stems; dried flower heads.
Summer: Round 6″ clusters of sterile flowers begin apple green, become pure white in midsummer, age to brown. Bold dark green foliage.
Autumn: Little fall color. Dried flower heads.
Description: Moundlike, to 3' tall and wide.
Comments: May die to ground in cold climates; blooms on new wood. Faded flowers less ornamental than other hydrangeas. Cut stems to ground in early spring. 'Annabelle', even larger clusters.

Hydrangea macrophylla var. *serrata*
LACECAP HYDRANGEA

H. macrophylla var. *macrophylla*
HORTENSIA HYDRANGEA
Zones 6-9 ☼-☒ ◖-◗ ▲-△

Winter: Upright, thick unbranched stems; persistent dried flower heads.
Summer: Coarse-textured green foliage; dramatic globes or flat lacecaps of blue or pink flowers in midsummer.
Autumn: Leaves drop with little color change. Flower clusters persist and fade to attractive earth colors.
Description: Rounded, 3'-6' tall; spreads by suckers.
Comments: Soil pH, controlled by aluminum, determines flower color; pH 6 to 6.5 usually gives pink flowers, and pH 5 to 5.5, blue. Prune immediately after flowering; blooms on previous season's growth. 'Variegata', a lacecap form with beautiful creamy white margins on dark green leaves. 'Blue Billow', blue lacecap flowers, 1990 Styer Award winner. 'Pink Lacecap', pink flowers even in alkaline soil. 'Nikko Blue', deep blue globes.

Hydrangea paniculata 'Grandiflora'
PEEGEE HYDRANGEA
Zones 4-8 ☼-☒ ◖-◗ ▲-△

Winter: Persistent dried flower heads; reddish brown peeling bark.
Summer: Huge pyramidal, snowball-like white flower clusters in midsummer; coarse dark green leaves.
Autumn: Flowers age to attractive old rose and then tan dried heads. Little foliage color change.
Description: Upright with arching branches; often trained to small tree. Reaches 10'-20' tall.
Comments: Prune shrub to strongest 10 stems for largest flowers; blooms on new growth. Leafs out late in spring. 'Praecox' flowers in early summer; 'Tardiva' flowers in late summer to early fall.

Hydrangea quercifolia
OAKLEAF HYDRANGEA
Zones 5-9 ☼-☀ ◖-◗ ▲

Winter: Cinnamon brown bark peels in long, shaggy strips. Attractive tan dried flower clusters.
Spring: Leaves emerge covered with silky hairs.
Summer: Huge, lobed leaves. Cones of flowers in midsummer start off apple green, change to snowy white, age to old rose.
Autumn: Deep rich red and purple foliage colors develop late; persistent dried flower clusters.
Description: Upright, forming mounded colonies of sparsely branched stems; to 4'-6' tall and wider, spreading by stolons.
Comments: Native American shrub. Excellent in woodland or mixed border. Keep soil mulched to retain moisture and coolness; needs ample moisture in sun. May topkill and thus not bloom in Zone 5, but worth growing for foliage alone. 'Snow Queen' noted for especially large blossoms; Styer Award winner 1989.

Hypericum kalmianum
ST.-JOHN'S-WORT
Zones 4-8 ☼-☒ ◖-◊ △

Winter: Warm brown stems and exfoliating bark on vertical branches.
Spring: Sea green new growth.
Summer: Blue-green foliage; showy golden yellow, 3" flowers borne in clusters of 3.
Autumn: Semievergreen, eventually turning cinnamon brown.
Description: Upright, to 4' tall.
Comments: Intolerant of heavy soil. Compact plant suited to small gardens. *H. calycinum* (Aaronsbeard St.-John's-wort), low groundcover, Zones 6-9, large yellow flowers in mid- to late summer. *H. patulum* (goldencup St.-John's-wort), Zones 7-9, low round shrub, showy midsummer flowers. *H. patulum* 'Hidcote' ('Hidcote' St.-John's-wort), Zones 6-9, spreading plant with early-summer flowers, persistent cinnamon brown leaves in winter. *H. prolificum* (shrubby St.-John's-wort), Zones 4-8, round to 5', showy midsummer flowers.

Ilex verticillata
WINTERBERRY
Zones 4-9 ☼-◐ ◖-◑ ▲-△

Winter: Outstanding red or orange berries on dense, bare branches, if berries are not eaten by birds.
Summer: Yellowish green leaves; darker green in selected cultivars.
Autumn: Good yellow fall color; showy red berries.
Description: Upright to oval, to 10′ tall; may spread to form large clumps.
Comments: Native shrub. Needs acid soil. Berries form on female plants only; locate male plant nearby for pollination. 'Winter Red', dark, rich green foliage and persistent bright red fruits. 'Afterglow', persistent, large, deep red fruits. 'Aurantiaca', orange fruits. 'Chrysocarpa', yellow fruits. 'Nana', compact with large red fruits. *I. laevigata* 'Hervey Robinson' ('Hervey Robinson' smooth winterberry), Zones 4-7, similar with orange berries. *I. serrata* var. *leucocarpa* (white-berried Japanese winterberry), Zones 6-9, white berries.

Itea virginica 'Henry's Garnet'
'HENRY'S GARNET' VIRGINIA SWEETSPIRE
Zones 6-9 ☼-◐ ⬧-◑ ▲-△

Winter: Evergreen to semi-evergreen in warm climates.

CULTURE KEY

✹	⬗	⬖	☼
Full shade	Light shade	Half sun, half shade	Full sun
⬧	●	◑	◊
Tolerates wet soil	Moist soil	Average–dry soil	Drought-tolerant
▲	△	△	
Rich soil	Average soil	Poor soil	

Summer: Long, cascading spires of fragrant white flowers, early summer; lustrous green foliage.
Autumn: Long-lasting, deep red-purple fall color.
Description: Rounded to arching, to 6′ tall, 8′ wide; forms colonies.
Comments: Cultivar of native shrub. Styer Award winner 1988. Needs acid soil and at least light shade in South.

Jasminum nudiflorum
WINTER JESSAMINE
Zones 6-9 ☼-◐ ◖-◊ ▲-△

Winter: Green bark on cascading branches. Yellow flowers with orange eyes, late winter.
Spring–Summer: Lovely, lustrous green leaves.
Autumn: Holds green color late before dropping.
Description: Spreading mound of trailing, rooting stems 3′-4′ tall, 4′-7′ wide; can grow 12′-18′ tall if trained on a trellis.
Comments: Grow against a sunny wall for good winter floral display. Train to cascade over a wall or down a slope. Not fragrant.

Kerria japonica 'Picta'
VARIEGATED JAPANESE KERRIA
Zones 5-9 ☼-◐ ◖ ▲

Winter: Upright thickets of slender, bright yellow-green stems and branches.
Spring: Golden yellow single blossoms in early spring with new leaves.
Summer: Gracefully cut, gray-green leaves with creamy white edges.
Autumn: Holds color late before dropping.
Description: Arching, to 4′-5′ tall; spreads by underground stems to form thicket 8′ wide.
Comments: Root-prune after flowering to control spread. Weak-stemmed in too much shade. 'Pleniflora', double pompomlike flowers, green leaves. *K. japonica* var. *aureo-vittata*, yellow stems.

Lespedeza thunbergii 'Gibraltar'
'GIBRALTAR' BUSH CLOVER
Zones 6-8 ☼ ◑-◊ ▲-△

Winter: Cut to ground in late winter.
Spring: May bloom lightly in the South.
Summer: Blue-green, trifoliate leaves.
Autumn: Abundant clusters of rosy purple flowers.
Description: Vase-shaped, to 3'-6' tall and wide.
Comments: May be killed to ground in cold areas; regrows and blooms on new growth; best cut back every year. *L. bicolor* (shrub bush clover), Zones 5-7, less showy, blooms midsummer to fall. *L. japonica* (Japanese bush clover), Zones 6-8, white flowers bloom in fall.

Myrica pensylvanica
BAYBERRY
Zones 4-9 ☼-◐ ◑-◊ ▲-△

Winter: Clusters of waxy, aromatic gray-white fruits line stems. Distinctive twiggy silhouette.
Summer: Bright to dull green leathery leaves.
Autumn: Remains green very late; semi-evergreen.
Description: Upright and twiggy, to 5'-10' tall; spreads by suckers to form thickets.
Comments: Tolerates seashore, roadside, and poor soil. Insignificant spring flowers. Fruits only on female plants; locate male nearby for pollination. Fruits used for scenting candles.

Potentilla fruticosa
BUSH CINQUEFOIL
Zones 2-7 ☼ ◑-◊ ▲-△

Winter: Reddish brown shredding bark.
Spring: Silky gray-green new leaves.
Summer: Showy yellow, red-orange, or white flowers all summer. Dark green, fine-textured foliage.
Description: Upright to rounded, twiggy, 1'-4' tall and 2'-4' wide.
Comments: Tolerates seashore, roadside, and alkaline conditions. Excellent border plant for summer

color, especially in Midwest. 'Abbotswood', white flowers, blue-green leaves. 'Goldfinger', large bright yellow flowers. 'Katherine Dykes', arching stems, lemon yellow flowers.

Rhododendron mucronulatum
KOREAN RHODODENDRON
Zones 5-7 ◐-◒ ◑-◊ ▲

Spring: Rosy purple (pink or white in cultivars) flowers on bare branches, earliest spring.
Summer: Leathery dark green leaves.
Autumn: Wine red to bronze leaves, late fall.
Description: Upright habit, to 4' tall and wide.
Comments: Needs acid soil. Blossoms susceptible to late frosts. Makes a good shrub for a foundation or mixed border planting because of compact size and shape. 'Alba', white flowers; 'Cornell Pink', clear pink.

Rhododendron schlippenbachii
ROYAL AZALEA
Zones 5-8 ◐-◒ ◑ ▲

Spring: Clusters of large pale, pure pink, or rose-pink flowers on bare branches in early spring with expanding leaves. Reddish new growth.
Summer: Whorls of dark green leaves with pale undersides.
Autumn: Bright orange, gold, and red foliage.
Description: Open, upright to rounded, 6'-8' tall and wide.
Comments: Protect from winter wind. A stunning specimen in a shade garden.

Rhododendron species and hybrids
DECIDUOUS NATIVE AND HYBRID AZALEAS

See "Native American Azaleas for Months of Bloom" on page 150.

Rhus typhina
STAGHORN SUMAC
Zones 3-8 ☼ ◐-◊ ▲-△

Winter: Picturesque gaunt and twisted silhouette; fuzzy, red, persistent fruits; velvety branches.
Spring: Velvety new foliage.
Summer: Dramatic, bright green compound leaves; tall panicles of greenish yellow flowers.
Autumn: Excellent orange and red fall color; tall, fuzzy clublike clusters of red fruits.
Description: Upright and sparsely branched, 15'-25' tall, spreading as wide by suckers.
Comments: Native shrub. Use in naturalistic landscape with plenty of space because of suckering habit. Prune to remove unsightly deadwood and contain plant; may cut to ground in late winter. 'Laciniata', lovely cutleaf form; *R. glabra* 'Laciniata' (cutleaf smooth sumac), similar but lacks velvety stems. *R. copallina* (shiny sumac), Zones 4-9, lustrous dark green leaves and bright red fruits.

Rosa glauca, syn. *R. rubrifolia*
REDLEAF ROSE
Zones 2-8 ☼ ◐ ▲

Winter: Persistent, shriveled dark red fruits, if not eaten by birds; purplish bloom on bark.
Spring: New growth purplish.
Summer: Clear pink, 2" flowers, early summer; attractive blue-gray foliage with purple margins and veins.

Autumn: Abundant cranberry-like fruits (hips).
Description: Vase-shaped, to 6'-8' tall.
Comments: Little pruning needed. Disease-free. Wonderful foliage plant; combine with red, blue, and lavender flowers.

Rosa rugosa
RUGOSA ROSE
Zones 3-7 ☼ ◐-◊ ▲-△

Winter: Thorny stems and large, glossy red fruits.
Spring: Light green new leaves.
Summer: Large pink, white, or rose-red flowers all summer. Attractively pleated, dark green leaves.
Autumn: Large, glossy orange-red berries (hips); occasional flowers; yellow to orange fall foliage.
Description: Heavy, upright stems; dense and rounded, to 5' tall and wide.
Comments: Japanese species naturalized along East Coast. Highly disease-resistant cultivars: 'Frau Dagmar Hastrup', pale pink flowers, extra-large hips; 'Blanc Double de Coubert', white semidouble to double flowers, no fruits; 'Hansa', semidouble purple-pink flowers, many hips.

Rosa virginiana
VIRGINIA ROSE
Zones 5-7 ☼ ◐ ▲-△

Winter: Glossy red canes and twigs; showy red fruits.
Summer: Pale purplish pink, 3" flowers, early summer. Glossy dark green foliage.
Autumn: Maroon then orange fall color; red fruits.
Description: Upright, to 5' tall and wide.
Comments: Disease-resistant. Cut back rangy plants. Sparse thorns. Very showy in fall and winter; best four-season rose. Native to eastern North America. 'Alba', white flowers.

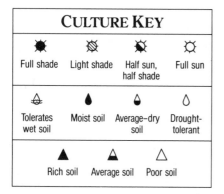

CULTURE KEY			
☀	⊘	◒	☼
Full shade	Light shade	Half sun, half shade	Full sun
⛲	●	◐	◊
Tolerates wet soil	Moist soil	Average–dry soil	Drought-tolerant
▲	△	△	
Rich soil	Average soil	Poor soil	

Salix alba 'Britzensis'
CORAL EMBERS WILLOW
Zones 3-8   ☼   ⬤-◗   ▲-△

Winter: Brilliant orange-red stems.
Spring: Silvery new leaves.
Summer: Bright green foliage with silvery undersides.
Autumn: Yellow fall foliage.
Description: Clumps of upright stems if pruned to maintain height. Grows 4'-5' each season.
Comments: Tough and adaptable. Cut back to 1' each year in late winter to encourage new colorful growth and maintain shrub habit. Best against a dark background. *S. daphnoides* (violet willow), bright violet twigs and buds; *S.* × *erdingeri*, coppery bark with bluish white waxy bloom; *S. lucida* (shining willow), lustrous orange bark.

Salix purpurea var. *nana*
DWARF PURPLE OSIER
Zones 3-9   ☼-☀   ⬤-◗   ▲-△

Winter: Lustrous purple bark on slender branches.
Spring: Catkins before the leaves, but not showy.
Summer: Narrow, blue-green leaves with pale undersides.
Autumn: Leaves dry up and turn black.
Description: Rounded and dense, to 5' tall.
Comments: Valued for winter effect. Prune to ground to rejuvenate. Leaves are a source of medicinal salicylic acid.

Sambucus racemosa 'Plumosa Aurea'
CUTLEAF GOLDEN ELDERBERRY
Zones 3-7   ☀-☼   ◗-◒   ▲-△

Spring: Highly effective bright yellow new leaves. Yellowish white panicles of flowers, midspring.
Summer: Foliage finely cut, becomes bright green. Red fruits, early summer.
Autumn: Yellow fall color.

Description: Upright, to 8'-12' tall.
Comments: Often cut completely to the ground in late winter to encourage vigorous, colorful new growth. Excellent foliage plant for mixed border.

Sorbaria sorbifolia, syn. *Spiraea sorbifolia*
URAL FALSE SPIREA
Zones 3-8   ☼-☀   ◗   ▲

Winter: Bold-textured stand of erect stems.
Spring: Reddish new growth emerges very early.
Summer: Deep green, bold-textured compound leaves; large, white feathery panicles, midsummer.
Description: Upright, 5'-10' tall and wide, spreads by suckers.
Comments: Outstanding in flower; blooms on new growth. Use in naturalistic setting. Needs room to spread. Good bank cover or soil stabilizer.

Spiraea × *bumalda*
BUMALD SPIREA
Zones 4-9   ☼   ◗-◒   △

Winter: Fine-textured twiggy mound.
Spring: New foliage emerges early, brownish red; may mature bright green, gold, or chartreuse, depending upon cultivar.
Summer: Lacy, carmine-pink flower heads in midsummer. Fine-textured dark blue-green foliage, colorful in cultivars.
Autumn: Bronze-red to purple fall color.
Description: Dense, rounded, 3' tall and 5' wide.
Comments: Excellent compact plant for mixed border. Removing faded flowers promotes second flush of bloom. 'Anthony Waterer', large carmine-pink flowers. 'Froebelii', taller and brighter pink. 'Goldflame', russet-orange new growth, changes to yellow, then yellow-green, and finally bright green by midsummer. 'Limemound', lemon yellow new growth matures to lime green. *S. japonica* var. *alpina*, pink flowers, early summer; 1' tall. 'Shirobana', deep rose, pink, and white flowers all on same plant, all summer; to 3' tall. 'Little Princess', deep

pink flowers; to 2'-3' tall. 'Goldmound', pink flowers, early summer; yellow spring leaves become yellow-green by midsummer. Excessive summer heat makes foliage greener in all cultivars.

Stephanandra incisa 'Crispa'
CUTLEAF STEPHANANDRA
Zones 5-8   ☼-☒   ◗-◗   ▲

Winter: Fine-textured zigzagged bare branches in spreading mound.
Spring: Red-tinged new foliage.
Summer: Fernlike, bright green leaves.
Autumn: Bright red-purple to orange fall color.
Description: Spreading, to 2' tall and 5' wide.
Comments: Needs acid soil. Useful as a groundcover or cascading down a slope or wall.

Syringa meyeri, syn. *S. palibiniana*
MEYER LILAC
Zones 4-7   ☼   ◗-◗   ▲-△

Winter: Dense and twiggy; tan bark.
Spring: Covered with dense clusters of highly fragrant violet-purple flowers in late spring, after purple-rimmed new foliage.
Summer: Neat dark green leaves, light undersides.
Autumn: Little color change.

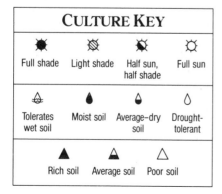

CULTURE KEY			
☀	☒	☀	☼
Full shade	Light shade	Half sun, half shade	Full sun
⬟	◗	◗	◊
Tolerates wet soil	Moist soil	Average–dry soil	Drought-tolerant
▲	△	△	
Rich soil	Average soil	Poor soil	

Description: Rounded, to 4'-8' tall.
Comments: Performs well in Midwest and South. 'Palabin' more compact. Mildew-free, as are similar-looking compact lilacs like *S. patula* 'Miss Kim' ('Miss Kim' dwarf lilac), Zones 3-7, with pale lilac flowers on 4'-6' upright plants, reddish fall color. *S. × persica* (Persian lilac), Zones 4-8, upright to 4'-8' tall and 5'-10' wide with violet flowers and neat dark green foliage. All are preferred over common lilacs in mixed borders.

Tamarix ramosissima
TAMARISK
Zones 4-9   ☼   ◗-◊   ▲-△

Winter: Sparse-looking, coarse silhouette.
Summer: Bluish green, fine-textured, needlelike leaves; large, fluffy, pink, fine-textured flower clusters in midsummer.
Autumn: Yellowish fall color.
Description: Vase-shaped, to 10' tall.
Comments: Shrub is pH- and salt-tolerant. Ideal seashore plant. Prune drastically to renew if becomes gangly. May be cut to ground each spring; flowers on new growth. Leafs out late. Unusual, airy-textured plant.

Viburnum × bodnantense 'Dawn'
FRAGRANT DAWN VIBURNUM
Zones 7-9   ☼-☒   ◗   ▲-△

Winter: Clusters of rose-pink buds open to pink-flushed, sweetly scented blossoms, early to late winter, depending upon climate.
Spring: Flowering continues into spring.
Summer: Dark green foliage.
Autumn: Purplish red fall color.
Description: Upright, to 10' tall and wide.
Comments: The earliest-blooming viburnum. Blossoms withstand light frost.

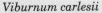

Viburnum carlesii
KOREANSPICE VIBURNUM
Zones 4-8 ☼ - ❄ ◗ - ◗ ▲

Winter: Dense twiggy outline; tan bark.
Spring: Midspring pink flower bud clusters open to white snowballs 4″ across with a pervasive sweet and spicy fragrance.
Summer: Neat gray-green foliage. Black fruits quickly eaten by birds.
Autumn: Vivid red fall color.
Description: Rounded, to 5′-8′ tall. Deciduous.
Comments: Similar highly fragrant plants: *V.* × *carlcephalum* (fragrant snowball viburnum), Zones 5-8, to 10′ tall, larger flower clusters, vivid red fall color. *V.* × *burkwoodii* 'Mohawk', Zones 5-8, red flower buds open to spicy white flowers, orange fall color. *V.* × *juddii* (Judd viburnum), small white flowers and open habit, Zones 4-8.

Viburnum opulus
CRANBERRYBUSH VIBURNUM
Zones 3-8 ☼ - ❄ ◗ ▲

Winter: Clusters of glossy cranberry-sized red or yellow fruits hang on well into winter on bare branches. Red twigs.
Spring: Flattened clusters of fertile white flowers surrounded by a ring of showy sterile flowers; late spring; showy against new foliage.
Summer: Deep green, 3-lobed leaves.
Autumn: Edible fruit colors in autumn. Foliage remains green well into autumn before falling.
Description: Rounded, to 12′ tall and wide.
Comments: 'Compactum' remains below 5′. 'Nanum' grows slowly to 3′ with outstanding red twigs but does not flower or fruit well. 'Xanthocarpum' has yellow fruits. *V. trilobum* (American cranberrybush viburnum), Zones 2-8, is similar but has reddish fall color.

Viburnum setigerum
TEA VIBURNUM
Zones 6-8 ☼ - ❄ ◗ ▲

Winter: Bright orange-red berries persist well into winter.
Spring: New foliage purplish. Small, flat clusters of white flowers in very late spring.
Summer: Soft blue-green, arrow-shaped leaves.
Autumn: Highly ornamental clusters of orange-red fruits color early in autumn. Foliage turns reddish purple.
Description: Vase-shaped, to 12′ tall and 4′ wide.
Comments: Can be leggy; best used with lower shrubs filling in around the base. 'Aurantiacum', orange berries.

Viburnum spp.
VIBURNUMS

See "Dr. Egolf's Best Viburnums" on page 194 for National Arboretum viburnum cultivars.

Vitex agnus-castus
CHASTE TREE
Zones 6-9 ☼ - ❄ ◗ - ◗ ▲ - △

Winter: Twiggy with gray bark.
Summer: Spectacular upright clusters of lavender-blue flowers, late summer. Aromatic gray-green leaves with gray undersides palmately cut.
Autumn: Holds gray-green color late.
Description: Rounded shrub or small tree, 15′-20′ tall in the South, often shorter in the North.
Comments: May be killed to the ground during severe winters in Zones 6-7 but will regrow. Leafs out late in spring. Blooms on new wood; prune in spring. 'Latifolia' is more cold-hardy and vigorous. White- and pink-flowered cultivars available.

Perennials
for Four-Season Landscapes

Achillea 'Coronation Gold'
'CORONATION GOLD' YARROW
Zones 3-9 ☼ ◖-◌ ▲-△

Summer: Flat-topped, 4″ golden yellow flowers all summer above gray-green, finely cut foliage.
Autumn: Gray-green, finely cut aromatic foliage.
Description: Sturdy plants reach 2′-3′ tall.
Comments: Avoid rich, moist sites. Shorter and better branched than green-leaved parent *A. filipendulina* (fernleaf yarrow), which grows to 3′-4′ and requires staking. *A.* 'Moonshine', similar to 'Coronation Gold' but with pale yellow flowers. *A. millefolium* (common yarrow), green mat-forming leaves; rapidly spreading; fine-textured white, orange, red, pink, or pastel flower heads all summer.

Amsonia tabernaemontana
WILLOW BLUE STAR
Zones 3-9 ☼-⌀ ◖ ▲

Spring: Silky gray-green willowlike leaves.
Summer: Clusters of pale blue flowers in early summer above dark green leaves.

CULTURE KEY

☀	⌀	☼	☼
Full shade	Light shade	Half sun, half shade	Full sun
⚘	◖	◖	◌
Tolerates wet soil	Moist soil	Average-dry soil	Drought-tolerant
▲	◭	△	
Rich soil	Average soil	Poor soil	

Autumn: Leaves turn brilliant gold.
Description: Forms sturdy clump to 3′ tall.
Comments: Old-fashioned plant of great elegance.

Anaphalis triplinervis
THREE-VEINED EVERLASTING
Zones 3-8 ☼ ◖-◖ ▲

Spring: Silvery stems and gray-green leaves with woolly, white undersides.
Summer–Autumn: Masses of small white flowers from midsummer into fall against gray leaves.
Description: To 2′-3′ tall and 2′ wide.
Comments: Best in moist sites, unlike most other silver-leaved plants.

Anemone × hybrida, syn. A. japonica
JAPANESE ANEMONE
Zones 4-8 ☼-⌀ ◖-◌ ▲-◭

Winter: Seedheads open to expose white cottonball-like puffs.
Spring–Summer: Handsome clumps of dark green lobed leaves. *A. tomentosa* 'Robustissima' begins blooming in late summer.
Autumn: Tall, wiry flower stems topped with clusters of 2″ pinkish mauve, rose, or white dogwoodlike blooms, early through midfall.
Description: Foliage clumps to 2½′ tall and wide-spreading by stolons; flower stalks 2½′-4′ tall.
Comments: May spread aggressively. Excellent fall display. 'Avalanche', semidouble white, 3′; 'Margarete', double, mauve; 'September Charm', single, silvery pink; 'Honorine Jobert', numerous small single white, to 4′. The following species may be sold as *A. × hybrida* or vice versa: *A.*

hupehensis (Chinese anemone); *A. sylvestris* (snowdrop anemone); *A. tomentosa* 'Robustissima', syn. *A. vitifolia* 'Robustissima' (Japanese or grapeleaf anemone).

Armeria maritima
COMMON THRIFT
Zones 3-8 ☼-◒ ◐-◊ ▲-△

Summer: Rounded 1″ heads of pink, mauve, red, or white flowers on bare stems rise above foliage tufts in early summer.
Autumn–Winter: Tufts of grassy blue-green leaves.
Description: Spreading evergreen cushion to 6″-12″ tall in bloom and 1′ wide.
Comments: Tolerates salt spray. Deadheading prolongs flowering. 'Alba', white flowers; 'Vindictive', deep vivid pink; 'Bloodstone', cherry red; 'Dusseldorf Pride', rosy red.

Artemisia ludoviciana 'Silver King'
'SILVER KING' WHITE SAGE
Zones 3-9 ☼ ◐-◊ ▲-△

Spring–Autumn: Silver, lance-shaped leaves on upright silvery stems.
Description: Upright plant to 3′ tall, spreading to form large clumps.
Comments: Very invasive. Does better in the South than many silver-leaved plants. *A.* × 'Valerie Finnis', very silvery, large, deeply cut leaves.

Artemisia schmidtiana 'Nana', syn. 'Silver Mound'
SILVERMOUND ARTEMISIA
Zones 3-7 ☼ ◐-◊ ▲-△

Spring–Autumn: Attractive cushion of silky, fine-textured silvery leaves.
Description: Woody-based, to 1′ tall and wide.

Comments: Mound may flop open in hot humid areas; prune back to rejuvenate when this happens. *A.* 'Powis Castle', Zones 5-8, 30″ mound, larger-leaved; tolerates heat and humidity of South better than silvermound artemisia.

Aruncus dioicus
GOAT'S BEARD
Zones 3-7 ◒-◓ ◐ ▲

Summer: Large, creamy white plumes, early to mid-summer; male plants are showier. Bold, deeply cut, dark green leaves form large, handsome clumps.
Autumn: Bold clumps of foliage.
Description: Plants reach 3′-6′ tall when in bloom and may be 6′ wide.
Comments: Native plant. Needs afternoon shade and plenty of moisture in hot areas. 'Kneifii', to 3′ tall, leaves more deeply cut.

Asclepias tuberosa
BUTTERFLY WEED
Zones 3-9 ☼ ◐-◊ ▲-△

Summer: Flat-topped clusters of brilliant orange to gold flowers attract butterflies. Bright green lance-shaped leaves.
Autumn: Showy seedpods split open to reveal silky long-haired seeds.
Description: Sturdy plants to 3′ tall and 18″ wide.
Comments: Native plant. Thrives in poor sites. Emerges late in spring. Taprooted; difficult to transplant.

Aster × *frikartii*
FRIKART'S ASTER
Zones 5-8 ☼ ◐-◒ ▲

Spring: New foliage growth makes bushy mound.
Summer–Autumn: Daisylike, 2″ lavender-blue flowers with yellow centers; midsummer into fall.

Description: Bushy plants to 2'-3' tall, 2'-3' wide.
Comments: Among the longest-blooming perennials. Mildew-resistant. 'Monch', very floriferous, well-branched, sturdy-stemmed plant with large lavender-blue flowers; 'Wonder of Staffa', clear lavender-blue, may flop.

Aster novi-belgii and *A. novae-angliae*
NEW YORK ASTER, NEW ENGLAND ASTER
Zones 3-8 ☼-◐ ◗ ▲

Summer–Autumn: Blanketed with a mist of tiny blue, purple, lavender, pink, cerise, or white flowers from late summer through fall.
Description: Clumps of fine-textured lance-shaped leaves, 3'-5' tall and 3' wide.
Comments: Native asters. Divide every 2 to 3 years. May need staking. Leaves may mildew; keep soil moist and leaves dry. *A. novi-belgii* cultivars: 'Eventide', semidouble purple, 3'; 'Professor Kippenburg', lavender-blue, 3'. *A. novae-angliae* cultivars: 'Alma Potschke', red buds open to hot pink, 4'-5' tall, resists mildew as does 'September Ruby', vivid cerise, 3½'; 'Harrington's Pink', light lavender-pink, 4'; 'Hella Lacy', deep purple, 4'; 'Purple Dome', purple, low-growing; 'Treasure', light purple, 4'. *A. tataricus* (Tartarian aster), Zones 4-9, blue-purple flowers in late fall, 4'-6' tall.

Astilbe × arendsii
ASTILBE
Zones 3-9 ◐-◒ ◗ ▲

Spring–Summer: Feathery plumes of pink, white, dark red, or rose flowers in late spring or early, mid-, or late summer, depending on the cultivar. Beautiful glossy, dark green deeply cut foliage.
Autumn: Foliage remains green late. Seedheads attractive.
Description: Clumps to 2'-4' tall when in bloom and 2'-3' wide.
Comments: Flowers last longest if plants are protected from direct sun and kept moist. Numerous cultivars. Late spring: 'Deutschland', white; 'Europa', pink; 'Rhineland', carmine-pink. Early summer: 'Diamond', white; 'Erica', rose-pink; 'Red Sentinel', deep red. Midsummer: 'Amethyst', lilac; 'Snowdrift', white. Late summer: 'Cattleya', rose-pink, 4' tall; *A. taquetii* 'Superba', bright lilac-pink into fall, 4' tall.

Aurinia saxatilis, syn. *Alyssum saxatile*
BASKET-OF-GOLD
Zones 3-7 ☼ ◗-◊ ▲-△

Winter: Gray, spoon-shaped leaves; trailing stems.
Spring: Dense heads of tiny, canary yellow flowers in early spring.
Summer–Autumn: Gray foliage.
Description: Woody-based; hummocks to 1'-2' tall, 2' wide.
Comments: Cut back hard after flowering. Needs good drainage. Excellent rock garden and wall plant. 'Citrinum', pale yellow flowers on compact plant; 'Compactum', golden yellow, compact plants; 'Sunny Border Apricot', pale apricot flowers.

CULTURE KEY

✹	✸	◉	☼
Full shade	Light shade	Half sun, half shade	Full sun
⚎	◗	◊	◇
Tolerates wet soil	Moist soil	Average–dry soil	Drought-tolerant
▲	△	△	
Rich soil	Average soil	Poor soil	

Baptisia australis
BAPTISIA, BLUE FALSE INDIGO
Zones 3-9 ☼ ◗-◊ ▲

Spring: Early asparagus-like new growth.
Summer: Showy, tall stalks of lavender-blue, pea-like flowers in early summer. Tall, bushy clumps of 3-part blue-green leaves.

Autumn: Showy, shiny black seedpods.
Description: Upright stalks to 3'-4' tall; forms clumps 4' wide.
Comments: Deep-rooted and long-lived. Doesn't need staking unless grown in shade.

Begonia grandis
HARDY BEGONIA
Zones 6-10 ✳-✸ ● ▲-△

Spring: New growth bright red.
Summer: Heart-shaped, shiny, and somewhat succulent, olive green leaves with ruby red backs and red veins.
Autumn: Sprays of pretty pink flowers from early fall until frost.
Description: Emerges late in spring. Clumps 1'-2' tall and wide. Leaves 6"-10" long.
Comments: Provide protective winter mulch in Zone 6. Adds texture and color to shade garden. Red veins dramatic when backlit. 'Alba', white flowers.

Campanula carpatica
CARPATHIAN HAREBELL
Zones 3-8 ☼ ●-◐ ▲-△

Spring: Dense hummocks of bright green, medium-textured, rounded to triangular, toothed leaves.
Summer: Blue, white, or pink, 2" cup-shaped flowers all summer.
Autumn: Green foliage remains late.
Description: Mounding plants to 12" tall and wide.
Comments: Needs good drainage, especially in winter. The longest-blooming *Campanula* species; deadhead to prolong flowering. 'Blue Clips', 3" blue flowers, 9" tall; 'Wedgewood Blue', dark violet-blue, 6" tall; 'White Clips', 3" white flowers, 9" tall.

Campanula glomerata
CLUSTERED BELLFLOWER
Zones 3-8 ☼-✸ ●-◐ ▲-△

Summer: Clusters of showy violet-blue flowers top tall flowering stems in early summer.
Autumn: Green foliage.
Description: Upright plants 1'-2' tall, 1' wide.
Comments: Plant in groups for best effect. Needs shade and plenty of moisture in the South. 'Crown of Snow', large white flowers; 'Superba', deep purple.

Campanula portenschlagiana
DALMATIAN BELLFLOWER
Zones 4-8 ☼-✸ ●-◐ ▲-△

Spring: Early-emerging rosettes of tiny heart-shaped, toothed dark green leaves.
Summer: Numerous deep lavender, bell-shaped 1" flowers in early summer.
Autumn: Foliage remains green late.
Description: Low plants, 6" tall and wide-spreading by underground stolons and trailing stems.
Comments: Ideal rock wall plant, but also does well as groundcover in mixed borders. Needs good drainage. Similar *C. poscharskyana* (Serbian bellflower), Zones 3-7, open star-shaped flowers with notched petals and *C. garganica* (Gargano bellflower), Zones 6-8, gray-green leaves, star-shaped flowers with white eyes, late spring.

Cerastium tomentosum
SNOW-IN-SUMMER
Zones 2-7 ☼ ●-◐ ▲-△

Winter: Evergreen mat of gray foliage.
Spring: Numerous small, bright white flowers cover mat-forming plants in late spring.
Summer–Autumn: Silvery gray mat of fine-textured foliage.
Description: Low plants, to 6" tall and spreading by rooting stems to several feet.
Comments: May die out in hot, humid climates. *C. biebersteinii*, similar with more silvery leaves.

Chrysanthemum nipponicum
NIPPON DAISY
Zones 5-8   ☼   ◑-◐   ▲-△

Summer: Mound of semi-succulent gray-green leaves.
Autumn: Large daisylike white flowers with yellow centers bloom all fall until frost.
Description: Woody-based perennial or subshrub, 1'-3' tall and wide.
Comments: Best if cut back severely each year in early spring; pinch until midsummer in mild climates. Grows well in seashore conditions. Very late- and long-blooming.

Chrysanthemum parthenium 'Aureum'
GOLDEN FEVERFEW
Zones 6-8   ☼   ◐   ▲

Spring: Finely dissected golden foliage.
Summer–Autumn: Clusters of small, white daisies, late summer into fall. Foliage becomes green.
Description: Semi-evergreen, 10"-18" tall, 1'-2' wide.
Comments: Short-lived but reseeds. Nice for sunny foliage effect.

Chrysanthemum weyrichii
Zones 3-9   ☼   ◑-◐   ▲-△

Winter: Reddish foliage until hard freeze.
Spring–Summer: Mounds of deeply cut, glossy dark green leaves.
Autumn: White or pink, 2" daisylike flowers in mid- to late fall. Withstands light frost.
Description: Plants to 1' tall and wide; spreads by stolons.
Comments: 'Pink Bomb', pink flowers; 'White Bomb', white flowers faintly tinged with pink.

Chrysanthemum zawadskii var. *latilobum*
HARDY GARDEN CHRYSANTHEMUM
Zones 4-9   ☼   ◐   ▲

Spring: Mounds of deeply cut, dark green leaves.
Summer–Autumn: Loose sprays of pink, rosy red, or yellow daisylike flowers from midsummer until fall frost.
Description: Plants 1'-3' tall, spreading by rhizomes into large clumps.
Comments: Also sold as *C. × rubellum*. 'Clara Curtis', bright pink blooms; 'Mary Stoker', buttery yellow aging to apricot.

Cimicifuga racemosa
BLACK SNAKEROOT, BLACK COHOSH
Zones 3-8   ⊗   ◐   ▲

Summer: 2' tall spires of white flowers tower over mounds of deeply cut, bold-textured, dark green leaves in mid- to late summer.
Autumn: Flowering continues into fall in the North. Seedheads remain decorative.
Description: Mounding foliage to 3'-4', flower stalks to 6'-8'.

CULTURE KEY			
☀	⊗	☼	☼
Full shade	Light shade	Half sun, half shade	Full sun
⟐	◐	◐	◊
Tolerates wet soil	Moist soil	Average–dry soil	Drought-tolerant
▲	▲	△	
Rich soil	Average soil	Poor soil	

Comments: Needs acid soil. Keep soil constantly moist to prevent leaf scorch. *C. ramosa* 'Brunette' ('Brunette' purple-leaf bugbane), similar with gorgeous reddish purple foliage, 3'-4' tall.

Cimicifuga simplex 'White Pearl'
'WHITE PEARL' KAMCHATKA BUGBANE
Zones 3-8 ◌ ● ▲

Summer: Mounds of bold-textured, deeply cut, dark green foliage.
Autumn: Arching, 2' long spires of dense, starry white flowers tower over foliage, late fall.
Description: Foliage to 2'-3'; flower stalks to 4'-5'.
Comments: Excellent for late-fall show.

Coreopsis verticillata
THREADLEAF COREOPSIS
Zones 3-9 ○ ●-◐ ▲-△

Winter: Dried foliage cinnamon brown; creates fine-textured effect.
Spring: Bright green new growth.
Summer: Fine-textured, bright green, linear leaves; numerous starry yellow or gold flowers, from mid- to late summer.
Autumn: Flowering may continue into fall.
Description: Wiry-stemmed, forms mounds 2'-3' tall; spreads wide by stolons.
Comments: Deadhead by light shearing in late summer to encourage reblooming. 'Golden Showers', bright yellow; 'Moonbeam', pale yellow, long-blooming, combines well with all colors, to 18"; 'Zagreb', golden yellow, to 15". *C. rosea*, pink flowers, to 18"; needs even moisture.

Corydalis lutea
YELLOW CORYDALIS
Zones 5-7 ○-◌ ●-◐ ▲-△

Spring: Ferny blue-green leaves.

Summer–Autumn: Clusters of spurred yellow flowers from early summer through late fall.
Description: Mounding plants 1' tall and wide.
Comments: Reseeds readily but never weedy. Charming plant for rock garden or in rock wall, between paving stones, or under shrubs in mixed border.

Dianthus deltoides
MAIDEN PINKS
Zones 3-9 ○-◌ ▲ ▲-△

Spring: Bright green linear leaves.
Summer: Numerous small, pink, rose, red, or white flowers with notched petals bloom all summer.
Autumn–Winter: Rose-flushed green leaves.
Description: Mat-forming, to 6"-12" tall and wide-spreading.
Comments: Needs well-drained, alkaline soil. Shear off spent flowers to encourage reblooming. *D. plumarius* (cottage pinks), Zones 3-9, usually double carnation-like flowers in early to mid-summer, 1'-2' tall, gray-green foliage; needs moist, humusy, neutral to alkaline soil.

Dicentra eximia
FRINGED BLEEDING HEART
Zones 3-9 ◌-◉ ●-◐ ▲

Spring–Summer: Vase-shaped clumps of ferny green to blue-green leaves and clusters of spurred pink flowers from early spring throughout summer.
Autumn: Flowering may continue into fall. Foliage turns yellow in late fall.
Description: Clumps to 18" tall and wide.
Comments: Native plant. 'Alba', white flowers; 'Bountiful', pale pink, prolific bloomer; 'Luxuriant', very vigorous, long-blooming, deep rose-pink flowers. Early-spring blooming *D. spectabilis* (old-fashioned bleeding heart), Zones 2-9, 3' tall and wide; goes dormant in midsummer in hot climates.

Dictamnus albus
GAS PLANT
Zones 3-8 ☼ ◐-◊ ▲-△

Spring: Glossy, dark green, deeply cut leaves on vertical stems.
Summer: Spikes of pure white to purplish pink flowers in early summer.
Autumn: Star-shaped seedpods.
Description: Woody-based, 3'-4' tall and wide.
Comments: Old-fashioned garden plant. Forms wonderful clumps; needs no division. Foliage causes an allergic reaction for some. 'Purpureus', mauve-purple flowers, dark-veined leaves.

Echinacea purpurea
PURPLE CONEFLOWER
Zones 3-8 ☼ ◐-◊ ▲-△

Spring: Coarse dark green leaves.
Summer: Daisylike, 4"-6", mauve-pink, rose, or white flowers with raised orange-brown centers and reflexed petals, mid- through late summer.
Autumn: Decorative seedheads.
Description: Upright stems to 4'; forms clumps 3' wide.
Comments: Remove faded flowers to extend flowering. Excellent with ornamental grasses. Native prairie plant; does best in lean soils. 'Magnus', broad pink petals; 'Bright Star', rose petals; 'White Swan', white with orange center.

Echinops ritro
GLOBE THISTLE
Zones 3-8 ☼ ◐-◊ ▲-△

Spring: Coarse, thistlelike green leaves with silvery white undersides.
Summer: Spiny globes of silvery blue to lavender flowers in mid- to late summer.
Autumn: Showy foliage and seedheads.
Description: Upright plants to 4' tall and 2' wide.
Comments: Architectural plant. Deadhead to avoid self-sowing. 'Taplow Blue', blue flowers, to 5'.

Foeniculum vulgare var. *purpureum*
BRONZE FENNEL
Zones 6-10 ☼ ◐-◊ ▲-△

Spring–Autumn: Stiff stems of dark purple-bronze feathery foliage. Yellow flower heads in summer.
Description: Upright, to 4'-6' tall, 2' wide.
Comments: Culinary herb excellent for red foliage effect in mixed border. Remove faded flowers to prevent reseeding. Grow as annual north of Zone 6.

Geranium sanguineum
BLOOD-RED CRANESBILL
Zones 3-8 ☼-◑ ◐-◐ ▲-△

Spring: Mound of dainty, deeply cut, dark green leaves.
Summer: Magenta 1" wide flowers (pink or white with red veins in cultivars) bloom all summer.
Autumn: Leaves turn reddish.
Description: Bushy plant 1' tall, 18" wide, spreading by stolons; makes good groundcover.
Comments: Var. *striatum* (syn. *lancastriense*), longest-blooming, pink with red veins. Many other excellent species with blue, purple, lavender, or pink flowers.

CULTURE KEY			
✸	✵	✺	☼
Full shade	Light shade	Half sun, half shade	Full sun
⬥	◐	◊	◊
Tolerates wet soil	Moist soil	Average–dry soil	Drought-tolerant
▲	△	△	
Rich soil	Average soil	Poor soil	

Helenium autumnale
COMMON SNEEZEWEED
Zones 3-8 ☼ ⬙-◗ ▲

Spring: Clumps of upright stems with coarse leaves.
Summer–Autumn: Large clusters of small yellow, gold, mahogany, or orange flowers with buttonlike centers, late summer into fall.
Description: Upright plants 3'-5' tall.
Comments: Native plant. Pinch tall-growing plants in spring to reduce height and encourage prolific flowering. Cultivars are shorter. Red-Gold hybrids, mixture of red, copper, orange, gold, and banded. 'Butterpat', rich yellow; 'Crimson Beauty', bronze-red; 'Riverton Beauty', gold.

Helleborus orientalis
LENTEN ROSE
Zones 4-9 �-☀ ◗ ▲

Winter: Pure white, rose, or maroon, nodding, buttercup-like flowers, mid- to late winter. Dark green leaves.
Spring: Flowers and seedheads showy, rosy pink. Light green new leaves.
Summer–Autumn: Leathery, dark green, lobed leaves.
Description: Foliage clumps to 18" tall and 2' wide.
Comments: Not difficult to grow if planted in shady, loamy, moist soil; provide winter shade. *H. niger* (Christmas rose), Zones 3-8, pure white flowers age to rose; *H. argutifolius*, syn. *H. corsicus* (Corsican hellebore), Zones 6-8, apple green flowers; *H. foetidus* (stinking hellebore), Zones 6-9, pale green flowers.

Hemerocallis hybrids
DAYLILIES
Zones 3-9 ☼-✕़ ◗-◌ ▲-△

Spring: Early-emerging, strap-shaped foliage.
Summer: Large funnel-shaped flowers in all colors but blue and true white, borne on tall scapes in early, mid-, or late summer, depending on the cultivar. Individual blooms last one day, but plants produce numerous flowers.
Autumn: Green foliage changes to golden yellow. A few cultivars bloom in fall.
Description: Grows from tuberous roots. Foliage clumps 1'-3' and flower scapes 1'-5', depending on the cultivar.
Comments: Indispensable summer flower. Cultivars too numerous to list. Rebloomers include: 'Stella d'Oro', orange-gold dwarf; 'Country Club', pink with green throat, 18"; 'Diamond Anniversary', peach-pink, 3'; 'Haunting Melody', fuchsia-rose, ruffled, 3'; 'Jenny Sue', pale peach, ruffled, 2'; 'Paul Bunyan', light gold, 3½'.

Heuchera micrantha 'Palace Purple'
'PALACE PURPLE' HEUCHERA
Zones 4-8 ☼ ◗ △

Spring: Clumps of wrinkled leaves, dark purple-bronze on top, wine red beneath.
Summer: Insignificant airy clusters of greenish white flowers, midsummer; foliage more bronze-green.
Autumn: Foliage becomes redder.
Description: Shrubby plants 2' tall, 18" wide.
Comments: Grown for handsome foliage. Use at the front of a mixed border. Seed-propagated plants not uniformly colored.

Heuchera sanguinea
CORALBELLS
Zones 3-8 ☼-✕़ ◗ △

Winter: Evergreen foliage.
Spring: Basal clusters of scalloped heart-shaped leaves; tall airy spires of pink, white, red, rose, or peach flowers.
Summer: May rebloom.
Autumn: Foliage remains green late.
Description: Foliage clumps 10" tall, flower stalks to 24" tall.

Comments: Provide shade in the South. Remove faded flowers to encourage reblooming. Neutral soil best.

Hosta species and cultivars
HOSTAS
Zones 3-9 ☀-☀ ◐-◊ ▲-△

See "Top-Rated Hostas for Foliage and Flowers" on page 174.

Iberis sempervirens
PERENNIAL CANDYTUFT
Zones 3-9 ☼ ◐-◊ ▲-△

Spring: Trailing mounds of linear, dark green leaves topped with circular clusters of pure white flowers, early to mid-spring.
Summer–Winter: Excellent evergreen foliage.
Description: Woody-based subshrub to 10"-12" tall and 18"-24" wide.
Comments: Cut back after blooming every year or two. Cultivars are usually more compact and thus more desirable. Excellent rock wall plant and combined with spring bulbs. 'Autumn Snow' reblooms profusely in fall. 'Little Gem', to 5"-8".

CULTURE KEY

☀	☒	☼	☼
Full shade	Light shade	Half sun, half shade	Full sun
⬦	●	◐	◊
Tolerates wet soil	Moist soil	Average–dry soil	Drought-tolerant
▲	△	△	
Rich soil	Average soil	Poor soil	

Iris, Bearded Hybrids
BEARDED IRIS
Zones 3-10 ☼ ◐ ▲

Spring: Sword-shaped, bright green leaves.
Summer: Large, gorgeous flowers with yellow-bearded falls, early or midsummer; cultivars in all colors.
Description: Rhizomatous plant; 1½'-4' tall and 2'-3' wide.
Comments: Numerous cultivars. Tops of rhizomes should be exposed at soil surface: They benefit from baking in summer sun. *I. pallida* 'Variegata' and 'Alba-Variegata' (variegated sweet iris), Zones 4-8, creamy white- or yellow-striped leaves.

Iris cristata
CRESTED IRIS
Zones 3-9 ☀-☼ ◐-◊ ▲-△

Spring: Bright green leaves; blue or white miniature iris flowers with yellow crests, midspring.
Summer: Excellent low, sword-shaped leaves.
Autumn: Foliage yellows.
Description: Upright plants 8" tall and spreading by rhizomes to cover large areas.
Comments: Native plant. Spreads well. Makes attractive groundcover in woodland or shade garden.

Iris sibirica
SIBERIAN IRIS
Zones 2-9 ☼-☒ ⬦-◐ ▲-△

Spring: Delicate blue, white, rose, or purple flowers with purple-veined white blotch, late spring.
Summer–Autumn: Graceful, narrow, grassy, bright green leaves form large, attractive clumps.
Description: Upright clumps 2'-3' tall and 2' wide.
Comments: Numerous cultivars. *I. ensata*, syn. *I. kaempferi* (Japanese iris), Zones 4-9; huge, flat blooms, midsummer; tolerates wet to very moist soil.

Lavandula angustifolia, syn. *L. officinalis*
LAVENDER
Zones 5-9 ☼ ◑-◊ ▲-△

Winter: Semi-evergreen.
Spring: Gray-green, aromatic, linear leaves on shrubby plant.
Summer: Fragrant lavender flower spikes, mid-summer.
Autumn: Gray-green foliage.
Description: Woody-based subshrub; to 2'-3' tall, 3' wide.
Comments: Prune back to 6" in early spring. Needs well-drained, neutral soil. Shear after bloom for rebloom and tidiness. 'Hidcote', deep purple, 18"; 'Munstead Dwarf', lavender, 12".

Ligularia stenocephala
NARROW-SPIKED LIGULARIA
Zones 4-8 ◕-◗ ◿-◑ ▲

Spring: Large, triangular to heart-shaped green leaves.
Summer: Spires of golden yellow flowers, mid- to late summer on purple stalks, tower over basal leaves.
Autumn: Dramatic foliage.
Description: Foliage clumps to 2'-3'; flower stalks to 3'-4'.
Comments: Wonderful plant for summer drama. Must have constantly moist site and afternoon shade. 'The Rocket', 2', lemon yellow spikes. *L. dentata* (bigleaf ligularia), dramatic leaves with purple undersides, orange flowers; 'Desdemona' and 'Othello', purple leaves in spring and fall.

Linum perenne
BLUE FLAX
Zones 4-9 ☼ ◑-◊ ▲-△

Spring: Small, pure blue, 1" saucer-shaped flowers among linear leaves on airy stems, late spring.
Summer: Flowering continues into summer.
Autumn: Fine-textured foliage.

Description: Airy plants to 2' tall, 1' wide.
Comments: Short-lived but reseeds. Individual flowers open for only one day, but plants produce numerous blossoms for several months. Excellent filler for textural contrast.

Lythrum virgatum
WAND LOOSESTRIFE
Zones 3-8 ☼-◕ ◿-◑ ▲-△

Spring: Upright stems and willowy green leaves.
Summer: Spires of magenta or pink flowers, mid- to late summer and into autumn.
Autumn: Foliage turns reddish.
Description: Upright plants to 4' tall and spreading into large clumps.
Comments: Cultivars are self-sterile; to keep this plant under control, choose one cultivar only, and don't grow any if loosestrife grows wild near your garden. This and similar *L. salicaria* outlawed in Minnesota and Wisconsin because they invade wetlands.

Mentha suaveolens 'Variegata'
VARIEGATED PINEAPPLE MINT
Zones 5-9 ☼-◕ ◑-◑ ▲-△

Spring–Autumn: Fuzzy gray-green aromatic leaves splotched with creamy white.
Description: Plant to 2' tall; spreads widely by underground stolons.
Comments: May be invasive; confine the roots. Leaves edible and scented minty pineapple.

Mertensia virginica
VIRGINIA BLUEBELLS
Zones 3-9 ◕-☀ ◿-◑ ▲

Spring: Early-emerging, blue-green rounded leaves and stalks of beautiful pink and bright blue bell-shaped flowers, early to mid-spring.

Summer: Dies to ground.
Description: Rosettes 1'-2' tall, spreading to form nice clumps.
Comments: Native plant. Excellent in woodland or shade garden. Combine with ferns to camouflage summer bare spot.

Monarda didyma
BEE BALM
Zones 4-8 ☼-☀ ● ▲-△

Spring: Tall stems with fuzzy, dark green, medium-textured, aromatic mintlike leaves.
Summer: Pinwheel-shaped red, pink, lavender, white, or mahogany flowers, mid- to late summer.
Description: Upright plant to 3' tall; spreads by underground stolons to form large clumps.
Comments: Mildew can be a problem just after flowering; to control, cut to ground and new foliage rapidly appears, usually disease-free. 'Adam', deep red; 'Cambridge Scarlet', vivid red; 'Croftway Pink', rose-pink; 'Mahogany', cranberry red; 'Prairie Night', violet-purple; 'Snow White', bright white.

Nepeta × faassenii
CATMINT
Zones 3-8 ☼-☀ ●-◊ ▲-△

Spring–Autumn: Dainty lavender-blue spikes above silvery gray foliage.

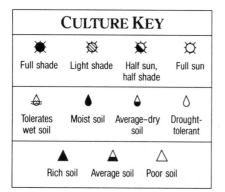

+---+
| **CULTURE KEY** |
+---+

☀	☒	☀	☼
Full shade	Light shade	Half sun, half shade	Full sun

⚘	●	◖	◊
Tolerates wet soil	Moist soil	Average–dry soil	Drought-tolerant

▲	◮	△
Rich soil	Average soil	Poor soil

Description: Sprawling plant to 1'-1½' tall and wide.
Comments: A sterile hybrid. Less sprawling and weedy than *N. mussinii*. Shear faded flowers to promote continuing flushes of bloom from spring through fall. A relative of catnip but doesn't attract cats.

Oenothera fruticosa
SUNDROPS
Zones 4-8 ☼ ●-◖ ▲-△

Spring: Fuzzy leaves on hairy, red upright stems.
Summer: Numerous bright yellow, 3" cup-shaped day-blooming flowers, early to mid-summer.
Autumn: Brilliant orange to red fall color.
Description: Upright plant to 2' tall; spreads to form large clumps by underground stolons.
Comments: Spreads invasively in rich soil, but easy to pull out. Makes dramatic display. Sometimes listed as *O. tetragona*. *O. missouriensis* (Ozark sundrops), Zones 4-8; low, sprawling, reddish stems; large pale yellow flowers, midsummer.

Oenothera speciosa
SHOWY EVENING PRIMROSE
Zones 5-8 ☼ ●-◊ ▲-△

Spring: Gray-green leaves on sprawling stems.
Summer: Soft pink, 3" bowl-shaped flowers borne mid- to late summer.
Autumn: Flowering may continue into early fall.
Description: Sprawling plants to 1' tall, 3' wide.
Comments: Spreads aggressively by stolons in moist, fertile soil. *O. berlandieri* (Mexican primrose), pinker flowers, even more aggressive.

Paeonia lactiflora
COMMON GARDEN PEONY
Zones 2-8 ☼-☀ ●-◖ ▲-△

Spring: Glossy, reddish purple new growth.
Summer: Dramatic single, semidouble, double,

or anemone-flowered blooms in pink, white, rose, red, or burgundy, early summer. Glossy, dark green leaves are deeply cut, quite handsome.

Autumn: Leaves turn burgundy to red.

Description: Bushy plants to 3' tall, 4' wide.

Comments: Double flowers very heavy; need individual staking. Very long-lived if sited correctly. Cultivars too numerous to list.

Perovskia atriplicifolia
RUSSIAN SAGE
Zones 4-9 ☼ ◐-◊ ▲-△

Spring: Silvery, finely cut, aromatic leaves on tall stalks.

Summer: Airy spires of lavender flowers, mid- to late summer.

Autumn: Flowers may continue into fall.

Winter: Dramatic airy gray stems.

Description: Woody-based, shrubby, to 4'-5' tall.

Comments: Cut back to 1' in early spring. Plants lean toward light, may need staking. Wonderful fine-textured effect.

Phlox carolina 'Miss Lingard'
'MISS LINGARD' CAROLINA PHLOX
Zones 4-9 ☼-◐ ◐-◊ ▲-△

Spring: Glossy green, lance-shaped leaves on upright stalks.

Summer: Dramatic, conical heads of white flowers, early summer; may rebloom.

Description: Upright plants to 3'-4' tall, spreading to form nice clumps.

Comments: Cut off faded flower heads to encourage reblooming. Earlier blooming, with more conical flower heads, than *P. paniculata* (garden phlox) and also mildew-resistant.

Phlox divaricata
WILD BLUE PHLOX, WOODLAND PHLOX
Zones 3-9 ◑-◒ ◐-◊ ▲-△

Spring: Clusters of blue or white flowers with notched petals, early to mid-spring.

Summer–Autumn: Nondescript after flowering.

Description: Clumps to 12"-15" tall; spreads slowly by creeping rhizomes.

Comments: Native plant. 'Fuller's White', very showy numerous white flowers on compact plants; subsp. *laphamii*, dark blue notchless petals.

Phlox stolonifera
CREEPING PHLOX
Zones 2-8 ◒-◐ ◐-◊ ▲

Spring: Clusters of blue, pink, or white yellow-eyed flowers on short stalks, early to mid-spring.

Summer–Winter: Creeping mat of small, dark green, rounded, evergreen leaves.

Description: Flower stalks to 10"; spreads vigorously by creeping stems.

Comments: Native plant. Very showy cultivars: 'Blue Ridge', pale blue; 'Bruce's White', white; 'Home Fires', magenta-pink; 'Pink Ridge', bright pink; 'Sherwood Purple', deep purple-blue.

Phlox subulata
MOSS PINK
Zones 2-9 ☼ ◐-◊ ▲-△

Spring: Leaves blanketed by brilliant magenta, pink, blue, lavender, or white flowers with notched petals and darker eyes.

Summer–Winter: Mat of green, needlelike leaves.

Description: Dense mats to 2" tall; spreads to cover large patches.

Comments: Thick groundcover for sunny spot. Cultivars too numerous to name.

Physostegia virginiana
OBEDIENT PLANT
Zones 3-9 ☼ ◐-◒ ▲-△

Spring: Tall stems with glossy, dark green sharp-toothed leaves, in opposite ranks up the stems.
Summer: Spires of magenta, pink, or white snap-dragon-like flowers, borne in rows, late summer.
Autumn: May continue flowering into fall.
Description: Upright plants to 3'-4' tall, spreading aggressively to form large clumps.
Comments: 'Summer Snow', white, early; 'Variegata', white-edged leaves, bright pink flowers; 'Vivid', large bright pink flowers, 18" plant.

Platycodon grandiflorus
BALLOON FLOWER
Zones 3-8 ☼ ◐-◒ ▲-△

Summer: Pale blue flower buds resembling inflated balloons open to cup-shaped, bright blue flowers with dark veins. Upright stalks of green leaves.
Autumn: Foliage changes to deep yellow-gold.
Description: Upright plant to 3' tall and 2' wide.
Comments: Emerges late in spring. Provide afternoon shade in the South. Needs staking. Deadhead to prolong flowering. Deep-rooted and long-lived. Var. *mariesii*, more compact. 'Shell Pink', pale pink flowers.

CULTURE KEY

☀	⊘	☼	☼
Full shade	Light shade	Half sun, half shade	Full sun
⚘	●	◐	◊
Tolerates wet soil	Moist soil	Average–dry soil	Drought-tolerant
▲	△	△	
Rich soil	Average soil	Poor soil	

Polygonatum odoratum 'Variegatum'
VARIEGATED FRAGRANT SOLOMON'S SEAL
Zones 3-9 ⊘-☀ ◐-◒ ▲-△

Spring: Early-emerging green leaves marked with creamy white edges, arranged opposite each other on tall curving stalks. Bell-shaped white flowers dangle in pairs beneath stems, midspring.
Summer: Green, pealike fruits dangle beneath dramatic variegated leaves.
Autumn: Foliage turns handsome bleached yellow.
Description: Arching plants to 3' tall, spreading to form thick stands.
Comments: Attractive foliage plant for woodland or shade garden.

Primula vulgaris
ENGLISH PRIMROSE
Zones 4-8 ⊘ ● ▲

Spring: Loose clusters of yellow tubular blooms with flared petals, very early spring; clumps of wrinkled, paddle-shaped green leaves.
Summer–Autumn: Leaves elongate to form rough-looking rosettes.
Description: Low rosettes, 6"-8" when in bloom.
Comments: *P.* × *polyantha* (polyanthus primrose), cultivars in a range of vivid flower colors with yellow eyes; best treated as annuals.

Pulmonaria saccharata
BETHLEHEM SAGE
Zones 3-8 ⊘-☀ ● ▲

Spring: Clusters of pink flower buds open to blue, bell-shaped flowers, blooming with the emerging foliage in very early spring.
Summer: Attractive, spoon-shaped green leaves spotted with silver.
Autumn: Leaves remain handsome late.
Description: Clumps to 1' tall, spreading to cover a wide area.

Comments: Keep evenly moist for best-looking foliage. 'Mrs. Moon', large leaves, pink flowers aging to blue; 'Sissinghurst White', large white flowers, boldly spotted leaves.

Rodgersia pinnata 'Superba'
FEATHERLEAF RODGERSIA
Zones 5-7   ☀-☁   ◦   ▲

Spring: Purple new growth.
Summer: Huge, toothed, fan-shaped, compound bronze-purple leaves; large panicles of bright pink, long-lasting flowers, midsummer.
Autumn: Foliage reddens; attractive seedheads.
Description: Huge plants to 3'-4' tall, 3' wide.
Comments: A bold plant for an accent in a mixed border or along a stream or pond.

Rudbeckia fulgida var. *sullivantii* 'Goldsturm'
'GOLDSTURM'
BLACK-EYED SUSAN
Zones 3-9   ☼   ◦   ▲-△

Winter: Dried seedheads turn dark brown.
Spring: Rough-textured green foliage.
Summer: Numerous yellow-gold, 4" daisylike flowers with brown centers, late summer.
Autumn: Flowering continues into fall.
Description: Compact plant to 1½'-3' tall; spreads by rhizomes to form large clumps but not aggressive.
Comments: A sturdy, large-flowered, long-blooming cultivar. *R. nitida* 'Autumn Sun', syn. 'Herbstsonne' (shining coneflower), Zones 4-9, bright yellow blooms on 5' tall stems, late summer through fall.

Ruta graveolens
RUE
Zones 4-9   ☼   ◦   △

Winter: Dried seedpods provide interest.
Spring: Blue-green, aromatic ferny leaves.

Summer: Clusters of greenish yellow, airy flowers, midsummer.
Autumn: Foliage remains green late.
Description: Subshrub; 2'-3' tall, 2' wide.
Comments: Grown for shrubby mounds of ornamental foliage. Cut back hard in early spring.

Salvia argentea
SILVER SAGE
Zones 5-9   ☼   ◦   △

Spring: Basal rosette of large, egg-shaped woolly white leaves.
Summer: Tall stalks of white flowers on woolly stems, midsummer.
Autumn: Foliage may become tattered.
Description: Basal rosette, 1' tall, 2' wide; flower stalks to 3' tall.
Comments: Best used as showy foliage plant; cut off flower stalk. May be short-lived.

Salvia officinalis
GARDEN SAGE
Zones 3-9   ☼   ◦-◌   △

Spring–Autumn: Spoon-shaped, pebbly, gray-green, purple, or variegated aromatic leaves. Insignificant blue flowers in summer.
Description: Woody-based; 2' tall and wide.
Comments: Cut back severely in early spring. Culinary herb; use in well-drained mixed border for foliage effect. 'Aurea', bright green leaves irregularly edged with yellow; 'Purpurea', purplish gray; 'Tricolor', gray-green leaves irregularly splotched with pink and white.

Salvia × superba 'East Friesland'
'EAST FRIESLAND' VIOLET SAGE
Zones 4-7 ☼ ◖-◊ ▲-△

Spring: Gray-green toothed leaves on upright stems.
Summer: Spikes of dense, deep purple flowers, early to mid-summer.
Autumn: May rebloom.
Description: Woody-based, 30″ tall and 24″ wide.
Comments: Best sage for the South. Cut back hard after flowering to encourage rebloom; cut back yearly in early spring. *S. azurea* (azure sage), Zones 5-9, to 5′, azure blue spikes in late summer and fall; stake or allow to rest on other plants.

Santolina chamaecyparissus, syn. *S. incana*
LAVENDER COTTON
Zones 6-8 ☼ ◖-◊ ▲-△

Winter–Autumn: Gray-green to bright green, needlelike, aromatic foliage on bushy plants.
Summer: Buttonlike yellow flowers.
Description: Subshrub; 1′-2′ tall and wide.
Comments: Does best in dry climates. Shear after flowering to rejuvenate.

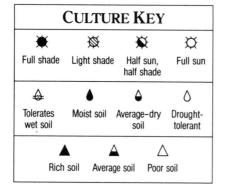

CULTURE KEY

✹	⊘	☀	☼
Full shade	Light shade	Half sun, half shade	Full sun
⚱	◖	◗	◊
Tolerates wet soil	Moist soil	Average–dry soil	Drought-tolerant
▲	△	△	
Rich soil	Average soil	Poor soil	

Sedum 'Autumn Joy'
'AUTUMN JOY' SEDUM
Zones 3-10 ☼ ◖-◊ ▲-△

Winter: Flower stalks dry into rust brown sculptures, stand all winter.
Spring: Jade green succulent leaves.
Summer: Stalks topped by pale green flower buds, which open to pale pink in late summer.
Autumn: Flowers become rosy pink, finally aging to rusty red as fall progresses.
Description: Upright fleshy plants to 2½′ tall and wide.
Comments: Cut dried stalks off when new growth appears in spring. Parent *S. spectabile* (showy stonecrop), bright pink flowers, does not stand through winter. *S. spectabile* 'Variegatum', green-edged leaves with creamy yellow centers, pink flowers. *S. maximum* 'Atropurpureum', foliage purple on weakly upright plants to 2′ tall and wide, pink flowers.

Sedum cauticola
Zones 5-9 ☼ ◖-◖ ▲-△

Winter: Sprawling, woody, purplish stems.
Spring–Summer: Blue-gray, fleshy oval leaves on short stems radiating from center crown.
Autumn: Clusters of purplish pink flowers, early fall.
Description: Woody-stemmed; 2″-4″ tall, spreading 8″ or more.
Comments: *S.* 'Ruby Glow', ruby flowers, to 12″, but may flop open if grown in fertile soil. *S.* 'Vera Jameson', dark purple leaves on sprawling stems with magenta-pink flowers, to 10″.

Sedum spurium 'Dragon's Blood'
'DRAGON'S BLOOD' TWO-ROW SEDUM
Zones 3-8 ☼-✹ ◖-◊ ▲-△

Winter: Semievergreen mat of purplish bronze leaves on sprawling stems.

Spring: Bright purple new leaves.
Summer: Clusters of brilliant red flowers.
Autumn: Foliage remains colorful.
Description: Fleshy plants to 2″-4″ tall, 12″-18″ wide.
Comments: Does poorly in hot, humid climates.

Stachys byzantina 'Silver Carpet'
'SILVER CARPET' LAMB'S-EARS
Zones 4-8

Year-round: Furry, silver-gray, ground-hugging leaves form thick mat.
Description: Woody-based, to 4″ tall; spreads by underground stolons to cover large areas.
Comments: Rake out tattered leaves in early spring. May rot in moist, humid areas. Excellent edging plant. The species has magenta flowers on furry stems, early summer.

Thermopsis caroliniana
CAROLINA LUPINE
Zones 3-9

Spring: Bushy clumps of bright green, trifoliate leaves on upright stems.
Summer: Tall spires of yellow flowers, early summer. Decorative flattened seedpods, late summer.
Description: Upright plants to 4′ tall, 3′ wide.
Comments: Native plant. Needs part shade in the South. Cut back foliage after flowering to rejuvenate.

Veronica spicata
SPIKE SPEEDWELL
Zones 3-8

Spring–Autumn: Small, tapered, dark matte green leaves with scalloped margins on upright stems.
Summer: Dense spikes of small blue, pink, or white flowers for more than a month in midsummer.

Description: Low, spreading clumps to 1½′ tall and wide.
Comments: 'Blue Peter', true blue. 'Icicle', white. 'Red Fox', rosy pink. *V. incana* (woolly speedwell), Zones 3-7, silvery gray leaves and tiny blue flowers. *V. teucrium*, syn. *V. latifolia* (Hungarian speedwell), prostrate plant, mass of tiny blue flowers in mid- to late spring.

Viola labradorica var. *purpurea*
PURPLE-LEAF LABRADOR VIOLET
Zones 3-8

Spring: Purple new growth, mauve flowers in early to late spring.
Summer–Autumn: Small, tidy purplish bronze leaves. Blooms sporadically in summer.
Description: Low plants to 4″ tall, spreading to form 12″ clumps.
Comments: Native plant grown for its handsome foliage. Makes excellent groundcover under shrubs or in woodland garden.

Yucca filamentosa
ADAM'S-NEEDLE
Zones 3-10

Year-round: Bold rosettes of sword-shaped succulent leaves, bright green or variegated, with peeling threads decorating the margins.
Summer: Tall spikes of showy white flowers, mid- to late summer.
Description: Woody-based succulent; 3′ tall and wide, flower spikes to 4′.
Comments: Excellent for textural contrast in a mixed border. 'Bright Edge', cream-striped leaf margins; 'Golden Sword', bright yellow-centered leaves with green margins.

Ornamental Grasses
for Four-Season Landscapes

Calamagrostis arundinacea var. *brachytricha*
FALL-BLOOMING
REED GRASS
Zones 5-9 ☼-☀ ◐-◌ ▲-△

Winter: Dried foliage creamy white.
Spring: Emerges rapidly in spring.
Summer: Upright, erect dark green leaves. Delicate, airy white flowers in early summer ripen to tan or cinnamon, wheatlike seedheads.
Autumn: Foliage turns chartreuse.
Description: Clump-forming; foliage 1½'-2' tall, flower spikes 4'-4½' tall.
Comments: Makes a strong vertical accent. Excellent in a meadow garden. Beautiful year-round. *C. acutiflora* 'Stricta' (feather reed grass), Zones 5-9, showy, summer-blooming, evergreen in mild climates.

Carex elata 'Bowles Golden'
'BOWLES GOLDEN' SEDGE
Zones 5-9 ☼-☀ ◐-◌ ▲-△

Spring–Autumn: Brilliant, golden yellow, gracefully arching leaves form open mound.
Description: 2' tall and wide.
Comments: Best in cool, moist areas; protect from hot sun. Wonderful color and texture contrast with hostas and ferns.

Carex hachioensis 'Evergold', syn. *C. morrowii* var. *aureo-variegata* 'Old Gold'
'EVERGOLD' JAPANESE SEDGE
Zones 5-9 ☼-☀ ◐ ▲

Winter–Autumn: Graceful clumps of cascading, bright yellow leaves with green margins.
Description: Evergreen mounds, 1½'-2' tall and wide.
Comments: Flowers inconspicuous. Cut off old foliage, if tattered, in late winter. 'Variegata' (silver variegated Japanese sedge), green leaves with silver edges.

CULTURE KEY			
☀	☀	☀	☼
Full shade	Light shade	Half sun, half shade	Full sun
⬡	◐	◌	◌
Tolerates wet soil	Moist soil	Average–dry soil	Drought-tolerant
▲	△	△	
Rich soil	Average soil	Poor soil	

Chasmanthium latifolium
NORTHERN SEA OATS
Zones 5-9 ☼-☀ ◐-◌ ▲-△

Winter: Bleached foliage.
Spring: Bright green new growth, early.
Summer: Bright green leaves; cascading spikes of dangling, flattened green flowers, late summer.
Autumn: Oatlike seedheads ripen to tan. Orange-brown foliage, mid- to late fall.

Description: Clumps 2'-3' tall and 2' wide.
Comments: Native to midwestern and southeastern United States. Reseeds but not terribly weedy. Flowers and seedheads pretty in arrangements. Use as specimen or in meadow.

Elymus arenarius 'Glaucus'
BLUE LYME GRASS
Zones 4-10 ☼ ◐-◊ ▲-△

Spring–Autumn: Bright blue leaves.
Description: Foliage 1'-3' tall, spreading by rhizomes to cover large areas.
Comments: Can be invasive in good garden soil and high-moisture conditions, but highly valued for its foliage color.

Erianthus ravennae
RAVENNA GRASS, PLUME GRASS
Zones 6-10 ☼ ◐-◊ ▲-△

Winter: Bleached foliage; dried plumes.
Spring–Summer: Huge clumps of blue-gray foliage.
Autumn: Dramatic feathery plumes of silky flowers in early fall, turning beige. Foliage turns chestnut brown late in season.
Description: Clumps 4'-5' tall and wide; spreads by runners; flower stalks 12'-14' tall.
Comments: Sometimes called hardy pampas grass. Use as a specimen in large gardens. Control size by growing in poor, dry soil.

Festuca cinerea, syn. *F. ovina* var. *glauca*
BLUE FESCUE
Zones 4-9 ☼ ◐-◊ ▲-△

Winter–Autumn: Tufts of blue-green to bright blue, fine-textured, narrow leaves.
Spring: Tall, airy stems of green flowers, turning brown, late spring.

Description: Evergreen; clumps 12"-18" tall and wide; may spread by short rhizomes.
Comments: Best in cool climates. 'Elijah Blue', very blue, low mounds. 'Solling', powder blue; does not bloom or brown out in heat.

Hakonechloa macra 'Aureola'
GOLDEN VARIEGATED HAKONE GRASS
Zones 6-9 ▨-☀ ◐ ▲

Winter: Bleached foliage.
Spring–Summer: Graceful cascading leaves fall to one side as if swept by wind. Golden green and green-striped leaves with overall golden effect.
Autumn: Delicate airy green flowers, early fall; variegations become peach-orange with cold.
Description: Slow-growing clumps to 2' tall and wide.
Comments: May be difficult in hot-summer climates; provide plenty of shade and moisture.

Helictotrichon sempervirens
BLUE OAT GRASS
Zones 4-9 ☼ ◐-◊ ▲

Winter–Autumn: Symmetrical clumps of blue-gray, fine-textured, stiff, spiky leaves.
Summer: Beige feathery flowers wave just above foliage, early to mid-summer.
Description: Evergreen; tufted clumps to 1½'-2' tall and wide.
Comments: Very pretty for color and texture contrast in a mixed border. Unlike most grasses, should not be cut back annually; instead, gently rake out spent blades of grass.

Imperata cylindrica 'Red Baron'
'RED BARON' BLOODGRASS, JAPANESE BLOODGRASS
Zones 6-9 ☼-☀ ◊ ▲-△

Spring–Summer: Upright blades, green at base with dark red tips.
Autumn: Leaves turn brilliant red.
Description: Foliage 20″ tall; spreads slowly by runners.
Comments: Colors best in sun. Effective as a specimen or mass-planted. Not effective in winter. Flowers insignificant.

Luzula sylvatica 'Marginata'
GOLDEN-EDGED WOODRUSH
Zones 4-9 ☀-☀ ◊-◊ ▲-▲

Spring: Loose clusters of chestnut brown flowers.
Summer–Winter: Shiny green, wide leaves with narrow golden yellow stripes along margins.
Description: Cool-season evergreen; tufts of foliage to 1′ tall, flower stalks to 3′.
Comments: Excellent dense groundcover for woodland garden. Tolerates dry shade.

Miscanthus sinensis cultivars
JAPANESE SILVER GRASS
Zones 5-9 ☼-☀ ◊-◊ ▲-△

Winter: Foliage bleached bright almond; persistent feathery seedheads.
Spring–Summer: Fountain of narrow leaves, dark green or variegated, depending upon cultivar.
Autumn: Brown to silvery feathery flowers and seedheads, beginning in midfall.
Description: Clumps 4′-8′ tall and wide.
Comments: 'Silberfeder' (silver feather maiden grass), very silky and silvery seedheads; 'Gracillimus' (maiden grass), fine-textured leaves, to 5′; 'Morning Light', very narrow leaves with silver margins, reddish flowers; 'Purpurascens' (flame grass), purple flowers early, red-orange fall color, spreading form; 'Nippon', slender leaves, 4′; 'Yaku Jima', 3′-4′; 'Variegatus', boldly striped with white; 'Zebrinus' (zebra grass), yellow horizontal bands, 6′-8′; var. *strictus* (porcupine grass), green leaves banded with gold, erect and narrow, sturdier than 'Zebrinus'.

Miscanthus transmorrisonensis
EVERGREEN MISCANTHUS, FORMOSA MAIDEN GRASS
Zones 7-10 ☼-☀ ◊-◊ ▲-▲

Winter: Glossy green, fine-textured evergreen leaves in attractive clumps.
Spring: New growth; flowering begins in late spring.
Summer: Feathery flower plumes borne above foliage; plumes open reddish brown, age to tan.
Autumn: Flowering continues into November.
Description: Warm-season, evergreen grass; clumps are 2½′-3½′ tall and wide; large flower spikes may reach 7′.
Comments: Lovely evergreen grass for gardens in mild climates. Attractive as a large groundcover, in groups, and as accent plants in the back of the perennial border. Ideal for small gardens. Don't let soil dry out or leaf tips will brown. Will grow in milder parts of Zone 6, but may suffer some winter damage.

CULTURE KEY			
☀	☒	☀	☼
Full shade	Light shade	Half sun, half shade	Full sun
⟁	◊	◊	◊
Tolerates wet soil	Moist soil	Average–dry soil	Drought-tolerant
▲	△	△	
Rich soil	Average soil	Poor soil	

Panicum virgatum
SWITCH GRASS
Zones 5-9 ☼ - ◐ ◆ ▲ - △

Winter: Beautiful bleached foliage and seedheads.
Spring: New growth.
Summer: Vertical blue-green leaves. Hazy flowers above the foliage create smoky effect.
Autumn: Foliage turns reddish brown.
Description: Clumps 4'-7' tall; spreads by runners.
Comments: Native to middle and eastern North America. May self-sow. 'Haense Herms', good red fall color; 'Heavy Metal', stiff blue-gray leaves; 'Rotstrahlbusch', best red fall color; 'Rubrum' and 'Rehbraum', red fall color; 'Strictum', blue foliage.

Pennisetum alopecuroides
FOUNTAIN GRASS
Zones 6-9 ☼ ◆ ▲

Winter: Attractive bleached foliage.
Spring: New light green growth.
Summer: Fountain of narrow arching green leaves.
Autumn: Bottlebrush mauve flowers, throughout autumn.
Description: Clumps 2'-3' tall and wide.
Comments: Wonderful voluminous grass for mixed border. 'Hameln', 1'-2'; 'Moudry', flowers dark brown-black. *P. setaceum* 'Rubrum' (purple fountain grass), Zones 8-9, dramatic purple foliage, pink flowers; used as an annual in Zones 5-7.

Pennisetum orientale
ORIENTAL
FOUNTAIN GRASS
Zones 7-9 ☼ - ◐ ◆ ▲

Winter: Attractive straw-colored foliage.
Spring: New growth; flowering begins in April in mild climates.
Summer: Upright clumps of fine-textured, glossy blue-green leaves; showy bottlebrush-like plumes of pearly pink flowers age to caramel.

Autumn: Flowering continues into October.
Description: Warm-season, deciduous grass; clumps are 12"-18" tall and wide; flower spikes arch out 12"-16" over foliage.
Comments: The prettiest fountain grass. Excellent grass for the perennial border. Attractive as accents or in groups. Will often survive winters in milder parts of Zone 6.

Phalaris arundinacea var. picta
RIBBON GRASS,
GARDENER'S-GARTERS
Zones 4-9 ☼ - ◐ ◆ ▲ - △

Winter: Attractive bleached foliage.
Spring–Autumn: Cascading bright green leaves boldly striped with white.
Description: Foliage 2½' tall, spreads rapidly by runners.
Comments: Beautiful groundcover. Can be invasive; contain with underground barrier. If becomes brown or stand splits open during hot weather, cut back to rejuvenate.

Schizachyrium scoparium
LITTLE BLUESTEM,
PRAIRIE BEARD GRASS,
BROOM SEDGE
Zones 3-10 ☼ ◐ - ◇ △

Winter: Dried foliage remains colorful.
Spring: Slender, light blue-green, hairy foliage.
Autumn: Leaves and stems turn coppery to bright orange.
Description: Warm-season, deciduous grass; upright clumps are 10"-12" tall; flower spikes are 3½' tall.
Comments: Native to North America. Effective groundcover for large areas. 'Blaze', brilliant pinkish orange to red-purple fall and winter color. Formerly *Andropogon scoparius*.

Vines and Groundcovers for Four-Season Landscapes

Actinidia kolomikta 'Arctic Beauty'
'ARCTIC BEAUTY' VARIEGATED HARDY KIWI
Zones 4-8 ☀-☀ ◉-◒ ▲-△

Winter: Glossy brown bark.
Spring: Purplish new foliage. Fragrant but insignificant white flowers, late spring.
Summer: Bright green, heart-shaped leaves with pink and white blotches.
Autumn: Edible green berries.
Description: Twining, deciduous vine, to 15'-20' high on trellis or tree.
Comments: Color best with sun and alkaline soil. Needs male and female plants for fruit production. Prune severely in late winter to control growth and improve fruiting.

Ajuga reptans
BUGLEWEED
Zones 3-9 ☀-☀ ◉-◒ ▲

Winter: Semievergreen foliage.

Spring: Purple, blue, pink, or white 6″ flower spikes blanket plants in late spring.
Summer: Rounded, ground-hugging shiny leaves, green, bronze, purple, or variegated.
Autumn: No color change.
Description: Mat-forming groundcover, spreading by stolons to cover large areas.
Comments: Excellent under shrubs and in foreground of mixed border. Invasive on lawn edges. 'Bronze Beauty' and 'Atropurpurea', dark burgundy leaves, deep blue flowers; 'Burgundy Glow', burgundy leaves splashed with pink and cream, blue flowers; 'Variegata' and 'Silver Beauty', gray-green leaves with creamy white edges, blue flowers. 'Alba', white flowers; green leaves turn bronze in winter.

Arctostaphylos uva-ursi
BEARBERRY
Zones 3-7 ☼-☀ ◉-◌ △

Winter: Fine-textured leaves turn bronze to red. Small red persistent berries.
Spring: Dainty, pale pink flowers.
Summer: Tiny rounded leaves, glossy dark green.
Autumn: Red fruits, late summer to fall. Leaves turn reddish.
Description: Woody, broadleaved evergreen, 1' tall, spreading widely, rooting along ground.
Comments: Needs acid soil; tolerates salt spray. Slow to establish. Protect from winter sun. Unusual groundcover for difficult sandy soil. 'Massachusetts', showy and disease-resistant. 'Vancouver Jade', establishes quickly.

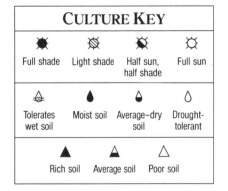

CULTURE KEY			
☀	⊘	☀	☼
Full shade	Light shade	Half sun, half shade	Full sun
⬯	◉	◔	◌
Tolerates wet soil	Moist soil	Average–dry soil	Drought-tolerant
▲	△	△	
Rich soil	Average soil	Poor soil	

Astilbe chinensis var. *pumila*
CHINESE ASTILBE
Zones 3-8

Spring: Mat of coarsely divided dark green leaves.
Summer: Spires of lavender-pink flowers in late summer for 4-6 weeks.
Autumn: Leaves green throughout fall.
Description: Deciduous, mat-forming groundcover, spreading vigorously by underground stolons to cover wide areas; flower stalks 8"-18" tall, depending upon soil moisture.
Comments: Does well in dry shade; spreads quickly. *A. chinensis* 'Finale', blooms late, to 18" tall.

Bergenia species and hybrids
BERGENIA
Zones 3-9

Winter: Evergreen to semi-evergreen, bold-textured foliage turns bronze to dark purple-red in winter.
Spring: Short stalks of bold-textured pink, mauve, or white flowers, very early spring.
Summer: Glossy, dark olive green, leathery leaves.
Autumn: Leaves redden with frost.
Description: Herbaceous, clump-forming groundcover with cabbagelike leaves to 1' tall; spreads by rhizomes.
Comments: Protect from afternoon sun. *B. cordifolia* (heartleaf bergenia), Zones 3-8, paddle-shaped leaves; 'Perfecta', large purplish pink flowers. *B. crassifolia* (leather bergenia), Zones 4-9, oval leaves, best winter color, tallest flowers. *B.* × *schmidtii* (hybrid bergenia), Zones 3-8; 'Evening Bells', pink flowers, good red winter foliage. Other hybrid cultivars include 'Bressingham White', lovely white flowers, spoon-shaped leaves color well; 'Silver Light', pink-tinged white flowers, bold leaves.

Calluna vulgaris
HEATHER
Zones 6-7

See "Heaths and Heathers for Year-Round Color" on page 32.

Ceratostigma plumbaginoides
LEADWORT
Zones 5-9

Spring: Foliage emerges late.
Summer: Fine-textured, rounded dark green leaves. Cobalt blue flowers with red calyxes, late summer through fall.
Autumn: Blue flowers; foliage turns wine red.
Description: Vining groundcover with woody base, 1' tall and 2' wide, spreading underground.
Comments: Excellent draping over low walls. Spreads best in part shade. Combine with fall bulbs. Cut back in late winter.

Chrysanthemum pacificum
GOLD-AND-SILVER CHRYSANTHEMUM
Zones 5-9

Spring: New silvery growth.
Summer: Gray-green, spoon-shaped leaves with silver margins and undersides radiate around stems.
Autumn: Numerous button-shaped gold flowers; blooms very late.
Description: Deciduous groundcover; 2' tall, 1½' wide. Spreads by underground stems.
Comments: Spreads rapidly. Cut to the ground in late fall or winter. Very attractive foliage. May not bloom before frost in the North. Roots easily from cuttings.

Clematis armandii
ARMAND CLEMATIS
Zones 7-9

Spring: Masses of small, fragrant, white starlike flowers in late spring.
Summer–Winter: Narrow, leathery, dense green leaves.
Description: Evergreen woody vine climbing by twining leaf stalks to 12' high.
Comments: Prune every few years immediately after flowering to reduce legginess. Keep mulched.

Clematis × *hybrida*
LARGE-FLOWERED CLEMATIS
Zones 4-9 ☼ ⬥ ▲

Spring: New green foliage growth.
Summer: Huge saucer-shaped flowers with prominent stamens, early to late summer; white, pink, mauve, blue, purple, or red. Medium-textured green leaves.
Autumn: Showy, silky, pinwheel-shaped seedheads.
Description: Deciduous vine climbing by leaf stalks to 10'-15'.
Comments: Keep mulched; flowers best with roots shaded and stems in full sun. Prune early-summer flowering types immediately after flowering; prune mid- to- late-summer flowering types in early spring. *C.* × *jackmanii* (Jackman clematis), deep purple, very free-flowering. Blooming in both summer and fall: 'Duchess of Edinburgh', pure white double flowers; 'Lady Betty Balfour', violet-blue; 'Mme. Baron Veillard', lilac-rose; 'Nelly Moser', huge mauve-pink flowers with rose stripes.

Clematis maximowicziana, syn. *C. paniculata*
SWEET AUTUMN CLEMATIS
Zones 4-9 ☼-☒ ⬥ ▲

Spring: Dense leathery green leaves.
Summer: Lacy white flowers blanket vines in late summer.
Autumn: Flowering continues well into fall. Foliage remains green late. Feathery seedheads.

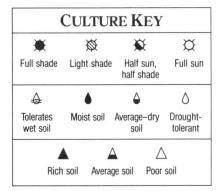

CULTURE KEY			
☀	☒	☼	☼
Full shade	Light shade	Half sun, half shade	Full sun
⬙	⬥	⬦	◊
Tolerates wet soil	Moist soil	Average–dry soil	Drought-tolerant
▲	△	△	
Rich soil	Average soil	Poor soil	

Description: Deciduous, woody vine climbing by twining leaf tendrils to 30'.
Comments: Vigorous grower. Prune hard in early spring to control. Native *C. virginiana* (Virgin's bower), Zones 3-7, similar, flowers earlier. *Polygonum aubertii* (silverlace vine), Zones 4-8, similar effect a bit earlier in late summer.

Clematis montana
ANEMONE CLEMATIS
Zones 6-8 ☒-☒ ⬥ ▲-△

Spring: Fine-textured, lobed medium green leaves.
Summer: Gorgeous dogwoodlike white or pink flowers blanket vines, early summer; vanilla-scented.
Autumn: Showy seedheads. Remains green late.
Description: Woody vine, climbing by twining leaf stalks to 25' tall.
Comments: Rapid grower. Prune immediately after flowering. Keep mulched. Var. *rubens*, pink.

Clematis tangutica
GOLDEN CLEMATIS
Zones 2-8 ☼ ⬥ ▲

Spring: Light green, fine-textured leaves.
Summer: Yellow, lanternlike flowers in mid- and late summer.
Autumn: Flowering continues into fall. Masses of showy, pinwheel-shaped, silky seedheads.
Description: Deciduous vine, climbing to 10' with twining leaf stalks.
Comments: Excellent for summer and fall color. Prune hard in early spring.

Clematis viticella
PURPLE VIRGIN'S BOWER
Zones 5-7 ☼-☀ ⬥-◊ ▲-△

Spring: Neat dark green leaves.
Summer: Numerous small purple, nodding bell-shaped flowers with prominent creamy stamens all summer.

Autumn: Decorative seedheads.
Description: Woody vine climbing by twining leaf stalks. Grows 15'-20' high each year after pruning.
Comments: Prune back hard in early spring. Keep mulched. 'Etoille Violette', deep purple; 'Madame Julia Correvon', ruby red; 'Rubra', bright burgundy.

Epimedium species
BARRENWORT, BISHOP'S-HAT
Zones 3-8 ☼-☀ ◗-◊ ▲-△

Winter: Leaves semievergreen, often die but remain on plant, turning attractive dry reddish brown.
Spring: Bright yellow-green or bronze-red new foliage; sprays of dainty white, pink, or yellow flowers, early spring.
Summer: Olive green leaves mottled with darker green or bronze, medium-textured, on wiry stems.
Autumn: Retains color throughout fall.
Description: Deciduous groundcover 1' tall, spreading widely by underground stems.
Comments: Thrives in dry shade. Excellent textural contrast with ferns and hostas or under shrubs and trees. Cut to ground in late winter before growth begins to reveal flowers and new leaves. *E. alpinum*, red-and-yellow flowers; *E. grandiflorum*, white-and-violet flowers, yellow in var. *sulphureum*; *E.* × *rubrum*, bright crimson; *E.* × *youngianum*, white in 'Niveum', pink in 'Roseum'.

Erica carnea
WINTER HEATH
Zones 5-7 ☼ ◗ ▲

See "Heaths and Heathers for Year-Round Color" on page 32.

Euonymus fortunei
WINTERCREEPER
Zones 4-9 ☼-☀ ◗-◊ ▲-△

Winter–Autumn: Dark glossy green, rounded leaves; variegated in cultivars.

Description: Vining groundcover, spreading by rooting stems and mounding to 2' tall, or climbing by rootlets to 30' high on wall or tree trunks.
Comments: Scale insects may be troublesome; use dormant oil sprays. 'Colorata' (purple-leaf wintercreeper), dark green leaves with purple undersides, turning completely purplish bronze in winter; 'Emerald Gaiety', Zones 5-9, small green leaves with creamy white edges turning pink in winter, may climb to 4'; 'Emerald 'n Gold', Zones 5-9, small green leaves with bright gold edges; 'Gracilis', variable variegation green and white, pink in winter, Zones 5-9; 'Kewensis' (little-leaf wintercreeper), Zones 5-8, very tiny green leaves.

Galium odoratum
SWEET WOODRUFF
Zones 4-8 ☼-☀ ◗-◊ ▲

Spring: Dainty white flowers, mid- to late spring, blanket fine-textured, light green whorled leaves.
Summer: Dark green fine-textured foliage.
Autumn: Remains green late.
Description: Deciduous to semi-evergreen groundcover forming thick mats 8"-10" tall and spreading widely by underground runners.
Comments: Naturalized in the United States. Beautiful plant for underplanting shade-loving shrubs, bulbs, and perennials in woodland garden. Can be invasive; locate with caution.

Hedera helix
ENGLISH IVY
Zones 5-9 ☼-☀ ◗-◊ ▲-△

Winter–Autumn: Attractive glossy green or variegated, usually triangular, lobed, evergreen leaves.
Description: Vine, climbing by aerial rootlets to over 15'. Mature plants bear round clusters of white flowers and poisonous small black berries.
Comments: Handsome groundcover or climbing vine. Many of the hundreds of available cultivars are not reliably hardy north of Zone 7; check with your nursery owner or the American Ivy Society

for recommendations if you live in Zones 5 or 6 and would like to grow a cultivar rather than the species.

Hydrangea anomala subsp. *petiolaris*
CLIMBING HYDRANGEA
Zones 5-7 ☼-※ ◐ ▲

Winter: Shaggy cinnamon brown bark peels off trunks of stout vines.
Summer: Huge clusters of lacy white flowers in early summer. Bold-textured dark green leaves.
Autumn: No color change; remains green late.
Description: Heavy deciduous vine climbing by rootlike holdfasts to 60' tall.
Comments: Needs acid soil. Provide shade in South. Forms massive framework of overhanging branches. Slow to establish. Allow to climb sturdy tree or masonry wall. Prune side branches and stems to control height immediately after flowering.

Jasminum nudiflorum
WINTER JESSAMINE
Zones 6-9 ☼-※ ◐-◌ ▲-△

Winter: Cascading branches with green bark. Yellow flowers with orange eyes, late winter.
Spring–Summer: Lovely, lustrous green leaves.
Autumn: Holds green color late before dropping.

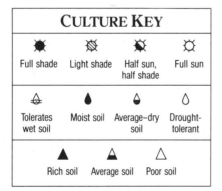

CULTURE KEY			
✹	✸	☀	☼
Full shade	Light shade	Half sun, half shade	Full sun
⬙	◐	◌	◌
Tolerates wet soil	Moist soil	Average–dry soil	Drought-tolerant
▲	△	△	
Rich soil	Average soil	Poor soil	

Description: Spreading mound of trailing, rooting stems 3'-4' tall, 4'-7' wide; can grow 12'-18' tall if trained on a trellis.
Comments: Grow against a sunny wall for good winter floral display. Train to cascade over a wall or down a slope. Not fragrant.

Juniperus conferta
SHORE JUNIPER
Zones 5-9 ☼-※ ◐-◌ ▲-△

Winter: Yellow-green to bronze-green needles.
Spring–Autumn: Bright green or blue-green needles.
Description: Ground-hugging coniferous groundcover 1'-2' tall and spreading to 9' wide.
Comments: Lovely, fine-textured, feathery groundcover. Does well in sandy soil and salt spray; tolerates more shade than most junipers. 'Blue Pacific', blue-green year-round; 'Emerald Sea', bright blue-green in summer, yellow-green in winter; 'Silver Mist', silvery blue in summer, purplish in winter.

Juniperus horizontalis
CREEPING JUNIPER
Zones 2-9 ☼-※ ◐-◌ ▲-△

Winter: Evergreen needles may turn bronze.
Spring–Autumn: Needles usually scalelike, dark green, blue-green, or golden.
Description: Coniferous woody groundcover with spreading horizontal branches, 1'-2' tall and 5' or wider; branches sometimes rooting.
Comments: Tolerates seashore and roadside conditions. Numerous cultivars. 'Douglasii' (Waukegan juniper), steely blue-green, silvery purple in winter; 'Bar Harbor', blue-green needlelike and scalelike foliage; 'Blue Chip', bright blue in summer, purplish in winter, very low; 'Wiltonii' (blue rug juniper), dense, silver-blue, very low; 'Livida', Zones 3-8, gray-green in summer, purple in winter; 'Mother Lode', gold-tipped needles, Zones 4-9.

Juniperus procumbens 'Nana'
JAPANESE GARDEN JUNIPER
Zones 5-9 ☼-◗ ◗-◓ ▲-△

Winter–Autumn: Fine-textured, light green needles.
Description: Conifer. Dense carpet, mounding to 1′ tall and 8′ wide, rooting along the ground.
Comments: Lovely juniper for groundcover or foreground of mixed border.

Lamium maculatum
SPOTTED DEADNETTLE
Zones 4-8 ◗-◓ ◗ ▲

Spring: White or lavender-rose flowers in midspring into summer.
Summer–Winter: Heart-shaped, green leaves spotted with silver; scalloped edges.
Description: Herbaceous groundcover. Sprawling stems form 8″ mounds, spread by rooting.
Comments: Good groundcover for small garden spots. Combines well with ferns, hostas, and other shade plants. 'White Nancy', white flowers, silver leaves edged green; 'Beacon Silver', rose-lavender flowers, silver leaves edged green; 'Aureum', soft yellow leaves with white midveins, pink flowers.

Liriope spicata
CREEPING LIRIOPE
Zones 4-9 ☼-◉ ◗-◓ ▲-△

Winter: Yellow-green or variegated leaves.
Summer: Grassy, dark green or variegated leaves; spikes of lavender, purple, or white flowers.
Autumn: Flowering may continue into fall.
Description: Evergreen groundcover forming grassy mat about 1′ tall; spreads by underground stems.
Comments: Leaves may yellow or brown in cold-winter areas; mow or cut back in early spring to rejuvenate. 'Silver Dragon', bright white stripes, lavender-purple flowers. *Ophiopogon japonicus* (dwarf mondo grass), Zones 7-9, similar but lower and more fine-textured, with flowers hidden by leaves; used as a lawn substitute. *L. muscari* (lilyturf),

Zones 6-9, wider and longer leaves, to 18″ tall; 'Gold Banded', narrow gold band down middle, lavender flowers; 'Big Blue', dark green leaves, large purple-blue flowers; 'Silvery Sunproof', almost-white leaves in sun, lavender flowers, Zones 6-9.

Lonicera sempervirens
TRUMPET HONEYSUCKLE
Zones 3-9 ☼-◗ ◗ ▲

Spring–Autumn: Flushes of orange flowers beginning in late spring; blue-green rounded leaves.
Description: Deciduous vine, climbing by twining stems to 10′-15′ high.
Comments: Prune back to large trunk and main branches in late winter. Provide trellis or other support to twine upon. 'Sulphurea', large yellow flowers. *L.* × *heckrottii* (goldflame honeysuckle), Zones 4-9, red buds with creamy insides. *L. japonica* (Japanese honeysuckle), highly invasive and smothering, spreads by seeds; do not plant south of New England.

Lysimachia nummularia 'Aurea'
GOLDEN CREEPING JENNY
Zones 3-8 ◗-◓ ◗ ▲-◮

Spring: Brilliant yellow-green, rounded leaves through autumn.
Summer: Golden inconspicuous flowers.
Autumn: Leaves remain colorful late.
Description: Deciduous creeping groundcover. Forms fine textured 6″ tall mats; spreads by rooting stems.
Comments: Brightens up shady garden spots. Spreads rapidly.

Microbiota decussata
SIBERIAN CARPET CYPRESS
Zones 2-8 ☼-◓ ◗ ▲-△

Winter: Needles turn bronze-purple.

Spring–Autumn: Bright green scalelike needles in flattened feathery sprays with nodding tips.
Description: Coniferous groundcover with woody branches to 8″ tall and spreading indefinitely, rooting along the ground.
Comments: An attractive juniper-like groundcover that performs well in light shade. Allow plenty of room to spread.

Pachysandra terminalis
JAPANESE PACHYSANDRA
Zones 5-7

Winter–Autumn: Glossy dark green whorled leaves.
Description: Herbaceous groundcover to 8″-10″ tall and spreading widely by underground stolons.
Comments: Best in moist soil; withstands dry shade. Common but useful groundcover under shrubs and trees. Can be invasive. 'Silver-Edge', variegated gray-green with creamy white edges, slow-growing; 'Green Carpet', more compact.

Parthenocissus tricuspidata
BOSTON IVY
Zones 4-8

Winter: Tracery of stems and branches.
Spring: Bronze to reddish new growth.
Summer: Dark glossy green, 3-lobed leaves.
Autumn: Brilliant glossy red leaves; blue berries.

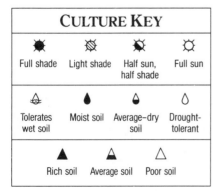

CULTURE KEY			
✸	✸	✸	☼
Full shade	Light shade	Half sun, half shade	Full sun
⬗	⬤	◖	◊
Tolerates wet soil	Moist soil	Average–dry soil	Drought-tolerant
▲	△	△	
Rich soil	Average soil	Poor soil	

Description: Vine or groundcover, climbing to 50′ high by tendrils and adhesive discs.
Comments: Grows well on masonry walls or tree trunks. Needs sun for fall color. Prune in late winter. *P. quinquefolia* (Virginia creeper), Zones 3-9, with 5-lobed leaves; use as vine or groundcover. Both require plenty of room to spread; can be invasive.

Schizophragma hydrangeoides
JAPANESE HYDRANGEA VINE
Zones 6-7

Winter: Interesting trunk and branch pattern.
Spring: Bright green new growth.
Summer: Large, coarsely toothed, heart-shaped rich green leaves. Large, lacy clusters of white flowers in midsummer.
Autumn: Remains green late.
Description: Deciduous woody vine climbing by clinging rootlike holdfasts; grows to 60′ high.
Comments: Needs acid soil. Provides shade in South. Vine stays flatter against surface than climbing hydrangea, blooms a few weeks later. Train on strong tree or masonry wall.

Sedum acre
GOLDMOSS STONECROP
Zones 4-9

Winter: Evergreen in warm climates.
Spring: Bright green new growth appears early.
Summer: Mass of golden yellow flowers, early summer. Tiny emerald green, triangular leaves.
Autumn: Remains green late.
Description: Ground-hugging carpet of succulent leaves, spreading rapidly by roots and seeds.
Comments: Shallow-rooted groundcover; easily weeded out if it becomes invasive.

Thymus × citriodorus 'Gold Edge'
'GOLD-EDGE' LEMON THYME
Zones 4-9

Winter: Evergreen green-and-gold leaves.

Spring–Autumn: Tiny bright green leaves with gold edges; rosy flowers in early to mid-summer.
Description: Creeping groundcover to 4″ tall; stems root to form large patches.
Comments: Lemon-scented foliage makes delightful border for walks or edging low walls.

Thymus pseudolanuginosus
WOOLLY THYME
Zones 2-9 ☼ ◐-◊ ▲-△

Winter: Evergreen leaves become purplish plum.
Spring: Rose-pink flowers, late spring.
Summer–Autumn: Mat of minute, silvery gray leaves.
Description: Mat-forming groundcover 2″ tall, spreading to make large patches.
Comments: Excellent fine-textured plant for stone walls and between pavers in hot, sunny locations. Not fragrant.

Tiarella cordifolia
FOAMFLOWER
Zones 3-8 ◙-☀ ◊ ▲

Winter: Evergreen leaves may turn bronze.
Spring: Foamy white flowers in 6″ spikes for 4-6 weeks in midspring. Lobed, heart-shaped leaves olive green with burgundy variegations.
Summer–Autumn: Variegations less pronounced.
Description: Creeping groundcover forming thick mat 10″ tall, spreading by above-ground runners.
Comments: Native to eastern North America. Wonderful for shade or woodland garden under shrubs or with perennials.

Vinca minor
PERIWINKLE, MYRTLE
Zones 4-8 ☼-☀ ◐-◊ ▲-△

Spring: Bright blue flowers decorate green leaves all spring. Starts blooming with daffodils.
Summer–Winter: Glossy, dark green, fine-textured evergreen leaves.

Description: Creeping groundcover forming thick evergreen mats 6″-8″ tall; spreads by rooting stems.
Comments: Popular groundcover very useful under trees and shrubs and in shade garden. A bit slow getting established. Protect from winter sun in North and summer sun in South and Midwest. 'Alba', pure white flowers, less vigorous; 'Bowlesii', numerous deep blue flowers, more clumping; 'Aureo-Variegata', gold-edged leaves.

Waldsteinia fragarioides
BARREN STRAWBERRY
Zones 4-7 ☼-◙ ◐-◊ ▲-△

Winter: Evergreen foliage turns bronze in winter.
Spring: Showy clusters of bright yellow flowers in late spring.
Summer–Autumn: Lustrous, deep green 3-parted leaves form thick mat.
Description: Herbaceous groundcover forming low mat of evergreen leaves 6″ tall; spreads by rooting runners to cover large areas.
Comments: Native to eastern United States. Best in cool, moist areas. *W. ternata* (Siberian barren strawberry), Zones 2-7, showier, harder to find.

Wisteria floribunda
JAPANESE WISTERIA
Zones 5-9 ☼-☀ ◐-◊ ▲-△

Winter: Network of massive trunks and branches; smooth gray trunk bark.
Spring: Huge clusters of fragrant, pendulous violet flowers (blue-violet, white, or rose in cultivars), midspring as new foliage emerges.
Summer: Bright green, bold-textured compound leaves.
Autumn: Leaves may turn yellow.
Description: Clockwise twining vine with massive trunks climbs to 40′ high.
Comments: Provide very strong support with metal posts. Do not allow to strangle trees. Specialized pruning needed. *W. chinensis* (Chinese wisteria), counterclockwise twining vine, blue-violet flowers opening all at the same time after foliage has enlarged in late spring; 'Plena', double violet.

Resources for Four-Season Landscapes

Here's an assortment of mail-order nurseries for four-season landscape plants. They are divided into nurseries that specialize in herbaceous plants and those that specialize in woodies. Of course, many nurseries offer both, but usually they offer more of one or the other, and they are listed accordingly. Some nurseries specialize in a plant or plants (like roses or irises); in these cases, you'll find the specialty in parentheses after the address if it isn't obvious from the company's name. Again, many of these specialty nurseries offer a selection of other plants as well. Happy plant shopping!

Perennials, Bulbs, Groundcovers, and Ornamental Grasses

Bakker of Holland
U.S. Reservation Center
Louisiana, MO 63353-0050
(bulbs)

Kurt Bluemel, Inc.
2740 Greene Lane
Baldwin, MD 21013
(ornamental grasses)

Bluestone Perennials
7211 Middle Ridge Road
Madison, OH 44057

Boehlke's Woodland Gardens
W. 140 N. 10829 Country
   Aire Road
Germantown, WI 53022
(wildflowers for the North)

Breck's
6523 N. Galena Road
P.O. Box 1758
Peoria, IL 61632
(bulbs)

Brookside Wildflowers
Rt. 3
Box 740-H3
Boone, NC 28607

W. Atlee Burpee and
   Company
300 Park Avenue
Warminster, PA 18974

Busse Gardens
Rt. 2, Box 238
Cokato, MN 55321

Carroll Gardens
P.O. Box 310
444 E. Main Street
Westminster, MD 21158

The Crownsville Nursery
P.O. Box 797
Crownsville, MD 21032

Daylily Discounters
Rt. 2, Box 24
Alachua, FL 32615

Daylily World
P.O. Box 1612
Sanford, FL 32771

Daystar
Rt. 2, Box 250
Litchfield, ME 04350
(alpine plants, perennials)

Peter de Jager Bulb Company
P.O. Box 2010
South Hamilton, MA 01982

Dutch Gardens
P.O. Box 200
Adelphia, NJ 07710

Endangered Species
P.O. Box 1830
Tustin, CA 92681
(bamboo, palms, grasses)

Fancy Fronds
1911 4th Avenue W
Seattle, WA 98119
(spore-propagated ferns)

Foliage Gardens
Dept. S
2003 128th Avenue SE
Bellevue, WA 98005
(ferns)

Four Seasons Nursery
Division of Plantron, Inc.
Dept. 8
1706 Morrissey Drive
Bloomington, IL 61704
(ferns, groundcovers)

Garden Place
6780 Heisley Road
Mentor, OH 44060

Heaths and Heathers
Box 850
Elma, WA 98541

The Herb Cottage
Heritage Gardens
1 Meadow Ridge Road
Shenandoah, IA 51601
(bulbs, ferns, groundcovers,
  grasses)

Hildenbrandt's Iris Garden
HC84, Box 4
Lexington, NE 68850-9304
(irises, peonies, hostas, lilies)

Holbrook Farm & Nursery
115 Lance Road
P.O. Box 368
Fletcher, NC 28732

Ed Hume Seeds, Inc.
P.O. Box 1450
Kent, WA 98035
(plants for the Pacific Northwest)

J. W. Jung Seed Company
335 S. High Street
Randolph, WI 53957

Kelly Nurseries
Highway 54
Louisiana, MO 63353

Klehm Nursery
Box 197, Rt. 5
South Barrington, IL 60010
(peonies, hostas, daylilies,
  Siberian irises)

Limerock Ornamental
  Grasses, Inc.
R.D. 1, Box 111C
Port Matilda, PA 16870

McClure & Zimmerman
108 W. Winnebago Street
P.O. Box 368
Friesland, WI 53935
(unusual bulbs)

Messelaar Bulb Company,
  Inc.
County Road, Rt. 1-A
P.O. Box 269
Ipswich, MA 01938

Michigan Bulb Company
1950 Waldorf NW
Grand Rapids, MI 49550

Milaeger's Gardens
4838 Douglas Avenue
Racine, WI 53402-2498

Moosebell Flower, Fruit &
  Tree Company
Rt. 1, Box 240
St. Francis, ME 04774

Niche Gardens
1111 Dawson Road
Chapel Hill, NC 27516
(native plants)

Oakes Daylilies
Monday Road, Rt. 4
Corryton, TN 37721

Oakwood Daffodils
2330 W. Bertrand Road
Niles, MI 49120

Owen Farms
Curve-Nankipoo Road
Rt. 3, Box 158-A
Ripley, TN 38063

Park Seed Company
Cokesbury Road
P.O. Box 31
Greenwood, SC 29647

Prairie Nursery
P.O. Box 365
Westfield, WI 53964
(prairie wildflowers and grasses)

Prairie Seed Source
P.O. Box 83
North Lake, WI 53064-0083
(prairie wildflowers and grasses)

Putney Nursery, Inc.
Putney, VT 05346
(alpines, perennials, wildflowers)

Quality Dutch Bulbs, Inc.
50 Lake Drive
P.O. Box 225
Hillsdale, NJ 07642

Rocknoll Nursery
7812 Mad River Road
Hillsboro, OH 45133
(ferns, groundcovers, wildflowers)

Savory's Gardens, Inc.
5300 Whiting Avenue
Edina, MN 55435
(hostas)

John Scheepers, Inc.
P.O. Box 700
Bantam, CT 06750
(bulbs)

Shady Oaks Nursery
700 19th Avenue NE
Waseca, MN 56093
(groundcovers, grasses,
  perennials)

Siskiyou Rare Plant Nursery
2825 Cummings Road
Medford, OR 97501-1524
(alpines, ferns)

Solomon Daylilies
105 Country Club Road
Newport News, VA 23606

Stoecklein's Nursery
135 Critchlow Road
Renfrew, PA 16053
(hostas, daylilies)

Sunlight Gardens
Rt. 1, Box 600-A
Hillvale Road
Andersonville, TN 37705
(ferns, perennials, wildflowers)

Thompson & Morgan, Inc.
P.O. Box 1308
Jackson, NJ 08527

Thon's Garden Mums
P.O. Box 146
Crystal Lake, IL 60014

Ty Ty Plantation Bulb
   Company
P.O. Box 159
Ty Ty, GA 31795

Van Bourgondien
245 Farmingdale Road
P.O. Box A
Babylon, NY 11702
(bulbs)

Van Engelen, Inc.
313 Maple Street
Litchfield, CT 06759
(bulbs)

Veldheer Tulip Gardens
12755 Quincy Street
Holland, MI 49424

Andre Viette Farm and
   Nursery
Rt. 1, Box 16
Fishersville, VA 22939

Wayside Gardens
1 Garden Lane
Hodges, SC 29695

White Flower Farm
Litchfield, CT 06759

Gilbert H. Wild & Son, Inc.
1112 Joplin Street
Sarcoxie, MO 64862

Nancy Wilson Species &
   Miniature Narcissus
571 Woodmont Avenue
Berkeley, CA 94708

Wright Iris Nursery
6583 Pacheco Pass Highway
Gilroy, CA 95020

Yoder Garden Mums
Yoder Sales
P.O. Box 230
Barberton, OH 44203

Trees, Shrubs, and Roses

Angelwood Nursery
12839 McKee School Road
Woodburn, OR 97071
(100 ivy cultivars)

Appalachian Garden
Box 82
Waynesboro, PA 17268

Armstrong Nurseries, Inc.
P.O. Box 4060
Ontario, CA 91761

Armstrong Roses
P.O. Box 1020
Somis, CA 93066

Bovees Nursery
1737 Southwest Coronado
Portland, OR 97219
(rhododendrons and azaleas)

Brooks Tree Farm
9785 Portland NE
Salem, OR 97305

Cardinal Nursery
Bill Storms
Rt. 1, Box 316
State Road, NC 28676
(rhododendrons for eastern
   gardens)

Carlson's Gardens
Box 305
South Salem, NY 10590
(rhododendrons and azaleas)

Catalpa Nursery
P.O. Box 1599
Easton, MD 21601

The Cummins Garden
22 Robertsville Road
Marlboro, NJ 07746
(rhododendrons and azaleas)

Del's Japanese Maples
4691 River Road
Eugene, OR 97404

Forestfarm Nursery
990 Tetherow Road
Williams, OR 97544
(unusual ornamentals and
   conifers)

Foxborough Nursery, Inc.
3611 Miller Road
Street, MD 21154

Girard Nurseries
P.O. Box 428
Geneva, OH 44041

Gloria Dei Nursery
36 East Road
High Falls Park
High Falls, NY 12440
(roses)

Greer Gardens
1280 Goodpasture Island
Road
Eugene, OR 97401

Heirloom Old Garden Roses
24062 N.E. Riverside Drive
St. Paul, OR 97137

Henrietta's Nursery
1345-C N. Brawley
Fresno, CA 93722

Heritage Rose Gardens
16831 Mitchell Creek Drive
Fort Bragg, CA 95437

Hidden Springs Nursery
R.R. 14, Box 159
Cookville, TN 38501

High Country Rosarium
1717 Downing Street
Denver, CO 80218

Historical Roses
1657 W. Jackson Street
Painesville, OH 44077

Hortico
R.R. 1, Robson Road
Waterdown, Ontario
Canada L0R 2H0
(roses)

Inter-State Nurseries
P.O. Box 208
Hamburg, IA 51640

Jackson & Perkins Company
1 Rose Lane
Medford, OR 97501
(roses)

Kalmia Farm
P.O. Box 3881
Charlottesville, VA 22903

Krider Nurseries
303 W. Bristol
P.O. Box 29
Middlebury, IN 46540
(modern roses)

Louisiana Nursery
Rt. 7, Box 43
Opelousas, LA 70570
(magnolias)

Earl May Seed & Nursery
208 N. Elm Street
Shenandoah, IA 51693

McConnell Nurseries
Port Burwell, Ontario
Canada N0J 1T0

Mellinger's, Inc.
2310 W. South Range Road
North Lima, OH 44452

Merry Gardens
P.O. Box 595
Camden, ME 04843

Musser Forests, Inc.
P.O. Box 340
Rt. 119 N
Indiana, PA 15701

Pacific Tree Farms
4301 Lynwood Drive
Chula Vista, CA 91910

Carl Pallek and Sons
Nurseries
Box 137
Virgil, Ontario
Canada L0S 1T0
(roses)

Pickering Nursery
670 Kingston Road
Pickering, Ontario
Canada L1V 1A6
(roses)

Roses of Yesterday & Today
802 Brown's Valley Road
Watsonville, CA 95076

Roslyn Nursery
211 Burrs Lane
Dix Hills, NY 11746

Wayside Gardens
1 Garden Lane
Hodges, SC 29695

We-Du Nurseries
Rt. 5, Box 724
Marion, NC 28752

Weston Nurseries
E. Main Street
Rt. 135, P.O. Box 186
Hopkinton, MA 01748
(rhododendrons and azaleas)

Woodlanders, Inc.
1128 Colleton Avenue
Aiken, SC 29801

Recommended Reading

Chapter 1

Cox, Jeff, and Marilyn Cox. *Flowers for All Seasons.* Emmaus, Pa.: Rodale Press, 1987.

Fox, Robin Lane. *Variations on a Garden.* Boston: David R. Godine, 1974.

Frederick, William H., Jr. *100 Great Garden Plants.* Portland, Oreg.: Timber Press, 1975.

Jefferson-Brown, Michael. *Leaves: For All-Year-Round Color and Interest in the Garden.* Newton Abbot, London: David & Charles, 1989.

Kelly, John. *The All-Seasons Garden.* New York: Penguin Books, 1987.

Lawson, Andrew. *Performance Plants.* New York: Viking, 1992.

Lloyd, Christopher. *The Year at Great Dixter.* New York: Penguin Books, 1987.

Chapter 2

Allen, Oliver. *Winter Gardens.* Alexandria, Va.: Time-Life Books, 1979.

Kinaham, Sonia. *The Overlook Guide to Winter Gardens.* Woodstock, N.Y.: Overlook Press, 1985.

Lawrence, Elizabeth. *Gardens in Winter.* Baton Rouge, La.: Claitor's Publishing Division, 1961.

Schuler, Stanley. *The Winter Garden.* New York: Macmillan Co., 1972.

Verey, Rosemary. *The Garden in Winter.* Boston: Little, Brown & Co., 1988.

Wilson, Helen Van Pelt. *Color for Your Winter Yard and Garden.* New York: Charles Scribner's Sons, 1978.

Chapter 3

Schenk, George. *The Complete Shade Gardener.* Boston: Houghton Mifflin Co., 1985.

Scott, George Harmon. *Bulbs: How to Select, Grow and Enjoy.* Tucson, Ariz.: HP Books, 1982.

Taylor's Guide Staff. *Taylor's Guide to Bulbs.* Rev. ed. Boston: Houghton Mifflin Co., 1986.

Chapter 4

De Bray, Lys. *The Green Garden: The Art of Foliage Planting.* Topsfield, Mass.: Salem House Publishers, 1988.

Glattstein, Judy. *Garden Design with Foliage.* Pownal, Vt.: Storey Communications, 1991.

Harper, Pamela L. *Designing with Perennials.* New York: Macmillan Co., 1991.

Pavord, Anna. *Foliage.* New York: Harper & Row, 1990.

Chapter 5

Clarke, Graham. *Garden Color: Autumn and Winter Colour in the Garden.* Topsfield, Mass.: Salem House Publishers, 1968.

Greenlee, John. *The Encyclopedia of Ornamental Grasses.* Emmaus, Pa.: Rodale Press, 1992.

Lacy, Allen. *The Garden in Autumn.* New York: Atlantic Monthly Press, 1990.

Ottesen, Carole. *Ornamental Grasses—The Amber Wave.* New York: McGraw Hill Publishing Co., 1989.

Chapter 6

Hobhouse, Penelope. *Color in Your Garden.* Boston: Little, Brown & Co., 1985.

Keen, Mary. *Gardening with Color.* New York: Random House, 1991.

Phillips, Ellen, and C. Colston Burrell. *Rodale's Illustrated Encyclopedia of Perennials.* Emmaus, Pa.: Rodale Press, 1993.

Reilly, Ann, and Susan A. Roth. *The Home Landscaper: 55 Professional Landscapes You Can Do.* Tucson, Ariz.: Home Planners, 1990.

Verey, Rosemary. *The Art of Planting.* Boston: Little, Brown & Co., 1990.

Williams, Robin. *The Garden Planner.* New York: Barron's, 1990.

Chapter 7

Armitage, Allan M. *Herbaceous Perennial Plants.* Athens, Ga.: Varsity Press, 1989.

Bennett, Jennifer, ed. *The Harrowsmith Gardener's Guide to Groundcovers.* Camden East, Ontario: Camden House, 1987.

Bond, Sandra. *Hostas.* New York: Sterling Publishing Co., 1992.

Clausen, Ruth Rogers, and Nicolas H. Ekstrom. *Perennials for American Gardens.* New York: Random House, 1989.

Dirr, Michael A. *All About Evergreens.* San Francisco: Ortho Books, Chevron Chemical Co., 1985.

———. *Manual of Woody Landscape Plants.* 4th ed. Champaign, Ill.: Stipes Publishing Co., 1990.

Editors of Sunset Books and *Sunset* Magazine. *Lawns & Groundcovers.* Menlo Park, Calif.: Lane Publishing Co., 1982.

Ferguson, Barbara, ed. *All About Trees.* San Francisco: Ortho Books, Chevron Chemical Co., 1982.

Harper, Pamela, and Frederick McGourty. *Perennials: How to Select, Grow and Enjoy.* Los Angeles: Price Stern Sloan, 1985.

Horton, Alvin, and James McNair. *All About Bulbs.* San Francisco: Ortho Books, Chevron Chemical Co., 1986.

Hudak, Joseph. *Gardening with Perennials.* Portland, Oreg.: Timber Press, 1985.

MacCaskey, Michael. *Lawns and Ground Covers: How to Select, Grow and Enjoy.* Tucson, Ariz.: HP Books, 1982.

Millard, Scott, ed. *All About Groundcovers.* San Francisco: Ortho Books, Chevron Chemical Co., 1977.

Reinhardt, Thomas A., Martina Reinhardt, and Mark Moskowitz. *Ornamental Grass Gardening.* Los Angeles: Price Stern Sloan, 1989.

Rice, Graham. *Plants for Problem Places.* Portland, Oreg.: Timber Press, 1988.

Scott-James, Ann. *Perfect Plant, Perfect Garden.* New York: Summit Books, 1988.

Shultz, Warren. *The Chemical-Free Lawn.* Emmaus, Pa.: Rodale Press, 1989.

Sinnes, A. Cort. *How to Select and Care for Shrubs and Hedges.* San Francisco: Ortho Books, Chevron Chemical Co., 1980.

Taylor's Guide Staff. *Taylor's Guide to Ground Covers, Vines and Grasses.* Boston: Houghton Mifflin Co., 1987.

———. *Taylor's Guide to Perennials.* Boston: Houghton Mifflin Co., 1988.

———. *Taylor's Guide to Shrubs.* Boston: Houghton Mifflin Co., 1987.

———. *Taylor's Guide to Trees.* Boston: Houghton Mifflin Co., 1988.

van Gelderen, D. M., and J. R. P. van Hoey Smith. *Conifers.* Portland, Oreg.: Timber Press, 1986.

Vertrees, J. D. *Japanese Maples.* Portland, Oreg.: Timber Press, 1987.

USDA Plant Hardiness Zone Map

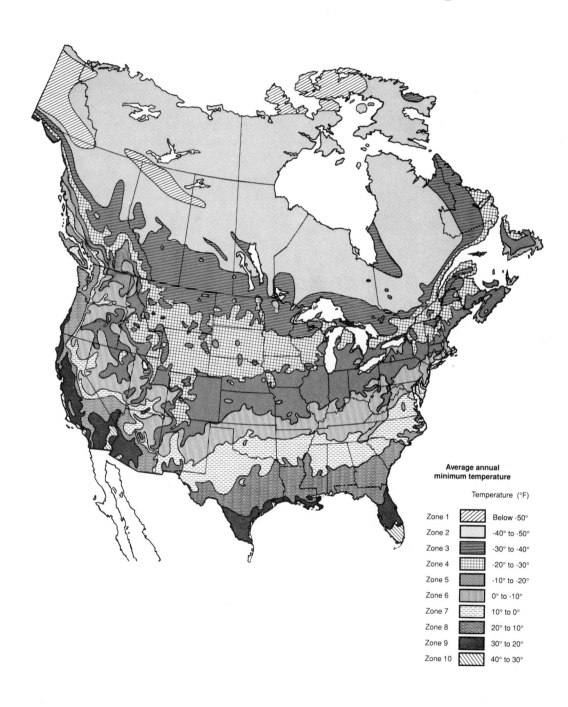

**Average annual
minimum temperature**

Temperature (°F)

Zone 1		Below -50°
Zone 2		-40° to -50°
Zone 3		-30° to -40°
Zone 4		-20° to -30°
Zone 5		-10° to -20°
Zone 6		0° to -10°
Zone 7		10° to 0°
Zone 8		20° to 10°
Zone 9		30° to 20°
Zone 10		40° to 30°

Index

Note: Page references in **bold** indicate photographs and illustrations.

A

Abelia, glossy, 154, 260
Abelia × grandiflora, 154, 260
Abeliophyllum distichum, 286
Accent, 236
Acer capillipes, 270
Acer ginnala, 186-87, 270
Acer griseum, 37, 42, 270
Acer japonicum, **185,** 271
Acer japonicum 'Aureum', **121**
Acer palmatum, 185-86
    best cultivars, 188-89
    leaf types, 185-86, **185**
Acer palmatum 'Atropurpureum', **168**
Acer palmatum 'Bloodgood', 175, **176,** 271
Acer palmatum 'Karagusawa', **161**
Acer palmatum 'Sango Kaku', 271
Acer palmatum var. *dissectum,* 271
Acer rubrum, 185, 271
Acer saccharum, 184-85, **215,** 272
Acer triflorum, 272
Achillea 'Coronation Gold', 300
Achillea millefolium 'Fire King', **157**
Aconite, winter, 50, 51, **51, 74**
Aconitum carmichaelii, 225, **225**
Actinidia kolomikta 'Arctic Beauty', 320
Adam's-needle, 315

Adonis
    Amur, 53
    spring, 53
Adonis amurensis, 53
Adonis vernalis, 53
Aesculus × carnea, 91, 272
Aesculus parviflora, 151, 286
Ajuga reptans, 246-47, 320
Alliums, 129
Allium thunbergii, 221
Alyssum, sweet, **217**
Amelanchier, 83
Amelanchier arborea, 83, 272
Amsonia tabernaemontana, 300
Anaphalis triplinervis, 300
Anemone
    grapeleaf, 226
    Japanese, 300-301
        in autumn, **206-7,** 225-26
Anemone × hybrida, 225-26, 300-301
Anemone pulsatilla, **111**
Anemone vitifolia, 226
Anemone vitifolia 'Robustissima', **206-7,** 226
Annuals, for mixed border, 253
Arborvitae
    American, 269
    oriental, 269
Arbutus unedo, 255

Arctostaphylos uva-ursi, 320
Armeria maritima, 301
Aronia arbutifolia, 193, 195, 286
Artemisia
    'Huntington', **213**
    silvermound, 173, 301
    'Valerie Finnis', **213, 216**
Artemisia ludoviciana 'Silver King', 301
Artemisia schmidtiana 'Nana', 173, 301
Aruncus dioicus, 301
Asclepias tuberosa, 301
Ash
    mountain, 196-97
        European, 196-97
        Korean, 196-97, 284
        'Longwood Sunset', 197
Aster(s)
    for autumn color, 182, **206**
    Frikart's *(Aster × frikartii),* 224, 301-2
    'Monch', **206-7**
    New England, **217,** 222, **225,** 302
    New York, 222, 302
    in perennial border, **213**
    Stokes', **162-63**
    types, 222, 224

Aster × frikartii, 224, 301-2
Aster × frikartii 'Monch', **206–7**
Aster novae-angliae, **217**, 222, **225**, 302
Aster novi-belgii, 302
Astilbe, **155**, 302
    Chinese, **156**, 321
    fall, **164**
Astilbe × arendsii, 302
Astilbe chinensis var. *pumila,* **156**, 321
Astilbe taqueti 'Superba', **164**
Aucuba, Japanese, 260
Aucuba japonica, 260
Aurinia saxatilis, 302
Autumn, 181-202, **203–18**, 219-28
    berries, 192-97, **196**, 198-99
    color garden, **200–201**
    color scheme, 182-84
    Indian summer, 182
    landscape features, 12
    mixed border, 228
Autumn flowers, 197, **225**
    border blooms, 221-22, 224-26
    bulbs, 202, 219-21, **220**, 223
    fall-blooming trees, 199, 202
    grasses, 226, **227**, 228
    perennials, 223
    shrubs and vines, 202
    wildflowers, **183**
Autumn foliage, 183-84
    ornamental grasses, 191
    perennials, 191
    shrubs, 187, 189, 190-91, 192
    trees, 184-87, 188-89, 190
    vines and groundcovers, 190-91
Azalea(s), **92**, **117**
    coast, 150
    Cumberland, 148, 150-51
    deciduous, 100
    deciduous species and hybrid groups, 100, 104, 148-49
    evergreen, 98-99, 143-46
        'Gumpo White', 17
        hybrids, zones and culture, 267
    flame, 150
    hammock-sweet, 150
    Korean, 93-94, 98
    midspring, 97-100
    native American, 150-51
    North Tisbury hybrids, 144-45
    pinkshell, 150
    pinxterbloom, 148, 150
    plumleaf, 148, 151, **167**
    pontic, 100
    Robin Hill hybrids, 144, 146
        'Sir Robert', 146, **147**

roseshell, **108**, 150
royal, 94-95, **96**, 295
Satsuki and Macrantha hybrids, 143
summer-blooming
    deciduous, 148-49
    evergreen, 143-46
swamp, 151
sweet, 150

B

Background, 236
Balancing mass and weight, 232, **233**
Balloon flower, 312
    compact, **170**
Bamboo
    clump, 56
    golden, 56
    heavenly, 265
    Kuma-zasa or Kuma, 56
Baptisia, 302-3
Baptisia australis, 302-3
Barberry, **155**, 189, 192
    Japanese, 287
    Korean, 286-87
    'Rosy Glow', **165**
    winter berries, 44
    wintergreen, 260
    choice for yellow flowers, 100-101
Bark
    ornamental, 36-43, **38–42**
    white, 37
Barrenwort, 323
Basket-of-gold, 302
Bay, sweet, 138, 257
Bayberry, 44, 295
Bearberry, 320
Beautyberry, 44
    Chinese, **196**
    'Profusion', 287-88
        in autumn, 193, **218**
        in winter, **63**
Bee balm, **155**, 310
Beech
    American, 49
    European, 49, **60–61**, 277
Begonia, hardy, 225, 303
Begonia grandis, 225, 303
Bellflower
    clustered, 303
    Dalmatian, 303
    Serbian, 17
Berberis, 189, 192
    winter berries, 44
Berberis julianae, 260

Berberis koreana, 286-87
Berberis thunbergii var. *atropurpurea,* 287
Bergenia, 321
Berries
    autumn, 192-97, **196**, 198-99
    winter, 43-47
Betula, 37
Betula jacquemontii, 273
Betula nigra, 24
Betula nigra 'Heritage', 37, **73**, 273
Betula papyrifera, 273
Betula pendula, **70**
Betula pendula 'Tristis' and 'Youngii', 273
Betula platyphylla var. *japonica* 'Whitespire', 37, 273
Betula sylvatica, **60–61**
Birch, 37
    canoe, 273
    European, **65**
    paper, 273
    river, 24
        'Heritage', 37, **73**, 273
    weeping European, **65**, **70**, 273
    white-bark Himalayan, 273
    white, 273
    'Whitespire', 37, 273
Birds, berries and, 43-44, 45
Bishop's-hat (barrenwort), 323
Black-eyed Susan, 'Goldsturm', 55, **167**, 313
Black snakeroot, 304-5
Bleeding heart, fringed, **96**, **111**, 305
Bloodgrass, Japanese ('Red Baron' bloodgrass), **214**, 318
Bloom sequence, 15-17
Bluebeard, 153-54, 288
Bluebells
    Spanish, **92**
    Virginia, **120–21**, 309-10
Blue star, willow, 300
Bluestem, little, 24, 319
Borders, mixed. *See* Mixed borders
Box, sweet, 268
Boxwood, common, 261
Buckeye, bottlebrush, 151, 286
Buddleia alternifolia 'Argentea', 287
Buddleia davidii, 287
    in summer, 154, **157**, **158**, **171**
Bugbane, Kamchatka 'White Pearl', 224, **225**, 305
Bugleweed, 246-47, 320
Bulbs
    autumn, 202, 219-21, **220**, 223
    how to group, **125**
    layering, 252, **252**

for mixed border, 250-53
spring, 104-6, 123-30
early, 81
late, 91
mid, 84
tips on growing, 128
summer, 178, 180
winter-flowering, 50-52, **51**, 54-55
Burning bush, 189, 291
Butterfly bush, 287
fountain, 287
in summer, 154, **157, 158, 171**
Butterfly weed, 301
Buttonbush, 288
Buxus sempervirens, 261

C

Calamagrostis arundinacea var.
brachytricha, 316
Callicarpa, winter berries, 44
Callicarpa bodinieri 'Profusion', 287-88
in autumn, 193, **218**
in winter, **63**
Callicarpa dichotoma, 196
Calluna vulgaris 'Cuprea', **71**
Calluna vulgaris (heather), 321
in winter, 31, 32-33
Camellia
common, 49, 261
sasanqua, 49, 261
Camellia japonica, 49, 261
Camellia sasanqua, 49, 261
Campanula carpatica, 303
Campanula glomerata, 303
Campanula portenschlagiana, 303
Campanula poscharskyana, 17
Candytuft, perennial, 308
Carex elata 'Bowles Golden', 316
Carex hachioensis 'Evergold', 316
Carpet cypress, Siberian, 325-26
Carpinus betulus 'Pendula', 274
Caryopoteris × *clandonensis,* 153-54,
288
Catmint, **158,** 310
Cedar
atlas, 255
Colorado red, 257
eastern red, 29, 257
'Snow Sprite' deodar, 261
Cedrus atlantica, 255
Cedrus deodara 'Snow Sprite', 261
Cephalanthus occidentalis, 288
Cerastium tomentosum, 303
Ceratostigma plumbaginoides, **167,
220,** 321

Cercidiphyllum japonicum, 274
Cercis, 274
Cercis canadensis, 82, 97, **116**
Cercis chinensis, 83
Cercis mexicana, 82-83
Cercis occidentalis, 83
Cercis reniformis, 82-83
Chamaecyparis, 28
Chamaecyparis lawsoniana 'Elwoodii',
168-69
Chamaecyparis nootkatensis 'Pendula',
255
Chamaecyparis obtusa, 261
Chamaecyparis obtusa 'Nana Aurea',
71
Chamaecyparis pisifera, 262
Chamaecyparis pisifera 'Lemon Drop',
61
Chasmanthium latifolium, 316-17
Chaste tree, 143, **161, 167,** 299
Cherry, 80
autumn-flowering, 199, 202
Japanese flowering, 282
'Kwanzan', 88, **110-11**
'Okame', 282
weeping higan, 282
Chestnut, red horse, 91, 272
Chimonanthus praecox, 49, 288
Chionanthus, 42-43, 275
Chionanthus retusus, 138
Chionanthus virginicus, 137
Chionodoxa luciliae, **66,** 124, 126
Chokeberry, red, 193, 195, 286
Chokecherry, Amur, 88, 282
Christmas rose, 52, **66**
Chrysanthemum(s), **209,** 221-22
gold-and-silver, 321
hardy, **212,** 221-22
hardy garden, 304
Chrysanthemum × *morifolium,* **212,**
221-22
Chrysanthemum nipponicum, 304
Chrysanthemum pacificum, 321
Chrysanthemum parthenium 'Aureum',
304
Chrysanthemum × *rubellum,* 222
Chrysanthemum weyrichii, 222, 304
Chrysanthemum zawadskii var.
latilobum, 222, 304
Chrysogonum virginicum, **112**
Cimicifuga racemosa, 304-5
Cimicifuga simplex 'White Pearl', 224,
225, 305
Cinnamon ferns, **112-13, 205**
Cinquefoil, bush, 149, 151, 295
Cladrastis kentukea, **118-19,** 137,
275

Clematis
anemone, 250, 322
armand, 321
golden, 322
Jackman, **160**
large-flowered, 322
sweet autumn, 202, **213,** 322
Clematis armandii, 321
Clematis × *hybrida,* 322
Clematis × *jackmanii,* 160
Clematis maximowicziana, 202, **213,**
322
Clematis montana, 250, 322
Clematis tangutica, 322
Clematis viticella, 322-23
Clethra, Japanese tree, 275
Clethra alnifolia, 288-89
in summer, 154, **162, 171**
Clethra barbinervis, 275
Clover, bush, 202
'Gibraltar', 295
Cohosh, black, 304-5
Colchicum, 219
Colchicum autumnale, 219, **220**
Color
autumn, 10, 183-84, **200-201**
(*see also* Autumn foliage)
for dormant season, 5
foliage for, 4 (*see also* Foliage)
for year-round landscape, 236-39
Color wheel, **237**
Columbine, **172**
Companions, 17
Coneflower
purple, 55, 306
shining
'Autumn Glory', **209**
'October Glory', **183**
Conifers
dwarf, 24, 28
shades, 28
Contrast, 235-36
Coralbells, 307-8
Coreopsis
threadleaf, 53, 55, 305
'Golden Showers', 53, 55
'Moonbeam', 53, 55, **210**
'Zagreb', **213, 216**
Coreopsis verticillata, 53, 55, 305
Cornelian cherry, 48, 276
Cornus alba, 43, 289
Cornus alternifolia, 275
Cornus florida. See Dogwood, flowering
Cornus kousa. See Dogwood, Kousa
Cornus kousa var. *chinensis,* 135
Cornus mas, 48, 276
Cornus × *rutgersenensis,* 89, 276-77

Cornus × *rutgersenensis* 'Stellar Pink', **121**
Cornus sericea, 43, **65**
Cornus sericea 'Flaviramea', 43, **65**, 289
Corydalis, yellow, 305
Corydalis lutea, 305
Corylopsis, 93
Corylopsis pauciflora, 93, 289
Corylus avellana 'Contorta', 23, 289
Corylus maxima 'Purpurea', 290
Cotinus coggygria, 151-52
Cotinus coggygria f. *purpureus,* 277
Cotinus coggygria 'Notcutt's Variety', 175
Cotinus coggygria 'Royal Purple', **157, 159**
Cotoneaster, **65**, 195
    rockspray, 290
    willowleaf, 262
Cotoneaster horizontalis, 290
Cotoneaster salicifolius, 262
Cotton, lavender, 314
Crabapple
    in autumn, 197, **209**
    choosing cultivars, 83, 85, 86-87
    in summer, **156**
    zones and culture, 280
Cranesbill, blood-red, 306
Crape myrtles, 142-43
    flowers, 199
    new cultivars, **144-45**
    zones and culture, 279
Crataegus, 89
Crataegus viridis 'Winter King', 45, 89, 196, 277
Creeping Jenny, golden, 325
Crocus
    autumn, 219-21
    saffron, **203, 220**, 221
    snow, 50
Crocus sativus, **203, 220**, 221
Crocus speciosus, 219-21
Crown imperial, 127
Cryptomeria
    Japanese, 256
        variegated, **65, 70**
Cryptomeria japonica, 256
Cryptomeria japonica 'Aurea', **65, 70**
Cupressus arizonica 'Blue Pyramid', **161**, 256
Cypress
    'Blue Pyramid' Arizona, **161**, 256
    false, 28
        Elwood, **168-69**
        golden, **65, 71**

    Hinoki, 261
    'Lemon Drop', **61**
    Sawara, 262
    weeping Nootka, 255
Cytisus × *praecox,* 290

D

Daffodil(s), 104-5, 106
    'February Gold', **61**
    winter, 202, **208-9, 220**
        bulbs, 52
Daisy
    Michaelmas (*see* Aster)
    Nippon, 304
Daphne
    'Carol Mackie' burkwood, 262
    garland (rose), 97, 262
    rose, 97, 262
    winter, 34
Daphne × *burkwoodii* 'Carol Mackie', 262
Daphne cneorum, 97, 262
Daphne odora 'Aureo-Marginata', 34
Daylily, 307
    in combinations, 251
    dwarf, **170**
    'Stella d'Oro', 17
Deadnettle, spotted, 325
    'White Nancy', **147**, 247
Deciduous shrubs, 286-99
    fall berries, 198
    spring
        early, 81
        late, 90
        mid, 84
Deciduous trees, 270-85
    fall berries, 198
Deciduous trees and shrubs
    with dramatic silhouettes, 20
    for winter, siting, 19, 21
Designing year-round landscape, 229-53
    background and accent, 236
    balancing mass and weight, 232, **233**
    colors, 236-39
    contrast, 235-36
    creating seasonal plantings, 230
    front yard, **240-41**
    layered look, 246
    mixed borders, 239, 242-53
    shade garden, **248-49**
    textures, 229-31, **231**
    tree and shrub shapes, 232, 234-35

Deutzia, 'Nikko' slender, 290
Deutzia gracilis 'Nikko', 290
Dianthus deltoides, 305
Dicentra eximia, **96, 111**, 305
Dictamnus albus, 306
Dogwood
    Chinese, 135
    for color, 43
    cornelian cherry, 48, 276
    flowering, 275-76
        in autumn, **210**
        in spring, 85, 88, **92, 114, 117, 121**
    golden-twig, 43, **65**, 289
    Kousa, 276
        in autumn, **196, 213**
        bark, 42-43
        in spring, **121, 135**
        in summer, **147, 166-67**
    pagoda, 275
    red osier, 43, **65**
    stellar, 89, 276-77
        pink-flowered, **121**
    tartarian, 43, 289

E

Echinacea purpurea, 55, 306
Echinops ritro, 306
Egolf, Donald R., 142, 192, **194**
Elaeagnus angustifolia, 290-91
Elderberry, cutleaf golden, 297
Elm, 'Emerald Vase' lacebark, 285
Elsholtzia stauntonii, 291
Elymus arenarius 'Glaucus', **168-69**, 317
Enkianthus, red-vein, **112**, 187, **210-11**, 291
Enkianthus campanulatus, **112**, 187, **210-11**, 291
Epimedium, 36, 323
Eranthis, 50, 51
Eranthis hyemalis, **51, 74**
Erianthus ravennae, 317
Erica carnea, 31, 33-34
Erica carnea 'Springwood Pink', **61**
Euonymus, winged, 189, 291
Euonymus alata, 189, 291
Euonymus fortunei, 323
Evergreens
    color changes, 29-31
    essential in winter garden, 24-35
    flowers, 49
    multicolored, 31, 34-35
    shades of foliage, 28
    siting, 19, 21, 242, **243**, 244

Evergreen shrubs, 260-69
autumn berries, 199
with colorful foliage, 29
spring
early, 81
late, 90
mid, 84
for winter garden, 25
purplish, red, or bronze color, 30
Evergreen trees, 255-59
with dramatic silhouettes, 20
Everlasting
three-veined, 300

F

Fagus grandifolia, 49
Fagus sylvatica, 49, 277
Fargesia nitida, 56
Fatsia, Japanese, 263
Fatsia japonica, 263
Fennel, bronze, 306
Ferns, **166–67**
cinnamon, **112–13, 205**
Fescue, blue, **213,** 317
Festuca cinerea, **213,** 317
Feverfew, golden, 304
Fir, Douglas, 259
Firethorn
'Mohave', **61**
scarlet, 195-96, 266-67
Flame grass, **217**
Flax, blue, **165,** 309
Flowers
autumn (*see* Autumn flowers)
spring wildflower garden, **78–79**
summer-blooming shrubs, 143-46, **147,** 148-54
in winter, 47-48
Foamflower, **120–21,** 327
Foeniculum vulgare var. *purpureum,* 306
Foliage
autumn (*see* Autumn foliage)
for color and form, 4
spring, 76
summer (*see* Summer foliage)
variegated
summer, 178, **179**
winter, 31, 34-35
Forget-me-nots, **118**
Form, foliage for, 4
Forsythia, white, 286
Fothergilla, 97
Alabama, 97

dwarf, 9, 291
in autumn, 189
in winter, 97, **122**
large, 97
Fothergilla gardenii, 9, 97, **122,** 189, 291
Fothergilla major, 97
Fothergilla monticola, 97
Fountain grass, 56, **210, 227,** 319
oriental, 319
Four-season landscaping, 3-17
design (*see* Designing year-round landscape)
Franklinia, 199, **218,** 277-78
Franklinia alatamaha, **218,** 277-78
Franklin tree, 199, 277-78
Fringetree(s), 275
Chinese, 138
in summer, 137-38
white, 137
in winter, 42-43
Fritillaria imperialis, 127
Fritillaria meleagris, 127
Front yard, **240–41**
Frost pockets, **82**

G

Galanthus nivalis, 50, 51, **51, 64**
Galium odoratum, **96, 111,** 323
Gardener's-garters, 56, 319
Gas plant, 306
Gayfeather, **170**
Gelsemium sempervirens, **114**
Genista, **115**
Geranium, hardy, **168–69**
Geranium platypetalum, **168–69**
Geranium sanguineum, 306
Ginkgo, 187, 278
Ginkgo biloba, 187, 278
Glory-of-the-snow, **66,** 124, 126
Goat's beard, 301
Golden-chain tree, 91
'Vossii', **108,** 278-79
Golden-rain tree, 139, 142, 278
Goldenrod, 182, 224
'Crown of Rays' Canada, **183**
Goldmoss stonecrop, 326
'Goldsturm' black-eyed Susan, 55, **167,** 313
Grape hyacinth, 126
Armenian, 126-27
common, 127
Grasses, ornamental. *See* Ornamental grasses
Green-and-gold, **112**

Groundcovers, 320-27
autumn-blooming, 219
berries, 199
foliage, 190-91
bulbs and, 129-30
for four-season landscaping, 3
for mixed border, 246-47
spring
early, 81
late, 91
mid, 84
winter, 30, 35-36
flowering, 54
Gum
black, 281
sweet, 187, 279

H

Hakonechloa macra 'Aureola', 317
Hakone grass, golden variegated, 317
Halesia carolina, 88-89, **96,** 279
Halesia montana, 88-89
Hamamelis, 48, **62,** 187, 189
Hamamelis × *intermedia,* 291-92
Hamamelis × *intermedia* 'Arnold Promise', 48, **62**
Hamamelis mollis, 48, **51**
Hamamelis virginiana, 202, 292
Hardiness zone map, **334**
Harebell, Carpathian, 303
Harry Lauder's walking stick, 23, 289
Hawthorn, 89
'Winter King', 89, 196
'Winter King' green, 45
Hazel
corkscrew, 23, 289
purple-leaf, 290
witch (*see* Witch hazel)
Heath
in autumn, **214**
'Springwood Pink', **61**
in winter, 31, 33-34, **65**
zones and climate, 323
Heather, 321
'Cuprea', **71**
'E. F. Brown', **214**
'Gold Haze', **214**
in winter, 31, 32-33, **65**
Hedera helix, 36, **73,** 323-24
Helenium autumnale, **214,** 307
Helenium autumnale 'Red-Gold Hybrid', **183**
Helictotrichon sempervirens, **162–63,** 317

Hellebore, 52-53
    Corsican, 53
    stinking, 53
Helleborus argutifolius, 53
Helleborus foetidus, 53
Helleborus niger, 52, **66**
Helleborus orientalis, 52-53, 307
Hemerocallis 'Corky', **170**
Hemerocallis hybrids, 307
Hemlock
    Canada, 259
        dwarf, 269
    Carolina, 259
Heuchera, 'Palace Purple', **172,** 307
Heuchera micrantha 'Palace Purple',
    172, 307
Heuchera sanguinea, 307-8
Hibiscus syriacus, 292
Holly
    American, 256
    blue, 263
        'Golden Girl', 45
        'Blue Maid', **70**
    Chinese, 263
    English, 256
    Japanese, 263
        'Hetzii', **161**
    Oregon grape, 101, 264-65
    red-berried evergreen, 44-45
Honeysuckle, trumpet, 325
Honeysuckle, bush, 48-49
Hornbeam, weeping European,
    274
Hosta(s), **170**
    in combinations, **231,** 251
    foliage, 172, **173,** 174-75
    in spring, **111, 118**
    in summer, **170**
    top-rated cultivars for foliage and
        flowers, 174-75
    zones and cultures, 308
Hosta 'Frances Williams', **170**
Hyacinth
    Dutch, 106, 123
    grape, 126
        Armenian, 126-27
        common, 127
Hyacinthoides hispanicus, **92,** 129
Hydrangea(s), 152-53
    climbing, **166–67,** 324
    flower types, **152**
    hills-of-snow, **161,** 292
    hortensia, **156,** 293
    lacecap, **168,** 293
        variegated, **168–69**
    oakleaf, 293
        color, 153, **165**

    in mixed border, **157, 162–63**
    panicle, 152-53
    peegee, 293
Hydrangea anomala subsp. *petiolaris,*
    166–67, 324
Hydrangea arborescens 'Grandiflora',
    161, 292
Hydrangea macrophylla, **156**
Hydrangea macrophylla var. *macrophylla,*
    293
Hydrangea macrophylla var. *serrata,*
    168, 293
Hydrangea paniculata, 152-53
Hydrangea paniculata 'Grandiflora',
    293
Hydrangea quercifolia. See Hydrangea,
    oakleaf
Hydrangea vine, Japanese, 326
Hypericum, 151
Hypericum kalmianum, 293
Hypericum patulum 'Hidcote', 49-50

I

Iberis sempervirens, 308
Ilex, winter berries, 44-45
Ilex aquifolium, 256
Ilex cornuta, 262
Ilex crenata, 263
Ilex crenata 'Hetzii', **161**
Ilex × *meserveae,* 263
Ilex × *meserveae* 'Blue Maid', **70**
Ilex × *meserveae* 'Golden Girl', 45
Ilex opaca, 256
Ilex verticillata, 44, **74,** 294
Imperata cylindrica 'Red Baron', **214,**
    318
Indian summer, 182
Indigo, blue false, 302-3
Inula, **155**
Inula helenium, **155**
Iris
    bearded, 16, 308
    crested, **122,** 308
    Japanese, **172**
    reticulated, 51-52, **64**
    Siberian, 16, 308
    winter bulbs, 50-52
    yellow flag, **117**
Iris cristata, **122,** 308
Iris reticulata, 51-52, **64**
Iris sibirica, 16, 308
Iris unguicularis, 52
Iris virginica, **117**
Island bed, 6-8
Itea virginica, 189

Itea virginica 'Henry's Garnet', 148,
    294
Ivy
    Boston, 326
    English, 36, **73,** 323-24

J

Jasminum nudiflorum, 294, 324
Jessamine, winter, 294, 324
Jessamine vines, Carolina, **114**
Juneberry, 83
Juniper, 28
    'Blue Star', 264
    Chinese, 263-64
    creeping, 324
        'Livida', 29
    Japanese garden, 325
    Rocky Mountain, 257
    shore, 324
Juniperus, 28
Juniperus chinensis, 263-64
Juniperus conferta, 324
Juniperus horizontalis, 324
Juniperus horizontalis 'Livida', 29
Juniperus procumbens 'Nana', 325
Juniperus scopulorum, 257
Juniperus squamata 'Blue Star', 264
Juniperus virginiana, 29, 257

K

Kalmia latifolia, 146, **147,** 264
Katsura tree, 274
Kerria, Japanese, 100
    variegated, 294
Kerria japonica, 100
Kerria japonica 'Picta', 294
Kiwi, 'Arctic Beauty' hardy, 320
Koelreuteria paniculata, 139, 142, 278

L

Laburnum × *watereri,* 91
Laburnum × *watereri* 'Vossii', **108,**
    278-79
Lagerstroemia indica, 142-43
    flowers, 199
    zones and culture, 279
Lamb's-ears, **165,** 173, 251
    'Silver Carpet', 315
Lamium maculatum, 325
Lamium maculatum 'White Nancy',
    147, 247

Landscape
    design (*see* Designing year-round landscape)
    four-season, 3-17
Larch
    European, 279
    weeping, **65**
Larix decidua, 279
Laurel, mountain, 146, **147**, 264
Laurustinus, 269
Lavandula angustifolia, 309
Lavender, 309
Lavender cotton, 314
Leadwort, **167, 220,** 321
Lenten rose, 52-53, 307
Lespedeza thunbergii, 202
Lespedeza thunbergii 'Gibraltar', 295
Leucojum aestivum, 127
Leucojum vernum, 127
Leucothoe
    fountain, **108, 161**
    'Scarletta', 264
Leucothoe fontanesiana, **108, 161**
Leucothoe fontanesiana 'Scarletta', 264
Liatris spicata 'Kobold', **170**
Ligularia, narrow-spiked, 309
Ligularia stenocephala, 309
Ligularia 'The Rocket', **164**
Lilac, 9
    Meyer, 102, 298
    'Miss Kim' Manchurian, 102
Lily, **168**
    checkered, 127
Lily-of-the-field, 202, **208-9, 220**
    bulbs, 52
Lilyturf, **168**
Lindera benzoin, 50
Linum perenne, **165,** 309
Liquidambar styraciflua, 187, 279
Liriodendron tulipifera, 279
Liriope, creeping, 325
Liriope muscari 'Variegata', **168**
Liriope spicata, 325
Little bluestem, 319
Lobularia maritima, **217**
Locust, black, 137
Lonicera fragrantissima, 48-49
Lonicera sempervirens, 325
Loosestrife, **162**
    wand, 309
Lungwort, common, 53
Lupine, Carolina, **161,** 315
Luzula sylvatica 'Marginata', 318
Lyme grass, **168-69**
    blue, 317
Lysimachia nummularia 'Aurea', 325

Lythrum 'Morden Pink', **162**
Lythrum virgatum, 309

M

Maackia, Amur, 142, 279
Maackia amurensis, 142, 279
Magnolia, 77, 80
    Loebner, 280
    saucer, 77, **115,** 280
    'Alexandrina', 80
    southern, 138-39, 257
    star, 77, 280
Magnolia grandiflora, 138-39, 257
Magnolia × *loebneri,* 280
Magnolia × *soulangiana,* 77, **115,** 280
Magnolia × *soulangiana* 'Alexandrina', 80
Magnolia stellata, 77, 280
Magnolia virginiana, 138, 257
Mahonia, leatherleaf, 265
Mahonia aquifolium, 101, 264-65
Mahonia bealei, 265
Maiden grass
    in autumn, **227**
    Formosa, 318
    silver feather, **206**
    in summer, **156, 159**
Maidenhair tree, 187, 278
Malus. See Crabapple
Malus 'Dolgo', **196**
Maple
    Amur, 186-87, 270
    coral-bark, 271
    fullmoon, **121,** 271
    Japanese, **168,** 185-86
        best cultivars, 188-89
        'Bloodgood', 175, **176,** 271
        cutleaf, 271
        'Karagusawa', **161**
        leaf types, 185-86, **185**
    paperbark, 37, 42, 270
    red, 185, 271
    snakebark, 270
    sugar, 184-85, **215,** 272
    swamp, 185, 271
    three-flower, 272
Mentha suaveolens 'Variegata', 309
Mertensia virginica, **120-21,** 309-10
Metasequoia glyptostroboides, 281
Microbiota decussata, 325-26
Mint, variegated pineapple, 309
Mint shrub, 291
Miscanthus, evergreen, 318
Miscanthus sinensis, **73**
Miscanthus sinensis 'Brookside', **70**

Miscanthus sinensis cultivars, 318
Miscanthus sinensis 'Gracillimus', **156, 159**
Miscanthus sinensis 'Morning Light', **206-7**
Miscanthus sinensis 'Purpurascens', **217**
Miscanthus sinensis 'Silberfeder', **206**
Miscanthus sinensis 'Variegatus', **179**
Miscanthus sinensis 'Zebrinus', **168-69**
Miscanthus transmorrisonensis, 318
Mixed borders, 13-14
    autumn, 228
    for four seasons, 239, 242
        annuals, 253
        bulbs, 250-53
        groundcovers, 246-47
        influential trees, 244-45, **245**
        perennials, 247
        shrubs for structure, 245-46
        steps to building, 242
        vines, 247, 250
        winter as primary focus, 242-44
    summer, **141,** 180
Monarda didyma, 310
Monkshood, azure, 225, **225**
Moss pink, 311
Muscari, 126
Muscari armeniacum, 126-27
Muscari botryoides, 127
Myosotis sylvatica, **118**
Myrica pensylvanica, 44, 295
Myrtle, **92,** 129, 327
Myrtles, crape, 142-43
    new cultivars, 144-45
    zones and culture, 279

N

Nandina domestica, 265
Narcissus 'February Gold', **61**
Narcissus hybrids, 104-5
Nepeta × *faassenii,* **158,** 310
Nicotiana alata, **165**
Nyssa sylvatica, 281

O

Oak, English, 21
Oat grass, blue, **162-63,** 317
Obedient plant, **213,** 312
Oenothera fruticosa, 310
Oenothera speciosa, 310
Olive, Russian, 290-91

Oregano, golden, **171**
Origanum vulgare var. *aureus,* **171**
Ornamental bark, 36-43
Ornamental grasses, 316-19
    autumn foliage, 191
    fall-blooming, 226, **227**, 228
    winter, 55-56
Osier, dwarf purple, 297
Osmunda cinnamomea, **112–13, 205**
Oxydendrum arboreum, 139, 187, 281

P

Pachysandra, Japanese, 36, 129, 326
    variegated, 34-35
Pachysandra terminalis, 36, 129, 326
Pachysandra terminalis 'Variegata',
    34-35
Paeonia lactiflora, **165**, 310-11
Pagodatree, Japanese, 143, 284
Pampas grass, dwarf, **227**
Panicum virgatum, 319
Pansies, **122**
Parrotia, Persian, 281
Parrotia persica, 281
Parthenocissus tricuspidata, 326
Pasqueflower, **111**
Pear
    'Bradford', 21, 80, 82
    callery, 187, 283
    ornamental, 187, 283
    'Silver Frost' weeping, 283
Pennisetum alopecuroides, **210,** 319
Pennisetum orientale, 319
Peony, common garden, **165,** 310-11
Pepperbush, sweet, 154, **162,** 288-89
    companions, **171**
Perennials, 300-315
    autumn, 223
        foliage, 191
    for mixed border, 247
    spring
        early, 81
        late, 90-91
        mid, 84
    summer, **155, 170,** 178, 180
        leaves, **172**
    winter-flowering, 52-55
Periwinkle, **92,** 129, 327
Perovskia atriplicifolia, **162–63,** 311
Phalaris arundinacea var. *picta,* 56,
    319
Phlox
    creeping, **120–21,** 311
        'Home Fires', **107**

    garden, **155, 165, 168**
    'Miss Lingard' Carolina, 311
    wild blue, **107, 120–21,** 311
    woodland, **107, 120–21,** 311
Phlox carolina 'Miss Lingard', 311
Phlox divaricata, **107, 120–21,** 311
Phlox paniculata 'Bright Eyes', **165,**
    168
Phlox stolonifera, **120–21,** 311
Phlox stolonifera 'Home Fires', **107**
Phlox subulata, 311
Phyllostachys aurea, 56
Physostegia virginiana, **213,** 312
Picea, 28
Picea glauca, **161**
Picea glauca 'Conica', 265
Picea omorika, 258
Picea orientalis 'Aurea Compacta', 265
Picea pungens, 258
Picea pungens 'Montgomery', 265
Pieris, 94
    Himalayan, 94
    Japanese, 30, 49, 131, 266
        'Valley Valentine', **69**
        variegated, **69**
    mountain, 94, 266
Pieris floribunda, 94, 266
Pieris formosa, 94
Pieris japonica, 30, 49, 131, 266
Pieris japonica 'Valley Valentine', **69**
Pieris japonica 'Variegata', **69**
Pine
    Austrian, 258
    dragon's-eye, 35, **69**
    dwarf mugo, 266
    Japanese red, 258
    lacebark, 43, 258
    Scotch, 259
    umbrella, 259
    white, **68,** 259
Pinks, maiden, 305
Pinus bungeana, 43, 258
Pinus densiflora, 258
Pinus densiflora 'Oculus-Draconis', 35,
    69
Pinus mugo var. *mugo,* 266
Pinus nigra, 258
Pinus strobus, **68,** 259
Pinus sylvestris, 259
Pistache, Chinese, 187, 281
Pistacia chinensis, 187, 281
Planting pyramids, 14-15, **14**
Platanus, 37
Platycodon grandiflorus, 312
Platycodon grandiflorus var. *mariesii,*
    170

Plum, purple-leaf, 131
    'Krauter Vesuvius' purple-leaf,
    282
Plume grass, 317
Polygonatum odoratum 'Variegatum',
    312
Potentilla fruticosa, 149, 151, 295
Prairie beard grass, 319
Primrose, **122**
    English, 312
    showy evening, 310
Primula × *hybrida,* **122**
Primula vulgaris, 312
Prunus, 80
Prunus cerasifera, 131
Prunus cerasifera 'Krauter Vesuvius',
    282
Prunus maackii, 88, 282
Prunus 'Okame', 282
Prunus serrulata, 282
Prunus serrulata 'Kwanzan', 88, **110–11**
Prunus subhirtella 'Autumnalis', 199,
    202
Prunus subhirtella var. *pendula,* 283
Pseudotsuga menziesii, 259
Pulmonaria officinalis, 53
Pulmonaria saccharata, 53, 312-13
Puschkinia, 126
Puschkinia scillioides, 126
Pyracantha coccinea, 195-96, 266-67
Pyracantha coccinea 'Mohave', **61**
Pyracantha, 195-96, 266-67
Pyrus calleryana, 21, 187, 283
Pyrus calleryana 'Bradford', 80, 82
Pyrus salicifolia 'Silver Frost', 283

Q

Queen-Anne's lace, **158**
Quercus robur, 21

R

Ravenna grass, 317
Redbud, 82-83, 97, 274
    Chinese, 83
    eastern, **116**
    Mexican, 82-83
    Texas, 82-83
    western, 83
Redwood, dawn, 281
Reed grass, fall-blooming, 316
Rhododendron(s), 94-97, **117**
    Carolina, 100, 267

Catawba, 102-3, 267
color changes of cultivars, 30-31
Dexter hybrids, 103
dwarf, 95-96, **120–21**
   cultivars, 267
Gable hybrids, 103
Korean, 295
large-leaved, 102-4, **108, 112–13**
late-summer blooming, 149
rosebay, 149, 267
Yako, 103-4, 268
Rhododendron 'Aglo', **205**
Rhododendron arborescens, 150
Rhododendron atlanticum, 150
Rhododendron bakeri, 148, 150-51
Rhododendron calendulaceum, 150
Rhododendron carolinianum, 100, 267
Rhododendron catawbiense, 102-3, 267
Rhododendron dauricum hybrids, 267
Rhododendron hybrids, 97-98, 102-4
Rhododendron × *indicum,* **92**
   zones and culture, 267
Rhododendron luteum, 100
Rhododendron 'Mary Fleming', 96-97
Rhododendron maximum, 149, 267
   cultivars, 267
Rhododendron mucronulatum, 93, 295
   cultivars, 93-94
Rhododendron periclymenoides, 150
Rhododendron 'P.J.M.', 30-31, 95, 132
Rhododendron prinophyllum, 108, 150
Rhododendron prunifolium, 148, 151,
167
Rhododendron schlippenbachii, 94-95,
96, 295
Rhododendron serrulatum, 150
Rhododendron vaseyi, 150
Rhododendron viscosum, 151
Rhododendron 'Windbeam', 96
Rhododendron yakusimanum, 103-4,
268
Rhododendron yedoense var.
poukhanense, 98
Rhus typhina, 296
Ribbon grass, 56, 319
Robinia pseudoacacia, 137
Rodgersia, featherleaf, 313
Rodgersia pinnata 'Superba', 313
Rosa glauca, **158,** 296
Rosa rugosa, 146, 148, **162,** 296
Rosa virginiana, 148, 296
Rose
   redleaf, **158,** 296
   rugosa, 146, 148, **162,** 296
   Virginia, 148, 296
Rose-of-Sharon, 292

Rudbeckia fulgida var. *sullivantii*
'Goldsturm', 55, **167,** 313
Rudbeckia nitida 'Autumn Glory', **209**
Rudbeckia nitida 'October Glory', **183**
Ruta graveolens, 313
Ryegrass (winter rye), 35

S

Sage
   Bethlehem, 53, 312-13
   'East Friesland' violet, 314
   garden, 313
   Russian, **155, 162–63,** 311
   silver, 313
   'Silver King' white, 301
   'Victoria' mealycup, **210**
St.-John's-wort, 151, 293
   'Hidcote', 49-50
Salix alba 'Britzensis', 297
Salix alba 'Tristis', 283
Salix matsudana 'Tortuosa', 23, **66–67,**
283-84
Salix purpurea var. *nana,* 297
Salvia argentea, 313
Salvia farinacea 'Victoria', **210**
Salvia officinalis, 313
Salvia × *superba* 'East Friesland',
314
Sambucus racemosa 'Plumosa Aurea',
297
Santolina chamaecyparissus, 314
Sapphireberry, 193
Sarcococca, fragrant, 268
Sarcococca ruscifolia, 268
Sasa veitchii, 56
Schizachyrium scoparium, 24, 319
Schizophragma hydrangeoides, 326
Scholartree, 143, 284
Sciadopitys verticillata, 259
Scilla, winter bulbs, 52
Scilla siberica, 124, 126
Scotch broom, **115**
Sea oats, Northern, **227,** 316-17
Seasonal groupings, 4-5, 8-10
Seasons, defining, 10-11
Sedge
   'Bowles Golden', 316
   broom, 319
   'Evergold' Japanese, 316
Sedum
   'Autumn Joy', 314
   in autumn, **209, 210, 217,**
224
   in summer, **156, 162–63**

   in winter, 53
   'Dragon's blood' two-row, 314-15
   'Vera Jameson', **213, 216**
Sedum acre, 326
Sedum cauticola, 314
Sedum sieboldii, 203
Sedum spurium 'Dragon's Blood',
314-15
Serviceberry, downy, 83, 272
Shadblow, 83, 272
Shadbush, 83
Shade garden, **248–49**
Shapes of trees and shrubs, 232,
234-35
Shrubs, **155**
   autumn, 202
      berries, 192-93, 195-96
      flowering, 219
      foliage, 187, 189, 190-91,
192
   deciduous (*see* Deciduous shrubs;
      Deciduous trees and shrubs)
   evergreen (*see* Evergreen shrubs)
   for eye-level color, 92-104, **96**
   for four-season landscaping, 3
   season-spanning color, 93-94
   shapes, 232, 234-35
   spring color
      early, 94-97
      late, 101-4
      mid-, 97-101
   for structure, 245-46
   summer blooming
      early, 143-46, 148, **157**
      late, 153-54
      mid-, 148-49, 151-53
   weather-defying, 48-50
   for winter
      flowering, 54
      showy berries, 46
      siting, 19, 21
Silverbell
   Carolina, 88-89, **96,** 278
   mountain, 88-89
Silver grass, Japanese, **73,** 318
   'Brookside', **70**
   'Morning Light', **206–7, 213**
   variegated, **179**
Skimmia, Japanese, 268
Skimmia japonica, 268
Smoketree, 151-52
   purple, **155,** 277
      'Notcutt's Variety', 175
      'Royal Purple' smokebush, **157,**
159
Snakeroot, black, 304-5

Sneezeweed
    common, **214**, 307
    'Red-Gold Hybrid', **183**
Snowbell
    fragrant, 285
    Japanese, 284-85
        in summer, 135, **136**, 137
Snowberry, white-fruited, 44
Snowdrops, 50, 51, **51, 64**
Snowflake
    spring, 127
    summer, 127
Snow in garden, 23-24
Snow-in-summer, 303
Solidago, 224
Solidago canadensis 'Crown of Rays',
    183
Solomon's seal, **172**
    variegated fragrant, 312
Sophora japonica, 143, 284
Sorbaria sorbifolia, 297
Sorbus, 196-97
Sorbus alnifolia, 196-97, 284
Sorbus aucuparia, 196-97
Sorbus rufoferruginea 'Longwood
    Sunset', 197
Sorrel tree, 139, 187, 281
Sourwood, 139, 187, 281
Speedwell, **165**
    spike, 315
Spicebush, 50
Spiraea × *bumalda,* 149, 297-98
Spiraea × *bumalda* 'Goldmound', **112,
    161**
Spirea
    bluebeard, 288
    Bumald, 149, 297-98
        'Goldmound', **112, 161**
    Ural false, 297
    for yellow foliage, 177
Spring, 8-9, 75-106, **107-22**, 123-33
    bulbs, 104-6, 123-30
    color clashes, 132-33
    color scheme, 130-31
    early-spring canopy, 77, 80-83
    landscape features, 12
    late-spring canopy, 89-91
    layers of bloom, 77
    midspring canopy, 83-85, 88-89
    shrubs for eye-level color, 92-104
    three seasons of, 76-77
    wildflower garden, **78-79**
Spruce, 28
    Colorado, 258
    compact golden oriental, 265
    dwarf Alberta, 265

    'Montgomery' dwarf blue, 156,
      265
    Serbian, 258
    white, **161**
Squill
    Siberian, 124, 126
    Spanish, 129
    winter bulbs, 52
Stachys byzantina, **165**, 173, 251
Stachys byzantina 'Silver Carpet', 315
Stephanandra, cutleaf, 298
Stephanandra incisa 'Crispa', 298
Sternbergia lutea, 202, **208-9, 220**
Stewartia, 42-43, 142
    Japanese, **72-73**, 142, 284
Stewartia pseudocamellia, **72-73**, 142,
    284
Stokesia laevis, **162-63**
Stonecrop, goldmoss, 326
Strawberry, barren, 327
Strawberry tree, 255
Styrax japonicus, 284-85
    in summer, 135, **136**, 137
Styrax obassia, 285
Sumac, staghorn, 296
Summer, 9-10, 134-54, **155-70**,
    171-80
    blooming shrubs for eye-level
      flowers, 143-46, **147**, 148-54
    early-summer canopy, 135, **136,**
      137-39
    easy-care garden, **140-41**
    landscape features, 12
    late-summer canopy, 142-43
    midsummer canopy, 139, 142
    mixed borders, 180
    perennials and bulbs, 178, 180
    plant combination, **171**
Summer foliage, 154, 171-78
    bicolored and tricolored leaves,
      178
    blue-green and gray-green, 171-72
    silver, 172-73
    sunny yellow, 177-78
    wine-dark, 173, 175, **176**, 177
Summersweet, 154, **162**, 288-89
    companions, **171**
Sundrops, 310
Sweetspire, Virginia, 189
    'Henry's Garnet', 148, 294
Switch grass, 319
Sycamore, 37
Symphoricarpos albus, 44
Symplocos paniculata, 193
Syringa, 9
Syringa meyeri, 102, 298

Syringa patula, 102
Syringa reticulata, 139, 285
Syringa reticulata var. *mandshurica,*
    139

T

Tamarisk, 298
Tamarix ramosissima, 298
Taxus, 268-69
Textures, 229-31
Thermopsis caroliniana, **161**, 315
Thistle, globe, 306
Three-veined everlasting, 300
Thrift, common, 301
Thuja occidentalis, 269
Thuja orientalis 'Juniperoides', 269
Thyme
    creeping, 130
    'Gold-Edge' lemon, 326-27
    woolly, 327
Thymus, 130
Thymus × *citridorus* 'Gold Edge',
    326-27
Thymus pseudolanuginosus, 327
Tiarella cordifolia, **120-21**, 327
Tobacco, annual flowering, **165**
Tree lilac
    Japanese, 139, 285
    Manchurian, 139
Trees
    for autumn
      berries, 196-97
      blooming, 199, 202, 219
      foliage, 184-87, 188-89, 190
    deciduous (*see* Deciduous trees;
      Deciduous trees and shrubs)
    with dramatic silhouettes, 20, **22**
    evergreen, 255-59
    for four-season landscaping, 3
    with ornamental bark, 36-43
    shapes, 232, 234-35
    spheres of influence, 244-45, **245**
    for spring
      early, 81
      late, 90
      mid, 84
    summer flowering, 135-43, **136,
      140-41**
    weather-defying, 48-50
    white-barked, 37
    for winter
      flowering, 54
      showy berries, 46-47
      siting, 19, 21, **22**

Tsuga canadensis, 259, 269
Tsuga caroliniana, 259
Tulip(s), **92, 115,** 123-24, 127-28
    perennial, 123, 126
    seasons, 124
    waterlily, 127-28
Tulipa batalinii, 128
Tulipa hybrids, **92**
Tulipa kaufmanniana, 127-28
Tulip poplar, 279
Tulip tree, 279
Tupelo, black, 281

U

Ulmus parvifolia 'Emerald Vase', 285
USDA plant hardiness zone map,
    334

V

Variegated foliage
    summer, 178, **179**
    winter, 31, 34-35
Verbena bonariensis, **210**
Veronica longifolia 'Blue Charm', **165**
Veronica spicata, 315
Viburnum(s), 94, 101-2
    for autumn berries, 192-93
        best cultivars, 194-95
    Burkwood, 101
    cranberrybush, 299
        American, 193
        European, 193
    doublefile, 101-2
    fragrant dawn, 298
    Koreanspice, 101, 299
    linden, 192-93, **204-5**
    ornamental, with winter berries,
        44
    tea, 193, 299
Viburnum × bodnantense 'Dawn', 298
Viburnum burkwoodii 'Mohawk', 101
Viburnum carlesii, 101, 299
Viburnum dilatatum, 192-93, **204-5**
Viburnum opulus, 193, 299
Viburnum plicatum var. *tomentosum,*
    101

Viburnum plicatum var. *tomentosum*
    'Shasta', 101-2
Viburnum setigerum, 193, 299
Viburnum tinus, 94, 269
Viburnum trilobum, 193
Vinca minor, **92,** 129, 327
Vines, **160,** 320-27
    autumn, 202
        blooming, 219
        foliage, 190-91
    for four-season landscaping, 3
    for mixed border, 247, 250
    spring
        early, 81
        late, 91
        mid, 84
    winter-flowering, 54
Viola labradorica var. *purpurea,* 315
Viola × wittrockiana, **122**
Violet(s), **111**
    purple-leaf Labrador, 315
Virgin's bower, purple, 322-23
Vitex agnus-castus, 143, **161, 167,**
    299

W

Waldsteinia fragarioides, 327
Walking stick, Harry Lauder's, 23,
    289
Warminster broom, 290
Waterlilies, **117**
White-barked trees, 37
Wildflowers
    autumn, **183**
    spring, **78-79**
Willow
    coral embers, 297
    corkscrew, 23, **66-67, 283-84**
    golden weeping, 283
Willow blue star, 300
Winter, 5-6, 18-58, **59-74**
    berries, 43-47
    bulbs, 50-52, **51**
    color scheme, 24
    creating garden, 56, **57,** 58
    early perennials, 52-55
    entrance garden, **26-27**
    flowers, 47-48

    garden design and, 242
    garden structure, 19-24
    landscape features, 12
    lawns and groundcovers, 35-36
    ornamental bark, 36-43
    ornamental grasses, 55-56
    plants with dramatic silhouettes,
        20
    weather-defying trees and shrubs,
        48-50
Winterberry, **44, 74,** 294
Wintercreeper, 323
Winterhazel, 93
    buttercup, 93, 289
Wintersweet, 49, 288
Wisteria, Japanese, 327
Wisteria floribunda, 327
Witch hazel
    'Arnold Promise', 48, **62**
    in autumn, 187, 189
    Chinese, 48, **51**
    hybrids, 291-92
    Virginia, 202, 292
    in winter, 48, **62**
Woodruff, sweet, **96, 111, 231,** 323
Woodrush, golden-edged, 318
Woody plants, fall-blooming, 219

Y

Yard, front, **240-41**
Yarrow
    common, **157**
    'Coronation Gold', 300
Yellowwood, American, **118-19,** 137,
    275
Yews, 268-69
Yucca, **206**
Yucca filamentosa, **206,** 315

Z

Zebra grass, **168-69**
Zelkova, 'Green Vase' Japanese, 285
Zelkova serrata 'Green Vase', 285
Zones, USDA plant hardiness zone
    map, **334**
Zoysia grass, 35